Public Opinion and Propaganda

LEONARD W. DOOB

Yale University

New York

Henry Holt and Company

THIS book seeks to analyze public opinion and propaganda from the viewpoint of modern social science. Instead of calling public opinion wise or foolish, it makes an effort to identify and explain the segment of human behavior known as public opinion, to describe how people react in social situations, and to assay the importance of public opinion in the modern world. Instead of presenting examples of the exotic or mundane results obtained from measuring public opinion, it utilizes such information incidentally and only to indicate the difficulties and the techniques of measurement. Instead of maintaining that propaganda is evil and tricky, it suggests that propaganda cannot be easily labeled and it focuses attention upon how propaganda functions. Instead of displaying grief or joy when the modern media of communication are contemplated, it tries faithfully to describe their accomplishments and potentialities as well as the reasons therefor.

The writer has only one thesis to advocate: public opinion and propaganda are intimately related because they both involve phases of human behavior. An understanding of human behavior, it is therefore contended, can provide insight into public opinion and propaganda. The reaction of public opinion to an atomic bomb or some propaganda fluff can be viewed in similar terms because the same principles of behavior are operating. In almost every paragraph an attempt is made to phrase the discussion in terms of human beings and thus to reduce apparently bewildering complexity to a common denominator.

Few people like principles, and principles can become unintelligible if they remain on an abstract level. To facilitate the analysis, consequently, specific illustrations of public opinion and propaganda are given at frequent intervals. On the whole these have been drawn from three fields: politics, business, and war. The selection is somewhat arbitrary, but seems justified because the fields are diverse and also important.

Social science, like all science, strives to be neutral. Facts are collected, collated, and fitted into theory. Or else theory in the first place demands their collection and collation. The utilization of social science is another problem—and, in this instance, the concluding chapter argues that the problem cannot be completely avoided. The argument is withheld from this preface: it is not an underlying motif of the book.

It must be said, however, that this volume aims to be useful to both the producer and the consumer of public opinion and propaganda. The producer is a fancy name for the individual who seeks to affect, measure, or control other people—and he may have the title of leader, politician, advertiser, public relations counsel, pollster, analyst, or journalist. Consumer refers to an individual in the group whose opinions are being affected, measured, or controlled—and he is either a student or a citizen. Specifically, for example, it is possible to learn how to conduct or to understand a public opinion poll; to plan or dissect an advertising campaign; to spray propaganda upon an enemy or to help immunize oneself from enemy propaganda. Let each reader decide for himself whether he is a producer or consumer. Perhaps, if he is really versatile, he can ride both horses through the chapters which follow.

The writer is deeply indebted to his friends in what was the Overseas Branch of the Office of War Information for the practical lessons they taught him; to Messrs. Edward W. Barrett, Elmer Davis, and Edward Klauber for having given him the opportunity to learn those lessons; and to his colleagues in the Department of Psychology and the Institute of Human Relations at Yale University for their intellectual stimulation. Dr. Burton R. Fisher and Professor Carl I. Hovland have critically examined a few sections but are absolved of all responsibility. The Institute of Human Relations has kindly provided assistance in preparing the manuscript for publication.

Permission to quote briefly from their publications has

been granted by Appleton-Century-Croft, Inc., Duell, Sloan and Pearce, Harcourt, Brace and Company, Harper and Brothers, The Macmillan Company, Oxford University Press, Princeton University Press, Simon & Schuster, *Survey Graphic,* and The University of Chicago Press.

L. W. D.

Woodbridge, Conn.
February 2, 1948

CONTENTS

vi

CHAPTER 1

The Importance of People

MEN seek to understand themselves and the forces affecting them. Such understanding, they feel, is essential if they are to obtain better control over their own destiny. The physical environment is now fairly well understood, and many parts of it can be manipulated. By and large, people know where and how to find and extract ores and fuels, how to build and run machines, and how to have these machines assist them in satisfying their needs. The weather, the tides, and the seasons cannot be directly regulated, but an analysis of them has enabled men and women to make reasonably good adjustments to their fluctuations. The understanding and control of people, however, has not been nearly so successful.

It is certainly true that some individuals do possess consumate skill in understanding and controlling their fellow men. The salesman who has swindled his customers may win their wrathful respect afterwards when the methods he employed to influence them are recalled. The bedside manner of the experienced physician brings comfort. The clever lawyer is able to sway juries. Dictators have understood and captured their people, and it is sometimes suspected that the chief difference between them and the party boss in a democracy is the greater influence they have exerted. Men, therefore, are not entirely bereft of human understanding.

Such examples of men who know and manipulate people, nevertheless, are not convincing. It is simply not possible to deny the existence of great gaps in man's knowledge about people. The human body, that complicated organism, still presents mysteries which medicine, even after centuries of research, has not yet been able to decipher. The human mind, that strange, strange phenomenon, has not been fully or even adequately grasped by psychiatry and psychology. The society in which men live, that web of infinite perplexities and vicissitudes, seems perpetually to emit problems that drive some men to unhappiness, insanity, or suicide and others to social conflict and war. Slightly more than a superficial glance is sufficient to indicate that few persons are satisfied or peaceful. The last war, pervading so many different lands, deprived civilized man even of the fantasy of the noble and happy savage whose simplicity and bliss he was supposed to envy.

Why do men know or why do they think they know more about the stars or cement than they apparently do about themselves and their society? The answers to this question are legion. They range from pleas concerning the difficulties of the task, through learned discussions about the differences between material and living matter, to denunciations of men and women for failing to heed the exhortations of some divine authority. It is not necessary to account for this ignorance, provided that the unhappy state in which men find themselves is acknowledged.

In no field of human activity is there a sure-fire path to perfect knowledge. Men everywhere are attempting to learn more about themselves. These students of behavior have various names: physicians, psychiatrists, biologists, physiologists, psychologists, economists, political scientists, journalists, historians, sociologists, jurists, anthropologists, semanticists, philosophers, artists, politicians, and ministers are some of the titles they have. The ordinary individual without a title is stimulated to become better acquainted with people whenever he is confronted with a crisis: a broken friendship, an unhappy love affair, a naughty child, the loss of a job, a defeat at election—all these are situations requiring additional knowledge and frequently requiring it quickly. The last war, its disquieting aftermath, and the atomic bomb have been serious crises that reveal our ignorance concerning people.

Some information about people is worse than no information at all only when it is misleading information. Additional insight is to be applauded if it represents a portion of the best and most valid that has been discovered and systematized. A valid analysis of any subject can alleviate somewhat the problems confronting mankind. The more that is known about the common cold, vitamins, the nervous system, economic cycles, political pressures, and the nature of art, for example, the more satisfactory social and personal existence is able to become.

The analysis of public opinion and propaganda is worthy of attention. It is worthy of attention but not necessarily more important than innumerable other problems which face people. For obvious reasons it is not possible to discuss the totality of one person or everything involving many persons all at once, no matter how long the treatise. What little knowledge men possess is not too well unified and, consequently, only segments of that knowledge can be grasped at a given moment.

Public opinion and propaganda represent a significant segment of behavior. As terms they pervade the vocabularies of many peoples and, when a word is in common usage, it usually refers to a phenomenon that affects men and women, or at least the fact of its being employed indicates that it is serving some kind of function. No matter how public opinion is defined, moreover, it is clear that many people and their beliefs are involved. No matter how propaganda is defined, it is equally clear that here is a man-made and man-directed force that is affecting large groups of people. Salvation will not be gained by reading this book nor even by knowing all there is to know or all that will ever be known concerning public opinion and propaganda. Not a leap but a step forward is all that should be desired and can be anticipated.

Since millions of words have been spoken and written

about public opinion and propaganda, it is only right to inquire at the outset concerning the approach of this volume.
The writer would prefer to say that no particular approach
with the conventional labels is being followed. Almost
everybody has had his say or his thoughts about these subjects, and each in his way has generally had some wisdom to
contribute. There is no reason, therefore, to concentrate
upon one approach and to exclude or underplay the rest.
From this point of view, the glib rationalization of the politician is as relevant as the pedantic generalization of the
political scientist; the quick observation of the shrewd journalist is as penetrating as are the vapid statistics of the
public opinion pollster; and the glittering phrases of the
public relations counsel are as interesting as the dull
principles of the social scientist. The source of knowledge
is less important than sagacity in evaluating what is being
offered.

It would be misleading, however, to claim that the
writer's approach is without bias. Probably as much sense
as nonsense has been expressed concerning public opinion
and propaganda. Some method of selection has to be
evolved if the subjects are to be helpfully analyzed and
understood. A collection of observations concerning public
opinion and propaganda by wise or learned men is not sufficient. Synthesis is needed, not merely judgments or anec-
dotes.

The common element in any social situation—and public
opinion and propaganda represent complicated social situations—is man. The more that is known about him as an
individual and the more that is known about the principles
governing his behavior, the greater can be our insight into
those situations involving many men. Writers and thinkers
do attempt to describe mass phenomena in collective terms:
they perch themselves, as it were, far above the whirling
multitude and then report what they see. Certainly it is
possible to analyze battles in terms of the opposing armies;
or crowds in terms of currents or movements; or differing
sentiments in terms of broad national trends; or propaganda campaigns in terms of devices and results. It is main-

tained, however, that such descriptions, exciting or as provoking as they are, remain in the realm of specificity. They produce uniqueness when what is needed is generality. Generality is needed so that knowledge can be obtained and predictions made concerning situations in the future which have not yet arisen

Since attention is being focused upon the human being, it is fair to call this book's method of approach a psychological one. No cheers are anticipated from other social scientists or from laymen. Except for the uncritical reader of the "pulp" and the "slick" magazines, psychology as a discipline or nascent science has won neither complete respect nor approval. Whether psychology deserves the reputation it possesses is a fascinating problem which happily requires no discussion at this point. It is felt, nevertheless, that the psychological approach can at least promise generality. It is potentially fruitful, although it cannot state the last word on the subjects of public opinion and propaganda.

At the same time psychology may not discard the approaches of other social sciences or of any discipline concerned with people. What is known systematically about the individual in psychology has been learned from observing him carefully in scientific laboratories or in clinics. Or an inferential understanding of his behavior has been secured by studying lower animal organisms whose lives can be more easily and efficiently controlled. When it is said that human responses are made to stimuli, all that is frequently accomplished thereby is to point out the need for attempting to discover what the stimuli are which have evoked the particular response. These stimuli may come from inside the organism (hunger pangs) or from outside (a loud noise) and, when they are outside stimuli in real life as distinguished from the laboratory or the clinic, they originate in social situations that are usually very complicated. Other social sciences and professions throw light on these very situations; consequently their contribution at this crucial point is absolutely essential.

Unfortunately psychologists are not in agreement con-

cerning principles of human behavior. In a real sense there
are schools of psychology as well as concepts and theories
which vary as a function of the particular psychologist's
training, bias, and interests. Most of the differences are
verbal but a few are quite fundamental. Some psychologists, for example, contend that an explanation of an individual's behavior in a given situation is not adequate until
it can be related to the basic, innate drives within all organisms like sex or food. Others maintain that drives, once
they begin to function within a personality, are self-sustain-
ing and that therefore an explanation is satisfactory when it
accounts for behavior in terms of the drives active at the
moment. Psychological evidence from all sources is unable
at the present time to substantiate or refute either theory.
The question behind the theory, moreover, is of vast practical importance. It underlies almost all assumptions concerning the nature of human nature that is involved in war,
competition or cooperation, and education. There can be
no completely satisfactory theory for public opinion and
propaganda until this and many other questions are settled.

It is unwise, however, to wait for psychology to settle all
the basic questions before the attempt is made to analyze
social phenomena. Men were able to build bridges before
physics and engineering had become sciences. They may
not have built them as well as they do now when they can
benefit from theoretical knowledge, but the structures served
a useful function. Advances in psychology may in fact have
to wait upon further research and systematization within
physiology, but in the meantime geniuses like Freud and
Pavlov have been able to make important contributions.
Similarly there can be progress if not perfection regarding
public opinion and propaganda in the absence of a mature
psychology.

There cannot be, or there should not be, separate discrete
disciplines studying nerves, learning under laboratory conditions, or men in a crowd. Naturally no one individual can
know all there is to know about such diverse phenomena,
but it is dangerous to overlook possible connections between
them or to forget that eventually different approaches must

be brought within a single universe of discourse. There must be temporary compromises or else knowledge concerning complicated phenomena will be retarded until more is learned about simpler matters. It is, moreover, quite superficial to brand one phenomenon complicated and another simple. A nerve may occupy less space than a crowd and it can be studied under more quiet and controlled conditions, but many of its properties are without question more elusive to grasp than is the crude behavior demonstrated by a lynching bee. What is done at one level of research should be related to the levels which are "beneath" or "above" it. Useful theories of public opinion and propaganda, therefore, cannot be solidly anchored in psychological principles because there are no thoroughly adequate principles; but their relation to the apparently fruitful principles that do exist as well as their implications in other fields should be continuously indicated.

In short, as many of the concepts and principles of precise psychology will be employed in the analysis of public opinion and propaganda as appear useful. What is proposed here is a tentative framework whose connections with the more exact discipline, it is hoped, can easily be discerned. In theory there can be no objection to this procedure, but in practice certain problems immediately arise. Scientific laws operate only under conditions which are always carefully specified. The qualifying clause, "other things being equal," which is so frequently tagged on to a generalization in physical and social science, does not represent a devious method of dodging responsibility for the verification of the principle. The law of the inclined plane in physics has to assume no friction and therefore in a sense cannot be verified unless a correction is made for the amount of friction actually present —and some always is. To make the correction in turn requires that the friction present be measured.

The application of psychological principles or laws to social situations involving many people is no easy matter because so often it is next to impossible to control or specify the other conditions which are supposed to be equal and which certainly in the realm of man's social life almost never are. In fact some historians and social scientists have argued that each situation in society is unique in some respect; that social phenomena do not repeat themselves; and that, therefore, there can be no social science as the word science is used in the natural sciences. This point of view, defeatist as it is, cannot be gainsaid: it deserves and herewith receives a bow, though a most perfunctory one. In an atomic age, to state the case against the view both briefly and unconvincingly, the search for lawfulness should not be impeded by complexity. Whether or not the complexity is subject to lawfulness cannot be contended with certainty, nor can the contrary be maintained. This does not mean that all social sciences must follow the example of classical economics and formulate laws under conditions (like free competition) which are almost never realized and which therefore prevent the theories from being adequately tested.

In addition to specifying the conditions which must be considered equal or—if unequal—measurable, a scientific law consists of a statement of relationship existing among certain significant variables. Again an example may be taken from physics. If the experimenter wishes to apply the principle of the lever to determine how far from the fulcrum Object A must be placed to balance Object B on the other side of the lever, he must know three things: the weight of Object B, its present distance from the fulcrum, and the weight of Object A. He has a simple equation in which the product of Object B's weight and its distance from the fulcrum must equal the product of Object A's weight and x, its distance from the fulcrum—and then the value of x can be quickly determined. He does not have to know the shape of the objects, their color, their ingredients, etc.

It is not easy or always possible similarly to identify and then weight the variables of a psychological law when social phenomena are being considered. A psychologist like Hull (1),[1] for example, has been able to write equations for

[1] Italicized numbers in parentheses refer to the citations which are listed separately for each chapter at the end of the volume. Some of these citations are recommended there as supplementary reading. Cross references are indicated only in a general way within the text; they can be easily located by consulting the Index.

many aspects of the learning process. To predict, on the basis of these equations, the outcome of a simple situation in which an organism is confronted with the problem whose solution must be learned, it is necessary to be able to measure the strength of previously existing habit systems. Such systems rarely can be measured directly. Their strength must be inferred and hence quantified by controlling, observing, and recording the conditions under which they have come into existence. In most social situations this process cannot be carried out: people already have habits whose strength can be inferred only vaguely from not very reliable indices, they are changing or learning as the situation is being observed, or they simply are not available or will not make themselves available even for a superficial interview. Specifically, how effective was allied propaganda to Germany during the war? Evidence exists which indicates that Germans perceived the propaganda and learned something from it. But what were the previously existing habits on the basis of which the learning occurred? This knowledge does not exist in any precise form, although every writer on Germany has his own theories or evaluations. How did the learning take place? Germans could not be questioned during the war and, even had they been available, the minute study of every German would not have been feasible. In fact the analysis of only one German in such detail that tendencies within him could be assayed and quantified is in itself a gigantic and almost impossible undertaking.

There is no reason to conclude, however, that because psychological principles cannot be easily applied to social situations, no principles at all should be applied. It happens that it is difficult to utilize principles in such situations. Rather than abandon them, it seems better to employ them with care and restraint. Naturally indices or inferences involve some amount of subjectivity, but at the very least psychological principles suggest the significant factors to be observed or discovered.

This book, therefore, begins with man as an individual. Then it examines many men simultaneously in the social situation called public opinion. There follows a detailed analysis of propaganda, which is one of the important forces affecting men in social situations as well as public opinion. Finally, special attention is given to the media of communication because they affect and are affected by public opinion and because through them propaganda is expressed.

CHAPTER 2

Social Behavior

THE most popular explanations of human behavior are simple and easily understood. People know and admit that behavior is complicated. They are convinced that it is difficult to understand why their friends and enemies and why they themselves act as they do or that it is precarious to predict reactions in the near or far future. It is uncomfortable, however, to be ignorant when ignorance brings pain, uncertainty, or insecurity. It is more satisfying to believe that behavior can be accounted for and foretold by reference to some one factor or to a limited number of factors.

Sometimes it appears that both primitive and civilized men have abandoned the quest for an explanation of behavior: all or most behavior is assumed to be inconsistent, irrational, or not subject to lawful principles. Spirits or demons, for example, have been posited to account for the actions of oneself and one's contemporaries. Social life, however, would be impossible if every judgment about people were in fact guided by a capricious theory. Men could not know what to expect—the expectation that anything may happen would preclude most cooperative activity such as hunting or living together in a family. The individual himself would be a hopeless victim of his own moods and whims. Through the process of learning, consequently, men inevitably gather experience about themselves and other people. The experience, even if it be unverbalized or unsystematized, guides them in new situations. They do know what to anticipate—more or less.

The guide is not perfect. Something unforeseen or unintelligible occurs. Adjustment must be constantly learned and relearned. Under these circumstances, then, an attempt is made to generalize from past experience and to evolve a theory of human behavior.

The path of human knowledge is littered with theories about people. What men do has been attributed to their will to survive, their sexual urge, their ability to imitate others, the functioning of their endocrine glands, the shapes of their bodies, the economic relations of their society, and the culture which is transmitted from generation to generation. Each of these theories has its merit in the sense that it appears to account for some part of behavior. Obviously men work so that they may eat, have shelter, and clothe their bodies. Courtship, dancing, and sonnets have some relationship to sex. Children imitate their parents: they learn the same language, they adopt many of the mannerisms observed in their home, and they acquire more or less identical values. A normal set of glands enables the individual to become a useful citizen but, when one gland malfunctions, he may display an over- or under-amount of activity. The strength and appearance of the human body can set the stage for an individual's accomplishments or reputation; and its overall form may be a reflection of an underlying physiological condition which has some relationship, perhaps, to intelligence or temperament. Poor men, in contrast with rich ones, have limited opportunities which affect the development of their personalities; and strikes or revolutions are certainly dependent upon economic circumstances. The average man in our society knows more about his universe than the most gifted of the ancient Greek philosophers not because he is more brilliant but because he automatically acquires as part of his formal or informal schooling the knowledge which has been developed in the meantime.

Any theory about people, whether it comes from Plato or Pareto, from Darwin or Dewey, from Marx or Mussolini, or from Spencer or Stalin, becomes useful when placed in perspective. The situation is truly like the ancient fable of the blind men exploring an elephant: what each reported was true in terms of his experience but no one report described the beast adequately. The reports differed, everyone would agree, because each man had been exploring a different part of the elephant. The situation is not quite so simple when theories about human behavior are discussed.

It is not so simple for a variety of reasons. Men like the theories they have because they would not have acquired them unless they had needed them. When their theories are criticized, they interpret what is said as a criticism of themselves, as indeed it is. They believe that their theories include the entire elephant and they therefore resent being told that they have been confining their thinking to the animal's head or hind quarters. Theories, moreover, must be expressed in language and the meanings of words are frequently numerous and unprecise. One of the reasons Marx, for example, could "explain" many aspects of the social struggle resulted from the fact that he used his key concept, "economic relations," occasionally to refer to the economic structure of society, at other times to the natural resources of society, at still other times to the stage of economic development, and almost never consistently. Then among laymen and social scientists there is no agreement concerning the nature of theory or principles. Too often it is believed that a mere observation of what has occurred in the past becomes a theory or principle merely by applying it to the present or the future.

The modest aim of this chapter is not to brush aside all previous theories of human behavior but merely to indicate the concepts or terms which can be employed to describe the behavior of the individual in relation to public opinion and propaganda. It is fair to compare the function of the vocabulary to be presented with the concepts employed by the physician who is seeking to diagnose the illness of a patient. He has learned a set of words which tell him what to look for: he knows he must ascertain the individual's temperature, pulse, respiratory rate, age, weight, etc. These words lead him to make certain formal or informal measurements, after which he attempts to arrange the facts into a pattern. The pattern is then incorporated into a theory or diagnosis which in turn leads to prognosis and treatment. But the words are the beginning of the process: they call attention to the principles involved.

Some of the principles underlying behavior will be suggested. As they stand they will not be adequate to describe or explain behavior like dreaming, insanity, anger, naughtiness, imitation, or poetry-learning. Elaboration is required before such applications can be made. Here and throughout the remainder of the book, however, there will be elaboration only when it is germane to an understanding of pubilc opinion and propaganda.

Stimulus and Response

The magic formula of most of modern psychology is to state that people respond to stimuli. A stimulus is a change in the environment, including internal changes (like an accelerated heart beat), which affects the individual. A response is what the person actually does or does not perceive or do after being affected by the stimulus.

The formula is very simple and hence many men, including psychologists, have criticized it for this very reason. They say that it affords no explanation of behavior because it neglects the fact that there is always an individual responding to the stimulus and that the response, therefore, depends not only upon the stimulus but also upon the individual. The same painting, even if it is not of the abstract variety and even if it is a simple, intelligible portrait, almost always arouses different responses in different people. Critics in the arts seldom agree with one another, except when all of them have been told that a product of the classics like Shakespeare is beautiful or great; and even then their ideas of beauty or greatness differ.

Such a criticism of the concepts of stimulus and response

is quite valid. When it is agreed, however, that organisms —including jackasses—respond more or less uniquely to the same stimulus, it is not agreed simultaneously that the formulation itself should be abandoned. To conceptualize behavior in terms of stimuli and responses is not to over-simplify human activity but to suggest that behavior can be thought of in lawful terms. The word "cause" could be substituted for stimulus and "effect" for response in an effort to point out the wider implication of the formula. If the objection is then raised that men's actions cannot be described in cause-and-effect terms, then no satisfactory re-ply can be made; the quest for generalizations must be abandoned.

The problem of ultimate causes need not be settled in order to proceed with an analysis of behavior. A man sees an apple on a tree and there is also some type of appetite within him; the response is eating. That the apple chances to be on the tree results from a long series of prior events which may include manure, the farmer who originally planted the tree, the bee which pollinated the seed, and perhaps even sunspots. The fact that the man has an appetite for an apple at the particular moment also presupposes a series of prior events: the heartiness of his breakfast, his experience with apples in the past, his feeling about picking fruit from trees, the amount of saliva in his mouth, and perhaps the original twinkle in his father's eye before he was conceived. This endless analysis, however, must be halted. No doubt it is sufficient merely to point out that the man likes apples, he sees the apple, he observes its ripeness, he believes he may pick it, he knows he can reach it, and he has teeth with which to chew it. The stimulus-response formulation en-ables those events which are involved in the situation to be selected from among the myriad of preceding and succeed-ing events. Whatever people do or whatever occurs in the organic or inorganic world stems from the cosmos. Since the cosmos cannot be grasped at a glance, men must be content with the humbler segments that are within their intellectual grasp.

Vocabulary differences make their trite appearance at

this point.   Only psychologists or physiologists, it can be
pointed out, use the words stimulus and response.   So they
do.   Stimulus does have other names which sound more or
less sweet: environment, social forces, culture traits, objects,
situations, people, etc.   And responses may also be called
actions, reactions, behavior, social movements, culture patterns, conduct, deportment, etc.   It matters not which words
are employed.   It would be just as useful to talk about the
environment-behavior or the object-conduct relationship.
Since a selection must be made—synonyms may promote
literary style but they are often a nuisance when a thought
is to be made consistently intelligible—the choice must be
arbitrary.

Personality

It has already been conceded that too little about human
behavior is known when only the stimulus and the response
are taken into account.   Even one of the simplest responses,
the jerking of the foot when a nerve on the knee cap is
struck (the so-called knee jerk or patellar reflex), not only
depends on the stimulus, the blow, which is applied, but may
also be affected by other responses which the individual is
making at the time.   Any reluctance to admit the role of the
individual or his personality in determining the response to
the stimulus is quite understandable: whereas most stimuli
and responses can be observed and measured directly, the
state of the personality can be observed only indirectly and
can be measured with difficulty.

A note is struck on a piano and an individual correctly
identifies it as middle C.   The stimulus can be described in
physical terms as a sound with a vibration rate of 260 per
second.   The response is the vocal vibration of "middle C."
A second individual calls the same note "D."   His response
is different from the first person's, and the difference between the two responses cannot be ascribed to the note
which was identical for each but to variations within the
two persons.   The state of the individual is not easily explained: perhaps the first person, one might say, has greater

"musical aptitude"; or the second may not have been paying close attention. Whatever explanation is given to account for the differing responses refers to other responses within the personality. Both the individual himself and the observer cannot immediately describe what those other responses are. Mankind possesses no psychic ray which reveals what is happening inside a person before his outside behavior is affected.

Since men's mental life is private and since they themselves are not always aware of what is determining and will determine their own response to stimuli, it becomes necessary to ascribe certain tendencies to people which cannot be directly observed. If it is known, for example, that an individual prefers Van Gogh to all so-called modern painters, then it becomes relatively easy to predict which of his responses to the pictures exhibited at a gallery will be favorable; the prediction can be more certain when a Van Gogh is included in the collection. Oh yes, out of sheer cussedness or perversion or for socially legitimate reasons he may suddenly prefer a particular Picasso to the Van Gogh—all that this means is that his behavior should not be predicted on the basis of knowing one of his preferences, or it may suggest that the conceptualization of the preference has not been accurate.

The question is: how can the state of the personality be determined? Various tests may be employed but, it must be said again and more emphatically, they all seek to measure tendencies which are not directly observable. The individual might be asked which modern painter he prefers. The paintings he has in his home or the books on painting he reads might be observed. Documents about his childhood and adolescence might be collected, with special emphasis upon his esthetic responses. He might be bribed to visit a psychological laboratory and there be confronted not with a collection of paintings but with various combinations of colors or forms which are believed to have some relationship to modern painting; from these preferences, perhaps, some kind of an inference could be made. All of these tests, except the first one, sound somewhat tedious, which is another way of pointing out that it is easier to make snap judgments concerning people than to study them carefully.

What is said about the state of the personality, in short, has to be inferred and usually it has to be inferred from the individual's behavior in the past. It is useful to know, for example, how intelligent an individual is. If we think we can look at him and discover his intelligence from his appearance, we are committing a commonplace error and more than likely will discover that our judgment is inaccurate. What we should do is to observe how he reacts to situations and on that basis—the observation of his behavior in the past—arrive at some decision as to how intelligently or unintelligently he will behave in the future. The standardized intelligence tests to which most children and many adults nowadays are subjected use the same approach: the individual is required to solve a number of heterogeneous problems; his solutions are scored; then this measure of adaptability or achievement gives an index of how he will solve new problems he must meet.

A friend says to us, "I would like to have you meet this man; he's from France and doesn't speak any English." The logical prediction we make, of course, is that the man speaks French. Why? Because we are told that he comes from France and we know that people who come from France speak French. We do not ordinarily carry our reasoning any further. Why do we know that individuals who come from France speak French? We know that French is spoken in France; that children born in France learn French unless they are imbeciles or segregated from normal French society; we believe, therefore, that anyone who comes from France has spoken French, possesses the capability of speaking French, and will speak it when we meet him unless he knows some other language or does not speak at all.

Tendencies to respond, then, arise from past experience. The statement is evident until explanations of behavior sometimes given by individuals in their rash or even in their rational moments are recalled. A person does something, it is said, because:

He is a Negro.
He is a member of a social class.
He has an ornery disposition.
He comes from a large family.
He has a low intelligence.
He is anti-social.
He does not think things through.
He is very ambitious.
He is a property owner.
He likes to do things that way.

A moment's reflection will reveal that each of these convenient or slipshod explanations assumes that, as a result of the specified circumstance, the person now has within himself a response tendency which affects his behavior. Being a Negro, for example, is crucial to an understanding of an individual's behavior only if this caste status in society has caused him to learn particular ways of reacting to problem situations. On the other hand, what he does at a given moment can be totally unrelated to the fact that he is a Negro, and hence ascribing the behavior to his caste may be nothing more than a semantic blunder.

The ways in which the tendencies within the individual are organized can be referred to as his personality. So much of behavior in a rather typical American community, it has been shown by Warner and Lunt (5), depends on the social situation in which the individual finds himself. He behaves in one way when he is in contact with members of his own class and he tends to be haughty or deferential toward another individual who is, respectively, beneath or above him in social class. If he is an aristocrat who belongs to the upper class, he expresses himself more freely at a cocktail party given by his clique than he does while talking with the attendant at a gasoline station or a distant acquaintance at an American Legion meeting. By and large the stimulus— and the vast conglomeration of furniture, dress, manner, symbols, etc., which compose class is conveniently summarized by this term—seems to produce more or less similar responses in individuals whose social-class membership has provided them with identical dispositions. The analysis of behavior through a concept like social class, as Warner and Lunt certainly point out, provides insight only into the social personality of individuals: it states in very general terms what they do in situations in which social class is important. Even in those social situations, however, individuals exhibit differences; and from situation to situation a particular individual may exhibit more or less the same personality traits. A member of the upper class, for example, may be shy whether he is talking to a banker, the attendant, or the Legionnaire—shyness characterizes him as a personality for reasons probably to be found not in his social class but in his own particular background.

When a woman argues with her husband, when a psychiatrist seeks to diagnose a patient, or when an artist describes an imaginary character, the primary interest is in personality with all its nuances, consistencies, and dispositional tendencies. The goal is knowledge of the personality not in the abstract but in the concrete. In studying public opinion and propaganda, however, personality is seldom the center of interest. What must be known is the dispositions which many individuals have in common, regardless of the unique role these dispositions play within each of them. Everybody cannot be analyzed at once, it must be admitted; but segments of many people's personalities can be simultaneously described.

Drives

The first and most striking characteristic of an organism is the need to make a response. Inanimate objects have no needs, except in a figurative sense: they respond to changes in their environments and the response depends upon their nature too, but that nature does not impel them to seek stimuli to which they must make a response if they are to survive or be happy. Where there is life, there is movement toward or in response to stimuli.

Almost everyone recognizes needs within himself which he calls instincts, urges, impulses, tendencies, sets, desires, motives, or drives. Here the term "drives" will be employed, again a very arbitrary choice. Unless a stimulus is extremely intense or otherwise outstanding or unless a drive is active, there is no response and a stimulus has no stimulating value for the individual. People eat food when they are hungry, not when they are satiated.

The individual realizes that a drive is active or unsatisfied when he is restless, tense, or plain unhappy. He knows he seeks a change or something which will make him feel rested, relaxed, or happy. What he seeks is a reduction in the drive and that reduction can be obtained only by altering his behavior, by making what has been called a *goal response*. In the simplest case of hunger, he craves food or feels pangs from his stomach and he reduces the strength of the drive or temporarily eliminates it altogether by finding, perhaps by cooking, but certainly by eating food. Frequently, of course, the individual is just vaguely driven to make a goal response he himself cannot even name. He is moody, for example, and cannot account for the mild depression except through a vague reference to the side of the bed from which he descended that morning. This conception of drives does not suggest that the goal of life is flabbiness or sleep, although there is a philosophical point involved when such a question is raised. Certainly most people, according to their own testimony and behavior, crave excitement which involves tension and not relaxation. The excitement does signify the arousal of drives, but simultaneously it implies that the aroused drives find satisfaction through a goal response. A meal may be enjoyed more when the person is extremely hungry than when he has no appetite because greater tension is involved—*and* then reduced. Without drives there can be no tension and unhappiness and also no reduction and satisfaction.

The relation of drive to stimulus may be twofold: a stimulus must arouse a drive and a drive may orient the individual to perceive another stimulus. Many of the stimuli that evoke drives are within the individual such as pain, hunger pangs, pressure on the bladder, movement of the liquid in the internal ear when equilibrium is disturbed, etc. Others are outside the individual and reach him through his sense organs. A man may feel hungry either when his stomach rumbles or when he sees a clock which indicates to him that it is time to eat. In short, some prior event or stimulus provokes a drive.

After a drive is active, then the individual is in a state of readiness to respond to other stimuli. He looks for a restaurant sign when he is hungry so that he can respond to that stimulus by entering the building, whereas he scarcely notices such signs when he is not motivated to eat. Sunsets, it has often been remarked, cannot be enjoyed by hungry men—presumably because men in that condition seek other forms of stimulation.

It is not always necessary, however, for a particular drive to have been previously activated before a stimulus is perceived. The audience watching and listening to a motion picture is experiencing a whole series of tensions, not one of which probably involves personal safety. As the hapless stimulus of a shouted "fire" is immediately perceived by almost everyone, another and overpowering drive is evoked. Then a variety of responses suddenly occurs which may lead to panic. This stimulus has become outstanding through sheer intensity—it may have been louder than the sounds accompanying the picture—or through its unusual character —ordinarily the only loud voices heard in a theater are those coming from the sound apparatus. It is not stretching a point too much, nevertheless, to maintain that there has to be some prior drive, the one which originally has led the audience into the building to see the picture. Such a stretch indicates a psychological fact of crucial importance to an understanding of propaganda : irrelevant as any drive may be to the perception of a stimulus, it can produce a state of readiness which facilitates that perception. As will be indicated later, for example, the individual listening at his radio set, reading his newspaper, or attending a motion picture, does not seek to be affected by propaganda but his interest in what he is doing may place him in the position of not being able to avoid perceiving the propagandist's message.

For a variety of reasons it is not necessary here to attempt to enumerate the drives with which people are born and which therefore, in modified form, determine their behavior. Lists of human instincts are no longer an academic pastime because it is clear that the practice is both arbitrary and useless. Whatever innate drives people possess, as will be subsequently suggested, are so thoroughly affected by their social environment that it is usually sufficient to know—or to attempt to know—the drives that are functioning within them at the moment of their behavior.

Reward and Punishment

When a stimulus has evoked a drive, the individual makes various responses. The responses which lead to reduction in tension are rewarding and those which do not decrease or in fact increase tension are punishing. The hungry man who finds inedible food or no food at all has undergone a punishing experience. In a less strict sense, a material object or a particular action may be said to constitute the reward or the punishment because it is intimately linked with the occurrence or non-occurrence of the goal response itself.

The rewards an individual seeks and the punishments he avoids when a drive has been aroused are determined by the original structure of his organism, by the experiences he has had while maturing, and by the particular drive that is active. A small child, for example, withdraws from an object like a pin which is lacerating his skin and is thus producing pain. The reward here is strictly negative: the avoidance of the pain and hence the reduction of the tension associated with that sensation. After one or more experiences with such an object, he avoids similar objects even before contact has been established. He has learned to anticipate pain and thus his withdrawal occurs sooner than it did at first. Later on, however, pins may acquire reward value for him. As a thoroughly normal individual, he learns that the function of pins is to fasten various articles together and he works or walks to a store in order to be able to buy some. If he is abnormally masochistic, he may conceivably like to puncture his skin with pins; thus the reward value of the pin has changed completely as a result of whatever pathological drive is functioning within him.

Original or primary rewards involve drive reduction through processes directly connected with physiological processes. The infant stops crying only when he is fed, when his clothing is made more comfortable, or when the pain from whatever cause ceases. Learned or secondary rewards soon become equally effective. Then the child's crying ceases when he sees his parent, when a light is turned on, and—much later—when he is told or bribed to stop. Whether these latter rewards are as important to the child's drives as the earlier ones presents a problem, but they do at least affect his behavior.

Rewards and punishments serve as the incentives to learning. Just as the individual will not begin to learn new responses unless he must reduce the tension of one or more of his drives, so it is likely that he will continue to respond until one response actually reduces the tension (*i.e.,* is rewarding) or that he will repeat a response which previously has reduced that tension (*i.e.,* has been rewarding). A response which leads to the reward of tension reduction and hence toward a goal response is thus *reinforced* and one that does not reduce or increases tension is *extinguished*. Simply expressed: reward reinforces, whereas punishment extinguishes responses.

Behavior is not so easily explained in terms of reward or reinforcement and punishment or extinction as might at first appear. For frequently there is more than one drive functioning and hence more than one reward or punishment involved. A man, for example, wishes to learn to ski. A superficial analysis might reveal that his drive is to participate socially with his friends who are ski enthusiasts and that therefore the reward he seeks is that participation. As a result, he responds to a whole collection of stimuli including snow, skis, hills, wind, sensations involving equilibrium, etc. Presumably the learning process continues until he can make the various responses required of a skier. Actually, of course, he may abandon skiing before he acquires the skill, and he may do so because the punishment he receives from hurting himself or from being ridiculed by his friends is stronger than the reward he has anticipated at the outset. Or he may conclude that he can achieve sufficiently rewarding social participation without learning to ski.

As a result of previous learning, the individual usually seeks to reduce drive-tension by responding in ways that have been rewarding in the past. His response to a stimulus outside or inside himself comes to be affected not only by the drive which moves him to action but also by these residues of previous experiences. The residues are habits.

Habits

The outstanding characteristic of human beings, it has been and should be said again and again, is their ability to learn. The progress of the infant to maturity is measured by what he learns. Some of the learning depends upon his physiological development and capacity, but the rest depends upon the experiences he has in his environment and then, subsequently, upon the effects these experiences have on his personality. The moot and tantalizing question of heredity and environment may remain unsettled since no black-white reply is possible : behavior involves both in varying degrees, depending on the person and situation.

Learning refers to behavior which becomes different as a result of past experience. The difference can be roughly described as a change in the stimuli to which approximately the same response is made or as a change in the response to approximately the same stimuli. A motorist learns to drive cautiously not only in response to stimuli like heavy traffic, darkness, and police regulations but also to other stimuli like snow or the presence of children playing anywhere on the street. A chess player learns new gambits which he employs defensively or offensively as similar complicated configurations confront him on the board. All learning, including the simplest type of conditioning, requires that a drive be active within the individual and that some kind of reward be attained (*3*). Those famous dogs of Pavlov, for example, which salivated after hearing the sound of a tuning fork when that sound had previously occurred before the unconditioned stimulus of food powder, exhibited this learning only under certain conditions: they had to be hungry, an optimal time interval had to separate the two stimuli, they could not be distracted by other sounds, and occasionally the conditioned response of salivating to the bell had to be reinforced by actually offering them food powder (2).

A learned connection between any stimulus and any response is defined as a habit. A habit, however, is not a mechanical bond between any one stimulus and any one response which functions automatically when the stimulus is perceived. Again a drive must be active, or else the stimulus is not perceived or no response occurs: habits serve drives. The stimulus, moreover, may be complex and patterned, such as the face of a person which habitually provokes an unfriendly response. It may be an internal response, like a thought after seeing a sign, which acts also as a stimulus to arouse other internal or external responses—such a response is called a stimulus-producing response or a response with stimulus value. It may be another kind of an internal response, like an ache after receiving a blow, which acts as a stimulus to evoke a drive—this type of response is called a drive-producing response or a response with drive value. The response components of the habit, in addition, need not be identical: a man who wants to smoke may habitually reach for a cigarette with his right or his left hand, he may smoke one of his own on one occasion or borrow one from a friend on another, or he may be content with any form of tobacco. The concept of habit, therefore, is being employed most broadly to include behavior as diverse as swimming and race prejudice. Learning can then be viewed as the process of establishing, weakening, strengthening, or eliminating habits.

Certain aspects of personality are so important that they must be singled out for special treatment. They are responses which are habitually evoked, but they also possess relatively unique characteristics. Here they will be termed attitude and knowledge.

Attitudes

An individual has attitudes toward other people and toward objects in his environment. Usually an emotional or evaluative reaction is involved: the attitude is friendly or unfriendly, favorable or unfavorable, positive or negative, respectful or disrespectful, etc. When it is said that a person has an attitude toward his country, other nations, democracy, communism, his friends, his enemies, Negroes, Jews, meat, oranges, contraception, or helicopters, the implication is that he always has either specific or general feelings regarding these concrete or symbolic stimuli and that his behavior is more or less governed accordingly. Actually, as employed by laymen and social scientists, attitude is a somewhat vague term which frequently merely calls attention to a psychological problem without contributing a coherent solution (*1*). It is, however, a convenient concept when a detailed analysis of individual behavior is not feasible—as is almost always the case in studying public opinion and propaganda—provided that its psychological attributes are specified.

An attitude is an internal response which the individual has learned as a result of past rewards and punishments. Attitudes are acquired and are not inborn; and a considerable part of human behavior depends upon the social environment rather than upon the germ plasm. The attitudes behind race prejudice, for example, are the culmination of previous experiences, and they therefore are inevitable only because such experiences are likely to occur and recur in a particular society. Similarly political attitudes develop as the individual matures.

Before an attitude can be aroused, some kind of stimulus has had to be present. The stimuli may be varied—the color of a face, the shape of a nose, the curl of the hair, the nature of the surname, the type of clothing, alleged forms of conduct, and the sound of a particular word are some of the stimuli evoking race prejudice—but almost always they are part of a pattern or are arranged in what has been called a *gradient*. This gradient may be one that exists in the physical environment (like the colors of the spectrum) or in the social environment (like the numerous appelations and epithets applied to a particular race), or it may be one which is peculiar to the individual concerned (like the size and breed of dog adopted for a pet). In any case, the individual has come to make the attitudinal response to some stimuli and not to others. When a group of stimuli arouses approximately the same response, the gradient is known as one of *generalization;* and when some stimuli arouse the response and others do not, the gradient is called one of *discrimination.* Gradients of generalization and discrimination can be learned: not only attitudinal responses but also all habitual responses, internal or external, are evoked by stimuli which are so arranged.

Attitudes, moreover, are a distinctive kind of internal response. When they are aroused, they predispose the individual to make certain overt responses. If the color green, Italians, or dachshunds provoke unfriendly or un-favorable attitudes, for example, the individual having these attitudes experiences a tendency to avoid the color, the group, or the animal. In the past presumably he has been punished by responding in a particular way to them and as a result the avoidance tendency, the attitude, has been set up within him. The attitude, consequently, has be-come an *anticipatory response* which is one occurring earlier in a response sequence than it did originally, just as a child who has been burned by touching a radiator soon learns to keep clear of all objects looking like radiators *before* he touches them(4). In addition, the internal response called an attitude possesses both stimulus and drive value: it in turn arouses other responses and it *always* evokes a drive. The responses to which it serves as a stimulus may be in-ternal or external, *i.e.,* they may be another attitude or involve relevant knowledge, or they may give rise to action. The drive value of the attitude may be strong or weak, and the drive evoked by the attitude may or may not be de-cisive in determining what the individual does in the situa-tion which is stimulating him.

The complicated character of an attitude becomes more

evident when its drive property is examined in relation to the entire personality of the individual. Some stimulus, for example, makes the individual aware of the fact that he is hungry. Such a drive, however, does not function by itself: he almost always has no generalized craving for food but seeks a particular kind more or less in accordance with the customs of his everyday existence. He wants food, but an attitude-induced drive must also be satisfied. The goal response—the eating of the food—is then determined both by the hunger drive and the accompanying attitude. As an individual he will be completely satisfied only when the tension connected with both drives is reduced. After eating a less preferred food, he will no longer be hungry but, although at that moment his attitude toward the preferred food may not be producing much tension within him, he will continue to feel somewhat frustrated. An attitude, in short, helps mediate a drive and few drives within socialized people are ever aroused without being accompanied by attitudes which have drive value of their own.

Almost every internal response involves, therefore, an attitude. Some differentiation between an attitudinal response and other internal responses, however, must be pointed out. On sociological but not on psychological grounds, internal responses with stimulus and drive value may be called attitudes only when the external responses to which they give rise are considered significant in the society. What is "considered significant in the society" is admittedly but deliberately vague, inasmuch as the evaluation of behavior is subject to enormous fluctuations from society to society and within a given society. The simplest act—and hence the attitude which helps determine it—is considered socially significant in some society. Many primitive people, for example, carefully dispose of their nail parings since they believe that damage inflicted on such exuviae by an enemy will actually bring pain or even death to themselves. Obviously they habitually make rather definite responses to the parings; the internal responses provoked by these stimuli are socially significant and hence attitudes. The responses produced among Englishmen and Americans by the same stimuli, on the other hand, have little or no social significance and are not called attitudes. Many of the emotions and feelings—which are also internal responses—are included in the classification of attitude when they represent or give rise to socially significant behavior.

Innumerable habitual responses occur within the individual which have no drive value, or at least their drive value seems to be at a minimum. The response to the stimulus, "What number comes after three?" is of course "four." Such a response will be called "knowledge."

Knowledge

Knowledge is ordinarily considered to be, very simply, that which is known about any kind of phenomenon. The implication is always that the knowledge either resides directly within an individual or is in a form (like a book) that can be readily learned by somebody. Knowledge is thus another residue of past experience which can affect present and future behavior.

Within the individual, knowledge assumes various forms. It may be a mental image such as is produced within many people when they are asked to think of the appearance of a person they have met or of a place they have visited. It may be a body posture which must be assumed preparatory to an overt act like swimming. More frequently it is a thought or an idea which in turn is closely related to or identified with a linguistic expression. The concept of knowledge, then, refers not only to what is formally called schooling or technical competence but also to what is informally termed experience or "know-how."

Knowledge as a habitual response is related to drive and hence to attitude. Some stimulus must arouse a response involving knowledge, and almost always a drive has been previously aroused. "What number comes after three?" is a simple verbal stimulus but, before it is perceived, the individual must be oriented to make the perception. The orientation represents a drive, such as the one pupils have when they are paying attention to their teachers. The

internal response of "four" which then occurs may itself
have no drive value: the individual will not say the word
aloud unless he is driven to cooperate with his questioner
for a reason which, in this simple instance, he himself can
doubtless explain. Sometimes, moreover, people seem eager
to display what they know. The child who is proud of his
arithmetical accomplishments responds to many stimuli
arithmetically and then quickly displays his erudition in
order to impress his parents and thus perhaps to improve
his status within the family group. In this case the same
question elicits both knowledge and an attitude-induced
drive, or the knowledge itself is able to evoke the attitude.
At any rate, by itself the knowledge is presumed to have no
drive value. The stimuli evoking knowledge, finally, are
extensive as a result of previous generalization—like attitudes, the same response can occur to a variety of questions
whose "meaning," consequently, is essentially identical.

A reference to knowledge usually raises the problem of
truth and falsity. From a strictly psychological viewpoint,
however, that problem is quite irrelevant. A person suffering from the delusion that he is Hitler or Satan has incorrect knowledge about himself according to the best
judgments of other people, but that "false" knowledge constitutes for him an extremely important internal response
which gives rise to an attitude affecting, perhaps, most of
his overt behavior. The delusion itself, therefore, is a
psychological fact, although it may be socially in error.

Apparently related to knowledge but basically different
from it is the factor of *skill* which must be mentioned at
least in passing. Skill can be said to represent a person's
more or less innate capacity to perceive stimuli and adopt
or modify habitual connections between stimuli and responses. Each sense organ, for example, possesses a certain
degree of skill. The average eye can perceive light only
when its wave length is between approximately 390 and 760
millionths of a millimeter; light whose wave length is below
or above this range is invisible. The eye of one person may
be more acute in detecting differences in the intensity of light
either as a result of innate skill or of practice—or of both.

Similarly individuals differ in respect to overall skill called intelligence, a term most generally referring to the ability to learn or at least to that part of the ability that is unaffected by previous experience.

In this chapter man has been presented as a creature who responds to certain stimuli that are arranged in his internal and external environment. His responses are affected by these stimuli as well as by the drives, attitude, knowledge, and skill which he himself possesses as a personality. He learns to seek rewards and to avoid punishments. The fruits of past experience are stored within him in such a way that they can be habitually evoked.

CHAPTER 3

The Nature of Public Opinion

THE Congress of the United States is discussing a bill involving a domestic problem. The debate inside and outside of the capitol building is prolonged and furious. Editorial writers, columnists, radio commentators, and cracker-barrel philosophers are stating their points of view. But, the question is asked, what do the American people think? How is "public opinion" really reacting?

From September 1, 1939, until December 7, 1941, almost every American was wondering whether or not the United States would enter the war. There were some individuals and groups who believed that the conflict was no concern of ours and that therefore we should avoid becoming embroiled. There were others who felt that, although Great Britain and then later the Soviet Union were fighting "our battle in defense of civilization," we should not actively participate but should help those countries defeat the Axis by becoming "the arsenal of democracy." And there were many who wanted this country to begin a shooting war immediately. Then the Japanese bombed Pearl Harbor. The next day war was declared on Japan and on December 11 the declaration by Germany and Italy was reciprocated. The American people, it was then felt, were no longer divided: "public opinion" was behind the war.

In a small American town in the Middle West the houses

are made of wood. Architectually they represent a variety
of styles ranging from late nineteenth century to imitation
classic and Cape Cod. On the whole people living there
consider them neither outstandingly beautiful nor too de-
pressingly ugly. The son of an old and wealthy resident
comes home from an Eastern college, enters his father's
business, marries a suitable girl, and begins building an
ultra-modern dwelling for himself and his bride. At great
expense rock is imported into the town and, as the construction progresses, it becomes evident that the house will have
a completely flat roof. Most people in the community are
outraged: they do not like the house and they say that it is
ruining the beauty of the street on which it is being built.
Feelings against the young man run high, there is talk of
enacting some kind of zoning regulation which will prevent
similar monstrosities in the future, and everyone says that
"public opinion" is hostile toward the man and the architec-
tural style he has selected.

A Negro is lynched in the Deep South. The members of
the mob admit privately that he may not have been guilty
but, they say, "public opinion" demanded that all Negroes
be taught a lesson. Besides a crime has been committed and
the girl, before she died, stated that it was a Negro who
attacked her. The governor of the state deplores the
lynching and declares that "public opinion" is against this
type of violence. Elsewhere editorial writers also point out
that in general "public opinion" in the South is opposed to
lynchings.

It is obviously unnecessary to belabor the point that the
concept of public opinion is often employed. "Public
opinion," it is stated variously, opposes or favors this or
that, is expressed or repressed, is a source of wisdom or
folly, or should or should not be heard. Perhaps the question may sound impudent, but it seems relevant to ask what
the term means.

Like brushing one's teeth, the act of defining a word is
both boring and essential. It is boring because it is more
interesting and exciting to think and talk without stopping
to decide on the meaning of words. Everybody knows what

"water" is; why define the word? Everybody knows what "justice" and "truth" are; why—but is there really agreement on how such abstract words should be defined? Definitions are essential if communication is to be intelligible. Most people are aware of this. Modern semanticists consider themselves startlingly original when they repeat the truism in their own complicated terminology. But it remains pleasanter and easier simply to maintain that "justice is being upheld" or that "truth is being defended" than to indicate the precise meaning of such terms by means of less abstract words or specific illustrations.

Although most writers who use the term public opinion seldom indicate its referent and thus contribute to general confusion, it is possible to come up with numerous definitions by conducting a diligent search through various intellectual sources. Definitions begin with the simple word "people" and end with the semi-mystical idea of "a more or less rational collective judgment formed by the action and reaction of many individuals" (*1*). No one can quarrel with a definition which is precise unless the question of its accepted usage is raised. "Public opinion," however, is such an ambiguous term that usage is no guide to clarity. Here is a definition that seeks to be precise and at least not sensationally different from the way in which the term is frequently employed: *public opinion refers to people's attitudes on an issue when they are members of the same social group.*

The key psychological word in this definition is that of "attitude." Before such a concept can carry the burden of the definition, it is necessary to recall from the previous chapter the characterization of an attitude as the socially significant, internal response that people habitually make to stimuli. Presumed, therefore, is a series of experiences which have produced within people more or less similar responses; various gradients of generalization and discrimination along which the evoking stimuli are arranged; and some connection with overt behavior. In this sense it might appear as though public opinion exists whenever people have attitudes. Most Americans, for example, drink coffee for breakfast and therefore may be presumed to have a favorable attitude toward this beverage; but should one say that American public opinion favors coffee?

According to common usage, it is fairly certain that this attitude would not be included in the category of public opinion. "American public opinion favors coffee"—no, it does not sound right. The definition of public opinion here proposed, moreover, also rules out the use of the expression to apply to coffee-drinking, *unless* an issue is at stake. An issue involves a controversy or conflict among people and therefore results in the interruption of a habit with consequent non-reduction of drives. If the price of coffee suddenly rises so high that it is beyond the budget of the average American family, then the attitude can no longer find its normal outlet in drinking the beverage but affects other behavior. There are public demonstrations or there is petty grousing against the government, coffee merchants, or the capitalist system. At this point public opinion regarding coffee arises.

In addition, the people who have attitudes more or less in common regarding an issue must be members of a social group before there is public opinion. Each group has a distinctive organization that regulates the behavior of its members. A crowd's organization is very simple: participants have face-to-face contact with one another and their behavior results from their pre-existing knowledge, attitudes, and drives as well as from mutual stimulation. Photographers scattered throughout the country belong to a social group, although they may not be members of a formal association: they are conscious of one another to a certain degree and they obviously share an interest in pictures. Citizens of a country also are members of a social group, the nation, while simultaneously they belong to local groups as well as those also scattered throughout the land.

The social structure of a group, as Warner and Lunt (2) have vividly demonstrated in the American society, assigns to each individual a status which in turn determines a large part but not all of his social behavior. The group, moreover, places at the disposal of its members certain media of communication through which public opinion can be expressed. These media can be quite diverse. Orally they range from the informal conversation of friends to the speaker whose voice is transmitted by a national hookup at one of the favorable evening hours. Visually they vary from a private letter received from a relative to a syndicated column reaching the more or less literate at their breakfast tables each day. They include the poorly focused snapshot in the family album as well as the most extravagant effusion from Hollywood.

The four illustrations given at the beginning of the chapter can now be critically examined in the light of this conceptualization of public opinion. Certain basic questions must be asked in connection with each:

1. *What group is involved?* The reaction of "the American people" to a Congressional debate seems to include all citizens of the United States. But does it? Are the insane and children under six interested? Are non-voters? In connection with the issue of American participation in the war before Pearl Harbor, it appears that many groups had varying viewpoints. What were these groups? Were they organized on a regional or an economic basis? It is said that "public opinion" looks with disfavor upon the young man who is building a modernistic home. Does this mean everyone in the community? "Most people," it is claimed "are outraged"—well, who is not? When the governor of the southern state claims that "public opinion" is opposed to lynching, is he referring to people like himself, to those with a college education, to poor whites, to Negroes? Certainly he cannot be thinking of the lynchers. Similarly, the mob is purported to claim that "public opinion" demands this form of pedagogy. Does the local minister advocate lynching? Do lawyers? Do Negroes? Who, moreover, opposes lynching in the South? Someone must, because editorial writers say they do. But who?

2. *What issue is involved?* The answer here seems easy at first glance: the bill being debated, America's participation in the war, the new style of house, and lynching. But are these the only issues? Maybe political or personal con-

siderations enter into people's reactions to a Congressional debate. No doubt patriotism and social philosophy were involved before and after Pearl Harbor. Perhaps people are considering not only the man's new house but also his reputation in the community—could the "suitable girl" from the East or the "old and wealthy" family be the issue? It is conceivable that the issue for the Governor of the state is not the lynching but the effect of the lynching on the state's ability to attract northern capital.

3. *Why have people responded to the issue?* Are people interested in the Congressional debate because the passage of the bill will affect their everyday lives or do they think that "matters of principle" are at stake? Why did isolationists who were opposed to American participation in the war suddenly become good soldiers or producers after Pearl Harbor? What happened to the isolationist attitudes? As a matter of fact, did all isolationists actually cooperate with the war effort? Why do people in a community worry about the appearance of houses when they are confronted with so many more pressing problems? For what reason do lynchers think that this kind of punishment will prevent Negroes from committing crimes in the future? Just who joins a lynching bee? Why do people in the South *and* the North take sides regarding lynching? This type of question could indeed be endless.

In fact, the series itself could be endless. It will be halted, however, at this point, though only three major questions have been asked. For these are the questions that are most relevant to the problem of understanding and analyzing public opinion. They are the questions which should be asked even before the term public opinion itself is employed.

A rough classification of public opinion is a first-step in identifying some of the problems. Since there can be public opinion concerning any conceivable issue, the classification cannot be based upon the attitude content; instead the criteria must refer to the psychological and sociological significance of the attitude. The first type of classification distinguishes between public opinion that, at a given moment, is expressed and unexpressed. The second points out the difference between public opinion which is already functioning and that which conceivably may come into being.

The distinction between the attitudes people possess regarding a particular issue and the actual expression of these attitudes either as overt opinion or in overt behavior must be made in order to indicate the social role being played by public opinion in a particular situation. If those attitudes are not expressed, reference can be made to *internal public opinion.* If they are expressed and hence are the important but not the exclusive determinants of action, reference can be made to *external public opinion.* The conditions under which internal public opinion becomes externalized can usually be specified only in general terms. One important factor is the drive strength of the attitudes involved. When people are extremely enthusiastic or indignant, for example, it is difficult for them to conceal or repress their feelings; their overt behavior almost inevitably is affected by their attitude; and under these circumstances public opinion can be said to be externally effective. Another factor involves the rules of the social group to which the people belong. Under a modern dictatorship the secret police make it patently clear that certain types of expression are prohibited. As a result, individuals are afraid to express themselves in front of their neighbors or even in the presence of their own children, lest they be denounced to the authorities. Here public opinion remains internal and only those aspects are externalized which are countenanced by the regime. In contrast, the inhabitants of a rural area in the United States pride themselves on the freedom of expression which they consider a priceless privilege. Actually, their freedom is also restricted, not by the government but by the rules of their own group. An advocate of nudism, atheism, bolshevism, or any unpopular doctrine is not ferreted out by an official gestapo, but he receives short shrift informally at the hands of his own contemporaries.

At other times, the expression of public opinion is limited by the available media of communication. One of the outstanding technological developments of the twentieth century has been the rapid growth of these media. Censorship permitting, most important events in the modern world can be described almost as they occur or—for those addicted to "dope" stories and for rumor-mongers—perhaps before they occur. Only the individual in our society who was disabled psychologically or the uncivilized man whose geographical isolation was left untouched by civilized warriors had not heard of Franklin D. Roosevelt or Adolf Hitler a few years ago. Under these conditions public opinion in theory has many more opportunities to express itself. In practice, however, it often happens that only a limited number of groups and of individuals within each group is able to employ these media.

When people react to an issue that has been presented to them, public opinion is either internal or external and it is also actual. *Actual public opinion,* consequently, indicates that attitudes have been aroused and that they are having some kind of effect upon internal or external behavior. Frequently, however, it is possible to anticipate public opinion before the issue arises, and so the term *latent public opinion* may be employed to refer to attitudes of people regarding an issue when those attitudes have not yet been crystallized or when they are not being evoked or are not affecting behavior. On the basis of their personality structure, it is likely either that potentially such attitudes can be learned and reinforced or that, being dormant at the moment, they can be aroused when and if the issue arises. During peace time public opinion about war tends to remain latent: the issue of fighting is not directly in front of people, although they continue to have attitudes which can be evoked by a conflict when it occurs and especially by the propaganda accompanying that conflict. Housewives have no specific attitude toward a new labor-saving gadget to be employed in their kitchens before that gadget is for sale and advertised. Potentially, however, they may be expected to express their approval, inasmuch as they are psychologically ready beforehand to learn to respond favorably: their desire to save labor and their readiness to accept gadgets are functioning attitudes which can be easily evoked.

Public opinion, however, should not be called latent unless certain attitudes which have not been previously learned or expressed are likely to be learned or expressed in connection with a future issue. It is perfectly true that potentially people can be made to approve or disapprove of any viewpoint or action, but there are also limits beyond which their behavior cannot be expected to range. Latent in the sense of potential should really mean probable or foreseeable. It is, for example, conceivable that Englishmen may some day change their form of government from a limited to an absolute monarchy. There is nothing in the English germ plasm, such a statement suggests, which precludes producing people on those blessed isles who could favor such a change. This state of affairs, however, is not likely to come to pass for a variety of reasons which either are obvious or else require a series of dull volumes to elucidate. English public opinion regarding an absolute monarchy, therefore, is both actually and latently unfavorable.

Another and final backward glance at the four illustrations in this chapter can reveal the applicability and utility of these distinctions:

1. *The Congressional Debate*

Public opinion of the American people on the question has not been ascertained. There is no way of knowing, therefore, whether that opinion is actual or latent. Since the debate is being reported in the mass media and since those media are perceived by people, there is presumptive evidence that public opinion has become actual. If the public opinion is actual, it certainly is internal rather than external; for the asking of the question—"how is 'public opinion' reacting?"—indicates that people's attitudes have not been expressed.

2. *Pearl Harbor*

Before the Japanese attack, the public opinion of various groups in this country was both actual and external. At the same time there was among the isolationists a latent public opinion, it must be assumed, which became actual after

Pearl Harbor: almost all Americans are willing to immerse themselves in the war effort after war has been declared. The "my-country-right-or-wrong" element in the American tradition is then actual. Isolationist sentiment, however, did not die during the war: it remained either internal or potential and then tended to burst forth in a new form during the postwar period.

3. *The Modernistic Dwelling*

Those people in the community who previously have never seen an actual house with a flat roof were ready to be critical, although they themselves may not have been conscious of their attitude: their background and habits predisposed them in one way rather than another, and hence their public opinion could have been called latent. The inhabitants who disliked the young man or his family were internalizing their attitudes before the great crisis arose. Since some or many people are now enraged by the new dwelling, it may be said that public opinion has become actual and external.

4. *The Lynching*

People who approve or disapprove of lynching in the South represent actual public opinion: the issue of lynching tends to recur to Southerners again and again, even when no lynching takes place. This public opinion, however, remains internal until there is a lynching or talk of curbing lynchings in general. Then it becomes external and has an overwhelmingly important effect on their behavior.

In summary, it must be emphasized that public opinion is a term not to be employed either easily or carelessly. It is not a synonym for people. It presupposes a social organization or group as well as a series of more or less common experiences which people have had. It is a concept, therefore, which should creep into a sentence or a description only when these conditions have been ascertained and, if possible, only when they have been appropriately though approximately measured.

The delimitation of behavior called public opinion merely

introduces the problem. Now it is necessary to relate public opinion to its context within a society, the subject to be discussed in the next chapter. Then it will be possible to suggest the ways in which public opinion reacts as well as the basis for those reactions. Additional insight into public opinion can also be obtained as the problem of measurement is considered; for that which is measurable exists and that which exists is measurable. Finally, public opinion must be evaluated: how important are the actual, the latent, the external, the internal attitudes of people in modern society?

CHAPTER 4

The Cultural Background
of Public Opinion

Ask a man why he likes beefsteak and he will reply in various ways. He may say that he likes the "taste" of it; thereby he uses slightly different words to repeat his preference without adding any additional information. Or he may state that he likes meat, especially thick, tender, juicy meat; thus he merely describes the food without revealing the source of his preference. Ask him then whether he prefers beefsteak or caterpillars as a main dish and, if he be an American, he certainly will choose the beef. Challenge him for a reason and he will state that he has never tasted caterpillars, that they are loathsome creatures, that perhaps he would become ill if he ate them—and, besides, he likes beefsteak.

Individuals give similarly inadequate analyses of their likes and dislikes when they are questioned concerning their favorite color, type of story, friend, automobile, house, religion, whiskey, relaxation, or way of life. They have preferences but they find it difficult to account for the determinants. Sometimes the simple and frank explanation is the only one they can express: "I like it because I am used to it."

When the individual claims he likes something because he is used to it, he is at least stating the problem in terms of

44

his life experience. He means that for complicated reasons a particular response has proven to be rewarding in the past, with the result that he feels favorably disposed toward repeating it: included in his personality structure is an habitual response or attitude on the subject which can be evoked by some stimuli and not by others. He knows he will like the color red in the future because he has generally liked it; but why has he generally liked it? Or, better, why has he learned to like it?

He has not always liked it. Maybe the first time he saw something red as a child he had a dreadful experience: the color may have come from a fire which actually burned him. Or maybe his initial contact with the color left him unmoved; it attracted his attention but stirred up nothing profound within him. It is only certain that eventually his experiences with the color became pleasant. Perhaps there was red ribbon on his crib and he liked his crib. Perhaps his father wore a red necktie and he liked his father. Perhaps at an impressionable age he drank a cool glass of grape juice which looked red to him and which pleased him. The reasons for his preference must be found, in short, by delving into past experience.

Eventually delving in this manner reaches some rather simple and basic drives in the infant. The human repertoire at birth is relatively limited but is sufficient to become the basis for a subsequent, complicated development. From the drives to eat, to avoid pain, to breathe, to sleep, etc., are derived the more complex attitudes which quickly develop in the child and then become increasingly intricate as he matures. It is clear that, if a child from infancy on had seen his parents consume nice, sweet, juicy caterpillars and if eventually he had been given the privilege of eating these animals, he might as an adult prefer a dish of them to beefsteak any day. As a matter of fact, caterpillars are roasted and eaten by the Aranda who live in Central Australia (5). There is, then, this cultural element, this dependence on past experience in a particular society, for human attitudes. Artists certainly are original, but their products are liked or disliked only if they evoke in other people responses bearing some resemblance to what has happened to them in the past.

The dependence of the present and the future on the past seems at first glance to be an obvious fact requiring no elaboration. Americans like the American flag because—it is superfluous to complete the sentence. Germans like strong leaders because—but here the explanation is not so easy to supply, though doubtless every reader can think of a reason according to his taste and prejudice. Men should be given a fair trial because—this sentence would have to be developed into many paragraphs before it could be completed satisfactorily. The past may not always be so easy to recapture.

Sometimes, moreover, the past does not appear to be a sure-fire guide to the present and the future. An explosive, apparently irrational or unpredictable element in human affairs cannot be dismissed as a nasty phenomenon because it seems to make the best laid generalizations about people go awry. Women unexpectedly become hysterical. Men suddenly cannot discharge their normal obligations and must be committed to mental hospitals. A well-trained, well-seasoned, and well-disciplined division goes into battle and then cracks under enemy shell fire: back at headquarters the relevant general wonders and wonders what has happened.

Few psychiatrists would boast that they can give a complete explanation of hysteria, the psychoses, or mass morale. Almost all of them, however, would maintain that the last event immediately preceding a mental upset is not in itself the sole cause of the event. The individual concerned has had a past history which disposed him to behave as he did. And yet the problem of why the last event did manage to lead to the upset remains, even when that event is placed within the perspective of the total personality.

Public opinion also produces its share of surprises. A piece of advertising copy that is considered excellent by technicians in an advertising agency who are supposed to be the experts does not actually promote sales. A Grade-B picture which has been produced with little meditation and on a modest budget becomes a box-office success; this occurs sufficiently frequently for Hollywood to have coined the word "sleeper" to describe the phenomenon. A Hitler arises and takes over the government, although wise men in and outside the country have predicted that Germans would not be swayed by a poor imitation of an Italian demagogue.

In general, an event is not anticipated or it is incorrectly anticipated when knowledge of the people or objects involved in the situation is inadequate, when the principles which have given rise to the prediction have been improperly applied, or when the principles themselves are incorrect. Since objects which are thrown into the air immediately fall to the ground, it might be predicted that a particular object —a balloon filled with nitrogen—will do likewise. The fact that it rises and does not fall should not lead to the abandonment of the principle of gravity. The nature of the gas has not been ascertained; the principle of gravity has been applied in a situation in which it is not strictly applicable; or the principle has been the crude one which states that, since objects in the past have fallen to earth, this object will also "obey the law." The new advertisement does not impress people because as a stimulus it fails to arouse the anticipated drives and attitudes or because at the time the consumers see the copy another and different drive is active as a result of other events which have occurred in the interim. Grade-B pictures may not usually be successful; but a particular picture can arouse drives which certainly have already existed within people. The new picture, moreover, may be in the general movie tradition but can contain elements of plot or acting which in turn evoke responses that are rewarding. In this case the classification of "Grade B" has been accurate in a production but not in a psychological sense. A Hitler's rise to power might be predicted more accurately if more were known about the people he seeks to impress and if what were then known could be carefully applied to the devices he employs to secure his adherents.

There is an element of glamour in the belief that the unexpected should be expected because it usually occurs. Exciting as the unexpected is, however, it occurs only because men are ignorant. Actual public opinion regarding an issue is predictable if—if so many things are known and if there are adequate principles on the basis of which the prediction can be made. Fortunately or unfortunately, the element of glamour will probably never be completely removed. The unpredicted will occur not because it is unpredictable but because the data needed to anticipate the phenomenon in lawful terms are difficult to gather. The fact that the pronostications concerning tomorrow's weather as made by competent experts are sometimes inaccurate should not induce men to lose faith completely in meteorology, nor suggest to meteorologists that they should abandon their discipline. A modern weather service can be improved when more data are gathered (an expensive process and, in a hostile world, an intricate one) and when the principles of forecasting are simultaneously improved. It is superficial to say that it would be jolly if each day's weather came as a complete surprise to us. Jolly it would be until people sought to plan a picnic or until they were caught above the Atlantic in an airplane by a swift storm whose genesis elsewhere on the North American continent and whose course thereafter no one bothered to ascertain.

In the culturally laden past, consequently, lie the basic determinants of the individual's behavior, of the attitudes he shares with others, and hence of public opinion. That past, however, is not a key which immediately unlocks all human mysteries and intricacies. It is the mere beginning of an explanation.

The Cultural Heritage

By making a very few assumptions it is possible to predict an important segment of an individual's behavior before his birth. There are, as Dollard (*1*) points out, certain obvious characteristics about an organism which can be broadly foreseen, such as "the kind of clothes it will wear, the language it will speak, its theological ideas, its characteristic occupation, in some cases who its husband or wife is bound to be, how it can be insulted, what it will regard as wealthy, what its theory of personality growth will be, etc." The more that is known concerning the particular social-class status of the family into which the child is born and will be reared, the more specific can the predictions become.

Attitudes can be anticipated but frequently with less certainty than other characteristics. If the child is raised in a staunchly Republican, rural area in the United States and if his family is also traditionally Republican, the odds are in favor of his voting the straight Republican ticket at the age of twenty-one. If his family is Catholic, he will be Catholic and will doubtless adhere to the Catholic viewpoint on the political, social, economic, and international issues of the day. If he is to be educated in upper-class surroundings, it is highly probable that he will never be an active supporter of a revolutionary movement. It is safe to say, too, that he will absorb the racial prejudice, if any, of his parents and his immediate milieu. The role of an embryo in the public opinion of the future, in short, is not completely unknown.

There is nothing mysterious about what the anthropologists call culture: it is a system of habits which all adults share in varying degrees, which aid them in making adjustments to their environment and to one another, and which children acquire from their parents and from other contacts with their society (2). To state that a country has a tradition of obedience or recklessness is to imply that people are obedient or reckless and that the habits associated with those traits are reinforced in the young. The various institutions in the society, especially the family, the church, and the immediate community have as their most important functions the perpetuation and transmission of culture or a segment thereof.

It must be recognized, however, that forecasts concerning very specific habits or attitudes which are based exclusively on a knowledge of cultural traditions can often go astray. In the first place, traditions are frequently perpetuated only after undergoing some change. Historical events leave their mark upon a society, which means that for some time their effects continue to be transmitted from generation to generation. The loss of the Civil War by the South, for example, led to the establishment of certain traditions which thereafter have been influencing southern public opinion on many crucial issues. The contemporary importance of these traditions as factors determining public opinion cannot be discovered from a detailed analysis of the Civil War, its aftermath, and even conditions in the South during the first four decades of this century: the social heritage in this respect has changed with the passing of time. Some southerners, for example, are still hostile toward the North, but their hostility has grown less intense and is evoked less frequently. The forms and strength of any tradition among the people whose public opinion is being analyzed, consequently, must be ascertained. Culture changes because the people who embody it respond to varying circumstances in their society.

Then, secondly, behavior at a given moment stems not only from cultural traditions learned in childhood but also from a combination of factors operating contemporaneously. Public opinion regarding political leaders is partially a function of the traditional respect and treatment accorded them. It is affected, too, by the ways in which the leaders themselves behave, by the strength of the opposition, and by other on-going responses among the constituents. Tradition may color public opinion without determining its precise content.

Public opinion on issues that are definitely related to the cultural heritage may be called *enduring public opinion,* whereas that which appears to be unrelated to solutions and decisions already agreed upon in the culture may be termed *momentary public opinion.* The opposition of most Americans to various forms of collectivism represents enduring public opinion: it has a tradition bound up with the history of the United States and it has been perpetuated—frequently for changing reasons—since the days of the pioneer. An example of momentary public opinion is the reaction usually provoked by a nation-wide strike. Here traditional elements concerning the rights of employers and labor are involved, but for the country as a whole there is no specific response which people automatically make to such an issue as a result of their childhood training.

Every member of a society does not indiscriminately acquire all of its cultural traditions. The specific customs he learns are those of the various groups to which he belongs. Individuals in our society, for example, are sex-typed. As a function of their sex, they are trained in different ways and are expected to assume different social roles. Dolls vs. engines, daintiness vs. toughness, sewing vs. arithmetic, restraint vs. freedom, marriage vs. career—it is almost automatically possible to associate the first of each of these five pairs with girls and women and the second with boys and men. At the same time the two sexes are also socialized somewhat similarly in respect to many issues such as religious beliefs and standard of living. Social groups frequently follow cultural traditions which present greater contrasts. When the public opinion of a group is being related to culture, therefore, the particular segment of the culture for that specific group must be specified.

Before culture can determine behavior, moreover, the individual's skill must be sufficiently adequate to permit more or less normal learning to occur. A blind or moronic infant's behavior will be markedly affected by that physical disability or the low intelligence. In certain respects he is constitutionally incapable of absorbing what his contemporaries can learn. Normal skill of this kind, however, can be assumed for public opinion in general, although occasionally an abnormal or outstanding individual like a leader may have to be surveyed in all his uniqueness.

Studies (6) have been made of identical twins who for fortuitous reasons have been reared apart in contrasting social environments. When examined later in life, they are found to differ in respect to personality traits and intelligence-as-measured-by-tests. The differences cannot be ascribed to the factor of skill. To a certain extent they must be attributed to variations in the cultural surroundings, but they must also result from divergent methods of socialization. It would seem that behavior in general is influenced by the content of culture as well as by the ways in which culture is learned.

Socialization

Many of the socializing influences upon the individual are themselves culturally determined. Parents employ traditional ways of caring for the infant. These include the feeding schedule, the time of weaning, cleanliness training, the role of the child in the home and in relation to the parents, etc. Almost all mothers and fathers believe that their solutions to these problems are correct in the same sense that a physician gives the correct prescription—it is hoped—when their child is ill. Actually the medical prescription usually has a scientific foundation, whereas the practices vitally affecting the infant's behavior have largely a cultural basis.

Some parents and teachers, moreover, are not able to follow the dictates of the culture. If they are neurotic, their neuroticism may find expression especially at those points where tradition is vague. They may over- or under-punish the child because they as well as less disturbed people honestly do not know under what circumstances and how often to encourage and discourage certain types of behavior in the young. Such treatment—whether good or bad—very likely will have permanent effects upon the children's adult personality and hence will influence them in their role as carriers or representatives of public opinion. Here is simply another application of the principle that present behavior results from experiences in the past, but it calls attention to the special importance of childhood experiences.

Reference has been made to neurotic parents and teachers, in order to indicate once again that in the process of socialization the cultural heritage of a particular group can be transmitted imperfectly. The child of Republican, Catholic, upper-class, or prejudiced parents may not simply reflect what he has been taught. There is a myriad of other forces affecting him besides the parental influence, some of which can prove more powerful than those bombarding him at home. The child may become a Republican, but the promises which he wishes to see included in the Party platform at a given election may be different from those desired by his father—and thereafter he may vote for the Democratic or even Communist candidates. He will most certainly, if his parents are devout, learn the ritual of the Catholic Church, but his rebellion against them on other grounds may eventually be generalized to the Church and produce atheistic learnings. The son of upper-class parents may never know there is a revolutionary movement in his country until the woman he marries introduces him to it; then the rewards from his family and their heritage can become weak in comparison with those offered by her. The racial prejudices of parents and the milieu may be so variously absorbed that the individual can learn to feel more or less intensely than his teachers. Culture loses some of its force as a factor determining behavior the moment a specific personality is examined: since that personality has been affected by a unique set of cultural circumstances which have had a unique impact on his organism, it is usually more economical to analyze him individually than to show concern for the common habits in his society or group.

Each generation apparently is doomed to face and experience its own difficult problems as it is being socialized. During the childhood of successive generations there are booms or depressions, wars in progress or repercussions from wars, slow or rapid social changes, a spirit of optimism or fatalism. The crisis or the peculiar condition of the society has an impact upon children. Youngsters during the last war inevitably had to learn about shortages, rationing, sacrifices, death, battles, and hatred. What effects these experiences will have upon them later on remains to be seen; and what will be seen no doubt will depend upon the kind of a world they find at their disposal when they begin to function as independent adults.

Recent students of culture, notably Kardiner (*4*), have indicated an important and continuing relationship between socialization and the institutions of a culture, a relationship which immediately raises the chicken-or-the-egg problem. *The chicken*: children in a society are socialized in a particular way as a result of the underlying structure of the culture. *The egg*: the underlying structure of the culture results from the particular way in which children of another generation have been socialized. The institutions in a society reflect the ways in which people have been socialized and in turn perpetuate those ways. Or, in older and less sophisticated words, children are like their parents, and parents are like their grandparents—but children are less like their grandparents. If the basis for enduring public opinion is established during socialization, then this type of public opinion is changed when the methods of socialization are altered; yet they cannot be easily altered because they are part of the culture. Here, then, is the important reason why basic social changes occur so slowly. The vicious interaction, however, can be affected when either youth as it is being socialized or the adults who are the socializers are changed. The great victors of the last war, for example, have been making an effort to modify Germans so that they will be less war-prone in the future. Presumably German public opinion has supported war as well as the institutions and individuals giving rise to war as a result of cultural traditions and of personality inclinations acquired during childhood. German children cannot be snatched from their parents and brought up in the tradition of the West or the East. Formal education is controlled, but the habits it promotes are frequently weaker or less fundamental than those transmitted in the home. At the same time, then, it is hoped that events and propaganda through mass media will affect German parents and teachers, so that eventually they will influence the permanent character structure of succeeding generations. In like manner, any event which affects the family—whether a trend toward urbanization in modern countries or the spread of contraceptives—has repercussions upon the children who are socialized under the changed conditions.

Much of actual public opinion springs from enduring public opinion which has been more or less moulded in the course of socialization. No sagacious seer, for example, is needed to predict that Americans will defend their flag, their Constitution, their heroes of the past, or their right to own gadgets when such subjects become issues: these are traditions belonging to American culture and are transmitted by the family and other institutions like the school. But the services of such a seer would be useful to forecast how Americans will react to the latest development in the control of atomic energy, to one of the lunatic movements which plague the United States (Long, Coughlin, Townsend, Divine, the Klan, etc.), or to a new novel launched by a large advertising campaign. Such actual public opinion seems to be more of the momentary variety, but to be based upon latent public opinion in the past.

In viewing history broadly, both the historian and the layman imbued with common sense have a tendency to flit back and forth between two viewpoints: sometimes it looks as though history is determined by social or economic forces and sometimes by great men or the leaders of the society. At this point—and most fortunately too—no decision has to be made concerning the relative merits of the two biases. Probably the quest for a decision is a foolish enterprise, inasmuch as the weight to be given to forces or to leaders largely depends on the particular historical event being examined. It is sufficient to state that leaders are important, on some occasions more important than on others, and that they therefore can affect the ways in which culture determines public opinion.

Leaders

Leaders are people and hence their nature, too, results in large part from their culture and the ways in which they have been socialized. The search for traits which clearly distinguish leaders from non-leaders has been largely futile (*3*), because the requirements of leadership vary so much from situation to situation. The differences between the personalities of political bosses, university presidents, and industrial foremen are greater than are their similarities, although conceivably they all possess some general skill in common like the ability to make a rapid decision. Hitler may have been psychopathic for a variety of reasons ranging from his endocrine glands to his childhood in a provincial Austrian town and the frustrations he encountered in his early career as a painter, but whatever gifts of leadership he eventually possessed—it can now be said with the great brilliance which comes only from hindsight—could be exercised because many Germans were predisposed to respond to him. His imitators throughout the world have been different people who operate with varying degrees of success in different situations.

Leaders both affect and are affected by culture and public opinion. This relationship is admittedly quite tortuous and dialectic like the one existing between culture and socialization. Hitler, for example, made Germany into a Nazi state because many Germans were ready to support him and were eager to be nazified. Without the latent and doubtless the enduring public opinion that existed in Germany, he could not have been successful—and without him and his organization German public opinion regarding national and international issues might have been altered quite differently. People may grow impatient and demand a more clearcut generalization about leaders and their public, but unfortunately such a demand, intelligible as it is in terms of the satisfaction secured from simplification, runs counter to the stubborn facts of social life.

It is well to understand the interaction between leaders and public opinion because a similar process pervades almost all of the relations which people have with one another. The master summons a dog by means of a whistle whose sound can be heard by dogs but not by human beings —its frequency is simply above the threshold of people's ears. He does not employ that whistle to call his child, nor does its manufacturer seek to have it adopted by traffic policemen. Dogs, not people can respond to its stimulation. The whistle is made for the dog and hence the dog can respond to the whistle.

One man wishes to persuade another to perform a task. If he is skilled in the use of persuasion, he will not seek to arouse a drive which his protagonist does not possess. He will not say that the task should be executed in the interests of the community where they both reside, if he knows that the man has no interest in the community. He will say that other people will respect him for his accomplishment if he has learned that the man is attracted by this kind of prestige. The appeal is adapted to the man and hence the man can respond to the appeal.

In more general terms, this principle of interaction suggests that responses occur only to stimuli which are arranged along an appropriate gradient and that consequently these stimuli must be presented if the responses are to occur. In social life, moreover, it is people who offer the stimuli to other people. As stimulators the former must find the stimuli which can affect the latter and, when once those stimuli have been found, the stimulators will very likely use them again on appropriate occasions in the future. The responses of the stimulators, it can be seen, have also been altered in the process of altering the responses of those who are stimulated. Hitler was not immediately successful even among his Munich followers in the early twenties. He had to find the arguments which would appeal to Germans; he was using a whistle at first which could not be heard by Germans. Then, as his oratory began to sway people, he must have noted which appeals were successful and which unsuccessful. His audience in a real sense was thus changing him as a propagandist, even while he was changing them through his propaganda.

The skilful leader is an individual who understands both public opinion and propaganda. The demagogue, for example, is able to swim with the prevailing tide: he is acquainted with public opinion, whether that opinion be actual or latent, internal or external, enduring or momentary. On the basis of prevailing attitudes among people, fascists and communists seek to attract their following; and at every point in their propaganda they make promises and suggest a future in which those attitudes or drives will be rewarded. They also single out certain groups in the society whom they call enemies ("Jews," "reactionaries," "capitalists," etc.) and onto whom they seek to drain the aggression which exists. Leaders who make fundamental changes in their society do so on the basis of latent public opinion: they are shrewd enough to realize that, with proper propaganda, people can be made to learn new responses. Any leader, moreover, usually begins his career by seizing upon issues concerning which there is actual public opinion. Eventually, if the changes are to be far-reaching, enduring public opinion must be changed.

Events

Psychologically an event is a collection of complicated stimuli which produce responses within people. Culture affects people by giving rise to an event like the celebration of a national holiday or the activities of the police force. The process of socialization is a series of events like weaning or like a conversation at the dinner table which deliberately focuses upon etiquette or which inadvertently reveals to the child the prejudices of his parents. Leaders create events, like a speech at a mass meeting or an administrative ruling, which have impact upon people.

Each event is an outgrowth of forces within the society, whether they be part of the cultural tradition, a consequence of socialization, or an expression of leadership. The relation of the event to the society, however, is not always easy to determine and, therefore, it is often pragmatically convenient to refer to the event itself as the determinant of behavior and public opinion. During an inflation, for example, there are many factors at work, some of which arise from social and economic strains having a long history of their own and others from momentary interactions among numerous peoples. These factors need not be determined to point out that the concrete stimuli accompanying the inflation influence people and public opinion.

Natural phenomena are events which sometimes are of crucial importance in the determination of human responses. A hurricane sweeps through a community and people's behavior toward one another is changed: they become more friendly and are mutually helpful and cooperative in a manner which represents a departure from their normal custom. At such a moment they tolerate or encourage actions which ordinarily are taboo. Or when a hot, sweltering heat descends upon an area, even the good-tempered become slightly irritable, traffic to cooler and pleasanter regions increases, bathtubs and showers receive a booming patronage, and both liquids and liquors are consumed with greater appreciation. Until the weather changes, public opinion on the subtler issues of life remains somewhat latent.

A hurricane or a heat wave is momentary and therefore public opinion is affected only momentarily. Some people, for better or worse, inhabit places where natural phenomena appear to have a more enduring effect upon them. This would be true in the arctic regions, near the equator at a low altitude, or anywhere at an extremely high altitude. The more enduring effect, however, is discernible within the culture itself: long-range adaptations to the environment are made and people's attitudes are thereby affected as they are socialized. Individuals who have been socialized elsewhere react both to the physical and the cultural environments when as explorers, warriors, tourists, or merchants they suddenly face conditions to which they are not accustomed.

As a matter of fact, almost all human reactions to natural events likewise contain a cultural element. It is misleading to believe that the natural in nature brings out the natural in man. During and after a hurricane, people may be terrified and behave atypically, but even then their cultural background affects a segment of their behavior. Most men in our society, for example, allow women to be rescued first from a sinking ship or a burning building. At such a time, too, almost all communities have more or less organized apparatus to alleviate distress. Actual public opinion during a catastrophe, therefore, is not completely dependent on the event and its consequences: more enduring elements may be at work.

External public opinion is itself an event that affects not only leaders but also the people themselves whose attitudes are being expressed. What they think and do in the future is largely dependent upon the extent to which their present behavior proves to be rewarding or punishing. If actual public opinion, for example, leads to a lynching, if the act of barbarism satisfies the participants, and if no punishments are meted out, then the chances of repeating the performance under similar conditions in the future are increased. The repetition may involve both the participants and their neighbors who have learned, or again realized from hearing about the event, that such behavior is tolerated. In no less mysterious fashion does lynching become a cultural tradition and part of enduring public opinion in an area. Then adolescents who themselves have actually never experienced a lynching will know, because their parents and associates have told them so, that they possess social permission to organize or participate in a bee.

Two kinds of events have especially heavy impact on public opinion: propaganda and the media of communication. They are events, as will be shown in later chapters, which are culturally determined in part but which also reflect the momentary problems of society and its leaders. In one sense they are an expression of culture; in another, they help mould that culture.

Public opinion, according to this chapter's viewpoint, is affected by culture because it is a part of culture. Only the background of public opinion can be explained by culture. A more complete explanation is possible when culture is viewed specifically through socialization, leaders, and events. Public opinion, moreover, is simply one kind of social behavior whose over-all relation to culture is no different from other behavior called criminal, insane, esthetic, religious, political, or economic. Behavior cannot be ripped out of the fabric of social life and examined in isolation. Public opinion, therefore, is an artificial, though useful segment of behavior which can be analyzed in its own right but always within its broader social context.

CHAPTER 5

The Behavior of Public Opinion

PUBLIC opinion has been defined and its relation to culture has been indicated. The next problem is to examine the characteristics of attitudes which people share. How does public opinion behave? The answer to this question may be a literary description of people in a social setting or an analysis growing out of their behavior as individuals.

Cantril's approach (7) can serve as the serious prototype of the literary or loosely impressionistic description. After observing the findings of public opinion polls in the United States from 1939 to 1941, he has formulated what he calls seventeen "laws of public opinion." Even as they stand, these "laws" do not reveal anything startling and many of them are vague and ambiguous. Most are applicable only to the period and the kind of opinion he studied. At least two are not "laws" in any sense but represent uncritical praise of public opinion and a gratuitous bit of sensible advice to democratic leaders. Cantril's "laws" are both tempting and vulnerable targets, tempting because they are superior to less systematic attempts and vulnerable because they are so glibly stated and so confused.

The first "law" states: "Opinion is highly sensitive to important events." Certainly such sensitivity is not always revealed. Many American experts, for example, consider a project like the Tennessee Valley Authority an important event, but there is little evidence to show that Americans by and large have concerned themselves intimately with the inception, development, notable achievements, and political adversities of that regional plan. What, moreover, is "important" and who is to make the judgment? In the fall of 1946, it seemed to many observers that the criticism of American foreign policy by Henry Wallace and his consequent resignation from the President's cabinet were important events. A Gallup poll on October 13 of that year, nevertheless, revealed that only 42 percent of a representative sample of Americans paid attention to the controversy, a figure scarcely indicating high sensitivity. The "law," consequently, must mean that people react to those events to which they have already reacted by considering them important—they react when they react.

The third "law" is: "Opinion is generally determined more by events than by words—unless those words are themselves interpreted as an 'event.' " This is a generalization derived directly from the war situation when battles speak louder than words. Or else the qualification of words being interpreted as an "event" means that people react to stimuli, which is certainly true. The gossip in a small community that rips apart an individual's reputation in the eyes of public opinion seems to be a series of phrases and sentences communicated in a provoking manner, as is an advertisement for a mouth wash. If gossip and advertisements be called "events," then every stimulus is an event.

The ninth "law": "When self-interest is involved, public opinion in a democracy is likely to be ahead of official policy." Here Cantril refers to evidence indicating that prior to Pearl Habor "a majority of the public" in the United States favored measures which helped Great Britain in her war against Germany and Italy "on an average of four months before legislation was passed." There is a definite value-judgment involved in the simple word "ahead": the implication is that, under the specified condition, public opinion somehow grasps the wiser policy before its representatives do and that public opinion, therefore, is wiser or more far-sighted than its representatives. The fact that people think something before their representatives act may simply demonstrate that leaders are affected by followers and that what eventually occurs is no sign of the leaders' wisdom but a reflection of public opinion. Cantril's own data (6) based on polls between September 1939 and December 1941, moreover, can be turned against this "law" if the answers to other polling questions are made the units of measurement. Presumably, for example, the same "self-interest" of the American people was involved in March of 1940 before the German invasion of Norway; yet only 1 percent believed then that this country "should declare war on Germany." In July of the same year after the fall of France the figure rose a mere 2 percent. In May 1941 after the sweep of the Germans through the Balkans and Greece it reached a high of just 10 percent. Why did not "self-interest" function during those critical days? One month before Pearl Harbor only about one-quarter of a polling sample thought the United States "should enter the war." A week or so before the Japanese attacked, less than one-third stated that they "would vote to go to war against Germany if a national vote were taken." Public opinion apparently needed some Japanese bombs before it could catch up with itself. If the United States had not entered World War II, Cantril could have then employed these data —rather than the ones he misleadingly chose—to pay tribute to the wisdom of public opinion.

The seventeenth and final "law" proclaims: "By and large if people in a democracy are provided educational opportunities and ready access to information, public opinion reveals a hard-headed common sense. . . ." This is a direct and no doubt laudable plea for public enlightenment. But it is not a characterization of public opinion because every man has his own meaning of "hard-headed common sense." In addition, the statement seems merely to suggest that the more information people are given, the better informed they will be—with the weasel provision—"by and large."

These "laws" of Cantril, it can be seen, reveal the pitfalls confronting anyone attempting to generalize about the behavior of public opinion on the basis of a loose conception of public opinion. Cantril has admitted (*8*) that his statements apply only "with respect to public opinion in a democracy." As a matter of fact, they are informally derived from the crudest type of public opinion measurement (the poll) which was applied to a particular group of people (Americans) on an unusual set of issues (mostly war) at a specific time (1939–1941) when the United States was organized or disorganized in a more or less unique fashion and when the media of communication were expressing a series of heterogeneous viewpoints.

The specificity of Cantril's type of approach to public opinion can be avoided—as he himself avoids it in three of his "laws" which will be mentioned in the course of this chapter—only by first considering the general characteristics exhibited by people in their thinking and behavior. Public opinion has the characteristics about to be enumerated and analyzed because people possess them. People possess them because they are learned during socialization and reinforced thereafter.

Consistency

It is a notorious fact that people are inconsistent. One day they like a painting, and the next day they are repelled by it. One week they are in love, and the next they avoid the person without whom, they have been saying, life would be unendurable. One month they like warm weather, and the next they seek the cold. One year they are enthusiastic about their occupation, and the next they make every effort to find a new position. In addition, the same individual may possess two or more beliefs which an outsider considers inconsistent, a view with which he himself might agree if he could be made to concentrate upon their strictly logical consequences. He may distrust or sneer at the judgments of the masses but also be in favor of "democracy"; or he may like and dislike the same individual simultaneously.

To call behavior inconsistent at a given moment or over a period of time is frequently misleading because, as Allport (2) has shown in his analysis of personality, apparently inconsistent actions may be consistent with a broader principle or set of attitudes within the individual. The man who distrusts the masses but who favors "democracy" may be quite consistent from his own viewpoint: as a social critic he is convinced that people have faults but that in the long run a system which takes their fumblings into account is "better" than the alternatives at hand. Socially and perhaps logically he is inconsistent; psychologically he is consistent.

The criterion of consistency is usually applied by an outsider: the individual himself may or may not appreciate the consistency or inconsistency of his own behavior. That outsider expects two responses to be aroused and to lead to a state of conflict. The conflict, however, may not occur. In the first place, one of the two internal responses which might produce the conflict is not evoked because past experience has not placed the present stimulus along its generalization gradient. To the stimulus "government-ownership-of-railroads" most Americans respond with something like "socialism-and-I-don't-like-it"; whereas to "government-ownership-of-mail" they do not respond "socialism-but-I-like-it" but "necessary-and-I-like-it." Here there is no conflict and hence no inconsistency because the different stimuli give rise to compatible responses. Approximately the same stimulus, moreover, can arouse different responses which may be labelled inconsistent or fickle by the outsider when he neglects to observe that the individual concerned has changed in the interim. In our society the young boy's contempt for girls almost completely disappears as he matures and is replaced by a positive attraction toward them. The explanation is fairly obvious: the initial reaction to girls has proved after a while to be more punishing than rewarding; hence it has been extinguished and has been replaced by a more satisfactory one. The question of inconsistency merely calls attention to the changed behavior over a period of time.

The conflict between two internal and "inconsistent" responses, in addition, can be quickly resolved when the drive strength of one is stronger than the other. The American who consistently demands ice with his highball may "inconsistently" consume a lukewarm whiskey-and-soda in England because there, unless he is willing to accept a drink without ice, he may not drink at all. Hartshorne and May (*16*) have shown that American school children in the twenties tended to be neither consistently honest nor dishonest: they cheated in one situation like the school and not in another like the home. The complex stimulus of the school elicited a drive to achieve a high grade and cheating became an instrumental act toward that end, in comparison with which any response involving "honesty-is-the-best-policy" apparently was much weaker. In the home, on the other hand, that latter response was stronger and the equivalent of the former was weaker as a result of punishments received for being dishonest. If a child is to be consistently honest in all situations, then he must learn that every situation falls along the gradient which evokes a strong drive in connection with honesty.

As Cantril (*9*) indicates in his sixteenth "law," inconsistency or fickleness of public opinion may be similarly viewed. Many people possess incompatible beliefs concerning the issues of the day without being in a state of conflict. The responses which could give rise to conflict may not exist, may be evoked at different times, or may be of different strength. The hero of yesterday, for example, becomes the villain of today or is forgotten altogether not because people are downright superficial or perversely whimsical but because their attitudes in the meantime have been altered as a result of the experiences they have had. Charles A. Lindbergh was not the same stimulus in 1927 after he had flown alone to Paris as he was in 1939 after he had expressed political and social views at variance with those to which many Americans were subscribing.

In short, the problem of the consistency of public opinion cannot be posed or settled for all time. What must be examined is not the end products as revealed by a poll or by other behavior but either the entire organization of attitudes and habits within people or their reasons for changing

—or both. People may continually disapprove of murder, they may change their style of clothing once every fourteen months, or they may grow to love a leader only after he is dead. They may be seduced into smoking one brand of cigarettes rather than another as a result of a high-pressure advertising campaign, they may refuse to use lemon juice to cure hangovers in spite of another vociferous campaign, or they may more or less spontaneously adopt zootsuits. Such descriptions—revealing inconsistency or consistency—require deeper probing before the reasons for the stability or the instability can be ascertained.

Rationalization

Life for most people, as the platitude would have it, seldom runs smoothly. Drives are evoked and the goal responses which would reduce their tension and bring satisfaction cannot be made. There is scarcity, whether natural or artificially created, in any society. Human relations produce friction. Socialization is not pleasant, for the neophyte is required to renounce many of his goals and modes of behavior and to learn to conform to society's demands. Crises continually occur in the life of the individual and his country. Frustration, conflict, and anxiety are always present.

Few people, however, accept frustrations and anxieties without seeking to make themselves feel less dissatisfied and more comfortable, nor do they tolerate conflicts without striving to resolve them. The avoidance or the reduction of frustration, anxiety, and conflict, therefore, is a constant problem. Public opinion can be understood in large part as a collection of responses to adversity.

Rationalization occurs when the pain resulting from one response sets up a stronger response which thereby reduces or almost eliminates that pain. "Sour-grapes" is the traditional way of describing what rationalization involves. The individual who fails to achieve an objective then explains to himself or others that he really preferred to fail because the attained objective would have been unsatisfactory. The rejected suitor sighs with relief when his lady love says "no," consciously because he manages to convince himself that married life with her would have been intolerable and unconsciously because he may have been afraid of marriage and the sexual, social, and economic responsibilities it entails. Sometimes a conflict is resolved by eliminating one of the conflicting responses through a response which in turn conflicts with it: the citizen who cannot decide whether to vote or play golf on election day weakens the first tendency by deciding that his one vote would be unimportant anyhow.

The ability to find an appropriate if misleading justification for behavior may have beneficial consequences. The individual can protect himself from the distress which conflict, anxiety, or failure produces. It is comforting to think that the grapes would have been sour since then the failure to obtain them becomes not a disappointment, but a piece of good luck. Dodging reality thus can diminish dissatisfaction. The soldier in combat who is afraid, bored, or disgusted feels happier and is probably more efficient if he can tell himself or be told that it is better to be in the armed forces during wartime than to remain a civilian and if he can also find other good reasons for seeming to prefer his present occupation. Middle-class people who actually envy the upper class find solace in pointing out that they themselves are more moral, respectable, or useful than their envied contemporaries.

Rationalizations, however, can also lead to difficulties. The anxiety, the frustration, or the conflict may be only superficially assuaged, and its pain can continue to affect the individual in ways which his rationalization prevents him from consciously detecting. He may feel vaguely discontent without knowing precisely why. He may dream about sweet grapes. He may forget about fruit or failure and displace his anger upon some innocent and irrelevant object. Or he may remain simply muddled or neurotic.

Many people exhibit more or less similar rationalizations when they are uncomfortable for more or less similar reasons. Under such circumstances it can be said that public opinion is rationalizing because the attitudes regarding the issue have resulted from the unsolved problems at hand. In spite of concentration camps, death marches, and other instances of "man's inhumanity to man," for example, it is not always easy for one group of people to exploit or be cruel to another group. There may be ethical principles in the society which oppose exploitation or cruelty, or individuals who are taught to be cooperative and kind in the family cannot automatically behave differently in relation to outsiders. Race prejudice, therefore, is almost always accompanied by theories which justify current practices and thus help to rid the dominant group of some of its guilt (*12, 22*):

> "They are lazy."
> "They are biologically inferior."
> "They are like animals."
> "They are just children."
> "They are immoral."
> "They love to be bossed."
> "They have no one but themselves to blame."
> "They are all alike."

Rationalizations like these may also be accepted in part by the subordinated group and thus serve to allay some of its frustration. Similarly, "good excuses" are offered whenever people feel guilty about aspects of their society, such as poverty, unemployment, imperialism, war, and the dropping of atomic bombs.

Rationalizations of groups appear to have at least three origins. In the first place, there are the traditional, ready-made explanations which are part of the culture and which are inevitably transmitted during socialization. Justification of race prejudice, through a commonly accepted theory about the subordinated group, is part of the dominant group's heritage which is accepted by each generation not merely because it is promulgated at home, in the school, and in the media of communication but also because each individual feels within himself—consciously or unconsciously—the need for such a theory as a result of the guilt he experiences after contact with the out-group. Then, secondly, there are rationalizations of new situations which are provided by leaders and propagandists. During a war men and women frequently must be told why they are fighting, since fighting is an activity in which relatively few of them are willing to engage until they are given good reasons for doing so. One of the most important techniques in propaganda is to offer hesitant people the effective rationalizations they require to alter their behavior in a manner that helps the propagandist achieve his objective. There are, finally, other rationalizations which seem to arise spontaneously among many people without previous provision by the culture or by leaders. Cantril (*10*) points out in connection with one of his "laws" that "there was invariably a rise of around ten percent" in the number of people favorable to measures which aided Great Britain before the United States entered the last war (like Lend-Lease) immediately after those measures became law. People changed no doubt because the measures were publicized as Congress was debating them, but they could not conceivably have experienced at the time any direct effects from the new regulations. At least in part they must have been rationalizing an accomplished fact.

Be it noted, in passing, that rationalization always raises a question of fact. The grapes may actually be sour, a condition which the individual can perceive by looking at them. The group against which discrimination is expressed may be "really just children" in some juvenile sense (though, of course, the reason for their childish characteristics is not their physiological structure but the subordination they have had to suffer). To accuse an individual or group of rationalizing, consequently, presupposes knowledge of their real psychological states or of the relevant factors in the external environment that are being perceived.

Displacement

When confronted with frustration, anxiety, or conflict, the individual may seek not only to rationalize the adversity but also to do something else which will bring him satisfaction. That something else is a substitute goal response evoked in large part by the pain which thus acts as a drive. One of the commonest forms of substitute activity is the partial reduction of the pain through responses involving destruction or the expression of hostility.

A drive to destroy or be hostile is one of the consequences of frustration (*13*) and in this sense frustration is the failure to reduce a drive, to eliminate anxiety, or to resolve a conflict. It appears as though the initial impulse is to express aggression toward the person, persons, or object that is thought to have brought on the frustration in the first place. The child strikes the chair into which he has bumped or hits the playmate who has been teasing him. Frequently, however, this initial impulse is inhibited because the individual knows that such behavior will bring him only additional grief. In this situation, a substitute target is consciously or unconsciously sought. The expression of aggression against such a substitute is called displacement. Instead of hitting his older and stronger playmate, the child hits a younger and hence less dangerous associate or he may even strike himself.

One of the important psychological functions of society is to provide its members who suffer from various frustrations with targets onto which aggression can be displaced. A favorite target seems to be another group which actually is, or which is considered to be, different from the individual's own. The ancient Hebrews sought each year to escape from the guilt generated by their sins and dispatched into the wilderness a goat that was supposed to bear these sins away. Usually, however, the scapegoat is less symbolic: it is much easier to hate and feel aggressive toward other human beings.

Germans were in a state of readiness to respond to the Nazis' anti-Semitism because, in addition to historical and cultural precedents for this form of persecution, they were eager to affix responsibility upon someone or something for the frustrations they endured or thought they endured during the period after World War I and especially during the depression of the early thirties. It seemed to many allied observers during the last war that Propaganda Minister

Goebbels launched an attack upon the Jews whenever Germans had experienced or were about to experience another military reverse or a cut in the food ration. Thus the Jews were used as scapegoats onto whom the bitterness and disappointment of many Germans could be displaced.

Frequently individuals in their more rational moments hesitate to displace aggression. The tired businessman tries valiantly to control his temper when he returns home after a miserable day at work. He knows that his wife and children are not the source of his annoyance and he inhibits himself, if he can, from considering them to be annoying. He presumably loves his family, moreover, and wishes to cause them no additional unpleasantness. The advantage of displacing aggression upon outsiders becomes apparent when it is realized that the individuals specified as the target by society or by leaders usually are those toward whom no or little affection has been previously felt. Shortly after the last war, some Germans inside Germany admitted to the writer—without guile, he believes—that they did not object to Hitler's anti-Semitic maneuvers until they themselves knew particular Jews who had been persecuted or until they came to learn in detail exactly what persecution entailed.

The presence of other people frequently facilitates displacement since individuals by themselves hesitate to inflict pain or injury upon a scapegoat. As members of a group, however, they may find the courage to do so because they feel that the involvement of the others legitimatizes their own actions or renders them less liable to punishment. Rationalization of displacement can also occur when people feel that others who cannot be immediately perceived but whose existence is suggested by the media of communication are similarly behaving. During a war the displacement of aggression upon the enemy is effectively promoted by propaganda among people who are widely separated.

Compensation

Aggression, whether displaced or not, is only one of the consequences of frustration. Another form of substitute goal response called compensation consists of reducing a different drive which has not been involved in the original frustration. Sometimes compensation is thought to be the healthy or sensible thing to do rather than to rationalize the pain or to be aggressive. The girl who cannot attract boys because she is not sufficiently beautiful may find in intellectual pursuits a form of compensation which brings its own rewards. Those rewards and the drives they satisfy, it must be quickly added, are probably not quite so satisfactory as the ones originally sought. For this reason the young lady may overcompensate by expending extra energy in achieving the substitute goal—and still remain unsatisfied.

Compensation is frequently necessary when there is no other way to reduce the blocked drive. Wishful thinking and day-dreaming, for example, represent innocuous forms of compensation to which the individual resorts because thoughts and dreams cannot be easily inhibited by environmental pressures. Much of the activity associated with the arts is compensatory: people escape from well-known harsh realities into a region of fantasy where life is pleasant and where problems are either solved or, if unsolved, can be gloatingly disassociated from the normal personality.

There are, in addition, social institutions which serve the psychological function of relieving misery and pain in a compensatory manner. Besides the arts, established forms of entertainment and games, festivals and holidays, and religious and other associations enable people to withdraw, temporarily at least, from their ordinary obligations and restraints. Each society has its own kind of circus and, after the performance has ended, the spectators are less reluctant to return to their customary way of life.

People demand compensatory activity especially when they are experiencing some kind of crisis. Forms of indulgence like drinking and sexual promiscuity are popular, for example, during a war. This drink-and-be-merry behavior seeks not only to drown the sorrows of the moment but also to diminish anxiety concerning the anticipated fate of tomorrow.

Public opinion in small and powerless countries tends to be both actual and intense regarding issues like national greatness of sovereignty. Such attitudes result in part from the ease with which group spirit can be established when the group is smaller and also from the need to cooperate which is produced by a somewhat hostile outside world. In addition they are compensatory reactions to feelings of inferiority: the country may be tiny, its inhabitants say and are told, but its water and milk are pure and its history is most ancient and honorable.

Projection

To understand another person is usually difficult. For the external behavior which he is exhibiting can be variously interpreted and the drives, attitudes, and knowledge which have produced the behavior also cannot be immediately deciphered. When faced with the problem of understanding someone else, therefore, the individual can adopt one of two shortcuts: he can believe that the other person is like himself or that he himself is like the other person. The first process is called projection and the second identification.

Among psychiatrists and laymen the classical illustration of projection which provokes both pity and mirth is the old maid who reports to the police that a man has designs on her. Consciously or unconsciously, the explanation goes, she wishes to be raped (or at least to experience some of the preliminaries thereto) ; she dares not acknowledge such feelings to herself; she protects herself, therefore, by ascribing her own drive to the hapless male; and the hostility she displays toward him is in fact a reflection of the shock which her own impulses have created within her. Ordinarily projection is neither so dramatic nor clearcut. The individual may have had a series of painful experiences with strangers or with people in general. He is afraid that social contact will bring additional punishment. He avoids people or becomes generally hostile toward them, though he still wishes to be sociable. He then rationalizes his own avoidance tendency and he smothers his desire to be with them by concluding that they are seeking to hurt him. He thus projects onto them his own hostility, while complaining that nobody is really interested in his welfare. If he is neurotic, he may never discover that he is the victim of his own delusions.

Projection, however, need not be motivated by repression or hostility. "We are all human after all" is a sentence which frequently introduces projection: the other people whose behavior is being called human are thought to be like the individual who utters the cliché. For each individual feels that to a certain extent he understands his own behavior. If others are felt to be similarly motivated, then their actions become clear—or at least clearer. Projection on a large scale usually permeates most of the institutions of a society. In the field of religion, for example, men make gods in their own images and project upon them their own foibles and virtues.

The attitudes at the base of public opinion exhibit projection for a variety of reasons. People have a tendency to rationalize some of their own displacements by concluding that others are similarly displacing. In-group solidarity, for example, is promoted by the presence of an out-group as Sumner (23) and others have pointed out: internal aggression is displaced upon members of the out-group and it is claimed that they and not one's own group is aggressive. Hitler employed this technique again and again to rationalize Nazi penetration of a foreign country.

Then socialization occurs primarily in the family, the one social group in which the members closely resemble one another. In this situation projection is more likely to be accurate, as it is whenever people are subjected to similar cultural stimuli and possess rather similar personalities from the outset. The habit of projecting, consequently, is reinforced and is later generalized to situations outside the family.

In addition, the leaders of a society frequently attempt to encourage projection. He who hesitates to leap on a bandwagon, for example, is told by a politician that the people already astride the vehicle are like himself: they want the same things, they are "plain folks" too. The citizen is supposed to ascribe to them all of his own feelings and hence to vote as they do.

Identification

Projection in reverse is identification: instead of ascribing his own behavior to other people and saying "They are like me," the individual feels that he is acting like them or tries consciously or unconsciously to do so. "I am like them," he maintains. Impulses may be projected upon other people who are loved or hated, but identification occurs only when the individual already possesses a favorable attitude toward the people with whom he identifies. A mother is torn with mental pain when she perceives that her child is undergoing physical suffering. Naturally her pain is not the same as the child's, but its drive strength is such that she becomes more attentive, perhaps over-attentive, and seeks means to reduce the suffering. Identification between an individual and a real or imaginary villain indicates that this villain or some of his traits are not thoroughly detested.

Projection and identification, though opposite in nature, may occur in the same situation and serve to complement each other. The follower, for example, projects his own reactions to a crisis onto a leader whom he respects. If he feels weary or ill-at-ease, he imagines that the leader is experiencing similar misery and, after making the assumption, he then identifies himself with the man and hence experiences what he believes would be his own responses in that position. The target of his projection and identification of course may be blasé and unmoved by the crisis, or he may be responding to it quite differently.

Many of the subtler forms of communication which occur between people involve identification. As poets have frequently observed and as every man in his own manner at some time in his life perceives with cosmic sorrow, each of us is dreadfully alone in the world. Every human experience is unique for the individual who has the experience. The unspeakable remains unspeakable or at least is never adequately expressed. People can break through the solipsistic crust which envelops them only by contact with other people. The contact consists of observation or the exchange of experience through language. Language is an imperfect means of communication because words, in the terminology of modern semantics, are only signs or symbols for the experience of the speaker or for the objects or situations to which they refer. By making every effort to place oneself in the psychological mood of the other person—the lover does this in reference to his beloved and the attentive reader in regard to the poetry before him—the individual is thus better equipped to understand someone beside himself and perhaps to be understood.

The earliest form of identification is that between the child and his parents and later perhaps between the child and his older or younger brother or sister. Gradually the individual learns to identify with more and more people as he matures until the good patriot believes that he himself experiences about the same emotions and feelings of all his countrymen. Psychologically, therefore, identification is one of the mainsprings of social or group life. Copious but not completely convincing evidence has been gathered which indicates that the success of a group leader is in part a function of his ability to act as a substitute for the person, usually the parent, with whom the individual first learned to identify. Certainly it is no coincidence that modern leaders occasionally employ family terms like "my children" and "my son" and that the Deity is referred to as Father. Such symbolic metaphors suggest, as Freud (*15*) in particular has pointed out, the original foundation for in-group loyalty.

Public opinion involves identification with leaders or with fellow members of the same group. Esprit de corps, for example, consists of the awareness not only of a common goal and of group traditions, but also of the members of the group who are striving for that goal. The individual is willing to make sacrifices and conform regardless of his own attitudes when he is convinced that others are enduring similar privations. People are moved by pity and hence the leader who can elicit this response and direct it toward himself has increased his chances of being effective.

Conformity

One of the characteristics of group life which almost always requires rationalization is the pressure to conform to the will of the majority. On the one hand, people know that conformity usually brings safety and security. They know this because the advantages of conforming have been stressed from earliest infancy: children in our society who do not conform to their parents' wishes are generally punished. As part of the socialization process they are quickly indoctrinated with a sense of family solidarity, for they can easily observe that their own welfare and rewards are dependent upon the ways they conduct themselves in relation to those who immediately engulf them. When they mature, they learn the immediate and ultimate value to themselves of esprit de corps or school or community spirit, phrases which automatically suggest that the group is more important than the individual. People are educated to be sensitive to the responses of others. They are reared to become parts of publics whose opinions they possess, reflect, and affect.

On the other hand, conformity can be frustrating. Individuals have their distinctive personalities and, more often than is usually imagined, they react unfavorably to the procrustean demands of their group. Sometimes conformity is then rationalized; at other times society is defied.

The very existence of public opinion on a given issue is an indication of conformity. For public opinion means that people agree to the extent that they have rather similar attitudes. The conformity may be more or less complete. If there is real conformity, the range of verbal or non-verbal responses may be represented graphically by a curve which, as Floyd H. Allport and his students have shown (*1, 20*), has the shape of an inverted J. Along the horizontal line or abscissa are plotted the various responses to the issues and along the vertical line or ordinate the number of individuals displaying the responses indicated on the abscissa. The curve connecting the points starts high up on the ordinate since many individuals make almost identical responses.

Then it slopes down steeply since few people exhibit the other or non-conforming responses. If responses were distributed by chance—and what chance would be is by no means clear since social responses tend always to be affected by conformity-producing institutions or situations—the so-called normal or Gaussian curve that resembles the shape of a bell would appear. Under these circumstances few individuals display extreme responses and hence both ends of the curve slope downwards (resembling the edges of the bell's profile) ; but many individuals are in a middle position and hence the curve has a hump in the center (resembling the top of the bell). Research has shown a marked tendency for external public opinion on a given issue to be J-shaped and for internal public opinion on the same issue to be normally distributed. The discrepancy between what some people openly say they believe and what they really believe indicates the pressure of conformity.

Whether the distribution of external public opinion itself is J- or bell-shaped on a given issue is a very important fact to know. The more the curve—hypothetical or actual—approximates the shape of the inverted J, the more conformity there is in respect to the response being observed. The external public opinion of a well-unified group on a variety of issues is J-shaped; the size of the tail of the J or the tendency of the curve to approach the form of a bell is a measure of the group's disunity (*14*). The shape of the curve, however, is a function of the group whose responses are being considered. The responses of an entire country on an issue like taxation may be normally distributed: a few people believe that taxes are much too high and approximately an equal number that they are much too low; the majority cluster around the position that taxes are about right or perhaps a trifle too high. The possibility must be recognized that public opinion on the issue may be stratified along social or economic class lines. The distribution of lower-class public opinion and that of upper-class opinion may be J-shaped, with the majority of the former believing taxes are much too low and the majority of the latter maintaining that they are much too high. The distribution curve for the entire country may thus be masking the real class-determined conformity which exists.

The opponents of democracy are fond of saying that people are like sheep: they conform to the wishes of their leader. This statement contains a grain of truth if its poorly concealed sneer is eliminated. It does require courage or a neurosis or both not to conform to public opinion, and few people have these qualifications. Many of the heroes of present-day American society, including historical characters like George Washington as well as products of folklore like Paul Bunyan, are now portrayed and praised as men who defied the convention of their times. A radical in any field who is still alive and exhibiting his nonconformity, however, is likely to be persecuted or shunned. In retrospect a man's motivation is not always considered as important as his social accomplishments, whereas at the moment all phases of him are judged and evaluated. Fortunately or unfortunately, there are always some individuals in any society whose constitutions and experiences are sufficiently peculiar or different so that they become non-conformers. It is they, the true leaders of a generation, who sense latent public opinion even while recognizing that actual public opinion is opposed to their efforts.

To be unconventional or to defy the culture is usually a punishing experience, and therefore individuality is freely and willingly sacrificed to achieve other gratifications or, at the very least, to avoid the penalities of being an out-grouper. The bandwagon of culture remains attractive because it is carrying other people and because so many human gratifications come from people. The conventionally dressed male in our society sometimes dreams of being able to toss aside his collar and to have his neck feel perpetually comfortable. He rarely gives expression to this impulse, except in the privacy of his home and in other situations where society is more tolerant. This is indeed a sacrifice which he makes because discarding collars on all occasions would produce inconveniences not worth the revolutionary gesture. William James's famous phrase describing habit as "the enormous flywheel of society, its most

precious conservative agent" (*18*) dramatically calls attention to the mechanism producing social conformity. Such
habits are continually reinforced because they lead to satisfaction. This is true in any society: men cannot or will not
live alone.

Simplification

It is a truism that nothing is simple. Or at least anything
can become complicated when the essence of its nature is
contemplated. "1 + 1 = 2" is not simple if it is recalled
that this elementary equation requires at least a knowledge
of language and a tacit agreement to abstract the characteristics of numbers from the concrete objects to which they
more often are applied. It is simple to turn on an electric
light, but the act involves an extremely complicated neuro-
muscular coordination as well as the electricity itself, both
of which are by no means thoroughly understood. Even
the spelling of "c-a-t" can be thought of as far from simple;
for example, why is the first letter of the word *c* and not *k*
or why is that same letter pronounced like *s* when it is
followed by the vowel *e* as in the word "cent"? Naturally
the equation is completed, the light is turned on, and the
word is spelled without raising the questions hastily mentioned here. No one could do anything unless he were to
make certain assumptions, forget certain problems, or simplify the problem at hand. Abstraction is inevitable.

One common form of simplification occurs when only part
of a stimulus is perceived and the rest is disregarded. Such
a partial response ensues because the individual is incapable
of making the complete response or because a prior drive
prevents him from perceiving the remainder of the stimulus.
Both the absence of the complete response and the presence
of the restricting drive in many instances are due to previous
cultural influences which have affected the individual who,
therefore, is heir to the simplifications of the past. In the
United States, for example, a favorite device of demagogy
is to brand an opponent with the label of "communist."
For that word elicits an unfavorable response among most

Americans. An unpleasant way of life or type of individual is associated with the word as a result of many factors: the historical belief of Americans that "free enterprise" represents a set of valuable institutions worth preserving; the ways in which the country's media of communication portrayed the Bolshevik revolution in Russia and the activities of the Soviet regime from its inception; the hysterical red-baiting of the early 1920's and the late 1940's; the hostility aroused or engineered by the strategy and tactics of the American Communist party; etc. The transition from these past associations to the present is accomplished by means of the stimulus "communist." The precise pronunciation by the political demagogue at the moment may be different from the way in which the individual has heard it spoken in the past, but the general form of the vocal vibration is sufficiently similar to evoke the pre-existing responses. To call an opponent a "communist" is to simplify a complicated situation in the interest of discrediting him. Disregarded are all the nuances of his personality and individuality; all the ways in which he differs from communists in the Soviet Union, in China, in Bulgaria, and in the United States; and all of his particular beliefs and ideologies. Instead only the hostile reaction is sought: he is a blinkety-blank communist and nothing more. Admittedly it is easier to think of him in such simple terms, and for this very reason demagogy has psychological advantages over rationality.

Most simplification consists of more than selective perception. The perceptual response may be a rather accurate reflection of the stimulus but what is learned and retained undergoes changes as time passes. The changes which occur are not haphazard, though they may be quite unconscious. They depend upon what has been originally perceived as well as upon prior habits which the individual already possesses and whatever other drives are active within him. Many of the metamorphoses through which handed-down reports and rumors go, for example, have been described (*3*) in terms of the levelling and sharpening of the original stimuli, both of which are forms of simplification. In an experiment (*4*) one person looked at an ambiguous drawing

of some people in what might have been a New York sub-
way car; he reported what he had seen to a second person;
that second person reported to a third what he had heard
from the first; and so on down the line, as in a well-known
parlor game. One of the figures in the original drawing was
a Negro. Chains of white and colored reporters had different attitudes toward the same drawing and hence they
introduced quite different simplifications and distortions.

According to Bartlett (5), some chiefs from an African
tribe once visited London and later recalled most vividly the
English policemen directing traffic whose uplifted hands
resembled the greeting they were accustomed to employ at
home. London for them had been simplified: as a result
of previous training, they perceived it as a city in which
certain persons followed one of their tribal practices. Naturally they observed other stimuli, but the one which impressed them was in accord with their habit systems. In like
manner, the novice sees and remembers an abstract painting
only as a confused blur which, from the viewpoint of the
artist, is a libelous simplification.

People who react to an event and find that their internal
responses have no appropriate or satisfying outlet are sorely
tempted to assign an explanation which has proven successful or satisfying in the past. This is especially true when
the correct or more adequate explanation is difficult or when
the event appears to defy rational analysis. Many super-
stitions, for example, are associated with events over which
the individual has no control. In our society, gamblers are
especially prone to be superstitious: they cannot regulate
their winnings and therefore seek refuge in actions which
from the scientific viewpoint have no relevance to success
or failure. The card player must have a particular ring on
his index finger and he feels vaguely that this symbolic act
in some way or other influences the cards he is dealt. Such
a belief may be founded on a single, fortuitous reinforcement in the past: on this occasion he was successful when he
happened to wear the ring on that finger. Thereafter he
sees a causal connection between the ring and success. Even
heavy losses may never extinguish the habit. He can always

assert that he might have lost more if he had not performed the ritual.

The simplified explanations which generally have proven most successful or satisfying are those which the individual has been accustomed to apply to himself and which he then projects upon events outside himself. He is really using a metaphor without realizing what he is doing. Anthropomorphism, for example, is the ascription of human characteristics to animals or deities. The master believes that his dog is devoted to him and may maintain that the animal has the same subtle feelings of attachment which one human being has for another; the dog prefers him to all other men "because" of his devotion. When the qualities of the human spirit are projected upon the inanimate object or upon the universe in general, the projector is said to be behaving animistically. Sailors even from "advanced" countries are traditionally animistic in regard to the sea which they say has moods, seeks revenge, lures them, etc. Sometimes, too, abstract words are made concrete by being considered persons or objects, a process labelled reification. The kind of preferred relationship among men known as "justice" is not always easy to grasp, and hence there is a tendency to reify the concept by thinking of a blindfolded woman with scales in her hand or of a physical restraint controlling human action.

Any metaphor tends to oversimplify the phenomenon it describes and thus to imply an explanation which at best is only partially correct. The ocean does have moods in the sense that it fluctuates like people, but these alternations are due to causes quite different from those which produce, for example, a manic-depressive psychosis in a patient. The use of the word "moody" to describe both calls attention only to superficial similarities and ignores significant differences.

Another method of simplification, as logicians and semanticists take delight in indicating, is the confounding of an object with the arbitrary name assigned it. If one individual is told that an ambiguous drawing of two slightly irregular circles joined by a straight line is a pair of "eyeglasses" and another that it is some "dumbbells," each is then corrupted by the verbal label and each subsequently tends to remember and draw a different version of the original drawing. The one with the word "eyeglasses" in his head retains the two circles but connects them not with a straight but a curved line. The other who had been told that the figure "resembles" dumbbells changes the width of the connecting line and makes it merge into the two circles (*11*).

To say that "this fruit is an orange" is to make a necessary but still a simplified statement; for the object referred to has many more attributes than the one suggested by calling it "an orange." Besides being an object which most men and some animals like to eat, it can also be considered to be a collection of seeds surrounded by a particular kind of substance; a weight which is heavier than a man's tooth; a weapon to throw at a spider or a motorist; a streak of color; etc. For practical purposes the designation "orange" is usually sufficient and it is the one which has been most heavily reinforced. It must be recognized, though, that the choice of a particular word, convenient as this is, masks other conceivable attributes. The individual who requires an object to heave at a tarantula would be a victim of his own language if he were unable to perceive that the piece of fruit could serve this function as well as the usual one of being eaten.

Language also encourages simplification by enabling individuals to designate an object, person, or situation as black or white and thus to forget the gradations of hues that separate the two extremes. According to Korzybski and his followers (*17, 19, 21*), this tendency in our society results from the influence of Aristotle who maintained that anything could be either A or B but not both A and B at the same time. These semanticists tend to overlook the logical justification for such simplified abstractions as they pounce upon what they call traditional logic.

Psychologically, however, they are on sounder ground when they call attention to the fact that there is an inclination to forget that abstraction has occurred after its purpose has been served. It is tempting to label people good or bad, honest or dishonest, moral or immoral, whereas in fact few if any of them are ever complete saints or devils. It is usually more difficult to choose a moderate hue or to add a qualifying adjective since moderation or qualification requires refined observation and cogitation. In addition, *if's* and *but's* suggest indecision, and hesitating individuals can resolve their conflicts and doubts more readily when they are confronted with apparently clear-cut alternatives. The black-white label assigned the issue then helps determine its appraisal.

The widespread quest for simple explanations and short-cuts suggests in large part why people are willing to accept simplifications offered them by someone else. Cantril *(8)*, for example, has observed in his fourth "law" of public opinion that "verbal statements and outlines of courses of action have maximum importance when opinion is unstructured, when people are suggestible and seek some interpretation from a reliable source." An event that affects people adversely is puzzling. They are ready to rationalize what has happened, to displace their insecurity, to engage in compensatory activity, to project themselves into the situation, or even to identify with what has happened—or they await an explanation of why the event has occurred and what its consequences for them are likely to be. The leader or propagandist with prestige then has the opportunity to give his version. For example, people ordinarily show little concern for public-health agencies until an epidemic breaks out. The disease arouses public opinion, and authorities are immediately consulted and heeded. The explanation of the epidemic which they give is as scientific as knowledge permits. In an earlier age the disease might have been blamed on a demon or on man's immorality.

Not all of the issues of public opinion need to be simplified in order to be grasped. Each issue falls along a kind of path, at one extreme of which the individual simply knows or states that he has a favorable or unfavorable attitude and at the other he tortures himself with all of the problems he believes to be involved. In this sense a well-informed public opinion is one whose decision rests not on simple acceptance or rejection, nor on tons of scholarship or soul-raking, but on a consideration of as many of the relevant factors as possible.

Principles of Public Opinion

The principal characteristics of attitudes and hence of public opinion have now been specified. It has been shown that public opinion may be consistent or inconsistent, may be based on rationalization, may represent displacement, may be functioning as a compensatory mechanism, may involve projection, may produce or reveal conformity, and very likely is a simplification of the issues. Some of the interrelationships of these characteristics have been described. Can principles be derived from the characteristics?

It is evident that the characteristics themselves are not principles. They are mere descriptions of what occurs or what may occur. In addition, their relation to social behavior in general has been suggested. But do they give rise to principles?

This question of principles cannot be dodged. More concretely stated, it is an inquiry concerning the conditions under which one or more of the characteristics will be demonstrated. The inquiry, in turn, is really much more general, for what is true of public opinion must be equally true of the behavior of individuals whether or not that behavior involves public opinion.

It is, in fact, premature to hazard a set of principles or "laws." Not enough is known concerning the behavior of the individual and still less concerning the simultaneous behavior of individuals. As a most tentative guess, however, the following principles may be stated:

1. Public opinion remains latent until an issue arises for the group; an issue arises when there is conflict, anxiety, or frustration.

2. Actual public opinion, therefore, is an attempt to diminish conflict, anxiety, and frustration:

   a. When these punishing circumstances cannot be avoided, there is rationalization.

b. When they cannot be avoided but when aggressive activity is rewarding, there is displacement.

c. When they cannot be avoided, when aggression is punished, but when substitute activity is rewarding, there is compensation.

3. Public opinion requires conformity:

a. When this conformity can be achieved by having some people attribute their own attitudes and knowledge to others, there is projection.

b. When it can be achieved by having some people assume that they possess the attitudes and knowledge of others, there is identification.

c. When it can be achieved by having people share almost identical knowledge, there is simplification.

4. Internal public opinion becomes external public opinion when:

a. The drive strength of the attitude is great.

b. Knowledge exists that the expression of attitude in action will be rewarding rather than punishing.

Crude principles like these, it is immediately admitted, merely state the kinds of problems which better principles must face. In connection with each one, there are questions involving the conditions under which a set of circumstances may be said to exist:

1. When and for what reasons do individuals experience "conflict, anxiety, or frustration?"

2. When and for what reasons can these "punishing circircumstances" not "be avoided" and when is "aggressive" or "substitute" activity "rewarding?"

3. When and for what reasons can conformity be "achieved" in the identical ways?

4. Just how "great" does the drive strength of the attitude have to be before action occurs; when and how do people know that they will be rewarded rather than punished; and how "great" must drive strength be before it can overcome a fear of punishment?

The answers to each of these questions in turn requires a set of elaborate sub-principles pertaining to the individual as well as to the stimuli in his society. And then each of the sub-principles demands some sub-sub-principles until—well, until all of social science and human knowledge are codified and systematized. Before the arrival of this great day at the time of the millennium, all that principles can accomplish is to call attention to the complexity of the problem and to caution as forcefully as possible against premature generalizations and glibness.

CHAPTER 6

Sampling Public Opinion

THE ability to measure phenomena and thus reduce them to quantitative form characterizes any discipline that has reached a scientific stage. Chemistry, physics, and astronomy are highly developed sciences because their data can almost always be expressed mathematically. Economics, sociology, political science, history, anthropology, and psychology are less scientific because frequently their data are not quantitative but qualitative. Compare, for example, the precision with which an astronomer can predict the time and observation sites of an eclipse, on the one hand, with the relative inability of the economist to state in advance where and when a depression or panic will occur. The astronomer has quantified information, such as the rate at which a star or planet travels and its orbit; but the economist is usually unable to obtain all the data he needs, for example, concerning supply and demand.

When phenomena can be measured, the investigator is in a better position to understand the problem confronting him and then to predict or to seek to control the outcome. The bacteriologist does not guess at the number of bacteria in a city's water supply; instead he measures the number present and then on the basis of this measurement declares the water safe or unsafe for human consumption. The airplane pilot does not consult his navel to decide whether he has enough fuel to reach a distant airport; instead he glances at his fuel gauge, notes the wind velocity and direction on other gauges, determines his distance or travelling time from the airport with the help of navigational instruments or landmarks, and then is able to conclude whether he should proceed, turn back, or seek a closer field. The city planner cannot rely on his own imagination to spin plans for a community; instead he seeks to estimate its present and future size, age distribution, occupations, recreational demands, etc.

In like manner public opinion can be adequately understood, controlled, or obeyed only after certain measurements have been made. The need for measurement in the case of the bacteriologist, the pilot, or the city planner is more or less universally recognized, but the same need does not exist in relation to public opinion. Many people are convinced that no instrument is necessary to measure public opinion. They feel that public opinion can be intuited and that refined techniques, therefore, are a waste of time and money. They may admit the need for measurement, while retaining complete faith in their own impressions or those of some gifted seer. There are others who are convinced that the task of measuring public opinion is hopeless because human beings are involved—and human beings, they say, cannot be placed under a measuring rod or a slide rule.

Public opinion, however, cannot be automatically or easily registered. A man who admits that he does not understand his wife after living with her for years will unhesitatingly announce what the American people are thinking. A series of studies (20) has demonstrated that judgments concerning the public are, in fact, affected by the opinions of the judges themselves. There is a tendency to project one's own attitude upon others.

Some of the confusion and controversy concerning the measurement of public opinion can be eliminated by recalling that the use of any kind of measuring instrument involves some error or at least the possibility of error. The individual who seeks to measure the area of a room, for example, may find that his measurements are not exactly the same each time he repeats them. Unless he is accustomed to measuring rooms, he doubtless will not trust the first figures he obtains. No matter how complicated or accurate an instrument is, eventually a human being must perceive the scales or dials and, in perceiving them, may make an inaccurate report. In many instances, too, the measuring instrument itself introduces an error for which a correction must be made. A voltmeter, for example, in measuring an electric current consumes a known amount of the current; hence the strength of the current is very slightly altered when it is measured.

Any public opinion instrument likewise contains errors, but there are methods available to diminish their magnitude, or at least to take them into account. Before judgment can be passed on an instrument, consequently, the corrective measures must be critically examined. Then it is possible to state whether or not a measuring device is better than intuition—and whether or not the distribution of attitudes among people can be reduced to mathematical form and the nature of public opinion reliably and validly measured.

Three principal errors are involved in measuring public opinion. The first two arise because the attitudes not of everyone but of a sample of the population are ascertained. Errors arising from the way the sample is selected from the population are called *biasing sampling errors* and those resulting from the sample's size are referred to as *chance sampling errors*. They are described in this chapter. The remaining errors occur as a result of people's reactions to the measuring instrument itself and may be called *instrument errors*. They are analyzed in the next chapter in connection with the mechanics of polling. Thereafter public opinion polls can be evaluated. Other more intensive devices to measure public opinion, together with the characteristic ways in which they seek to avoid or diminish these three errors, are appraised in Chapter 9.

The Nature of the Sample

A journalist arrives in a city from which he intends to file stories to his newspaper about an important strike occurring there. He reports the number of workers on strike and describes the picket lines. He interviews or secures statements from both sides of the controversy. He attempts to determine the conditions which have led to the strike and he gives abbreviated portraits of the leaders involved. Then his editor requests a less conventional story: "How," a telegraphed message asks, "is public opinion reacting to the strike; which side do people favor and why?"

Most American reporters believe they know how to determine public opinion. They talk to a certain number of people, secure a general impression of what those people are thinking, generalize to the entire population, and then write their story. Such an approach is frequently unreliable, as can be demonstrated by comparing two newspaper stories on the same event which have been written by different reporters. The journalist who has the assignment of reporting public opinion on the strike, even though he is working against a deadline, may casually ask himself the first question confronting any pollster: who should be interviewed?

Unless he asks himself this question, he may confine his interviewing to the unrepresentative people with whom strangers like himself are most likely to have contact. He may speak only to taxicab drivers, hotel clerks, waiters, bartenders, etc., and thus neglect to poll the wealthy, the extremely poor, and the affluent middle class. His method of selection results in a biased sample. In like manner the public servant abroad may send to the Foreign Office or the State Department an unreliable report concerning the public opinion of the country where he is stationed because—unless he makes a special effort to see all types of people—the ones he does meet in all likelihood are unrepresentative: they may include only those who can speak his own language, who frequent diplomatic gatherings, or who have business with his embassy or legation.

Surveys of public opinion are almost always based on a sample of the population. The process of sampling consists of measuring a small segment of the entire population or universe and on the basis of that measurement drawing a conclusion concerning the measurement that would be obtained if the entire population or universe itself were measured. The entire group is not measured because it is too expensive, impractical, or time-consuming to do so. The sample must be representative of the entire group, or otherwise the result is biased.

A distinction must be drawn between homogeneous and heterogeneous populations or universes (*19*). A population or universe is homogeneous when any sample drawn at random does represent the whole. A person who wishes to know whether he likes a cocktail must assume that he is drinking a liquid which is so well mixed (that is, homogeneous) that any one sip will be like all the rest. To be more certain of its representative character, he may occasionally stir the drink, thus ensuring a more perfect blend of the components. Similarly the manufacturer tests his product by examining a few samples. He makes the assumption that the product has been homogeneously manufactured and hence that a randomly selected sample represents the entire production.

A heterogeneous population or universe is not uniform. In principle, therefore, a completely random sample will not necessarily be representative of the whole, regardless of the size of that sample. The cocktail would be heterogeneous if it were poorly mixed: one sip might then contain an excess of distilled liquor and another an excess of vermouth or fruit juice. A product would come from a heterogeneous universe if it were not manufactured under identical conditions: one sample would be different from another because of varying production. If the reader wishes to know how many words there are on this page, he cannot adequately sample the page merely by counting the words in one line selected at random and then multiplying the result by the number of lines on the page: the one line may not be typical. What he can do is to count the number of words in three or four lines, secure an average, and then multiply that average by the total number of lines. This will involve less work than counting all the words on the page.

A sample of public opinion is almost always drawn from

a heterogeneous and never a completely homogeneous universe. People differ so much from one another that they cannot be chosen at random to make up a sample unless evidence exists that they accurately reflect the entire group. When the *Literary Digest* in 1936 predicted that Mr. Roosevelt would be defeated by his opponent, Mr. Landon, it committed almost every conceivable polling error except that of interviewing too few people. It mixed its poll with a promotion campaign to boost its own circulation. It had people register their preferences on postcards rather than in interviews: some types of individuals are more likely to respond to a written communication than others. It lumped together results obtained earlier in the campaign and those obtained later. Its greatest blunder, however, was its biasing sampling error: it polled only people whose names were in telephone books and such people tended to be wealthier (and at that time more pro-Republican) than those without telephones. Its sample, therefore, turned out to be representative not of the voting population as a whole but of the upper-economic group in the United States. As a matter of fact, Gallup was able to predict within one percent the *Digest*'s false prediction before its ballots were even distributed simply by conducting a survey of a sample from which the lower-income groups and people on relief had also been excluded (*4*).

The importance of securing a representative sample can also be illustrated by a hypothetical poll during an election. Assume that 1200 people are interviewed and that Candidate X is favored by 550 and Candidate Y by 650 of the sample. A simple prediction in the tradition of the *Literary Digest* would be that, within the range of the chance sampling error, Candidate X can be expected to obtain 46 percent of the votes and Candidate Y 54 percent. Assume, in addition, that the various economic groups in the society— ranging from the wealthiest, Group 1, to the poorest, Group 4—have different political preferences. The population, then, is heterogeneous and hence it is necessary to determine whether or not the sample is representative in respect to income. When the sample is broken down into income groups, the following distribution of the votes within each group might be observed:

	Group 1	*Group 2*	*Group 3*	*Group 4*	*Total number*	*Total percent*
Candidate X	100	100	150	200	550	46
Candidate Y	200	200	150	100	650	54
Total number	300	300	300	300	1200	100

It can be seen that the four economic groups are equally represented in the sample—in each, 300 people have been interviewed. The assumed fact, however, is that the four groups are represented in different strengths within the population; for example, there may be fewer very wealthy people (Group 1) than there are very poor people (Group 4). Only an empirical investigation can determine the proportion of the total population which each group may be said to represent.

If it be further assumed that 4 percent of the population is in Group 1 and that Groups 2, 3, and 4 have, respectively, 12, 52, and 32 percent of that population, a representative sample would have to contain three times as many individuals in Group 2 as in Group 1, thirteen as many in Group 3, and eight times as many in Group 4. In the above table each of the four groups contributes to the sample exactly 25 percent (300 ÷ 1200) and not its correspondingly correct proportion within the total population. The sample, as a result, is unrepresentative of the population. The prediction that Candidate X will secure 46 percent of the votes contains a biasing sampling error.

At this point the pollster can do one of two things. He can interview more people in order to secure the required increase in representation from the last three groups which in his present sample are differentially under-represented. Or he can weight the figures he has by multiplying those in each group by the proportion of the total population represented by that group. In this illustration, the 100 votes for Candidate X in Group 1 become 400, since the obtained figure of 100 is multiplied by 4, the percentage of the total population represented by that group. That same candidate's figure of 100 in Group 2 becomes 1200 (100 x 12), the figure of 150 in Group 3 becomes 7800, and that of 200 in Group 4 becomes 6400. Candidate Y's figures can be similarly weighted. When the data in the above table are thus weighted, the result is that Candidate X who received 46 percent of the unweighted sample has 53 percent of the weighted sample. Thus making the sample a representative one through statistical means has completely changed the prediction concerning the outcome of the election.

Gallup (5) refers to his representative sample for a national election in the United States as a "miniature electorate." This means that he strives to obtain a sample which is just like the entire voting population in respect to the attributes presumably related to voting, except that it is smaller. Before Gallup or anyone else working with a heterogeneous population can secure a representative sample or weight an unrepresentative one, it is necessary to know or at least anticipate something concerning the composition of that population. The cocktail sipper might conceivably but not probably determine whether a given sip is representative of the entire glass or shaker by asking a chemist to compare the proportion of distilled liquor and vermouth it contains with that in the entire glass or shaker.

The composition of a population which is being polled in the United States is not easily obtained. All reliable sources of statistical knowledge must be consulted, such as the United States Census, census-like material collected by other federal and by local authorities, special studies made for research or polling purposes, etc. Frequently reliable data of this kind are elusive or expensive. The information is lacking for a specific locality, as is often true of income data. It is out-of-date, as is a Census report in the later years of the ten-year census period. Or sudden changes in the society, such as the migration toward large industrial areas during the last war, require that existing information be corrected. The data describing the composition of a population, in short, almost always have been collected before the sample is obtained and therefore judgments concerning the sample's representativeness are difficult or risky to make.

Obviously a sample cannot be representative of the entire population in every respect. By and large, half the population of the United States is male and the other half female. A representative sample of the American population should contain, consequently, an equal proportion of both sexes. If 49 percent of the entire population of a state is Negro, as is the case in Mississippi, then the same percentage of Negroes should be represented in the sample. Forty-nine percent of the sample should not be drawn from Negroes (nor 48 percent, which is the actual proportion of Negroes in the population of Mississippi 21 years of age or over), however, when public opinion regarding an election is being measured and when it is known, from the past and from a current estimate, that only a small percentage of Negroes will actually vote. To have the figure for Negroes so high or to weight it that much would be to distort the sample: the political preferences of Negroes in this instance are largely irrelevant.

Suppose that 60 percent of the population prefers a white bread, 25 percent whole wheat bread, and 15 percent other kinds of bread—then should the sample reflect these bread preferences in the proper proportions? The answer might be affirmative if public opinion regarding a new type of bread or perhaps food in general were being measured. It would undoubtedly be negative if the issue were an election or birth control, unless it is thought or can be shown that bread preference determines political opinions or attitude toward contraceptives. A negative answer would mean that the sample might be unrepresentative in respect to bread preferences but perfectly representative in respect to the other characteristics of the population which appear related to the issues at hand. Conceivably, moreover, if bread preference is unrelated to those issues, a sample collected on the basis of other criteria will not necessarily turn out to contain about the correct proportion of people preferring the various kinds of bread. The same reasoning applies to the million-and-one other attributes of a large population; most of them can be disregarded in favor of a selected group of attributes which seem directly related to the issues whose impact upon public opinion is being measured. Securing a sample representative of the beliefs Americans have concerning the fate of the human soul after death would probably be quite superfluous when public opinion on the possibility of another world war within the next decade is being ascertained, again because these attitudes seem unrelated.

The criterion of relatedness, however, is not an infallible guide to the selection of the attributes in respect to which the sample is made representative. On many issues, the public opinion of men is no different from that of women. Males and females, for example, are usually equally patriotic, though the latter sometimes are more pacifistic. There are, nevertheless, enough issues on which the sexes can be expected to have divergent opinions because their socioeconomic status in our society is different and because in the past divergencies have sometimes been noted; hence sex must generally be accepted as one of the attributes of a national cross-section. The criterion, at any rate, suggests an important principle of sampling: attributes should be selected in respect to the issues provoking the public opinion being measured and the population being sampled. In practice, the polling agency has its own list of attributes which have proven useful and which therefore serve as the basis for collecting representative samples.

In conducting a poll, the problem arises as to how the respondents whose opinions are to be ascertained should be selected so that a representative sample can be obtained. When the central office plans the precise method of selecting respondents and leaves almost nothing to the interviewers' judgment, the method is known as that of specific assignment. When that office, on the other hand, plans only in a general way the type of respondent to be interviewed and leaves the selection of particular informants to the interviewers' judgment, the method is known as that of quota control. There is no question that the method of specific assignment secures a more representative sample but it tends to be expensive to administer; whereas the method of quota control is usually much more economical, but is likely to produce a less representative sample.

The Method of Specific Assignment

The method of specific assignment is also called the method of area sampling to emphasize the design of the sample rather than the instructions given the interviewers. At the outset the investigator must decide which people are of interest to him—does he want to poll the entire population above the age of 21 or only those eligible to vote; does his problem concern farmers or both farmers and city dwellers? Then he must select as the primary sampling area some convenient locality in which such people are to be found. In the United States the county is frequently the area for a national sample, since the 3,070 counties are scattered throughout the country, they can be easily identified by their recognized boundary lines, and almost all of them can be used as sites in which a corps of interviewers can comfortably travel and be supervised.

The next problem is to choose from a large group of primary sampling areas the particular ones in which the interviews are to be conducted. To do this, all the sampling areas are first grouped into strata, a process called stratification. Usually this grouping is done on the basis of some attribute like population density (the number of people per square mile) or the extent of urbanization (the percentage of people living in communities of a certain size), concerning which up-to-date information is available. Or the criterion or criteria may relate directly to the study in question. Thus the counties of the United States may be grouped into 30 or more strata in terms of their population density. One area—like a large city—can be considered a separate stratum because its inhabitants are of special interest to the pollster. With respect to the attribute or attributes which form the basis for this process of stratification, sampling experts advise that all the units within a given stratum be as homogeneous as possible but that the strata themselves be as heterogeneous as possible. If the counties

are stratified on the basis of population density, for example, each stratum should contain counties of approximately
the same density, but all the strata should differ markedly
from one another in regard to that attribute.

The principal reason for stratifying in this fashion is
statistical in nature and will become clear in the next section.
Here part of the rationale can be appreciated by considering
the next step in designing a sample. At least one and sometimes more than one primary sampling area is selected at
random from each of the strata. The areas, therefore,
should be as homogeneous as possible since only one or a
few of them is made to represent all the rest. "As homogeneous as possible," however, suggests that they will not
be completely identical in respect to the criteria of stratification; for this reason each area should *not* stand an equal
chance to be selected at random, but its chance of being so
selected should be proportionate to the degree to which it
represents those criteria (*9*). If three counties make up a
stratum and one has a population of 10,000, another of
15,000, and the third of 20,000, they are homogeneous in
the sense that they all lie between 10,000 and 20,000 but
obviously the third has twice the population as the first. If
pure randomization be employed to select one and only one
county in which interviewing will be conducted, then the
first which has only one-half the population of the third
would stand just as good a chance of being selected as the
third. In this way a biasing sampling error might be introduced into the sample, since by chance the polling results
may be expected to differ for each county. Giving each
county a chance proportionate to its size would mean that,
out of a total of nine possibilities, the first county would
have a chance of 2, the second a chance of 3, and the third
a chance of 4 of being selected.

A similar procedure may then be repeated within each of
the primary sampling areas selected from the various strata
in the indicated manner. The primary sampling area itself
is substratified and then a subsampling area is chosen from
each of the substrata. Such substratifying and subsampling
are required when it is not possible or feasible to select in-

formants at random from within the primary sampling area. Definitive mathematical statements on the entire sampling procedure—statements which can be understood only by those with mathematical training—are given by Hansen and Hurwitz (*7, 8*) ; but, as they emphasize, the decisive factor in substratifying and subsampling is frequently not statistical but economic. Both the cost of interviewing and the required reliability of the results must be considered simultaneously and perhaps weighed in the balance. The sampling units which emerge may be city blocks or portions of counties.

At this point only the sampling units have been chosen and it is still necessary to pick out the particular individuals to be interviewed. While the selection of the units has been partially deliberate and partially random, the individuals must be selected completely at random to avoid bias. The problem here is to work out a procedure whereby every individual in the sampling unit stands an equal and known chance of being interviewed. If the unit be a city block and if everyone within that block cannot be interviewed, then the quotient obtained from dividing the total number of individuals known or estimated to be in the block by the number of interviews to be conducted there provides a preliminary basis for deciding which people will be interviewed on a random basis. Assume that there are 1,000 people in a block and that 100 interviews are planned as a result of statistical and budgetary considerations. Divide 1,000 by 100. The resulting figure of 10 means that one in ten persons or every tenth person must be interviewed. Every tenth name can next be selected from an alphabetic list of all the inhabitants in the block, if alphabetization itself does not introduce a bias. When no list is available, the interviewers can be instructed to interview some one in every tenth family. But how can every tenth family be selected? Here rules must be worked out to insure randomization. Without these rules, corner houses, penthouses, basement dwellers, apartments near stair cases or elevators might be over- or under-represented in the final sample for the simple reason that interviewers may have a tendency to seek out or avoid such places. The rules lead the interviewers to the dwelling units in which the interviews are to be conducted. Additional guides are necessary, however, to enable them to select the particular respondent in the family if, for example, an individual's and not the family's opinion is to be ascertained—should the person who opens the door be questioned or someone else?

No matter what rules are formulated, the goal is to leave absolutely nothing to the judgment of the interviewers: they must find their respondents only in accordance with instructions. If a respondent is not available, interviewers are then instructed to call back until they find these persons, in spite of the extra expense involved. For it is known (*12*) that respondents who are at home when interviewers call may differ in certain respects (for example, number of children) from those who are not so readily accessible.

This method of specific assignment thus ensures randomization by deliberately setting up a sample design which gives each individual of interest to the investigator an equal and known chance of being interviewed. It strives to be as economical as possible by having the interviews concentrated in a relatively large number of randomly selected sampling units. It is an expensive method because the selection of those units in the first place is a time-consuming process and because call-backs are generally required. But, as advocates of this method point out (*11*), the initial investment in carefully designing the sample "may be calculated to more than pay for itself" particularly "when the investigator is contemplating a more or less continuous series of surveys, because the same fundamental sample design with slight variations in the selection of primary or subsampling units can be used over a considerable period of time for many continuous or independent studies." The method, moreover, almost always results in a representative sample (as measured afterwards by comparing the sample's attributes with those of the entire population when the latter's are known), even though the original stratification may have been based on only one of the known attributes and the substratification, if any, on only one other.

The Method of Quota Control

The method of quota control has been employed by most commercial survey agencies, although after the last war private groups like the Columbia Broadcasting System began to change to the method of specific assignment. When the method of quota control is followed, the central office decides only what the composition of the representative sample should be in respect to certain attributes and assigns to its interviewers the task of finding—more or less at random—a group of respondents whose total attributes are specified. At least five attributes are generally employed to secure a nationwide sample in the United States on most social, economic, and political issues. Aside from *sex,* the attribute of *age* is usually taken into account since the attitudes of youth, for example, are frequently different from middle-aged and older people. Sometimes the sample is made representative only with respect to two age groups, those below and those above 40. At other times there may be three groups—such as from 16 to 20, from 21 to 39, and 40 and above—or even four or five. Then an effort is always made to obtain a sample containing appropriate representations from groups of different *economic* or *social status.* That status may be measured by determining the individual's net or gross income, the size of that income in relation to other incomes in the same community or locality, or his actual occupation. It may also be estimated from the amount of education a respondent has had, a fact closely related to economic status and less closely connected with social class; or from his possession or non-possession of an automobile, a telephone, a bathtub, etc. In practice, regardless of the criteria employed, this attribute is most difficult to control (*21*).

The *population size* of the community in which the individual resides is a fourth attribute of the polling sample. Here a simple distinction may be made between urban and rural by defining rural arbitrarily, for example, as a community with a population under 5,000. Or there can be a scale containing four or five steps, ranging from communities under 1,000 to those above 100,000. A fifth attribute usually considered is that of *section of the country,* since within a country like the United States there are frequently regional differences in public opinion on many issues. The country may be divided simply into the Northeast, Southeast, North Central, South Central, Northwest, Southwest, and West, or this arbitrary seven-fold classification may be further broken down into a dozen or more areas or into the forty-eight states.

For other purposes, different attributes may be employed and then the sample is made representative with respect to them. On appropriate occasions, the following have been taken into account: color (whether Negro or white), race (national origin such as English, German, Irish, etc.), religion (generally Protestant, Catholic, Jewish, and "others"), politics (in terms of party membership or the party of the candidate supported at the last election), education (as distinct from economic or social status), membership or non-membership in the armed forces, etc. Sometimes, as in market research, the population may be limited to a particular group in the society like housewives, and very specialized attributes—such as marital status, number of children, type of dwelling inhabited, size or type of farm, etc.—become the basis for drawing the representative sample. The investigator of public opinion who uses the method of quota control is constantly experimenting to ascertain not only which attributes should determine his representative sample but also how each of them should be weighted.

After the attributes have been selected, the central office carefully instructs certain interviewers located in various parts of the country to obtain a specified number of interviews (*22*). In this way, since the interviewer interviews in his own locality, the variables of population size and section of the country are automatically controlled from the outset. The interviewers are further instructed to obtain, for example, 24 interviews distributed among five economic groups ranging from top to bottom as follows: 2 from the first, 6 from the second, 11 from the third, 4 from the fourth, and 1 from the fifth. Thus the attempt is made to secure a population distributed in respect to economic status. The interviewers are also required, for example, to have approximately half of their informants under and half over 40 and to divide them approximately in respect to sex. Since it is not feasible to have each of the economic-status groups divided equally on the basis of age and sex—an interviewer might have to spend too much time attempting to find, for example, an individual in the top economic group who is also both a female and under 40—the pollster hopes that from the data of many interviewers his sample as a whole will have these two factors properly distributed. As a further check on the representative character of the total sample and also as clues to interpret the results, the interviewers may be asked to record on the ballots additional facts concerning the respondents, such as political preference or educational status.

An interviewer operating under a system of quota control, where the choice of actual interviewees is left to his discretion, will obviously have no trouble in recording the variable of sex: all he has to do is to make the simple decision as to whether his informant is a man or a woman. Age can also be determined with almost equal dispatch if not quite so reliably, either by estimating it from appearance or by asking a direct question to which perhaps only women beyond their twenties hesitate to reply. In connection with the attribute of economic status, real difficulties arise. Most interviewees are about as loath to state what their income is as they are to give intimate details concerning their sex life. As a result, pollsters must instruct their interviewers to obtain indirect measures of economic status in various ways: to have the respondent name his occupation, which few people are reluctant to do and which has some relationship to economic status; to ask or to observe whether there is a telephone or a bathtub in the home; to size up the individual from his clothing, the neighborhood, or the kind of a house he occupies, etc. It has been shown (*17*) moreover, that agreement between two interviewers regarding an individual's economic status is very far from perfect and

that in fact one interviewer may not even agree with himself
when he appraises the economic status of the same individual
on a subsequent occasion.

The sample secured through the method of quota control,
consequently, is never perfectly representative and hence a
biasing sampling error is present. Rugg (*18*) for example,
compared the types of samples used by two typical polling
organizations with figures obtained from the United States
Census. He found that pollsters' samples did not differ appreciably from Census figures in respect to attributes the
central office controls like section of the country, rural-urban
distribution, and sex; but he had indirect evidence suggesting that the polls were "usually somewhat biased toward the
upper economic levels." Polling samples—perhaps because
Rugg made this analysis during the war—also had too
great a proportion of the population in the older brackets.
The most serious discrepancies between the sample and the
Census figures occurred in connection with two attributes
the central office does not seek to control: polls secured
far too many people of superior education and too many
from the white-collar and professional occupation. In fair-
ness to polling organizations, however, it must be pointed
out that they continually make every effort to diminish such
deviations and many of them, in attempting to predict a
national election, deliberately correct for the biases they
know they possess (*13*).

It has been indicated (*14*) that this method of quota control may yield a reasonably accurate cross-section for the
population as a whole but that the sub-groups into which the
sample is divided may not necessarily be representative.
Even though the entire sample, for example, contains approximately the correct proportion on a national basis of
individuals who are Catholics and of individuals who belong
to a medium-income group, the sample of individuals who
are both Catholic and members of the medium-income group
may not be representative. These two attributes can be
correctly distributed throughout the entire sample and not
within the particular sub-group. The risk becomes greater
when the results are interpreted in terms of an attribute

which has not been originally considered in setting up the sample. Ordinarily belonging or not belonging to a labor union is not one of the attributes determining a national sample, but pollsters sometimes present results which compare the two groups without any assurance that representative samples of them have been obtained.

Breakdowns, therefore, may reveal some kind of relationship but not necessarily a casual one. A hypothetical example—similar to one employed by Crespi and Rugg (*3*) —will be considered in detail, in such detail in fact that, it is hoped, the reader will remain suspicious toward breakdowns for the rest of his life. Let the question be concerned with attitude toward China. A national sample in the United States is polled by means of the method of quota control and the following hypothetical results are obtained:

> 55%: favorable
> 35%: unfavorable
> 10%: don't know
> ———————
> 100%: total

In this poll it will be assumed that 2,000 individuals have been questioned. According to the method of quota control, the sample may contain 1,000 individuals below 40 years of age and 1,000 above 40. When the data are broken down into the percentage of each age group having a favorable opinion toward China, the following table appears:

Age group	Number in group	Percent favorable
below 40	1000	49
above 40	1000	61

From this table it is tempting to conclude that age has something to do with attitude toward China, since more people above than under 40 have a favorable attitude toward that country. The difference is 12 percent and is statistically significant. Does such a conclusion make sense?

It is also possible to see whether there is any connection between an individual's sex and his attitude toward China. The sample of 2,000, it will be further assumed, contains

1,000 males and 1,000 females, whose favorable attitudes are distributed as follows:

Sex group	Number in group	Percent favorable
males	1000	70
females	1000	40

These figures obviously indicate that sex has something to do with attitude toward China: more males than females have a favorable attitude. Now the question is: is it age or sex that affects the attitude? Sex seems to be more important, since the difference between the two groups is 30 percent, whereas the difference between the two age groups is only 12 percent.

Another crucial question must be asked: how does it happen that at first glance both age and sex are related to the attitude? The answer to this question can be a function of the method of selecting the sample by the quota system. The sample as a whole may be equally divided into the two age and the two sex groups, but each age group may not contain the same number of the two sexes or each sex group may not contain the same number of the two age groups. Such a distribution of the two attributes within the sample is possible if not probable, and it was somewhat more likely to occur during the last war when the polling agencies using the method of quota control had difficulty finding younger males. If a more elaborate breakdown is provided, then the mystery disappears:

Sex group	Number in group	Percent favorable
males		
below 40	200	70
above 40	800	70
total	1000	70
females		
below 40	800	44 (or 43.75)
above 40	200	25
total	1000	40

From this table it becomes immediately clear that the tentative conclusion concerning the relation between age and attitude toward China was not simply misleading but false. When age is examined with sex held constant, there is no difference between the two age groups among the males, and more younger than older females are favorably disposed toward China. Only simple arithmetic is involved in the calculations, and the outcome in the above table, it is repeated, results from the uneven distribution within the sub-groups. If the number of males below 40 had been almost equal to the number above 40 and if the same distribution had occurred among the females, then the table could not have been obtained; in addition, the differences in the two previous tables would not have been the same. The method of quota control thus can produce a sample of sub-groups that are not representative of the whole. When comparisons between sub-groups are drawn, therefore, the critical observer of the polls must know whether those groups are correctly represented—and the commercial polling agencies almost never provide this information. In the illustration employed, the attributes of age and sex were interrelated for sampling reasons: young males and old females were under-represented. Sometimes two attributes are interrelated in the population itself. In the United States, for example, older people tend to be wealthier than younger people. For this reason, polls which show alleged differences in age groups must always be analyzed to determine whether those differences are in fact a reflection of economic status. Age may be called the crucial factor only when age differences appear within each economic group.

The biasing sampling error of a sample secured through the method of quota control may often be decreased not by changing the attributes or the weights assigned to each but by introducing a correction for an uncontrollable phenomenon which seems to be affecting the polling results. During the closing week of an election campaign, for example, polling may reveal that one candidate's popularity is slowly increasing—perhaps voters who have not previously come to a decision are now turning in his direction. The last sample, therefore, may be unrepresentative in the sense that it will be out-of-date on election day and thus be biased because of this time factor. The pollster may then make the unprovable assumption that the observed trend will continue up to and perhaps on election day itself, and he can correct his final prediction in accordance with what he believes would have been the result of sampling right before the voters enter the voting booths. An unusual situation arose during the 1944 presidential campaign in the United States when servicemen who had the privilege of using an absentee ballot could not be polled by the agencies. Without them, there was no assurance that a national sample would be representative. Many of the major polling organizations, as a result, attempted to make shrewd guesses as to how many of the armed forces would vote and next, on the basis of trends among their civilian counterparts in the same age brackets, to estimate how they might have responded to a poll. These guesses and estimates were then employed to correct the total obtained from the national sample of civilians who had been polled (*13*).

During the years since the *Literary Digest* neglected the problem of sampling, pollsters have made considerable progress in the field of forecasting elections not only in the United States but also in various other democratic countries. Even with the method of quota control, the discrepancies between their predictions and election results have almost always been within their chance sampling error. In 1942 Cantril and his associates (*1*), moreover, demonstrated the essential soundness of statistical and sampling methods for political behavior by predicting within 5 percent a New York gubernatorial vote on the basis of only 200 interviews; within .6 percent a Republican primary in an eastern county on the basis of 233 interviews; and within 4.5 percent a Canadian plebiscite concerning conscription on the basis of 208 casually obtained interviews. They most correctly and emphatically warn, however, that "small samples are highly unlikely to represent opinion faithfully *unless* opinion is fairly uniform throughout an area and within different interest groups and *unless* such differences are already fairly well known and can be adjusted for in constructing the sample" (*2*).

In most polling situations, moreover, there is no outside check on the extent of the biasing sampling error as there is when election returns are available. In addition, the ability to predict the results of an election is by no means infallible proof that this type of error has been eliminated. Ordinarily polling officials must rest content with comparing the attributes of their sample with the known distribution of these attributes in the population, if that distribution is accurately known—as it seldom is. If two comparable samples are obtained at the same time from the same population and if the polling results differ by more than what can be expected through sheer chance, then the pollster must immediately conclude that some error other than the chance sampling error has been introduced. That error may be the result of a biasing sampling error and probably is; hence improved methods of sampling are required. Or, less probably, instrument errors may be involved. In addition, as McNemar points out (*16*), results which agree may simply show that they are "biased in the same direction."

The reader, therefore, is strongly advised not to place too much faith in polling results obtained through the method of quota control merely because that method enables pollsters to predict election returns. The sample of the population which is obtained may be biased in innumerable respects other than voting preferences. Besides, voting is a special case with respect not only to the biasing sampling error but also to the instrument errors which will be analyzed in the next chapter.

The Size of the Sample

While selecting his sample, the pollster must also decide how many people should be interviewed. Common sense immediately suggests that the sample should be as large as possible. For almost everybody has been confronted with the problem of sampling and automatically has sought to check his first impression by securing, as it were, repeated

measurements.   Do you like this cocktail?   You take a sip
and cannot make up your mind.   You take another sip and
then perhaps by the third sip or the third round you come
to a decision.   Do you like this person?   You cannot quite
decide after meeting him for the first time.   You see him
again and, after another sample of his behavior, you begin
to form an opinion of him.   The more frequently you see
him, the more confidence you have in your judgment.   In
sampling, then, there is the possibility of obtaining an unrepresentative group when too few samples are taken.   This
chance sampling error can be reduced by increasing the size
of the sample.

It is not quite true, however, that confidence in a sample
increases directly with its size.   Even when the sample is
representative, the relationship is not a simple one: the reliability of results obtained from a sample which is selected
completely at random depends on the square root of the
sample's size.   This means that, other things being equal,
confidence does not increase fourfold when four times as
many people are interviewed, but twofold: the square root
of four is two.   The reporter whose editor has requested a
story on how public opinion in a community is reacting to a
strike may seek to write a more accurate story by interviewing sixteen people rather than four; in so doing, he has
quadrupled his work, but only doubled the confidence he may
have in his results.

Another factor affecting the chance sampling error is not
quite so obvious as the number composing the sample.   The
individual attempting to determine whether or not he likes
a cocktail feels that he has to sample no further if each successive sip is pleasant to him; but suppose he likes the first
sip, dislikes the second and third, likes the fourth, dislikes
the fifth, etc.?   Similarly the problem of sampling another
person's behavior becomes more complicated when the first
meeting produces an unpleasant one, the second a pleasant
one, the third and fourth an unpleasant one, the fifth a
pleasant one, etc.   Departures from complete conformity,
then, appear to diminish confidence.   The reporter who interviews four or sixteen people and finds half of them in

favor of the strike and half opposed will feel—and correctly too—that he can depend less on his survey than if he had discovered all of them in favor or all opposed. This factor is called the variability of the sample and, like the number in the sample, its effect even under conditions of complete randomization is not direct but involves a square-root sign: confidence in the results obtained from polling a sample selected at random decreases or increases as the square root of the variability of the responses, respectively, increases or decreases.

Statisticians have a mathematical symbol which expresses neatly the chance sampling error of a measurement: the *standard error* of the proportion of individuals giving a particular response. The term indicates the fluctuations in the obtained percentage which can be expected from successive samples of the same population when these samples are selected at random under identical conditions. The investigator can thus estimate the probable or possible deviation of the results of his sampling from those which might have been obtained if he were able to interview the entire population. When the judgment is "like" rather than "dislike" for example, 80 percent of the time—as determined from eight successive sips or meetings—and since the standard error of this proportion is approximately 14 percent, then it is quite possible that the figure of 80 percent will vary by 14 percent in either direction as more sips or more meetings occur. Any elementary textbook on statistics (*e.g., 6*) will offer the reader an explanation for the following which can be stated here only dogmatically: the chances are approximately two out of three that an obtained percentage will vary within limits indicated by a percentage plus its standard error and by that percentage minus its standard error; and it is practically certain that those limits can be indicated by the percentage plus three times its standard error and by the percentage minus three times its standard error. In two out of three times, if successive samples are taken, 80 percent will not be higher than 94 (80 + 14) or less than 66 (80 − 14); or almost always 80 percent can reach 100 (80 + (3 × 14) = more than 100) and can sink as far as

38 $(80 - (3 \times 14))$. The assumptions are being made, it will be noted again, that each sip or meeting occurs at random under essentially identical conditions and that therefore each stands an equal chance of leading to either of the two judgments. In these illustrations the assumptions certainly do not hold. The cocktail drinker may be gradually getting drunk as he continues to sample the drink and the person with an opened mind regarding another person will be meeting that person under varying circumstances.

The reader who has the common aversion toward mathematics and statistics will find it, nevertheless, a relatively easy task to calculate the standard error of a proportion if he can multiply two numbers together, divide the result by another number, and then extract the square root of the result (or use a square-root table to do so). For the standard error of the proportion under conditions of completely random sampling is expressed by the simple formula:

$$\sqrt{\frac{p \times q}{n}}$$

The terms of this formula may also be comprehended with dispatch, if the mathematician or statistician will tolerate a somewhat liberal and hence not literally correct interpretation. The letter p stands for the percentages of instances in which a given result (liking the cocktail or person, or favoring the strike) has been obtained in the sample. The letter q stands for 100 minus p or the percentage of instances in which any other kind of a result (disliking and feeling neutral toward the cocktail or person, or opposing and feeling neutral toward the strike) has been obtained in the sample. And the letter n stands for the number of cases on which the sample is based (the number of sips, the number of times the individual has been seen, the number of people interviewed by the reporter). In manipulating the formula, the reader must remember that, since both p and q represent percentages, they are in fact decimals and must be so treated when they are multiplied. The product of 70 percent and 30 percent, for example, is represented as follows: $.70 \times .30 = .21$.

This formula, it can be seen, embodies the two factors already discussed: the number in the sample and the variability of that sample. It demonstrates, moreover, the square-root relationship which exists and places the factors in relation to each other. Thus the standard error of a proportion varies inversely with the square root of the number in the sample: n is the denominator of the fraction. It also varies directly with the square root of the variability: p and not -p (or q) is the numerator. The measure itself indicates the chance sampling error by revealing the limits within which the obtained p may be expected to vary *if* the method of selecting is completely random, and it consequently shows how much confidence the investigator may have in his sample.

Consider again the reporter who has interviewed four people on the subject of the strike and has found that 50 percent of them are in favor of it. N is the number interviewed or 4; p is the percentage in favor or .50; and q is .50 (1.00 — .50) or the percentage disapproving. Then these values are substituted in the formula as follows:

$$\sqrt{\frac{.50 \times .50}{4}} = \sqrt{\frac{.25}{4}} = \frac{.5}{2} = .25 \text{ (or 25 percent)}.$$

Thus on purely chance grounds, about two out of three times the obtained percentage of 50 percent in favor of the strike will vary between 75 percent (50 + 25) and 25 percent (50 — 25) within the total population. Or, if the standard error of this proportion is multiplied by 3 — .25 × 3 = .75 — the outside limits for all practical purposes then would be 100 percent (50 + 75 = more than a hundred) to zero (50 — 75 = less than zero), which means that everyone else in the remainder of the total population might actually be in favor *or* opposed to the strike. This reporter, therefore, should have absolutely no confidence in his measure of public opinion: he has interviewed too few people whose opinions have varied too much.

If sixteen people instead of four are interviewed, it can be readily seen that the standard error of this proportion becomes 12.5 percent by substituting 16 instead of 4 for n

in the formula. The expected variability to be obtained from securing a larger sample of the population has been diminished from 25 to 12.5 percent. The reporter's confidence in his poll has been doubled because he has quadrupled the number of people interviewed. Such a result should also inspire little confidence, since the possible variability of 37.5 percent within the entire population ($3 \times .125 = .375$) is still very large. If he interviews 100 people, his standard error is then only 5 percent and—provided his sample is representative—he would be able to report to his newspaper that public opinion is rather evenly divided, inasmuch as the chances are practically certain ($3 \times .05 = .15$) that the percentage of 50 could vary only between 65 ($50 + 15 = 65$) and 35 ($50 - 15 = 35$) and its probable range is between 45 and 55.

It will be noted, too, that the size of the numerator in the formula—obtained through multiplying p by q—diminishes as p approaches 100 or zero percent and increases as p approaches 50 percent. Thus when $p = .99$ (99 percent) and $q = .01$ (1 percent), the product of the two is .0099; but, when $p = .50$ and $q = .50$, the product increases to .25 or over twenty-five times the product obtained when $p = .99$. This is another demonstration of how the formula takes the factor of variability into account. If the reporter interviews sixteen people and finds that twelve of them (or 75 percent) are in favor of the strike and the remaining four (or 25 percent) are opposed to it, the standard error of the proportion can then be calculated as follows:

$$\sqrt{\frac{.75 \times .25}{16}} = \sqrt{\frac{.1875}{16}} = \frac{.433}{4} = .108 \text{ (or 10.8 percent)}$$

If sixteen people are interviewed and p equals 50 percent, it will be recalled that the standard error is 12.5 percent; with the same number of interviewees but with p equalling 75 percent, the figure is reduced to 10.8 percent. The reporter, consequently, can have slightly greater confidence in his survey either when he interviews more people or when he finds more respondents in agreement with one another.

The formula for the standard error of a proportion is

the mathematical foundation for estimating the chance sampling error of any instrument that seeks to measure public opinion. Statistical refinements, however, are frequently necessary. Two will be considered very briefly. In the first place, the formula as it stands is based on the assumption that the number of individuals in the population is infinite, an assumption which is not true when a relatively small group is sampled. On purely commonsense grounds a random sample of 1,000 people may be expected to give more reliable results if the total population is 5,000 than if it is 5,000,000. In the first case 20 percent of the population has been sampled, whereas in the second only one-fiftieth of a percent. The following formula for a standard error takes into account the size of the universe being sampled:

$$\sqrt{\frac{p \times q}{n}\left(1 - \frac{n}{n'}\right)}$$

Note that the basic relationship of $\sqrt{\dfrac{p \times q}{n}}$ remains and

that the only new term introduced into the formula is n' which represents the total population in the finite universe. This correction in the standard formula, however, is of no great significance in large-scale polling operations: usually the correction is so small that it need not be taken into account, and most polls are based on samples of populations sufficiently large that for practical purposes they may be considered infinite in size. Thus when p equals 75 percent and n is 1,000, the standard error calculated in the usual fashion is 1.4 percent; when a correction is made for the fact that 1,000 out of a total of 5,000 have been interviewed, the figure becomes 1.2 percent; and when a correction is made for the fact that 1,000 out of a total of 5,000,-000 have been interviewed, the figure remains virtually 1.4 percent. A population of 5,000,000, therefore, can be considered to be infinite in size and the simpler formula may then be employed.

It may have been noticed throughout the previous discussion that another assumption has been constantly expressed

in connection with the use of the basic formula for the standard error: it has been stated that sampling has been occurring under conditions of randomization or chance. As indicated in the previous section, public opinion polls usually
draw their samples not completely at random but at random
from within specified strata of the population which have
been determined on the basis of attributes related to the
particular poll in question. When this is done, the standard
error can usually be expected to be smaller than if complete
randomization were employed: a greater scattering of the
interviews is assured since they are deliberately selected
from many strata. The formula then becomes:

$$\sqrt{\frac{p \times q}{n} - \frac{(s.d.)^2}{n}}$$

Again p, q, and n have the same meaning as before and
there is the same basic relationship of the product of p and
q divided by n, but a new term, $s.d.$ (which is squared), has
been introduced. That term is an abbreviation for standard
deviation and represents, roughly expressed, the weighted
deviations of the p's of all the strata from the p of the entire
sample; for further statistical details, the reader is referred
to an article by McNemar (*15*). Without these details,
however, it may be noted that the expression containing $s.d.$
is *subtracted* from the basic formula; when that expression
is high, then the standard error is correspondingly lowered.
The expression becomes high when there is great variation
in the responses given by individuals in the various strata.
In the method of specific assignment, therefore, the different
strata are made as dissimilar as possible in respect to the
sampling attributes: such dissimilarity is likely to give rise
to a dissimilarity in replies to the poll, hence to an increase
in the $s.d.$, and thus ultimately to a reduction of the standard error of the proportion. If strata differ markedly in
degree of urbanization, the percentage of respondents approving or disapproving of a question on taxation may also
be expected to vary—whether or not this latter variation
occurs depends of course on the relationship between urbanization and the attitude being measured.

In any case, regardless of which formula is employed, the basic relationship between confidence or chance sampling error on the one hand and variability and size of the sample

on the other—as given by the ratio of $\sqrt{\dfrac{p \times q}{n}}$ —remains the

same. The formula, therefore, indicates how many people must be interviewed to reduce the chance sampling error to whatever the investigator desires or finds necessary, and it reveals the limits within which a figure obtained from a particular sample may be expected to vary through chance if a larger sample or the entire population were to be interviewed. When sub-groups within the sample are to be compared, it is necessary for each of them to be sufficiently large to make the comparison statistically significant. Then the number of interviews to be conducted within each stratum is made proportional, for example, to the size of the entire stratum if size is the criterion for selecting the strata in the first place. Sampling experts (*10*) also advise that in the case of substratification the number of interviews to be conducted within each substratum be proportionate not to its own size within the sampling area but to the size of all the substrata within the entire stratum.

The basic formula's utility can be demonstrated by considering a poll during a national election in a country like the United States. Again, only the number of people to be interviewed is being considered; the more difficult error to correct—the biasing sampling error—for the moment is assumed to be at a minimum. A pollster, for example, interviews 100 people and discovers that 60 percent of them favor one candidate, 35 percent another, and 5 percent the remaining candidates. The standard error of the figure 60 percent is then approximately 5 percent, which means that the candidate represented by this figure could conceivably receive only 45 percent of the votes $(60 - (3 \times 5) = 45)$; if the other major candidate, the one who polled 35 percent of the sample, gained the 15 percent, he would then have 50 percent of the votes and win the election. Obviously, then, the standard error of this sample is too high for the pollster to be able to predict the outcome of the election. He must reduce that error. Mathematically the formula appears at first to suggest that the numerator—the product of $p \times q$—must be decreased by increasing p or decreasing q, but both are figures which the pollster must accept since they are results of his poll and hence represent what he set out to discover in the first place. All he can do, therefore, is to reduce the standard error by increasing the size of n, the denominator of the fraction. Increasing n means securing a larger number of interviews.

At this point the pollster is more dismayed by the square-root sign in the formula than is the average reader. For interviews cost money, and that sign tells him that his standard error will decrease much more slowly than the number of interviews he will conduct. The table which follows is derived from the formula and indicates in the first column the number interviewed; in the second column the corresponding standard errors based on that number and under the assumption that the obtained p for the first candidate continues to be 60; and in the third column the range within which p can be expected to vary with practical certainty (*i.e.*, the obtained p plus and minus three times the standard error).

Number interviewed	Standard error (*in %*)	Range of variability (*in %*)
100	4.9	74.7–45.3
200	3.5	70.5–49.5
500	2.2	66.6–53.4
1,000	1.6	64.8–55.2
2,000	1.1	63.3–56.7
5,000	.7	62.1–57.9
10,000	.5	61.5–58.5

From examining a table like this, the pollster can decide that he needs at least over 200 interviews to be able to make the very simple prediction that the leading candidate will win the election. For with 200 interviews his standard error will be 3.5, which will enable him to state with practical certainty—so far as chance sampling error is concerned—that this candidate will receive at least 49.5 percent of the votes.

To raise 49.5 to 50 percent, as a matter of fact, about 215 people have to be interviewed.

In practice, however, the formula or any table derived from it has to be applied somewhat differently to determine the number of interviews to be conducted. In the first place, the assumption of the above table that the leading candidate will continue to receive 60 percent of the votes as larger samples of the population are taken will not necessarily be true. In fact, on a purely chance basis, the standard error of 3.5 percent based on 200 cases suggests that p can be expected to vary as the size of the sample is changed. If the candidate's lead over his rival decreases, then p will draw closer to 50 percent, which will increase the standard error and hence require still more interviews to compensate for that increase. There is also the possibility, of course, that he will receive a higher percentage of the vote in the larger sample and, consequently, fewer interviews will be necessary to obtain the same standard error.

Then, secondly, it has been assumed that no biasing sampling error is present or, in other words, that the sample is truly representative of the entire population. It has been repeatedly emphasized that such an error does in fact plague the pollster, and for this reason the total variability which should be expected will be greater than the chance sampling error calculated from the formula. Gallup warns his readers—usually only during an election campaign— that his polls have a 4 percent "margin of error." This figure includes both the chance sampling error obtained through the use of the formula as well as biasing sampling errors resulting from faulty or inadequate sampling; it is, therefore, an empirical estimate based upon his years of polling experience.

Finally, pollsters seek to predict not only which candidate will win but approximately what percentage of the votes he will receive. To accomplish the latter, the last column in the above table must be consulted. There it can be determined not merely whether the percentage of the votes for one candidate may drop below 50 percent but the lower and upper limits within which that percentage may be expected through chance to vary. A polling organization likes to score a bull's-eye by predicting the precise percentage. It will be noted in the table above that as many as 10,000 interviews still result in a standard error of .5 percent and hence allow a variability of 1.5 percent above and below the obtained percentage. In the same illustration, approximately 1,360 interviews would have to be conducted to obtain a standard error of 1.33 percent (or a variability range of 4 percent above and below 60 percent).

The table under discussion also demonstrates that the standard error of 4.9 can be reduced to one-tenth of its original size only by securing 100 times as many interviews. The diminishing rate at which an increased sample decreases the standard error makes the prediction of a close election extremely precarious, as was the case the last two times Mr. Roosevelt was re-elected. In this situation, a fluctuation of a percent or two means that one candidate rather than the other will receive the majority of the votes. Aside from biasing sampling errors resulting from faulty sampling, it is so agonizingly difficult to reduce a standard error especially when that percentage tends to be large anyway around the 50 percent mark. In the United States, moreover, there is always the possibility that a successful presidential candidate may run behind in the popular vote and still win the majority of the electoral votes and hence the election, as Mr. Hayes did in 1876 when he defeated Mr. Tilden. In addition, a successful candidate can win a bare majority in many states and yet sweep the electoral college; polls based on the popular vote, as a result, give an accurate but a journalistically misleading impression. For an American presidential election, therefore, the problem of how many and which kinds of individuals to interview should occur forty-eight times—and in some states the race may also be close. Few polling agencies have the facilities or the courage to attempt a state-by-state prediction.

The *Literary Digest*'s ill-fated poll of 1936 was based upon 2,376,523 people, of whom 57 percent favored Mr. Landon. The standard error of this proportion from so large a sample was about .03 of a percent and hence the outside limits within which the obtained figure might have been expected to vary by chance were between less than 58 percent and more than 56 percent. The *Digest* obviously had polled enough people to make its chance sampling error infinitely small, but its method of selecting respondents from telephone directories had introduced the large biasing sampling error. This latter type of error cannot be reduced through the application of a statistical formula but only through a careful sampling design. The pollster, in short, must show simultaneous concern for both types of error.

CHAPTER 7

The Mechanics of Polling

In the last chapter only the elementary and preliminary problems of measuring public opinion have been considered: the nature and the size of the sample to be interviewed. These are problems which must be faced before a single interview has been conducted or a single questionnaire distributed. In this chapter the instrument errors introduced into a conventional poll by the act of measurement will be surveyed.

Any instrument leads to error when it fails to possess three properties. In the first place, its effect upon the object being measured must be known and taken into account in arriving at the final measurement. A thermometer influences the temperature of the object being measured if the instrument itself at the outset is decidedly warmer or colder than that object. The practical effect is unimportant in a large room, but it becomes significant in a very small space. In this connection, it must be added that an instrument is utilized when the phenomenon which it is constructed to measure is thought to be present and that the phenomenon is not expected to appear merely because the instrument is employed. A thermometer designed to measure only freezing temperatures cannot reveal the temperature of a hot oven, and measuring its temperature with such an instrument does not temporarily make the oven become a refrigerator. Secondly, an instrument must be reliable, an ambiguous term which shall mean here that essentially identical results are obtained when measurements are repeated under identical circumstances. A reliable thermometer registers the same amount when it is repeatedly submerged in water whose temperature is carefully controlled to remain constant. Finally an instrument should be valid: it must measure what it has been designed to measure. If the thermometer is valid, it will register 32 degrees Fahrenheit whenever water begins to freeze and 212 degrees Fahrenheit whenever water begins to boil at sea level; or under varying conditions it will give the same readings as another instrument that is known to be accurate. Inexpensive thermometers that are on the same shelf in a store and hence are being affected by the same amount of heat frequently register different temperatures. They may be quite reliable in the sense that they consistently over- or under-estimate the temperature, but only those are valid which register the "correct" temperature as determined by some independent criterion.

The public opinion poll is not perfect in all of the above respects and, therefore, pollsters are continually faced with the problem of reducing or correcting various instrument errors.

The Interview

The interviewer operating under the method of quota control approaches a prospective respondent who appears to satisfy some of the sampling requirements set forth by the home office: he is a white male obviously below the age of 40 and he probably comes from a lower economic group because he is wearing overalls and because—at five o'clock in the evening—he seems to be walking home from work and is approaching a poor neighborhood. Sex, age, color, and economic status are thus wholly or partially accounted for, in addition to the attributes of population size and section of the country which the polling site and the particular interviewer have automatically registered. The interviewer

greets the man and asks him whether he is willing to answer
a few questions for a national polling agency. He is assured
that his name will not be requested and hence that he should
reply frankly and honestly. In less than a quarter of an
hour the interviewer then asks him a series of questions to
which he replies after consulting the alternatives presented
to him on a series of cards. The interviewer records these
replies in terms of the alternatives and, if so instructed,
makes note of some of the interviewee's free-floating comments. The interview ends with a few questions, for example, concerning the man's occupation, the candidate for
whom he voted at the last presidential election, etc. The
interviewer thanks him and is off to fill the rest of the quota.

In this and in any other interview, the respondent has
been going about his business before the interviewer approached him. He has been thinking his private thoughts
or he has been responding to other stimuli. Suddenly a
new series of stimuli is presented to him: the interviewer,
his request for an interview, and the questions themselves.
Almost as suddenly he produces a new series of responses.
The pollster wants the questions stated by the interviewer
to arouse a particular attitude and he also wants the attitude to determine the verbal response. Compare these reactions of two other interviewees:

	Individual A	*Individual B*
Stimulus	"For whom will you vote?"	"For whom will you vote?"
Internal response	"For Candidate X and I might as well tell this man."	"Hasn't he beautiful eyes and doesn't he ask the question adorably? Now I wonder whether . . ."
Verbal response	"For X."	"Oh, I really don't know; why are you asking poor little me this question?"

This is admittedly a caricature of the interview situation,
but it suggests an ideal reaction in the case of Individual A
and an unrevealing reply in the case of Individual B, ideal
and unrevealing from the pollster's viewpoint. Individual

A has responded to the stimulus of the question, and his reply rather directly depends upon a pre-existing attitude. Individual B, on the other hand, has pushed the stimulus of the same question far into the background, has concentrated instead on the personal charm of the interviewer, and certainly has not revealed much about her political thinking, except perhaps that it occupies a less central position in her personal life than sex.

The pollster knows that the temperature of a thermometer should not affect the temperature of the room which the instrument itself is supposed to measure. All he can do, however, is to instruct his interviewers to be pleasant and to appear interested in what the respondents have to say. They should ask the questions in the form devised by the central office and they may add explanatory comments only when these are absolutely necessary. They should politely but firmly insist that interviewees answer the questions and not wander off on to tangents. They should interview one person at a time and not in the presence of other people, lest an audience affect the expression of attitude.

Investigations in the United States have shown, however, that interviewers can affect the results of a poll by biasing the sample and by influencing the replies to questions. In one study (*10*), for example, interviewers regularly employed by a polling agency obtained results on issues of the day which were quite different from those secured by other interviewers who ordinarily worked as mill hands. When the issues involved labor, the worker-interviewers elicited more radical or liberal replies than the regular interviewers. These differences did not result from a biasing sampling error: although it may have been anticipated that worker-interviewers would tend to interview too many respondents from their own class, the presence of a few clerks in this interviewing group and the interviewers' mistaken belief that they would do a better job by getting "the opinions of better dressed people" produced the opposite effect. The fact that the worker group had had no experience at interviewing accounted for some of the discrepancy, but much more important was the tendency for workers to respond more freely when interviewed by fellow-workers. Rapport appeared better when the interviewer's and the interviewee's class as conveyed by similar clothing and speech mannerisms was the same. There tended, finally, to be a correspondence between the interviewers' own opinions and the replies they received. In like manner, a group of investigators (*21*) reports similar and striking differences in the direction of the interviewers' own opinions, especially in smaller communities. An analysis has also been made (*16*) of polling results obtained by trained and untrained interviewers: the inadequately documented but anticipated conclusion is drawn that trained interviewers tend to conduct slightly—but very slightly—superior interviews.

There are selective factors that induce some people rather than others to work as interviewers for the polling organizations. Many American interviewers, for example, tend to be middle-class women who are seeking to supplement their families' income through this type of part-time work. It has been suggested (*11*) that women in that class are prone to interview more respectable-looking individuals since they may be afraid to approach tough-looking strangers on the wrong side of the tracks. Their middle-class status as well as their sex can also have an effect not only on the kind of people they interview but also on the attitudes they elicit. It is conceivable that some men reply differently to the same question as posed by a woman from the way they do when questioned by a man.

Here, then, is another demonstration of the fact that the method of quota control can lead to an unrepresentative sample since the interviewers select the particular people to be questioned and their selection may be biased. The method of specific assignment, in contrast, can practically eliminate this type of error. The elimination of the biasing sampling error, however, does not mean that the interviewers do not affect the outcome of the interviews.

There is, in fact, clearcut evidence demonstrating how important the mere presence of the interviewer may be under certain circumstances. A direct interview and a poll by mail can produce different results from identical questions even when the same individuals are involved (*6*). Then the interviewer can be partially eliminated, as it were, when the respondents state their preferences on a secret ballot in the interviewing situation. Sometimes different and at other times essentially identical results are obtained (*1*) when two representative and comparable samples are polled regarding political preferences: the one is interviewed openly in the usual fashion and the other records its choice on a ballot which is then dropped into a box marked "secret." In a Maine community during 1940, for example, the secret ballot was 5 percent closer to the election returns than was the interview in the senatorial contest; it was 7 percent closer in the gubernatorial contest; but it was only less than 1 percent more accurate in the presidential contest. For the 1944 presidential election, the same investigators report, the interview gave a 2 percent more accurate forecast than the secret ballot, but the latter was slightly better on a state-by-state basis especially in the South. It would seem, then, that the secret ballot may decrease the instrument error slightly under certain conditions; yet it may also increase the biasing sampling error by reducing the number of literate respondents willing to be questioned. Another investigator (*22*), using the same technique, has demonstrated that occasionally but not always respondents are less willing to express themselves freely in an interview situation.

A survey of Negro public opinion (*15*) was conducted during the last war in a large southern city on the treatment Negroes would expect if Germany or Japan conquered the United States and on the issue of concentrating "on beating the Axis" versus making "democracy work better here at home." The replies of Negroes were markedly affected by the skin color of the interviewer: these informants tended to give white interviewers answers acceptable to white people. On the other hand, essentially identical results were obtained (*23*) by white and Negro interviewers in Harlem (where Negroes are more at ease in front of white people) on less provocative issues.

Such studies suggest that all polling results must be interpreted cautiously. The presence of the interviewer elicits not internal but external public opinion. Or as a stimulus that interviewer produces additional responses within the interviewees, and those responses rather than the attitude to be measured can affect the replies he records. It matters not that the interviewer may not always influence the results or that he is more likely to have an effect when the interviewees are somewhat tense or when the issues are tension-producing, inasmuch as it is difficult to anticipate in advance when such an effect will appear or to prove afterwards that it has or has not appeared. In theory it is quite possible that the conflicting biases of the interviewers can cancel each other in the final tabulation; but in practice, as McNemar (*13*) has pointed out, it does not necessarily follow that "the biasing effect of the pro-interviewers is the same in amount as that of the anti-interviewers."

In large polling agencies, moreover, there have been instances in which the interviewers have actually faked the ballots they send into the central office. Respondents are not interviewed or only a few of the questions on the ballot are asked; then the interviewers complete the ballots on the basis of their own imagination. Although the agencies usually attempt to eliminate such practices by making a careful analysis of the work each interviewer submits, it appears (*4*) that they have not been completely successful in doing so.

The Existence of the Attitude

Out of politeness, curiosity, ego-enhancement, or civic responsibility most people at least in democratic countries are willing to answer a series of polling questions. Some drive to cooperate with the interviewer quite readily becomes active. Cooperation, however, is not enough from the pollster's viewpoint. He wants his informants to respond in terms of the attitudes they already possess.

In some instances it appears as though people do not have the attitude to be measured but instead their answers are formulated and then expressed during the interview.

Gallup himself (7) has forcefully indicated this possibility when he was engaged not in measuring public opinion throughout the United States but in attempting to determine reader-interest in various features of newspapers. At that time he observed that "seldom do readers know what they read, or what interests them most" but that "when they are questioned by an interviewer, they fall back upon the answers which they believe they should give."

The order of questions on the polling ballot, for example, may affect the results (*17*). A national sample of American people was asked the following two questions in the indicated order on September 1, 1939, right at the outbreak of the last war:

1. "Should the United States permit its citizens to join the French and British Armies?"
2. "Should the United States permit its citizens to join the German Army?"

Forty-five percent of the sample replied affirmatively to the first and 31 percent to the second question. But the figure of 45 was reduced to 40 percent and that of 30 to 22 percent when a comparable sample was asked the same questions *in the reverse order*. The investigators state that under the first condition "after endorsing enlistments in the armies of the Allies, people evidently felt obliged to extend the same privilege to those wishing to join the German Army," whereas "when the question of joining the German Army came first . . . fewer people were willing to grant this right to American citizens." The two questions, regardless of order, apparently aroused favorable attitudes toward the Allies and unfavorable ones toward Germany since in either case a greater number favored direct assistance for the French and British. The attitude regarding the particular issue being investigated, however, must have been formed by some people while they were being interviewed.

Similarly the alternatives provided respondents can be crucial stimuli which form rather than channelize the verbal response. Here is a somewhat dramatic illustration from Gallup's files (*18*). The time: April 8, 1941. Question for Sample A: "About how soon do you think we will be in the war?"   Question for Sample B: "Do you think we will be in the war within two months?"   Sample A gave any reply it wished, but Sample B was restricted to three alternatives: "yes," "no," and "don't know."   The contrasting replies were as follows:

Sample A		Sample B	
2 months or less	12	Yes	25
3 months	8		
4 to 6 months	22	No	46
Later estimates	31		
No opinion	27	Don't know	29
Total	100		100

More than twice as many people predicted America's entry into the war within two months when that period was suggested as a reply than when they themselves had to formulate their own prediction.

It is difficult indeed to interpret the meaning of polling results which depend on the order of the questions or on the alternate replies that are offered.   Usually the pollster can determine whether or not the interviewees have previously had an attitude only by asking them questions, a test which is obviously misleading since the act of interviewing may itself form the attitude.   Perhaps the attitude has been latent and the interview makes it actual.   If this is the case, then the drive strength of such an attitude may be relatively small and, as a result, the attitude can be expected to have little or no effect upon subsequent behavior.

The fact that the pollster asks a given question indicates at least his own belief that an issue is confronting public opinion.   The interviewees, however, may not have previously recognized the issue.   Their knowledge may be deficient or they may not have been affected by the problem.   Or the issue may be apparent to no one except a small group in the society.   In the latter case, the issue is meaningful only for that group, and one of the pollster's problems may be first to identify and find the individuals to whom the issue is real.   One writer strongly advises that the percentage of "no opinion" answers on a poll "should always be carefully scrutinized" (*12*). When this percentage is large, however, it is dangerous to draw a conclusion concerning the state of public opinion of those who have replied positively or negatively: they may have decided "impulsively" during the interview—and the impulse may or may not represent potential public opinion—or they may really have possessed determining attitudes. Unfortunately, the conventional type of poll seldom if ever makes such a distinction.

Polling organizations sometimes seek to eliminate respondents who do not have pre-existing attitudes by determining first whether their knowledge concerning a question is correct or incorrect. The assumption here is that those who are informed are more likely to be predisposed one way or the other. The device is called the "filter question": a preliminary question filters out the ignorant or the disinterested and then only the attitudes of those remaining are measured. In September 1946, for example, Gallup sought to measure the reactions of Americans to the issue of "balancing the budget" versus "cutting income taxes." Instead of immediately asking a representative sample which alternative they favored, he began with this question: "Can you tell me what is meant by 'balancing the Federal budget?'" Forty-nine percent were able to give a correct reply, and only those were presented with the next question: "Which do you think is the more important in the coming year—balance the budget or cut income taxes?" Parenthetically this writer must remark that no doubt the 51 percent who did not know the meaning of "balancing the Federal budget" may have been perfectly willing to answer the second question too—and he would leave to the reader the problem of interpreting their replies!

The Nature of the Question

It has already been pointed out that people's replies under certain circumstances may be dependent upon the alternate replies that are suggested to them by the interviewer. In this section the wording of the question itself will be considered since in many instances its form can affect the replies. The pollster's problem, in brief, is to devise a question which will evoke the attitude of interest to him and not some other attitude.

The question must be understood. The interviewees should have sufficient prior knowledge so that, when they perceive the stimulus, similar or identical internal responses are evoked within them. The stimulus, "For whom are you going to vote at the next election?" is undoubtedly unambiguous to people who speak English and are aware of the fact that an election is about to occur. Frequently stimuli have been previously arranged along a gradient so that variation in the wording of a question nevertheless produces essentially similar responses which in turn evoke essentially similar attitudes. A national cross-section of the American people right before the outbreak of the last war in 1939, for example, responded almost identically to these three different questions whose "meaning" to them must have been practically identical (8):

1. "Would you like to see England, France, and Poland agree to Germany's demands regarding Danzig?"
2. "Do you think Hitler's claims to Danzig are justified?"
3. "Do you think Hitler's claims to the Polish Corridor are justified?"

At other times, however, what appears to be a clear-cut question turns out to be quite ambiguous and hence to arouse initially varied responses in different people. During the last war, for example, Roper polled a cross-section of Americans on the question, "After the war is over, do you think people will have to work harder, about the same or not so hard as before?" By means of careful and detailed interviewing of individuals, it was discovered (2) that this question contained at least three ambiguous words or phrases. Interviewees gave different responses to the word "people": some responded with "people in all walks of life," some considered only "one class or group of people," and the rest claimed they simply did not know to whom the word referred. Responses to "work harder" included "longer hours," "more competition," and demand for "a higher quality of work." Finally, "as before" elicited responses which drew a comparison either with "war times" or "the old days of peace"—or else the interviewee did not stop to consider the temporal basis of the comparison he was making.

To be reasonably certain that the question does produce internal responses related to the attitude being measured, the pollster can do two things. In the first place, he himself must know precisely which attitude he is measuring. In the illustration above, Gallup obviously was attempting to measure American reactions to German (or Nazi or Hitler's) designs on Danzig and the closely connected question of the Polish Corridor. Roper, on the other hand, apparently had not decided or did not express adequately the "people," the conception of "harder" work, and the time period he must have been considering. Secondly, the pollster can pre-test one or more versions of a question on a preliminary sample before he begins his formal poll. These individuals can reveal whether or not they make meaningful responses according to his criteria. Evidently Gallup decided in September, 1946, that an issue facing public opinion was that of budget-balancing vs. income-tax-cutting, for at that time the problem was being discussed by politicians and the various communication media. A pre-test, however, must have revealed to him the ignorance which prevailed concerning the meaning of budget-balancing and for this reason, as pointed out in the previous section, he may have employed a filter question.

The "meaning" of a question can be adequately understood, but the responses which are that "meaning" may in turn arouse an attitude different from the one the pollster seeks to measure. In this case, the question is an inadequate stimulus because it is not part of the stimulus gradient capable of evoking the attitude. When slight variations in the form of the question lead to marked alterations in the replies, then it must be presumed that different attitudes are being aroused or that one of the questions is incapable of arousing all of the responses which determine the verbal expression of that attitude. One writer (*3*), for example, points out that 64 percent of a sample secured by one polling organization in January 1945 replied "Join" to the question, "After the war, would you like to see the United States join some kind of a world organization, or would you like to see us stay out?" Three months later 81 percent of a similar sample of another polling group said "Yes" to the question, "Do you think the United States should join a world organization with police power to maintain the peace?" It is assumed that the two samples were comparable and that public opinion remained more or less constant during the three months interval; the difference in the results is attributed to "the magic quality of the phrase 'to maintain the peace.'" If this interpretation is correct, then the attitude aroused in January involved only the abstract idea of a world organization, whereas that elicited in April included also people's desire to have peace rather than war (and perhaps the notion of "police power").

A similar and more striking illustration is given by Rugg and Cantril (*19*) who report that 76 percent of a national sample polled by them on September 17, 1941, replied "No" to the question, "Should the United States enter the war now?" Eighty-eight percent of a strictly comparable sample polled by Gallup on exactly the same day said "No" when the wording of the question was: "Should the United States go into the war now and send an army to Europe?" The difference of 12 percent cannot be due to a chance sampling error, nor is it likely the result of a biasing sampling error. It cannot be ascribed to the word "enter" in the first question and the words "go into" in the second because the two expressions are completely synonymous even from a psychological viewpoint. The phrase, "and send an army to Europe," must represent the significant alteration in the stimulus. It would be difficult to argue that people answering the first question could possibly have conceived of the United States engaging in war without sending an army to Europe—how, in heaven's name, could this country go into or enter a war and keep its army at home? It must be concluded that the first question failed to evoke responses

relating to one of the fairly obvious consequences of a declaration of war and that, therefore, these interviewees replied "impulsively." At that time, moreover—less than
three months before Pearl Harbor—the problem of
whether or not the United States should enter the war was
an issue which must have occurred to most Americans, inasmuch as by then the United States was giving rather active
economic and semi-military support to Great Britain and
the Soviet Union. In spite of the clamor, some people's attitudes must have been more latent than actual.

Not only must a question be understood and elicit the attitude being investigated, but it also must *not* evoke some
other attitude which perhaps deserves to be measured separately in its own right. Gallup (*20*) asked a representative
sample of Americans in August, 1940, whether they agreed
or disagreed with the proposal that "if Germany wins the
war in Europe, the United States should try to have friendly
trade and diplomatic relations with Germany." Only 25
percent of one sample disagreed when the proposal was introduced with "It has been suggested that . . . ," but 41
percent of another sample rejected the same idea, worded
also in identical fashion except that it began with "Lindbergh says that. . . ." Apparently, the introduction of the
stimulus "Lindbergh"—who at that time had been losing
prestige as a result of his isolationist sentiments, his statements deprecating English and Russian strength and boost-
ing German power, and his dire predictions about England's
slim chances of winning—produced within the second sample a response relating to the famous flyer, and this attitude
for approximately 16 percent of them was stronger than
their response concerning the proposal itself. Such a question was double-barreled: it elicited two sets of responses
when only one was of interest to the investigator, and the
relative strength of the two attitudes within the interviewees remained unknown. The first form of the question beginning with "It has been suggested . . ." was obviously
preferable if public opinion on the proposal was to be measured. Public opinion regarding Lindbergh would have had
to be determined through a separate question devoted exclusively to him.

The impression must not be gained that the answers to a poll always depend so dramatically on the phrasing of the question. Any polling organization can produce many, many more illustrations of how a variation in the question produces practically no variation in the replies of representative samples. It is much more common to obtain practically identical results from the different forms of a question—as indicated above by the three questions concerning German demands for Danzig and the Polish Corridor— than it is to secure the kinds of divergencies reported throughout this section. More frequently than not, polls are able to achieve a high degree of constancy under varying conditions of measurement.

In addition, pollsters usually seek to determine the importance of the wording of the question, especially during the pre-testing period. Actual verbal responses of interviewees are obtained and, either from them or from more detailed interviewing, it is possible to induce what kinds of internal responses are being elicited by specific types of questions and answers. When pre-testing reveals responses— internal or verbal—which do vary considerably, the polling agency can decide to employ in its survey not one but two ballots, each of which contains different forms of question and/or answers on the issue involved. The two ballots are then given to different but comparable samples. The technique, known as the split-ballot, enables the pollster to measure directly the effects of variation in wording. Most of the illustrations in this chapter, for example, have been derived from split-ballots. When the results on the two ballots are essentially equivalent, either version may be published. When they differ, the publication of only one version is definitely misleading.

Constancy and Reliability

Pollsters seek to make their questions and suggested replies clear, unbiased, and brief. In this way they hope to diminish various instrument errors and thus to increase the reliability of their results. Such questions and answers, they rightly assume, are more likely to yield similar results when they are given a second time to the same set of informants or when they are administered to a comparable sample.

On the score of diminishing instrument errors in order to increase reliability there can be no quarrel with this procedure. There are, however, two questions which must be raised. The first involves the problem of validity and will be discussed in the next chapter as the polling instrument is evaluated; do such sterilized questions and answers produce results which are related to actual behavior? The second question which is related to but different from the first involves what may be called constancy: will the results remain constant under slightly or markedly different measuring conditions?

The answer to the second question, unfortunately, seems to be negative. This chapter has repeatedly demonstrated how the interviewer, the order of the questions on the ballot, the suggested replies, and the wording of the question *may* affect the results because a change in the measuring instrument is able to elicit different attitudes. While it has been pointed out that dramatic changes in the results are quite unusual, the mere fact that these changes are sometimes possible requires that they always be anticipated. Each poll, therefore, is a new adventure which demands a careful pre-test and—at least in theory—the use of numerous split-ballots to weigh the importance of the various factors in the act of measurement.

This is not to say that the results of a given poll are without interest or value. The least that is always known is how people react under the particular polling conditions. And it may also be possible to infer how they might react, for example, to a different version of the same question. The danger arises when an inference concerning constancy is drawn without adequate grounds for doing so. The untested assumption is then made that the second version of the question will fall along the same stimulus gradient as the first—and this may or may not turn out to be the case.

To diminish instrument errors and to increase reliability, polling has to be somewhat artificial. Questions in real life are not always clear, unbiased, and brief. Frequently they are fuzzy, prejudiced, double-barrelled, and interminable in length. The answers, too, are often not clear-cut. When public opinion, however, is actual rather than latent and when it is external rather than internal, polling results are more likely to be constant and less likely to be dependent on the particular standardized conditions of measurement. Under these circumstances, the single question and the clip reply represent a more adequate sample of the individuals' verbal behavior.

Constancy should not be confused with reliability, merely because each involves a second interview with the same or with a comparable sample. When constancy is tested, the measuring conditions are altered. When reliability is tested, all polling conditions are kept the same. In general, the reliability of polls in this strict sense appears to be either suspect or unproven. It is frequently impossible to say whether dissimilar results are due to the unreliability of the polling instrument or to real changes in attitude that have occurred in the interim. Too many pollsters assume the reliability of their instrument and convince themselves, after different results are obtained from a second administration of the same question, that real attitude changes have been detected.

One study (*14*) has shown that different replies may be given when the same informants are re-interviewed by the same interviewers at the end of three weeks. Only 79 percent of a small sample which was asked in the early forties to decide whether President Roosevelt was doing a "good," a "fair," or a "bad job in running the country" gave identical replies on both occasions. To a question pertaining to ownership or non-ownership of an automobile, 96.5 percent replied consistently. The failure to obtain perfect correspondence was probably not due to changes in attitude or in ownership but to the unreliability of the instrument. As might be expected, the same study revealed fewer identical replies (86 percent) concerning car ownership when the second interview was conducted not by the same but by a different interviewer.

Another investigator (*5*) required college students to

answer the same series of polling questions twice, with twelve weeks elapsing between the two tests. After the second test, the students were interviewed at some length and it was discovered that only 52 percent of the apparent changes which occurred were acknowledged to be "real" ones. The remaining 48 percent seemed to be dependent on instrument errors. Some questions, moreover, were more reliable than others.

The reliability of the simple questions usually employed in market research, on the other hand, is rather uniformly high. In one study (*9*), for example, consumers were asked "What brand of . . . did you buy last?" The same question was repeated two days later. It was found that 97 percent of the informants named the same brand of beer both times, 93 percent the same tomato juice, and the lowest figures obtained were 87 percent and 85 percent, respectively, for hand lotion and automobile tires.

Another problem relating to reliability involves the interpretation of the overall figure obtained from a sample. It is conceivable that this figure may be reliable for the group and not for all the individuals therein: the instrument errors of the separate informants can cancel one another. Such a discrepancy between group and individual reliability is of no consequence when the group is the center of interest, but it cannot be overlooked when the social or political importance of the separate informants whose attitudes are reliably or unreliably measured is taken into account. Similarly, more or less identical results obtained after re-measuring the same or an equivalent group do not necessarily mean that public opinion has remained correspondingly constant. Counterbalancing changes may have occurred within the group or groups, a fact which can be neither affirmed nor denied until an examination is made of the responses of the individuals themselves. These counterbalancing changes are illustrated in one of the studies previously mentioned (*14*). Although only 79 percent of a sample rated President Roosevelt in identical fashion during the two successive interviews, the following table indicates that the overall percentages varied very little:

	"Good job"	"Fair job"	"Bad job"
First interview	56	33	11
Second interview	50	41	9
Difference	−6	+8	−2

During the second interview, it can be seen, 6 percent less thought the President was doing a "good job," 8 percent more considered the job "fair," and 2 percent less subscribed to the "bad" alternative. A surface examination of these differences might suggest that only 8 percent had altered their opinion or had been measured unreliably: the 6 percent changing from "good" to "fair" and the 2 percent changing from "bad" to "fair" could be thought to account for the 8 percent rise in the "fair" category. As a matter of fact, there happened to be in this instance no changes from "good" to "bad," although such extreme changes would have been concealed in the above table. All of the individuals who changed either moved into or out of the "fair" category: in rounded figures, a gain of 10 percent from the "good" and 4.5 percent from the "bad" categories was accompanied by a loss of 4.5 percent to the "good" and of 2 percent to the "bad" categories, which accounted for the 8 percent *net* gain of the "fair" category and for the entire change of 21 percent.

The Evaluation of Polls

AT THE beginning of the last chapter a relatively facile distinction was drawn between the reliability and validity of an instrument. It was said that an instrument is reliable when repeated measurements under identical conditions produce the same results and that an instrument is valid when its measurements correspond with some outside criterion. The validity of an instrument, however, cannot be determined if its reliability is unknown. An unreliable instrument which gives a valid reading on one occasion may give an invalid one on another and, unless the extent of its unreliability has been ascertained, its validity remains a mystery.

The reliability of most polls is always in doubt, it has been shown, because differences in people's responses to questions may be due either to instrumental errors or to genuine changes within them. Conditions for people are never "identical" as they must be if reliability is to be conclusively determined. It is difficult, therefore, to discuss the validity of polls when their reliability is so uncertain. For purposes of this analysis, nevertheless, their reliability must be assumed—and this is admittedly a very risky assumption to make.

In addition, the question of the polls' validity raises a much more general question which is a variant of a problem already mentioned in Chapter 3 : the relation of internal to external public opinion. Here the question is more specific; if an attitude is an internal response with drive value, when or under what circumstances does any attitude affect overt behavior? This problem intrudes itself again for a very important reason. An attitude, since it is an internal response, can be measured only by means of overt behavior like the answers to a question or some observable action. Validity can be determined by comparing what is measured with some outside criterion. The validity of a poll which measures an attitude by means of the answers to a question, therefore, cannot be established by comparing the attitude with the answers because the answers themselves are the indices of the attitude. The only satisfactory solution to this complicated situation is to compare the answers with other types of overt behavior; but this solution has its difficulties.

One concrete investigation will clarify this somewhat abstruse problem. In 1930, LaPiere (*32*) sent a questionnaire to hotels, motor camps, and restaurants in the United States which he had previously visited while accompanied by two Chinese students. Without identifying himself and exercising suitable controls, he asked the proprietors whether they would be willing to "accept members of the Chinese race as guests in your establishment." All but one of the replies was negative, and less than 10 percent stated that their policy regarding Chinese guests might "depend on the circumstances." As a matter of behavioral fact, however, LaPiere and his friends had been rejected, six months before, by only one proprietor. Was his questionnaire, which was essentially a poll of unknown reliability, valid or invalid? It certainly was invalid in the sense that the actual behavior of the proprietors did not correspond to their expressed attitudes. But it may have been valid in another sense: although the anti-Chinese attitudes of these individuals did not affect their behavior in the situation created by LaPiere and his friends, it was perhaps quite influential in determining other behavior, such as voting for representatives who favored laws involving the segregation of Chinese in this country. Something was being measured by the questionnaire.

The testing of a poll's validity by comparing the verbal replies with some other behavior criterion, consequently, is a rigorous but not necessarily a fair procedure. Which behavior should be selected as the criterion? The pollster who deals with this problem generally singles out behavior which, *he* thinks, will be decisively affected by the attitude. He may be wrong. His error, however, is understandable and forgivable because he is confronting himself with one of the most complex problems in human behavior, the relation between words and deeds. Many investigators who employ polls or some other instrument to measure attitudes, it must be added, dodge the problem altogether: they are satisfied if their instrument proves to be constant or reliable and they are then happy in their verbal realms. This position takes refuge in the assumption that a poll is valid if it is constant or reliable. A man who consistently and deliberately lies during successive interviews, for example, is certainly being measured constantly or reliably as indicated by his consistency. It is necessary, however, to know that he is lying before his consistent answers can also be considered a valid index not of his attitude toward the questions but of his deceit—and this additional information is not provided by those answers.

Forecasting Elections

There is one pernicious error which must be avoided if the validity of polls is to be properly understood. That error consists of calling all polls valid because pollsters are able to predict election results. Polling during a political campaign is a very special and unique case of measuring public opinion. Polls, consequently, cannot coast along on the prestige they have acquired from this single instance.

The pollster's ability to predict the outcome of elections results from the virtual elimination of all sources of error. More people are polled to reduce the chance sampling error; only increased costs prevent the pollster from having the standard error of his proportion infinitely small. Then the biasing sampling error is kept at a minimum by making heroic efforts to interview a representative sample. American pollsters who generally use the method of quota control, as previously pointed out, have been enormously lucky in this respect. So far voting preferences apparently are not too closely related to the attributes of the population which this method frequently distributes in a slightly biased fashion.

There is of course another risk involved in political forecasting: the polling sample may be representative of the potential voting population at the time the poll is taken, but not of the people who actually vote on election day. The difference between the two populations results from the failure of qualified voters to vote, from last-minute changes in political preferences, from the differential effects which the state of the weather on election day has upon prospective voters, and from bribery and fraud which distort people's behavior at the polls. In a real sense, it is fair to contend that voting preferences obtained by surveying a polling sample are a more accurate representation of actual public opinion than the sample which votes. Polling officials seek to correct their sample by experimenting with various questions which estimate in advance whether or not individuals will cast their votes (*11*). Last-minute changes in voting preference are taken into account either by attempting to determine voting trends as the campaign draws to a close—as indicated in Chapter 6—or by conducting the final poll as close as possible to election day. An organization like Gallup's American Institute of Public Opinion keeps polling right up to the Saturday preceding the Tuesday on which a national election is held in the United States. When the race is close, it may even instruct its interviewers to poll on Sunday and telegraph their results to the central office at Princeton, New Jersey, where they are quickly tabulated and released in time to appear in the Monday morning newspapers. Little of a political nature can occur between Saturday or Sunday and Tuesday to affect the behavior of the voters. Weather, bribery, and fraud, however, cannot be controlled or forecast by pollsters who can only point out to their readers that these factors may influence the election and hence the polls' validity.

One study of 358 individuals regarding the issue of legalizing pari-mutuel betting in the state of New Jersey (*34*) clearly indicates the need to take the time factor into account. They were polled two weeks before a state referendum on the subject and then their actual votes were obtained a week after the vote. When the "no opinion" in the first interview and the "didn't vote" individuals are realistically disregarded, then the original figure of 55 percent in favor of the proposition dropped to 47 percent. With such a small sample, this change might have been expected as a result of the chance sampling error. In this case, however, only 52 percent expressed the same attitude during the poll and actually registered it in the voting booth. The remainder included those who changed from "favor" to "against" or vice versa (9 percent), from "don't know" to "favor" or "against" (5 percent), or from "favor" or "against" to "didn't vote" (34 percent).

Instrument errors are also reduced to a minimum in political forecasting. The question, "For whom are you going to vote?" can be easily understood by anyone above the level of a moron. There is no need to employ an elaborate pre-testing procedure to determine the clearest wording, nor to resort to a split-ballot to discover whether nuances in wording will affect the results. The simple question, moreover, is almost certain to arouse the attitude toward the political candidates and not to evoke other irrelevant or stronger attitudes. Although it has been previously shown that in a few situations secret ballots on a poll may give results slightly different from those obtained through interviewing, by and large it is true that citizens of democratic countries are not reluctant to express their political preferences. Unless they support a political party which is unpopular—such as the Republican party in Mississippi, the Democratic party in Vermont, or the Communist or Socialist party almost anywhere in the United States—they have no reason to conceal their choice from the interviewer.

An election in a democratic country, furthermore, is a well-publicized event. People know that, when they enter the voting booth, they will have to record their choice. Many or most of them have reached a decision before election *and* before they are approached by an interviewer from a polling agency. The instrument of the poll, therefore, is measuring an attitude which exists and not one which is formed during the interview. Actual rather than latent public opinion is involved.

In addition and most important of all, the political attitude is the exclusive determinant of the interviewee's behavior both in the polling interview and in the voting booth, and it tends to affect that behavior in almost identical fashion because the two situations are so similar. On the stimulus side, the names of the candidate whether spoken by the interviewer or thought of by the interviewee during the interview are no different from the names which are seen on the printed ballot or the voting machine. On the response side, the act of expressing a choice after being questioned by an interviewer is about the same as placing a cross next to a name or pulling a lever in the voting booth. Between these similar stimuli and responses is just the attitude.

Forecasting Public Opinion and Behavior

The record of the very few polls whose validity has been determined by comparing the results with actual behavior is not particularly impressive. Most of the studies confirm LaPiere's conclusion which has been previously mentioned: behavior does not correspond to the attitude measured by the polling instruments. A commercial agency (*39*) has discovered that the discrepancy between answers given to the simple question, "What brand or make of automobile tire did you buy last?" and actual use of the tire named "was so large that this question was abandoned" in its survey work; there was a 100 percent agreement between brand reported and sales-slip records for bread and 93 percent for salad dressing, but only 63 percent for cheese and 62 percent for flour (*25*). Another investigator (*24*) checked on the validity of replies to questions involving prestige. He found that 17 percent of 243 individuals who had actually redeemed war bonds during the last war stated when questioned that they had not sold their bonds; the percent rose to 43 in the upper-income brackets. In addition, 14 percent of 790 storekeepers who had received a government poster through the mails denied having received any posters and another 58 percent disclaimed having received the particular poster; 42 percent of those admitting receipt of the poster claimed it was on display, a claim that was shown to be false. Finally, 34 percent of 134 workers who had been absent from war plants—activity of course with low prestige—reported that they had not been absent. On the other hand, common purchases in the United States during the last war were estimated (*43*) by interviewing a sample of 5,000 households and by figures made available to the War Production Board: a remarkable agreement between the two sets of figures was discernible.

Two ingenious investigators (*17*) initially polled a representative sample of a Colorado community on the candidates running for public office and on three public issues. They compared these results with a secret ballot filled out by the voters at the election booths immediately after they had cast their votes (thus approximating the actual voting situation as far as possible). The poll, they found, had made an extremely accurate, in fact almost perfect prediction concerning the votes obtained by the political candidates and a sufficiently accurate one concerning two of the issues. The actual error in predicting people's attitudes toward a national sales tax, however, exceeded the one to be anticipated from the standard error of the proportion by almost 100 percent.

Results like these lead inevitably to a conclusion: in general, with the exception of political preferences in a democracy and with other exceptions not too easy to specify, the validity of a poll should be accepted only with extreme skepticism. From such a conclusion it definitely does not follow that the polls themselves are to blame for their low validity. That which the polls measure under ideal conditions, the attitudes of people, affords only a small amount of insight into overt behavior in the future. A good thermometer—one which is both reliable and valid—can measure the temperature of a room at a given instant of time, but from any one or several measurements it is not possible to predict what later readings will be. The sun may go down, the furnace in the house may be turned on or off, the season may change, a hole may develop in the roof. No one thinks of discarding the thermometer because it gives different results at different times or because it does not measure the factors which affect temperature. Nor does anyone ascribe predictive power to this instrument on the basis of the height of its mercury at the moment. Thermometer readings fluctuate with conditions; if the conditions remain constant, its readings are more or less the same.

In different words, the validity of a poll as a guide to future behavior can be no higher than the degree to which attitudes themselves determine such behavior. An attitude expressed in the polling situation may not be the decisive factor in determining behavior in a real-life situation and, for this reason, a knowledge of the attitude will be a good predictive guide only when the real-life situation resembles or is similar to the polling situation. The similarity is so marked in the case of political attitudes that in this instance the polls are remarkably valid. But usually there is great dissimilarity between the two situations.

The polling situation, therefore, does not arouse all the attitudes and drives which the real-life situation does. If it is known that an individual has an unfavorable attitude toward a political candidate, LaPiere (*33*) has suggested, the investigator is more likely to predict his vote than he is his behavior while meeting the candidate face-to-face. In the latter situation other attitudes come into play and the individual may be both polite and friendly. Naturally pollsters and polling devotees like to convince themselves and their financial supporters that they have their fingers on the public "pulse." Like the physician, however, they can employ their measurements of that pulse only as one and just one symptom. More of the patient has to be examined before he can be diagnosed. And just as the pulse at one moment may be misleadingly rapid as a result of violent exercise, so public opinion may be made deceptively violent regarding a particular issue as a result of events and propaganda.

From a strictly theoretical viewpoint it is possible to conceive of attitudes which not only determine the answer given to a polling question but which also are likely to have a corresponding effect upon other behavior in future situations. An attitude with great drive strength, for example, can be counted on to be the crucial factor whenever it is aroused. People who were extremely hostile to Mr. Roosevelt when he was President certainly told pollsters that they were going to vote against him, just as certainly did cast their ballots for his opponents, tended to explode whenever his name was mentioned, and perhaps would have been uncordial toward him if they had ever met him. It has been suggested (*14*) that individuals who are not neurotic or who tend to "think things through" may be expected to possess attitudes which induce them to do in real life what they tell the pollster they are going to do. Such individuals presumably do not express an opinion until they have considered the additional complications that will face them in the real-life situations. If this reasoning—which admittedly is not supported by evidence—is correct, then it may follow that measurements of enduring public opinion are more likely to be valid guides to future behavior than measurements of momentary public opinion. It is interesting to note that few polling agencies ever interest themselves in issues involving enduring public opinion. They are afraid to raise basic questions concerning sexual practices, race relations, or the democratic form of government, they are convinced they know the results beforehand, or they have decided that the data are not newsworthy.

Still in the realm of theory is the suggestion that polls can conceivably extend their validity by seeking deliberately to arouse not only the attitude to be measured but also the other attitudes and drives which are likely to be evoked in the real life situation. If this were feasible, then there would be a greater psychological similarity between the polling and the real life situations. Consider, for example, a specific illustration. In January 1944, a little less than a year and a half before the war in Europe ended, *Fortune* magazine listed a "number of things . . . that might be done with Germany when we are victorious." One of the questions to which a national sample replied was: "Do you think the United States should or should not govern Germany with an occupation force for several years?" Seventy-three percent of the sample replied affirmatively, 11 percent negatively, and the remaining 16 percent had no opinion. Presumably a truly representative sample was obtained; the standard error of the proportion was low; the question appears to be unambiguous; public opinion of the issue must have been more actual than latent inasmuch as there was at the time considerable discussion concerning ways of dealing with and re-educating a defeated Germany. But within two years or shortly after Japan surrendered, Americans began to demand that the soldiers stationed in Europe return home as quickly as possible, the Congress of the United States had to engage in a long struggle before it found the political courage to extend draft legislation even in diluted form, and in general it seemed as though public opinion was opposed to those very measures which are the prerequisites for an army of occupation. There is no reason to assume that this external public opinion reflected only the 11 percent who at the start of 1944 believed that Germany should not be governed by an occupation or the 16 percent who had no opinion. Some of those represented by the figure of 73 percent supporting the occupation force must also have been involved. People could not have appreciated the consequences of their attitude toward occupation upon other attitudes which they simultaneously possessed. In January 1944 it was relatively easy to believe that Germany should be occupied after her defeat; but in January 1946 it seemed more important to parents, for example, to have their sons with them in the United States. Occupy Germany, yes, but let another mother's boy do the job or be drafted to do it. Or in 1944 the interviewee may not have considered the personal consequences which occupation would entail. From the answers to the *Fortune* question, it would have been foolish to attempt to predict people's future reaction to the very policies that logically required their support to attain the objective favored by the 73 percent.

Suppose *Fortune* had followed a methodological procedure once proposed semi-seriously by the *New Yorker* magazine and had phrased its interview as follows:

"Do you think the United States should or should not govern Germany with an occupation force for several years? Before you answer this question, please bear in mind the following facts on which experts are agreed:

1. If there is such an occupation, it will mean that:
   a. Many soldiers—perhaps including your son, husband, or friend—will have to remain away from you.
   b. Many other boys or men—perhaps including your son, husband, or friend—will have to be drafted even though the war is over.
   c. It will cost so many millions of dollars each year and hence you as a taxpayer will actually be contributing X dollars and Z cents over a ten-year period.
   d. American soldiers stationed in Germany will begin to feel that Germans cannot be allowed to starve; their voice will be added to the demand that American food be sent to that country and, if other countries also require food from us, you and all your relatives and friends will either eat less or have a more restricted choice of food.
   e. There will be fewer men who are seeking civilian jobs; as a result, there may be less unemployment in the postwar period, you yourself may find the competition for jobs less keen, or industrial reconversion may be more difficult.
2. If there is no such occupation, it will mean that:
   a. American influence on Germany and on United Nations' policies for that country will be negligible.
   b. The Soviet Union, Great Britain, and France will undoubtedly send in their occupation forces.
   c. Germans may not feel defeated and may be ready to start another war within our lifetime.
   d. There will be fewer marriages between American soldiers and German girls.

Please go ahead and answer the question."

Such a question and its accompanying exposition obviously present more stimuli to the interviewees and would have produced a variety of different implicit responses within them. But would their verbal responses have been affected, would a smaller number have favored an occupation?

As a matter of fact, almost a year earlier one investigator (*38*) tried essentially this approach by means of a series of discrete questions concerning American participation in European and world affairs after the war. Although the samples interviewed were extremely small, it is important to note that the majority of the respondents not only favored active participation but also claimed they were willing to make various personal sacrifices in order to preserve the peace. These sacrifices, however, were phrased as possibilities or contingencies, not as certainties. The desire to prevent another war, in short, appeared to be so strong during the last war that at the time it could not be affected, on the whole, by other responses. It is highly unlikely, though, that attitudes concerning other issues would remain unaffected by a poll which dramatically and authoritatively pointed out the consequences of favoring one position rather than another.

A poll of course does not or should not be employed to educate public opinion: it is a measuring instrument and nothing more. A thermometer is not criticized for failing to register the temperature of a well-heated living room when it has been placed in an unheated attic. Similarly a polling question can measure only the response or responses which it actually arouses, not those which it might or should arouse or which may be aroused in the future. *Fortune* presented the reactions of a representative sample to a perfectly sensible question in a very limited situation. If the readers or editors of the magazine concluded that this kind of public opinion would endure beyond the war into a society which would be bombarding people with different stimuli *and* would affect their attitudes and behavior in logically related situations, they were misinterpreting the poll's results. Such a conclusion neglected to take into account those changes which a more thorough analysis of actual and potential public opinion could have at least partially anticipated. It was based, moreover, on a superficial examination of the attitudes and drives even then functioning within the American people. Certainly most wives' desire to have their husbands at home was stronger than any conceivable drive they possessed relating to Germany. The thermometer must be brought into the living room and not left in the attic if the temperature of the attic is to be ascertained; it is extremely difficult to calculate the temperature in the living room from the instrument's level in the attic.

That the response to the *Fortune* question was perhaps constant and reliable without being a valid guide to postwar situations is shown by a Gallup poll taken in September 1946. Essentially the same question was asked close to three years later. By then the occupation of Germany had been in effect and the strength of American forces there had been considerably reduced. Approximately identical replies were obtained. In fact, the percentage approving an occupation increased from 73 to 80. Even reality apparently failed to indicate to most Americans the logical inconsistency of their attitudes.

One illustration (*28*) demonstrates that the simple polling question can attempt to extend its validity by presenting some of the facts related to the issue. In the fall of 1945 organized labor in the United States was agitating and striking to retain the "take-home" wages that had been received during the war. A national cross-section was polled by the Psychological Corporation and by Gallup through the use of these questions:

Psychological Corporation	*Dr. Gallup*
If a man was paid $50 a week for *48* hours in wartime and he is now working only *40* hours a week, should he still be paid $50?	Because of loss of overtime, the total weekly pay of many factory workers is less than it was during the war. So that their total weekly pay will be the same as it was during the war, these workers want a 30 percent increase in their hourly rates. Do you think they should or should not receive this increase?

It was to be expected that the question of the Psychological Corporation whose clients include business organizations and which has been known in the past to present somewhat biased questions in its surveys (*15*) produced fewer replies in favor of the wage increase than did Gallup whose clients are newspapers and hence the readers of newspapers, including workers. Gallup, moreover, determined that there was less opposition to the increase than did the Psychological Corporation by asking "those opposed to a 30 percent increase whether or not they would favor a 15 percent increase of hourly rates." The wording of a question should not be decided by the biases of the pollster or his clients but in terms of the stimuli which are likely to evoke all the relevant responses in the people concerned.

Pollsters seek to increase validity—as well as consistency and reliability—by asking several questions on the same ballot. The usual ballot contains at least a half-dozen questions in addition to those which help locate the respondents sociologically for sampling and breakdown purposes. The questions may pertain to various unrelated issues or a battery of them may be fired in the direction of one issue. It is uneconomical simply to ascertain opinion on one or two issues since, for example, only a little extra time is required to secure additional information when once the time-consuming procedure of setting up, locating, and punching cards for a representative sample has been begun. As many as thirty questions can appear on a ballot; but usually it is better to limit the number, lest the interviewees object to being interviewed for too long a period or otherwise lose interest in the interview. When a battery of questions on approximately the same issue is employed, more or less similar internal responses are aroused within the interviewee and determine variously the replies he gives. The devout Communist or the equally devout Communist-hater respond consistently to any stimulus containing the word "communist" or to any word or phrase along the gradient of communism; hence their replies to a battery of questions on the Soviet Union are likely to be consistent. The attitudes of other individuals who assume less extreme positions regarding communism can be scaled to show variations in degree of sympathy or antipathy toward the Soviet Union.

The exponents of the method of specific assignment point out in this connection that their approach permits them, without sacrificing the advantages of random sampling procedures, to obtain answers to a long list of questions. As a short series of questions is given to the large sample, a small but representative sample is located; later this small sample is given the longer list.

Drive strength can also be estimated by having interviewees state how strongly they feel about a given issue, by offering them alternate answers which suggest varying degrees of intensity, or by asking them with what degree of certainty they hold their opinions (*8, 27*). A very slightly improved guide to the future is thereby obtained: attitudes that are called certain or important are a little less likely to change than those considered uncertain or unimportant (*16*). Such additional information, however, is not too trustworthy, inasmuch as knowledge of the strength of an attitude may give a clue concerning the relation of that attitude to the individual's personality but little more. A person who feels deeply may change his attitude overnight because that attitude has been only a means of expressing some deep-rooted drive which later leads to a more satisfactory goal response. The war-hater whose pacifism in peacetime springs from his desire to be accepted by a pacifistic clique of friends changes his opinion quickly when that clique, after the outbreak of conflict, begins to support the war effort.

Interviewers frequently are instructed to record the spontaneous remarks made by interviewees as they reply to the formal questions on the ballot. Or they may be asked to inquire why their informants believe as they do on a specific question. The answers are then jotted down more or less as they are given, or else the interviewer uses the shorthand device of a check list which contains a half-dozen principal reasons (obtained from pre-testing the question) together with a miscellaneous category. The information can be tabulated in the usual way after it has been thrown into categories. It can then be presented either as another polling result or as human-interest material accompanying the analysis of the conventional questions. By and large American polling agencies have not utilized these spontaneous comments as much as they might, perhaps because tabulation is frequently difficult and almost always expensive. In addition, such comments cannot be easily interpreted—except as rationalizations frequently prescribed by the culture —without additional knowledge concerning the interviewees. People are neither willing nor able suddenly to account for their attitudes.

The Practical Importance of Polls

Public opinion polls have contributed little or nothing to scientific theory. Their function has been almost solely that of a measuring instrument dedicated to very practical and useful objectives. Social sciences like history and political science have seized upon polling data not to improve whatever theories they have nor to formulate brand new ones, but as sources of more concrete and more accurate information.

The survey has proven to be exceedingly valuable in determining short-range facts about people and in measuring their attitudes after an issue has produced actual public opinion. Advertising agencies, large commercial groups, and some media of communication employ polling techniques to become better acquainted with their "market" and thereby to anticipate or learn the reasons for the momentary demands and attitudes of the consumer. Since polling is usually an expensive operation, however, few private groups can afford to have their own polling organizations and hence, when they feel the need for precise data on public opinion, they may utilize a company whose sole function is to gather such information for a number of clients.

Government, too, is concerned with public opinion and hence has shown an interest in polling. The bureaucracies of Germany and Japan during the last war utilized the secret police and other government officials to collect data about public opinion, not in the interest of "adapting their policies to public wishes," but in order "to determine the extent to which the population was filling its obligation of obedience and the extent to which officials had been successful in 'leading' the people" (*42*). The polling, moreover, was conducted unsystematically: a representative sample was not obtained and there was a "tendency for the reporting official to give his superiors the type of material they wanted." The reports themselves received only a limited circulation in government offices.

In Great Britain and especially in the United States, on the other hand, government officials have used polls to help formulate policies in accord with the desires of people, to discover general or specific reactions to governmental programs, and to secure census-type information not immediately available through any other source. Much of the interest in polling arose during the last war when the cooperation of people with their government was considered essential if what was popularly called "high morale" was to be created or maintained. At least one old-line agency in the United States, the Department of Agriculture, however, felt impelled before that war to study the reactions of farmers to its various plans and hence created a competent Division of Program Surveys under the able direction of Rensis Likert (*44*).

When food and other consumer commodities were rationed in Great Britain and the United States after the outbreak of the war, polls were employed to discover the needs of people and their reactions to various restrictions and regulations. In the United States, the Treasury Department borrowed the polling organization of the Department of Agriculture to carry on fundamental research in connection with its various drives to sell war bonds and otherwise to strengthen patriotic attitudes through the kind of propaganda which its Secretary somewhat righteously chose to employ. One of the pollsters, Angus Campbell, has indicated (*5*) the kind of information which this surveying group secured:

The Treasury Department was able, for example, to find out within a few weeks after each bond drive how many people had known the drive was on, how many knew the individual and community quotas which had been set, how many knew the slogans which had been featured, how many knew the relation of bonds to inflation control, and other related items. It was able to determine which parts of the population had been most effectively reached and which were least well informed. Most important of all, it was able to assess the influence of these items of information on the individual's inclination to buy bonds.

Campbell also points out (6) how policy was affected by such a survey. When it had been determined, for example, that "a good many prospective buyers said they would buy more bonds" if their investment were in a more liquid form, the decision was made by the Department "to reduce the time delay in the redemption of War Bonds." Not as an aside, however, the writer would like to suggest to those who, like Campbell, are so enthusiastic about the function of polls in the service of a democratic government that their polls serve not to formulate overall policy but merely to help determine specific sub-policies which are really only means to predetermined ends. After all, it was the government which had decided to ration scarce consumer goods and it was the government which had decided to help control inflation through bonds and not through compulsory savings; the polls then became rather humble servants in the interest of these decisions. This is not to say that people can or should be expected to make technical decisions over which so-called experts disagree, but to indicate the limited field of activity allocated to polling.

During the last war, there were also a few attempts by Americans to study public opinion in foreign countries through the use of modified polling techniques. The reading and listening habits of some Latin American countries were determined, so that American propaganda could be more skillfully designed—dogmatism and ethnocentrism among the officials and not the polling results tended to produce maladroit propaganda. In at least one instance a small poll rather accurately predicted in advance how certain groups would react to an invasion by Allied forces. The attitudes of Frenchmen toward world events and American propaganda were ascertained shortly after part of France had been liberated. The morale of necessarily small but successive samples of German prisoners was measured by American authorities for nine months beginning in June of 1944 by means of questions pertaining to Hitler, Germany's chances of winning, and the "secret weapons" mentioned at the time in Nazi propaganda (*22*). The United States Strategic Bombing Survey sought to estimate the effect which bombing had had upon German and Japanese morale by carefully questioning representative samples in each country that were selected in accordance with the method of specific assignment. Through surveys the American occupation authorities in both countries from time to time obtained greater insight into the basic attitudes of the conquered peoples as well as into their own efforts at "re-education."

The propagandist, whether in or out of government, can utilize the polls to his own advantage. Some high officials in the United States privately and quite surreptitiously have secured from existing private polling organizations information concerning their own popularity and that of some of their policies. In a few cases they have sought help in gauging public opinion in advance by learning how people react to situations which are phrased as hypothetical possibilities. An aspiring politician can decide what his chances of being elected are by conducting a poll *before* he risks his reputation by seeking the office. The results of such a poll are likely to be more reliable than the opinion of a wise political boss, no matter how good and numerous the latter's informal contacts with the constituents are. If he decides to enter the campaign, a poll can tell him what progress he is making and whether one type of appeal is more effective than another. As a matter of fact, more and more prominent figures in American life are using surveys for just such purposes. All do not depend on polls for the facts of public opinion because some still prefer the old-fashioned, intuitive methods and others cannot afford the relatively high cost of having a representative sample interviewed and the results tabulated.

The polls may be criticized for measuring only superficial

reactions on a verbal level, but their very superficiality can frequently be exploited by the propagandist. According to a Gallup poll (9) toward the end of 1940, for example, 97 percent of a national sample of Americans stated that they "believe in freedom of speech." The belief in "freedom of speech" may be called by the semanticists a verbal reaction which has no referent; or anyone can label it simply a "cliché" or a "stereotype." And yet this is a valuable bit of information which every Fourth-of-July orator, every demagogue, and every citizen knows and sometimes utilizes. The phrase, in fact, is in the Atlantic Charter. Neither the orator nor the demagogue, moreover, should be deterred by the second Gallup question asked of those 97 percent: "Do you believe in it [freedom of speech] to the extent of allowing Fascists and Communists to hold meetings and express their views in this community?" Only 23 percent apparently believed that these unpopular groups should enjoy "freedom of speech." He who would exploit the cliché, consequently, can learn one of two things from the second question: the phrase should be used only vaguely and without the slightest implication that it applies to brown or red sheep; or it is politically expedient, so far as the majority is concerned, in another context to deny the privilege to all sheep considered black. Merely to point out the inconsistency of replying affirmatively to the first and not to the second is to express the belief that ordinary people are nothing more than logical machines and that, as a result, they always and carefully consider all the implications of the knowledge and attitudes they possess.

One of the most astute critics in the United States of public opinion polls (29) has called attention to "the confusion between problems of fact and problems of opinion about fact" sometimes involved in polling. During the last war, for example, Colonel Rickenbacker and others complained publicly about the absenteeism among workers in war plants. Katz points out, however, that "factual researches indicated that the incidence of absenteeism was exaggerated, that it was due in large measure to the mushrooming of war industry with increased employment of working wives and mothers." Gallup at the time asked this question: "What do you think should be done with workers in war factories who are regularly absent from work without a good cause?" His "release to the press reported the answers to this question under a headline stating that the great majority of the American people supported Rickenbacker in his campaign against absenteeism." Katz maintains that Gallup contributed nothing to learning the extent of absenteeism but rather "assumed malingering on the part of war workers—the very problem that called for factual investigation." What was being measured in large part was an attitude toward absenteeism partially created by Rickenbacker's propaganda. As such the poll seems to this writer to have been useful though misleading. Katz is absolutely correct in maintaining that "it is necessary to distinguish between what people *think* are the facts and what the facts actually are." Polls can obtain the facts in a situation only if they seek those facts; otherwise they obtain a measure of attitudes toward facts or pseudo-facts. By asking people the question and treating their answers as he did, Gallup was unintentionally supporting the prevailing propaganda on absenteeism.

There is a question of interest to political theory which the polls at this point raise: to what extent should leaders in public life be guided by polling results? The question is puzzling because of the uncertain reliability and validity which most polling inquiries have been shown to possess. Planning wisdom cannot be automatically anticipated from people who answer questions impulsively or who have not the technical competence to pass judgment (though they do so for the benefit of the pollster). The people themselves do not expect some of their answers to be taken too seriously by legislators; for, as has been pointed out (*10*), there are many instances in the United States of legislation going contrary to wishes expressed in polls without noticeable clamor or protest from the people concerned. Many of those blindly in love with pollsters refuse even to discuss this problem; they angrily say that merely raising such a question "parts company with Democracy also" (*12*). Invective will not solve the problem of when or under what conditions the voice of the people has such drive strength that it dare not be disregarded.

Four studies have attempted with little success to show the extent to which polling results actually do affect the voting judgment of legislators in the United States. In each case the representativeness of the sample is unknown and hence the importance of the investigations must be seriously questioned. One investigator (*23*) in 1942 induced 58 out of 197 New York State legislators to reply to a poll. These men indicated their interest in polls: 59 percent claimed that either "always" or "frequently" they "study the published public opinion polls relating to an issue before voting on that issue in the Chamber"; and 67 percent claimed they were "interested" in "the particular findings (or the figures released on specific propositions) reported by the different polling organizations." Approximately two years before another investigator (*36*) submitted a somewhat similar poll to every United States Senator and 200 Representatives, to which 117 or approximately 40 percent replied. To the question, "Do you think that public opinion polls . . . correctly portray and measure public opinion?" 13 percent replied "yes" and 72 percent "in part." To "do the results of public opinion polls aid you in deciding upon the desires of your constituents?" 9 percent said "yes" and 30 percent "in part." These latter percentages rose to 23 and 47 respectively when essentially the same question was asked about "other men in public life." On the other hand, a 1944 poll of 52 Congressmen and Senators (*30*) indicated that polls rank fifth as measures of public opinion, with the following in the indicated order being the more preferred methods: personal mail, visits to the public, newspapers, and visiting from the public. Forty percent of this sample considered polls "usually" accurate, 36 percent accurate "half the time," and 23 percent "seldom" accurate—and in general the respondents showed that they misunderstood polling techniques. A sample of administrators in the executive branches of the government, however, rated polls first as a method of ascertaining public opinion and ranked personal mail and visits from the public, respectively, fourth and fifth. Finally, when thirteen Congressmen were interviewed in 1939 (*20*), only one was willing to state that his vote on the repeal of the Neutrality Act had been affected by the polls—and even for him polls had been of only secondary importance.

The fact that polls are more or less widely used, does not prove that they are either reliable or valid instruments. One of the members of the American polling cult has naively argued against the suggestion that "public opinion measurement is almost totally lacking in merits" by asserting that "it is singular to find so many groups whose functioning is based upon dependable information—government administrators, politicians, editors, industrialists, and labor leaders—uncomplainingly paying out larger and larger sums for public opinion analysis" (*13*). Anyone actually familiar with the professions mentioned will agree that the decision to employ a device is not made completely rationally but may result from irrelevant factors like a fad or persuasion by an enthusiastic person. Certainly polls have proven useful according to people's judgments, but it is these judgments that must remain suspect until the reliability and validity of polls have been more carefully determined.

The Bandwagon Effect of Polls

The poll of the 117 Senators and Congressmen mentioned above (*37*) contained a question which plagues and disturbs present-day pollsters: "Do you think public opinion polls are capable, by themselves, of influencing the public's opinion?" The replies: 32 percent "yes," 18 percent "in part," and 50 percent "no." Such a question is delicate because it suggests that polls may contribute to the bandwagon tendency of voters in a democracy: some people wait until they learn from the polls what the result is going to be and then they leap in the indicated direction.

The pollster reacts sharply to the bandwagon charge because he does not wish to be accused of influencing the election he is forecasting. Gallup (*18, 19*) in particular is eager to be the spokesman for the polling guild. He suggests that, if the polls point out the bandwagon that is likely to win, there should then be a substantial rise in the popularity of the candidate who, according to the polls, is ahead of his opponents as the election draws to a close. The *Literary Digest*'s prediction of a Roosevelt defeat in 1936 was loudly sung over the radio and somewhat enthusiastically printed by the press, but Mr. Roosevelt was not defeated. He cites evidence from his own records which indicates that frequently the candidate who is leading loses ground as the campaign proceeds. In the 1938 Kentucky primary election, he points out, the Gallup poll published in the *Louisville Courier-Journal* was "given wide publicity throughout the state." Polling results published on April 10, May 15, July 8, July 24, and August 5 (the day before the primary) showed that Mr. Barkley was leading Mr. Chandler, but indicated too that this lead was slowly being diminished, from 67 percent on April 10 to 59 percent on August 5. Even though many of the voters of Kentucky presumably knew which candidate, according to the poll, was slated to win, fewer of them supported him as the campaign progressed. Since Mr. Barkley actually secured 57 percent of the votes, the implication is that polling had no influence on the election. Gallup has also attempted to show that actual knowledge of polling results does not influence political preference. In July 1939, for example, there was no difference in preferences between those who had and those who had not seen polling figures on the leading Republican candidates for the presidential nomination.

Such reasoning by no means constitutes an adequate refutation of the bandwagon charge. In fact one study (*35*) has shown that the voters in Erie County, Ohio, who had not selected their candidate as the presidential campaign of 1940 began, tended eventually to vote for the man they expected to win and "polls as a source of change in expectation were explicitly mentioned" by 7 percent of the entire sample that was questioned. Another investigator (*1*) found that slightly more American college and university students changed their attitudes on social issues in a two to four week

period when they were shown the results of a Gallup poll
than did another which was tested and retested under similar
conditions without seeing the Gallup data—and, in spite
of Gallup himself, the changes were in the direction of the
majority opinion indicated by the poll.   Perhaps Americans
are more eager to conform to majority opinion involving less
certain social issues than they are when the opinion concerns
such a clear-cut decision as voting.   In addition there are
experimental studies galore (*e.g.*, *2, 4, 31, 40, 41, 45*) revealing that people's judgments and attitudes change after
they have been told what the majority is thinking.

A national poll on the polls in the United States in 1944
(*21*) demonstrated that by and large the poll had not become a potent force which conceivably can affect public
opinion.   Of the sample questioned, 56 percent had "heard
of a public opinion poll" and only 9 percent claimed to read
polling results "regularly" and 19 percent "occasionally"—
in other words, almost three quarters either were not acquainted with polls or paid no attention to them.   When the
56 percent claiming acquaintance with polls were asked
whether election results could be predicted from polling, 57
percent replied affirmatively, 21.5 percent negatively, and
another 21.5 percent stated that they did not know.   The
effect polls might have if they were more widely and regularly perceived and if they were accorded greater credibility,
therefore, remains unknown.

It is conceivable that knowledge of voting trends derived
from polls can stimulate the candidate who is in the rear to
carry on a more vigorous campaign.   Perhaps this increase
in political propaganda can counteract whatever advantage
there is from being in the lead.   But it is also possible that
the candidate or his followers may become discouraged when
the polls reveal the state of public opinion.

The bandwagon charge has been at the bottom of the
criticisms hurled at polls by government officials and private
citizens.   Many of both groups, to be sure, have been critical
because they themselves do not understand the sampling
procedures employed by the pollsters or the ways in which
the raw figures have to be weighted or corrected to make

the sample representative or to reflect estimated unknowns. It has also been said that polling results on occasion have been accompanied by misleading headlines or textual explanations. Sometimes, in fact, the uncritical reader may be misled by a perfectly legitimate statistical breakdown which nevertheless underplays the no-opinion vote (*26*). Gallup's release on January 9, 1946, to his newspaper clients contained this headline: "THREE OUT OF EVERY FOUR IN U. S. FOLLOWING DISCUSSIONS WANT JEWS ALLOWED TO SETTLE IN PALESTINE." Although the headline is quite accurate and the accompanying text most explicit, the impression might have been gained that 75 percent of Americans wished Jews to be permitted to migrate to Palestine. Actually only 56 percent of the sample stated that they had been following the discussion and *of these* 76 percent favored granting the permission; in short, the headline could have been: "TWO OUT OF EVERY FIVE IN U. S. WANT JEWS ALLOWED TO SETTLE IN PALESTINE."

A congressional investigation after the presidential campaign of 1944 vindicated the Gallup organization. No reputable polling agency has anything to conceal from an investigation and no pollster in his senses would dare fake a poll: he might thereby affect an election but, if his bandwagon powers proved ineffective and the actual result wandered too far from his deceptive prediction, the loss of prestige would undoubtedly compel him to share the fate of the *Literary Digest*. At any rate, polls in the United States will doubtless remain a public issue which will be kept alive by unsuccessful campaign managers, and there will be proposals from time to time for governmental authorities to audit, control, or take over the polling agencies.

The Analysis of Results

Frequently American polling agencies try to interpret the results of their interviews, since they realize that some data by themselves reveal nothing or can be made more interesting by means of a breakdown. A national sample, for example, is accidentally or deliberately polled before an important event. A comparable sample is interviewed after the event has occurred. The differences, if any, are attributed to the event, or else a more cautious reference is made to that event as a possible explanation of the change in public opinion. Poll questions that are repeated again and again enable the pollster to reveal trends over a period of time, and such trends can be similarly interpreted. The trend of American public opinion from the outbreak of the last war in Europe up to Pearl Harbor, for example, was studied by Cantril (7) with the aid of this technique. On one of his charts, he is able to show the percentage of Americans believing that England or Germany would win the war, the percentage who were undecided, the percentage thinking that the United States would enter the war as well as selected points from the Dow Jones Stock Market Reports. The time periods represented along the horizontal axis are illuminated by recalling the significant events in the war which were simultaneously occurring, like the invasion of Norway by Germany or the election of Mr. Roosevelt for a third term.

The pollster is able at least to begin an analysis of the determinants of public opinion regarding an issue by breaking down his data into sub-groups. Any one or more of the attributes determining his sample can be studied. Comparisons like the following emerge: young vs. old people; rural vs. urban dwellers; women vs. men; East vs. West; lower vs. upper economic status; etc. By planning breakdowns in advance, it is also possible to have interviewers collect supplementary information from people so that other comparisons can be made, such as between Democrats and Republicans, members and non-members of labor unions, Protestants and Catholics, ex-servicemen and civilians, etc.

More than two groups of course can be compared by means of a breakdown. Instead of contrasting the opinions of older and younger people, sub-groups within each of the age groups may be established. The age groups, for example, may be divided into regional groups and then, if the investigator wishes, he may compare the responses made by younger people in the West with older people in the South.

The breakdown may be based not only on the attributes of the sample (such as economic groups) but also on the attitudes themselves (such as attitude regarding Russia). When this is done, two types of presentation can be made: the attitudes of those belonging, for example, to the different economic groups or the economic groupings of those holding the various attitudes. In the first instance, if attitude toward the Soviet Union be polled as "favorable," "unfavorable," or "uncertain" and if the sample be stratified into five economic groups, the investigator can indicate how each economic group feels about the Soviet Union. Are rich people more or less favorably disposed toward Russia than poor people? In the second instance, the investigator can indicate the economic composition of the individuals holding the three attitudes. Are there more or fewer rich people among those who feel favorably disposed than there are among those who are unfavorably disposed toward Russia?

In addition, the sampling attributes can be neglected altogether in making a breakdown and instead relationships can be shown between two or more attitudes that have been measured. If the same ballot containing the question on the Soviet Union also has one on American foreign policy, the sample can then be divided into three groups on the basis of "favorable," "unfavorable," and "undecided" opinions concerning Russia. Thereafter the attitudes toward American foreign policy characterizing each of these three groups may be calculated. A question like the following can then be answered: what do those people who have a "favorable" attitude toward the Soviet Union think about American foreign policy? Or what do those people who approve of American foreign policy think about the Soviet Union?

Two asides must be made in connection with breakdowns. In the first place, the labor involved in making a statistical breakdown can be greatly reduced through the use of special cards and tabulating machines manufactured by the International Business Machines Corporation (3). Skilled operators punch holes into special cards at specified places which represent in a pre-established code the essential data concerning the respondent and his replies. The cards are then automatically assorted and counted at the rate of over 400 per minute by a machine which is guided by the particular holes punched thereon. The modern public-opinion analyst, therefore, requires not patience but money with which to hire punch-card operators, to purchase the cards, and to rent the machine from the IBM.

Then, secondly, a difference between two percentages in the sample may not necessarily indicate a real difference between the two groups in the entire population. For the difference may be due to any one of the three errors—chance sampling, biasing sampling, or instrument—which all polls commit. There are statistical means to determine whether the chance sampling error can account for the difference or, in different words, whether the difference is greater or less than might have occurred as a result of chance. There is, however, no statistical procedure which can help the investigator determine whether faulty sampling techniques— especially those employed in the method of quota control— or any one of a score of instrument errors is or is not responsible for the difference.

A concrete illustration will quickly show how the chance sampling error can be disposed of statistically. In this instance, it may be assumed that 41 percent of Group A and 38 percent of Group B reply "yes" to the same question. Purely in terms of the chance sampling error, it does not necessarily follow that 3 percent more of Group A than Group B favors the affirmative reply. The standard errors of the proportion of both groups may be sufficiently large so that, if other samples had been drawn from both groups, the difference might not have appeared or might have been in the opposite direction. Let it be further assumed that the standard error of both proportions is 2 percent. Then it is practically certain that each proportion can vary by 6 percent; hence the 41 percent of A may be as high as 47 or as low as 35 percent, and the 38 percent of B may likewise fluctuate between 44 and 32. It is quite conceivable, therefore, that the difference between the two groups can be as high as 15 in favor of A or 9 in favor of B, or there can be gradations in between these extremes. The original difference, in short, is not statistically significant just on the basis of the chance sampling error.

The problem of finding relationships between attitudes and sub-groups based on the attributes of the sample or between attitudes on different issues measured on the same ballot increases in complexity as more than two factors are taken simultaneously into account. In the hypothetical illustration employed above, the pollster may discover that attitude toward Russia is more closely related to attitude toward American foreign policy than it is to economic status, age, sex, or age-with-sex-held-constant. Closer analysis than can be obtained in a polling interview might also reveal that one individual is favorably disposed toward the Soviet Union because as a worker he has become convinced that the Communist Party furthers his interests. Inasmuch as that Party's constant line is to be pro-Russian, he then approves of American foreign policy which he interprets to be oriented toward closer and more friendly collaboration with the Soviet Union. In another individual, approximately the same pro-Soviet attitude may be a symptom of rebellion against his parents which lingers within him even though the parents are dead, he is living off an income inherited from them, and he is now past 50. A breakdown of polling data as such, no matter how often the cards are run through the IBM sorting machines, cannot take into account such subtle psychological differences. Only tentative hypotheses can be suggested and these subsequently must be verified by an examination of the attitudes and drives giving rise to the opinions expressed in the interviews. It is an empirical and useful fact for a poll to demonstrate that Republicans or Protestants tend to have specified beliefs which are different from Democrats or Catholics; but a more complete understanding of the fact requires that the difference in the opinion be traced to other factors which may turn out to be more basic than party or religious affiliation. Even on the surface, however, polling results become more meaningful when they are given in terms of social groups which have real psychological significance to their members and not in terms of the statistical groups which were arbitrarily selected by the pollster to enable him to obtain a representative sample.

CHAPTER **9**

Intensive Measures of
Public Opinion

A PUBLIC opinion poll seeks to measure the attitudes of a representative sample of a selected population in order to infer the attitudes of the entire population. What a poll gains in extensiveness it loses in intensiveness: it is difficult or impossible to probe very deeply into less superficial attitudes, to reduce instrument errors, and to relate the final results to future behavior. In marked contrast is the carefully collected case or life history. Here the investigator seeks to discover by appropriate but by no means standardized techniques all there is to know about one individual or a segment of his personality like his attitudes on public issues. Such a time-consuming investigation can give rather complete insight into the individual and his attitudes, but little or no knowledge of other members of his group, inasmuch as the person analyzed may not be typical or certainly cannot be called a representative sample.

Efforts are frequently made to measure public opinion in a manner which avoids these extremes of extensity and intensity, while retaining the advantages of sampling from the poll and of the additional knowledge from the life-history approach. Unfortunately such compromises almost inevitably also have varying degrees of the disadvantages of the two methods. The art of measuring public opinion consists or should consist, consequently, of finding that compromise which gains as much and loses as little as possible from a modification of the extreme approaches. The investigator seeks to know the maximum about as many people as are necessary to have a representative sample.

The Panel

The interviewers employed by polling agencies are usually warned not to interview the same individuals more than once or twice each year. The reasoning seems to be that, if the interviewer knows the general or specific attitudes of a group of people from a previous interview, he is more likely to secure a biased sample from seeking them out too frequently. As a result, each ballot is a new adventure: he must find and establish rapport with another collection of strangers, and he must repeat census-type questions to locate them sociologically.

The panel technique deliberately violates the rule against repeated interviewing of the same individuals. A representative sample is located, is motivated to cooperate with the interviewer, and thereafter is repeatedly interviewed. The advantages of this procedure are many. In the first place, there is sometimes a financial saving: the interviewer does not have to spend time securing his sample whenever he receives a ballot, nor does the central office have to show concern for the representativeness of the replies it receives from its interviewers when once the representative character of the group has been ascertained. In commercial work, however, a panel is considered (*24*) "among the most expensive methods of obtaining information on the American consumer." Then a friendly relation can be established between interviewer and interviewee which enables the former to begin questioning the latter without repeating his explanation of why polls are conducted and without making the effort he must always make to win the individual's confidence. The interviewer, instead of securing replies to the census-type questions, can ask new and sometimes more personal questions as the interviews proceed. Both through these questions and from repeated observations, the astute interviewer gradually becomes acquainted with some of the nuances of the interviewees' personalities, knowledge which may help him as well as the central office in evaluating and interpreting the results of the surveys. The interviewer of a panel, moreover, can be instructed from time to time to rate informants on personality traits or attitudes. When two comparable but different samples are interviewed at different times in a conventional poll, it is only possible to compare the attitudes of both groups and then to infer that public opinion has or has not varied. With a panel, the individuals who have remained constant or have changed can be identified, and then the reasons for their constancy or inconstancy can be determined. In experimental or controlled situations, moreover, one group can be exposed to a set of stimuli (like propaganda) to which a comparable group is not exposed: if the groups have the same attitude before they respond to the stimuli and different ones afterwards, then the investigator comes as close as he ever can come to testing the effects of those stimuli.

The panel has at least two disadvantages. Some respondents always drop out for various reasons. The panel director, therefore, may begin his investigation with a much larger sample than he needs so that at the end of the survey enough people will remain to be interviewed. In one panel study (*19*), however, it has been shown that fewer college graduates than non-graduates and fewer interested than disinterested individuals drop out. Such a biasing sampling error can be corrected only by seeking to keep the panel together or by beginning with a larger representation of the individuals who can be expected to have a high rate of non-cooperation.

The more important disadvantage of the panel, it is claimed, is one of its psychological by-products: the interviewees who anticipate that they will be re-interviewed grow self-conscious. Between interviews they may formulate or note their opinions more carefully and seek to discover reasons for their beliefs because they know they will be subsequently questioned and do not wish to appear inarticulate. They may reply consistently to the same questions to avoid giving a wishy-washy impression and thus mask real changes in attitude. They may even make special efforts to increase their information by reading a newspaper or magazine or by listening more carefully to particular radio programs. In short, the panel which begins as a representative sample of the population on the basis of its sociological attributes or through random selection may soon become psychologically unrepresentative in respect to its attitudes. People are not like chemicals which are affected by measuring instruments in a constant and predictable manner; they react to the measuring instrument, the interviewer, and hence affect the reliability and validity of survey results.

The panel advocates maintain that this disadvantage is highly exaggerated and that, at any rate, it is overshadowed by the advantages of the technique. In a study of the presidential campaign in Erie County, Ohio, during the presidential campaign of 1940 (*21*), the investigators selected four representative groups, each containing 600 individuals. One of the groups, constituting the panel, was visited once a month beginning in May and ending after the election in November. Each of the other three groups was interviewed only once, one in July, another in August, and the third in October. These latter groups thus served as checks on the panel's representative character. A comparison of the panel with the groups which were strictly equivalent before the study began (*22*) reveals that the political preference of the panel members was not affected by being repeatedly interviewed: the same distribution of Republican and Democratic votes emerged from them as from members of the other groups. But more panel members voted and they showed a "somewhat" greater interest in the campaign. The latter effect, the investigators admit, was due to the repeated interviews which they granted.

The technique of this Erie County study suggests a way of having one's cake and eating it too: have two cakes if the polling agency can afford the expense or if a foundation official allows himself to be bewitched into supporting the project. The panel can be employed to secure more intimate information and to observe the same people as they and their society change. Other comparable samples can simultaneously be interviewed in order to determine to what extent panel members are being affected by repeated interviews. A panel, moreover, can be kept alive indefinitely by obtaining replacements at regular intervals for those members who have served their time as interviewees and who then deserve to be set loose again into the fields of un-self-consciousness.

The Open Interview

Critics of public opinion polls point out that the interviewing situation tends to be quite artificial. The interviewee is self-conscious because he knows that his opinions are being deliberately sought. He must accept one of the standardized replies the interviewer offers him. In real life, it is said, people express their attitudes spontaneously. To make the interview more lifelike and hence to elicit more valid replies, therefore, the open interview and question have been developed, especially by Likert and his associates who from 1939 until 1946 constituted the Division of Program Surveys in the Department of Agriculture. The technique is simple: the interviewee is asked a question of a very general nature and he replies in any way he wishes. "Tell me, what do you think of the United Nations?"

When this method is employed, the interviewer may or may not reveal his true purpose. In some instances he may deliberately deceive the interviewee. The writer (*10*), for example, discovered in 1940 that it was extremely difficult to investigate the war attitudes of a rural group in one of Canada's maritime provinces. These individuals are of Scotch-Catholic origin and have a distinctive community structure into which the investigator as an outsider did not fit. He was, moreover, a stranger and some of the inhabitants considered him a German spy. Under the circumstances, it was necessary to adopt a role which would arouse little or no suspicion. He pretended that he was writing a history of the community and, during the interviews, carefully took notes on historical facts which almost all of the interviewees were happy to give. Then he ostentatiously put his notes and pencil away. At this point, however, the real interview began, for the conversation could be made to drift gracefully and easily from talk about the weather and crops to the war itself. The respondent was thus caught off guard; he was then less reluctant to express himself.

Some form of deception can be involved in any attempt to measure attitudes and public opinion. Even the conventional pollster does not reveal to his informants precisely which breakdowns and analyses he will make—to that extent he is deceiving them. A market survey concerned with an advertising campaign may contain a "tricky" question which is designed to elicit information indirectly. The interviewees, for example, can be asked to state why they purchase a particular product. From their viewpoint the interviewer is interested in their product preference, when in reality he is attempting to discover whether his advertising slogan has been learned or what type of slogan he should adopt in the future. Sometimes questionnaires and attitude scales contain "decoy" questions whose sole function is to mislead informants and prevent them from suspecting the true purpose of the survey. In the open interview, however, the interviewee may not even realize that he is being interviewed. The use of any kind of deception raises of course an ethical question which each investigator must answer in terms of his own conscience and research interests. The matter of conscience is less troublesome if the identity of the informant is completely protected, as it always should be.

Whether or not he reveals his true purpose, the interviewer can use an open type of question by simply asking the questions on the ballot *without* offering alternate answers. Then the individual replies in his own words as he wishes and not as dictated by the pollster. The interviewer is usually instructed to memorize the exact wording of each question, so that this part of the interview can remain standardized. The technique makes an interview seem very informal, since the questions are raised in the midst of the give-and-take of a more or less normal conversation. A well-trained and skillful interviewer allows his informant to select some of the topics for conversation and thus increases rapport, but eventually he must take gentle steps to prevent the conversation from wandering too far away from the questions of interest to his polling agency (6). He may take notes in the presence of the interviewee or he may wait until the interview has been terminated; or he may take only a few notes during the interview and then later write down more details. In any case, the exact or the approximate words of the informants are recorded, or else the interviewer checks those items on his schedule which come closest to reflecting what the informant has said. If such a schedule is used, it is constructed on the basis of a pre-test and is never shown to the interviewee.

The open question prolongs the interview. It enables the interviewer to cover a wide range of topics related to the issues at hand. It can provide rich, colorful data which the more conventional type of question-and-answer fails to elicit. And yet this method has certain patent disadvantages. More time, energy, and money have to be expended to conduct each interview. The skill and training of the interviewers must be greater. The task of tabulating the results in the home office is made more complicated. If the final report on public opinion is to be statistically reliable and intelligible, the data for each question must be thrown into a limited number of categories and the percentages calculated for each of the answers. Someone must decide whether a freely given reply, for example, falls in the category of "favorable," "unfavorable," or "no opinion" regarding the issue at stake. That someone, whether he be the interviewer himself or an analyst in the home office, may thereby introduce an instrument error unless extra precautions are taken to train him in this type of coding procedure and to be certain that he follows with few deviations a set of standardized instructions. The results of a survey based on an open question can sometimes be interpreted with greater subtlety, inasmuch as the analysts have at their disposal not only the distribution of public opinion in statistical form but also part of the verbal and psychological context of the relevant attitude.

Pollsters and students of polls continue to debate the advantages of the open question and the conventional or closed type of question (20). No one doubts that the open approach provides more information, but the issue is whether that information is a more or less valid reflection of the attitudes being measured: is it worth the extra effort? It appears that the approach can provide more valid information when the interviewee's confidence must be patiently won or when he has to be browbeaten into giving a truthful reply. In the previous chapter it was pointed out that 34 per cent of a group of industrial workers during the last war replied truthfully to a conventional polling question regarding their absenteeism from war plants. On the other hand, only 4 percent of a similar sample—unfortunately not under strictly comparable conditions—lied when they were interviewed intensively (17).

Even the staunchest opponent of the open question has to employ this technique at some point in his polling procedure when the alternative answers to a question involve shades of opinion more refined than "yes," "no," and "don't know." He employs it on himself or on his associates in order to formulate the replies which are to be pre-tested or during the pre-testing in order then to discover with which replies he should later confront his representative sample. In like manner, as has been suggested, even the staunchest advocate of the open question has to abandon the "naturalistic" procedure when tabulating and presenting his results. The writer feels, consequently, that both approaches have their usefulness. The type of interview and the type of question should be determined by considering the interviewing situation and the issues at hand. The use of the open question to ascertain political preferences in the United States is doubtless a complete waste of time, unless the investigator wishes simultaneously to estimate the strength of the conviction and perhaps to relate it to probability of actually voting. The use of the closed question on many issues involving only potential public opinion is to be deplored, unless the investigator wants only superficial and rather meaningless results which he can publish.

Attitude Scales

The most refined method for measuring public opinion is through the use of attitude scales. What distinguishes an attitude scale from other polling methods is not the fact that people check with a pencil instead of signifying orally the one answer to a question with which they most fully agree, for the polls and surveys have also been conducted in writing and sometimes by mailed ballots. The attitude tester, rather, seeks to obtain a quantitative measure of the degree to which an individual or a group of individuals possesses an attitude. In many ways an attitude scale resembles a battery of questions on a polling ballot, but it usually differs from that technique by including more questions which have been previously not only pre-tested but also scaled or which can be subsequently scaled.

Reference again is made to the thermometer as a measuring instrument. This device enables an individual both to predict when water will boil or freeze and to compare its heat under varying conditions whether or not boiling or freezing is involved. Water at 80 degrees Fahrenheit is hotter than water at 70 and still hotter than water at 60. An attitude scale attempts to serve a similar function in measuring a response within an individual: it tries to relate his attitude to a similar attitude within other individuals at the same moment or within himself at various time periods.

Attitude scales are of various types and almost all of them involve a degree of statistical complexity beyond the scope of the present section which aims only to outline their general procedures and the philosophy of measurement. The simplest type of question on the poll—the one which offers some version of the three alternatives of "yes," "no," and "uncertain"—can merely divide the population into three groups. If six alternatives to one question are offered, then there can be six groups. If there are two questions of the yes-no-uncertain variety on the same issue, then there can be nine groups: those who answered "yes" on both questions, those who answered "no" on both, those who answered "uncertain" on both, those who answered "yes" on the first but "no" on the second, those who answered "no" on the first but "yes" on the second, etc. If there are three questions of the same type, then the population can be divided into 27 groups—and, if four, then 81 groups. The difficulty with this procedure is that the resulting groups are quite arbitrary and bear no logical or statistical relation to one another. If race prejudice, for example, is being measured by means of three questions, each of which can be answered by "yes," "no," or "uncertain," then it is clear that Individual A who answers "yes" to all questions is more prejudiced than Individual B who answers "no" to all three—provided the investigator in some way or other has decided that a "yes" answer displays prejudice and a "no" reveals lack of prejudice. But what can be said in comparing Individuals C and D when the former answers "yes" to the first two questions and "no" to the third and the latter "yes" to the first and third questions but "no" to the second? Has each an equal amount of prejudice? If the third question (the one on which Individual C displays no prejudice as defined by the investigator) involves approval or disapproval of lynching and the second question (the one on which Individual D reveals no prejudice as similarly defined) involves approval or disapproval of shaking hands with a Negro in public, then from a social viewpoint Individual C must be considered less prejudiced than Individual D. Such a conclusion can be made in quantitative form only by giving the reply to the second question a higher score than that given the reply to the third. The procedure is known as weighting.

Weighting enables the investigator to assign numerical values to each answer. Then the total score of an individual on an attitude scale is obtained simply by adding together his scores on each of the individual questions. If in the above illustration a numerical score of 2 is assigned to every "yes" answer, one of 1 to every "don't know" answer, and one of zero to every "no" answer, an individual's prejudice score on this scale can range from 6 when he replies "yes" to all three questions to zero when he replies "no" to all three. Only in a figurative and misleading sense, however, can it be said that an individual with a score of 6 has twice as much prejudice as one with a score of 3.

But how should the answers to the questions be weighted? Various methods are employed. A list of questions thought to be related to the attitude being measured is assembled and perhaps pre-tested to be certain that they are understood. Then an arbitrary score or weight is assigned to each answer by the investigator whose personal judgment thus colors the entire scale. The investigator may also show his questions and proposed answers to a group of experts (like students of race relations) and ask them, first, whether the each question is related to the issue and, second, how the alternatives under each question should be scored (*15*).

A more elaborate method for scoring the questions of a scale has been designed by Thurstone and his associates (*27*). They also submit a list of questions to a group of judges who are asked not to give their own opinions but very carefully to rank the questions in terms of the degree to which the answers reflect the attitude being measured. The judges are instructed to place each question in one of eleven piles, with the last pile representing the most extreme expression of the attitude (such as prejudice), the first the least extreme (such as the complete absence of prejudice), the sixth the midpoint of the attitude, and the remaining eight piles various degrees in-between. After the judges have placed the questions into the eleven piles, each question is subjected to careful statistical scrutiny largely in terms of the various piles to which it has been assigned by the different judges. If the same question has been placed in many different piles (and thus, in the judges' opinion, is said to reflect degrees of prejudice varying from very strong to very weak), it is discarded because it is obviously ambiguous. A set of questions finally emerges which, according to the hard-working judges, are relatively unambiguous. These compose the attitude scale. The score each question receives is the average numerical value of the piles in which it has been placed by the judges. The score of the individuals who then answer the questions is the average score of the questions to which they have replied affirmatively or of the statements with which they have agreed. A person with a score of 8.4, for example, is more prejudiced than one with a score of 4.1, but he is less prejudiced than one with a score of 10.2. What is being measured is thus the degree of prejudice on a standard provided by a group of judges.

This procedure of obtaining numerical values for questions through the use of a large number of judges is most painstaking and time-consuming. It has been argued by Likert (*23*), therefore, and to a certain extent demonstrated—if not to the complete satisfaction of those adhering to Thurstone's method (*11*)—that the labor involved is unnecessary and that the arbitrary assignment of numerical scores to the replies to a question gives approximately the same results and is just as reliable and valid. This controversy cannot be described in further detail at this point. For general purposes, however, it must be pointed out that investigators who assign arbitrary scores to the questions making up their scales must also make what is called an item analysis of each question before it is retained in their scale. The procedure behind such an analysis is not difficult to understand. The scores a group receives on each question are compared—in statistical language, correlated with —the scores that group obtains on all the other questions making up the scale. If those who favor lynching under certain circumstances, for example, tend to receive higher scores on the other questions of the scale than those who disapprove of lynching under all circumstances, and if a high score has been made to represent a high degree of prejudice, then it is concluded that the question has been correctly scored and belongs on the attitude scale. But if those with high scores on the lynching question receive low scores on the other questions (a most improbable result of course), then it is concluded that this item has been incorrectly scored and hence it is scored to make approval of lynching one item indicating lack of prejudice (just as improbable) or the question is dropped from the scale. Finally, if no difference on the question of lynching exists between those with high and low scores, that question is considered to be unrelated to the scale and dropped.

Investigators of attitude, regardless of the technique they employ, show concern for the reliability of their scales. In general, the more questions a scale has, the more reliable it is likely to be. The total score of an individual who misunderstands one question, for example, will be less affected by this instrument error when there are thirty other questions which he understands then when there are merely three. The best way to determine the reliability of a scale is to administer it a second time to the same group and then to note the differences. This method, however, is usually impractical for the same reasons that polling questions are seldom repeated: the group may not be available or willing to take the test a second time; its replies the second time may be dependent upon what is recalled from the first test; the obtained differences may result not from the unreliability of the scale but from real changes which have occurred within the individuals in the interim. Usually, therefore, reliability is determined by administering the scale only once and then calculating the differences between (*i.e.,* correlating) the scores obtained on the first half with those obtained on the second; or the scores obtained on the even-numbered items are compared (correlated) with those obtained on the odd-numbered items. By means of a simple statistical procedure—the use of the Spearman-Brown formula (*12*)—the resulting reliability figure is then raised to approximate the one which would have been obtained if the calculation had been based not on a comparison of one half of the scale with the other but on the entire scale. Sometimes two forms of a scale are prepared, each of which contains different but similar questions; then both forms may be administered to the same group and the resulting scores compared.

The validity of an attitude scale, like that of a poll, cannot be easily determined. Again some outside criterion involving the actual behavior of the people answering the questionnaire must be found. An attitude scale measuring race prejudice, for example, is considered valid if individuals who are already known to be prejudiced and unprejudiced from their reputation or their deeds receive, respectively, extremely high and low scores on the scale. Indirect criteria have also been employed, such as the ratings on the attitude which the individuals themselves or people who know them well have given, autobiographical material of the subjects which is then converted into quantified scores by a set of judges, the scores obtained on other attitude scales whose validity has previously been determined, etc.

If the scale proves to be valid on the basis of some criterion, the assumption is made that it will be more or less equally valid for other individuals whose attitudes eventually will be measured. This procedure assumes a certain constancy in the reactions of individuals to the questions of a scale. It is analogous to believing that a thermometer which accurately measures temperature somewhere in the United States will be equally accurate in Ecuador or Alaska. The belief about the thermometer is correct, provided it is not injured in transit; but the faith in the attitude is unfounded. Prejudice at one time in the United States may be provoked by certain stimuli (like the question of whether Negro children should be allowed to attend elementary school with white children) which later become a moot issue no longer related to prejudice. And certainly the stimuli provoking prejudice in the United States are different from those operating in Ecuador or Alaska. An attitude scale, therefore, is usually validated only for a specific group in society at a particular time-period. A very large percentage of existing attitude scales, moreover, has been designed and validated for American college students, many of whom have been students of psychology and especially of social psychology. These students have good-naturedly agreed to serve as subjects—they usually find an attitude scale more intriguing than the lecture of their instructor. Such a group is obviously unrepresentative of the entire population.

A significant advance over previous methods of scaling has been proposed by Guttman (*13*) and was evolved and extensively employed during the last war by the Research Branch of the United States Army's Information and Education Division under the auspices of Stouffer, Hovland, and their associates. The method possesses at least two unique features. In the first place, the scale's existence is not assumed on the basis of opinions given by outside judges or the investigators, but is tested by studying the replies of individuals whose attitudes are being scaled. Then, secondly, an individual's score on the scale not only ranks him in respect to other members of the group but also, with a very small degree of error, indicates the precise way in which he has answered *all* the questions.

In ordinary practice about a half-dozen questions make up such a scale. For simplicity's sake, however, only three questions will be considered here:

1. Do you think that Negroes are inferior to whites?
2. Do you think that Negroes should be segregated in public conveyances?
3. Do you think that lynching of Negroes is sometimes justified?

At the outset all the investigator must decide is that an affirmative answer to any of these questions is an indication of prejudice. He does not have to decide that question #3 shows more or less prejudice than question #1. In theory, if the answer to each question can be only either "yes" or "no," the individuals to whom the scale is given can be divided into eight groups. The practical problem is to discover the actual groups into which the individuals divide themselves; there may not be any one individual, for example, who replies "yes" to questions #1 and #3 and "no" to #2. The individuals' attitudes toward Negroes are considered scalable if—within an error of from 10 to 15 percent—they can be divided into a smaller number of groups which can be arranged in a regular series ranging from all affirmative to all negative replies to the three questions.

As hypothetical results, consider the following: 90 percent of a sample replies affirmatively to question #1, 20 percent to question #2, and 10 percent to #3. If the individuals' attitudes as measured by these questions are scal-

able, then they should be divisible into groups on the basis
of their answers to all three questions. Here, for example,
are four conceivable groups:

	Percent total group	Answer to question: #1	#2	#3
Group #A	10	yes	yes	yes
Group #B	10	yes	yes	no
Group #C	70	yes	no	no
Group #D	10	no	no	no
Percent "Yes"		90	20	10

It will be noted in the above table that the percentages
answering each question affirmatively or negatively have
not been altered; for example, question #2 is represented
by two "yes" groups (#A and #B) of 10 percent each,
making a total of 20 percent which is the percent said to be
replying affirmatively in the first place. Group #A can be
called the most prejudiced because it has replied "yes" to
all three questions; Group #B is less prejudiced because it
said "no" to question #3 but "yes" to the other two; etc.
Each group differs from its neighbor only in respect to one
of the questions; thus Groups #B and #C think the Negro
inferior and both disapprove of lynching, but #B favors
Jim-Crow practices while #C does not. If it is known that
an individual is in Group C, then it is immediately indicated
how he answered all three of the questions.

Not all questions are so easily scalable. When a large
number of questions is employed, it is usually discovered
that only a small percentage of them can be scaled in this
fashion. It may then be presumed that the non-scalable
items measure other attitudes. Those that are scalable,
moreover, may be evoking an attitude different from the
one which the investigator thought he was measuring. The
nature of this different attitude can be determined by adding
more questions to the scalable items and discovering whether
they fit into a scale. The question, "Do you think Negroes
are honest?" for example, would not be included in the
above scale if the answers bore no relation to the answers

given to the other three questions: individuals replying affirmatively might reply in every conceivable combination to questions about Negro inferiority and lynching. That question, however, might be related to an attitude concerning ethnic groups in general. With more than three questions in the scale, the investigator could find that the scalable attitude concerns not Negroes as an entire group but only Negroes in the South.

It has already been indicated, moreover, that from 10 to 15 percent of the individuals will not fall so neatly into one of the four groups. One person, for example, might not consider Negroes inferior and might be opposed to segregation in public conveyances but could be in favor of lynching. The pattern of "no" on questions #1 and #2 and "yes" on #3 does not happen to correspond to any one of the four groups which have been empirically established. His position regarding Negroes may be quite in keeping with his personality or social philosophy, but it differs from the patterns found in from 85 to 90 percent of his group. There is also the possibility that an instrument error has occurred: perhaps he did not understand one of the questions or was careless in answering it. Such an error, therefore, would decrease the scale's reliability.

The questions which form a scale for one group at one time may not form the same scale for another group or for the same group a different time. For this reason the scaling procedure may be repeated whenever a new group is examined. Happily the statistical procedures are not very complicated or time-consuming. The problem of validity, moreover, must continually be attacked in the usual manner by comparing the individuals' scores with some outside criterion involving behavior.

An important additional feature of this type of scaling may be mentioned in passing (*14*). If the individuals are asked not only to answer the questions but also to indicate how certain they feel about each answer or how important each question is to them, then the investigator can obtain two scales: one for the attitude and the other for the attitude's intensity. Empirical investigation has revealed that individuals who hold an extreme view (for example, those with the most and the least prejudice) tend to be more certain of their views or to consider them more important than those who subscribe to a position between the extremes (for example, those with some but not very much prejudice). The individuals whose attitude is least intense, therefore, can be thought to be at the mid-point of the attitude scale. In this fashion, it is possible to discover the individuals who have a favorable and those who have an unfavorable attitude toward the issue not by deciding arbitrarily that scores above a certain figure (like the average of the group or a point selected by outside judges) shall be called favorable and those below that figure unfavorable but by finding the point at which the group itself begins to feel strongly one way or the other.

Systematic Observation

Most reports on public opinion are based upon casual observations of people and therefore they are likely to be neither reliable nor valid. The journalist may not interview even an unrepresentative sample of informants. Instead he may observe what people are saying and doing, and then base his reports on the impressions he receives. These impressions, of course, will be incorrect or misleading if they are derived from unrepresentative or too few people and if they are affected by the reporter's own bias and other instrument errors he commits.

It is possible to observe people both systematically and continually and thus to obtain data which, though they cannot be thrown into statistical form, nevertheless can be perhaps as reliable and valid as a poll or an attitude scale. The anthropologist investigating a so-called primitive people lives among them, observes their customs, notes how they react to crises or ordinary events, and records their verbalizations under varying circumstances. He may never ask them what their opinions are and he most certainly will never administer an attitude scale, but he will be able to report on the popularity of their native chief, of a missionary, or of a colonial official. His report, however, may refer only to external and not internal public opinion if the people of the tribe are supposed to like the chief, the missionary, and the official; if they fear punishment from not doing so; or if he has not won their confidence.

In like manner no Gallup poll was necessary to verify the fact that the majority of Germans—externally at least—supported the Hitler regime from 1935 at the latest until its downfall in 1945. Nazi theorists, nevertheless, recognized the distinction between external and internal public opinion. The former they called *Haltung* (or behavior) and the latter *Stimmung* (or inner mood). They frequently and cynically asserted that they were interested only in *Haltung* which they maintained through force and that *Stimmung* was a democratic luxury which they found superfluous. The straightforward observer could perceive only the *Haltung* of Germans. *Stimmung* might be inferred with great risk from overt behavior and could be ascertained with much difficulty by somebody who, the Germans decided, would not report them to the Gestapo.

The observer of public opinion increases his opportunities of determining internal public opinion by becoming assimilated as far as possible into the community he is observing. This approach has been descriptively termed the method of participant observation and, in another connection, is employed by detectives who join criminal cliques in order to gather necessary evidence and then eventually to expose and apprehend the members. Ordinarily it is not easy for a stranger to participate actively or typically in a group: he may speak their language differently, he may commit social blunders, or he may find them inhospitable. To be a successful observer, he must make his behavior conform to theirs as best he can, so that his foreign characteristics become scarcely noticed and the group behaves as if he were one of its members. Many Americans who travel abroad return with the impression that people in other countries spend a considerable part of their lives discussing, analyzing, or being critical toward the United States. Such an impression is probably an exaggeration of the fact; the presence of an American promotes the United States as a conversational topic in deference to or as an expression of hostility toward the visitor and his country.

Systematic and especially participant observation enables the investigator to secure public opinion data in their social context. Warner and his associates (*29*), for example, entered a New England community to study its class structure. Although they did not conceal their general purpose, they became convinced that people soon tended to forget why they were there and to accept them as more or less equivalent to members of the in-group. As a result, they were able to dissect the community and to present data on the enduring and momentary public opinion of social classes, ethnic groups, cliques, and organizations.

The reliability and validity of observations depend completely on the capabilities of the observer. What he reports only he himself has perceived and frequently there is no one who is able or willing to check his findings. "Should the researcher expect to be believed . . . ?" Dollard (*7*) asked himself after he had participated in the life of a small southern community in the United States, and in reply he could only describe the methods he employed to secure his data. There is thus the implication that his readers could make their own observation if they did not believe him. It must be remarked that most of Dollard's readers probably have neither the ability nor the opportunity to make this kind of analysis. As a result, the author himself has to be trusted and, realizing this, he frankly stated his own biases at the outset of the report (*8*) so that others might be in a better position to evaluate his observations. When a staff of investigators participates in a community, reliability can be determined by comparing the impressions of more than one investigator.

A group of Englishmen (*16*) evolved in 1937 a method of measuring public opinion which they call "Mass Observation." In addition to conducting poll-like interviews, full-time observers stationed in Lancashire, one borough of London, and occasionally elsewhere in England and Scotland eavesdrop on conversations in public places; observe and record "incidents, street scenes, and rituals"; and secure information concerning "opinion-forming channels" which range from sermons to wall drawings. A panel of part-time observers scattered throughout England is asked to write reports on how people in their communities are reacting to specified issues; some keep diaries which are later examined by the central office in London. The results from the national panel are sometimes given in statistical form, but the figures are always accompanied by the qualitative statements of these informants or the full-time observers. The proponents of Mass Observation claim that this combination of heterogeneous approaches enables them to dig beneath "public" opinion and thus to determine "private" opinion. One report (*28*), for example, noted that conventional polls indicated an increase in Prime Minister Chamberlain's popularity during the first six months of the last war; yet "in the privacy of the darkened cinema, applause for Mr. Chamberlain, when he appears on news reels, has gone *down*." Without doubt spontaneously expressed opinions are obtained in this fashion, and the published reports of the organization possess a warmth and color no conventional poll ever displays. The varied types of information, however, are pieced together most subjectively without systematic regard for their representativeness. A kaleidoscopic impression of public opinion is given, but it is the editors who turn the machine.

One technique of Mass Observation was employed during the last war in the United States by the Domestic Branch of the Office of War Information (*5*). Key individuals in communities—such as clergymen, newspaper and labor editors, social workers, farm leaders, businessmen, etc.— agreed to serve on a "Correspondence Panel" and to write letters to the O.W.I. reporting how people with whom they had personal contact were reacting to the issues of the time. These reports contained colorful and meaningful details, and they reflected grassroot opinions in an informal and natural fashion. The conscious and unconscious biases of the amateur or professional reporters produced an instrument error which, however, was noted by comparing the

Panel's trends with those obtained by the conventional polling organizations.

Another method, though not based on direct observation, must be mentioned. Under some circumstances it is possible to make inferences concerning public opinion from observing the content of the media of communication. The actual technique of analyzing these media are considered in Chapter 13, and so here it is only necessary to suggest how content analyses can serve as an indirect measure of public opinion. Many government agencies during the last war made elaborate analyses of enemy newspaper and domestic radio broadcasts. Before insight into German public opinion could be obtained, however, at least one fact had to be known and one assumption made. Analysts had to know that German authorities, especially Propaganda Minister Goebbels, were aware of public opinion trends in Germany. Intelligence did reveal at the time—and this was confirmed after the war (26)—that Goebbels and his associates employed the machinery of many Nazi organizations to ascertain these trends, much in the manner of the political boss in the United States. In addition, the propaganda astuteness of Goebbels had to be assumed: he would make an effort to affect public opinion when it was to the advantage of the Nazi cause for him to do so. Thus, if Goebbels began a campaign against grumbling, as he sometimes did, it could be concluded that Germans were grumbling to such an extent that he was compelled to deal with the problem by staging the campaign. Similarly, if Goebbels devoted space in his newspapers and time on his radio to claims that allied bombing was not interfering with the German war effort, the deduction could be made that many Germans were convinced that bombing was having precisely that effect. Inferences and deduction of this kind were naturally most hazardous to make, but frequently no alternate method was available to American and allied intelligence organizations. Under normal conditions in a democracy it is equally risky to employ editorial opinion in a newspaper as a guide to public opinion since it both affects and reflects the attitudes of its readers.

Letters from foreign countries which had been intercepted by censorship authorities (*18*) were also subjected to analysis in order to throw some light on the state of "morale" in an enemy or occupied country in Europe. Here at least were concrete expressions of attitude written, for example, by Germans to friends in neutral countries. The letters, however, had to pass through the hands of enemy censors before they could leave their country of origin; complaints might very well have been deleted and hence an instrument error would be introduced. Even if attention were focused only on the small number of letters written by enemy nationals who temporarily evaded their own censors by writing or posting them from Switzerland and Sweden, the analyst might then be concentrating upon a biased sample without knowing just what the bias was. There was always the possibility that enemy officials would deliberately "plant" letters in order to create a false impression abroad; and the civilian population certainly had been told which topics it could and could not mention in its written communications. The representativeness of the letter-writing sample, moreover, was difficult to determine from the few clues which the letters themselves provided. In employing intercepted letters as one source of information concerning German "morale," therefore, the writer never even attempted to say whether that "morale" was high or low, improving or declining. Instead he collected the reasons offered by the letter-writers for their high or low "morale" and analyzed shifts in those reasons. One extremely valuable study of intercepts conducted outside of the United States was based essentially on a panel technique: the letters to a group of German prisoners from their relatives were analyzed over a period of years.

A final variant of observation that is also useful in democratic societies during peace time is the analysis of current rumors. For rumors—whether deliberately planted or not—are indices of what people consider important and at the same time reflect the situations and issues that are ambiguous to them (*1*). In the three months after the bombing of Pearl Harbor, rumors circulated throughout the United

States that American losses there had been greater than official statements indicated. According to Allport and Postman (*2*), these tales were given currency because Americans felt impelled to rationalize the reasons for the fears they were experiencing as the war began; because for security reasons the news about actual losses had been vague and inadequate; and because the government in Washington and especially its news policies were distrusted by many people. About two and a half months after the Japanese attack, in fact, President Roosevelt officially recognized the uncertain state of American public opinion on this issue by attempting to expose the rumors in one of his radio fireside chats. The same writers (*3*) also suggest that "each rumor has its own public" as a result of the particular group's more or less unique responses and its limited knowledge. The rumors pervading a group, in short, indicate its problems and perplexities.

Rumors, however, are a very equivocal index of public opinion. They may show what is important and ambiguous to a group, but without further investigation it is not possible to deduce which drives have been active to give currency to them and precisely what aspects of which situations are ambiguous. Both the facts in the original situations and the first report of those facts, as Allport and Postman (*4*) have shown on the basis of rather convincing experimental evidence and much more convincing case histories of rumors, undergo a variety of changes as the rumors spread from mouth to mouth or from newspaper to newspaper. The public opinion analyst who collects rumors, consequently, obtains only clues: he cannot know what his net has brought in until he also investigates the past distortions which have produced the version in his possession. It is also necessary to discover which groups in a society are spreading and giving credence to the tale. These various investigations are so time-consuming and difficult that it is generally easier to assay public opinion by any one of the more direct methods. When public opinion data concerning the enemy during a war are scarce, then rumor analysis permits sagacious guesses to be made—but they are guesses.

Prolonged Interviewing

A prolonged interview, it has been pointed out, represents the most intensive and the least extensive method that can be employed to measure public opinion, just as the conventional poll based on the "yes," "no," and "don't know" type of question is the least intensive and the most extensive. Without doubt more intimate and psychologically meaningful data can be obtained from interviewing an individual over long periods of time. In addition to determining his attitudes, insight into his general personality structure can be obtained and the attitudes can be related to that structure (*25*). No one, however, should imagine that a corps of psychiatrists, psychologists, social workers, vocational counsellors, or individuals otherwise trained in interviewing techniques can provide ideal knowledge concerning public opinion. Such a corps, if sufficiently large and sufficiently well-subsidized, might find a representative sample, but the problem of coding the data so that they could be thrown into statistical form would still have to be faced. This is the same problem confronting those who use any type of open interview or question. Interviewing at its best, moreover, is an art and not a science: the very best specialists do not agree with one another concerning how the data shall be secured or interpreted. The type of case or life history obtained from a prolonged interview, finally, reflects the uniqueness of the person who has been interviewed; a thousand intensive interviews, therefore, cannot be fully represented by a statistical average or a proportion.

The prolonged interview, nevertheless, can serve at least three functions in the measuring of public opinion. Occasionally public opinion may be so J-shaped and people in the society so homogeneous that data obtained from a few individuals adequately represent the entire group in respect to certain issues. Naturally individual differences will be present, but they may be disregarded when they do not bear on the issues. Under such circumstances a small, random sample is sufficiently representative. Intensive interviewing of a few individuals from one social class when class structure in society is rigid, for example, may be all that is required to understand the opinions of their class. This procedure, it must be hastily added, is most risky and should be employed most cautiously, since the investigator can never be completely certain of the homogeneity of the total group.

The intensive interview can be utilized as a device to supplement the general survey. Extensity is obtained from the answers to relatively superficial questions by a representative sample. And intensity results from the prolonged interviews of a few individuals more or less randomly selected for illustrative or anecdotal purposes. The more intimate interpretation of the survey findings through case-history data from a small number of interviewees, however, may produce the spurious impression that a similar interpretation might have been made for the entire sample if everyone in that sample had also been intensively interviewed. The survey data come to life when incorporated within specific individuals, consequently, but the limitations of the additional dramatic or psychological insight must be clearly recognized.

In addition, the significant polling questions to be asked a large and representative sample of individuals can be ascertained by interviewing intensively a small number of informants. When two investigators (9), for example, wished to study the fear reactions under battle conditions of former members of the Abraham Lincoln Brigade who had fought against Franco in Spain, they first recorded the prolonged interviews they conducted with twenty of these volunteers. From the interview data they were able to formulate much more telling questions which they then submitted to 300 respondents than if they had simply chosen questions on the basis of a superficial pre-test or of ideas they themselves considered relevant to the problem of fear.

CHAPTER 10

The Importance of Public Opinion

Both the words and the deeds of every tyrant have revealed at least a grudging but respectful recognition of the importance of public opinion. In spite of a thorough contempt for the intellectual capacity of the masses, the dictator has been compelled to admit that his own ruthlessness is limited by what people are willing to accept. Ordinary men and women may be stupid, but they cannot be completely misled or corrupted.

At the other extreme are individuals who express their faith in democracy by extolling the virtues of public opinion. The American polling cult—for example, Bruner (*1*), Cantril (*3*), Childs (*4*), and Gallup (*11*)—states bluntly and also interprets poll data to indicate that the common man is frequently if not always wiser than his leaders. Gallup in particular is addicted to quoting Lord Bryce who apparently also loved public opinion in the abstract and who qualified as the patron saint of polling by once suggesting that democracy would function more effectively if people's opinions could be continually and systematically ascertained. The pollsters, of course, are seeking to justify their own preoccupation with the data of public opinion by emphasizing the importance of those data. This viewpoint, moreover, is shared by those who have no professional interest in polls and, as a matter of fact, is a key tenet of democratic ideology: *vox populi, vox Dei.*

Whether the voice of the people is the voice of the ignorant or of God involves, among other things, an issue of fact. Whether the voice of the people should be listened to or not is a philosophical-political problem. The issue and the problem are of supreme importance at a time when the relation of people to their government is in a state of crisis.

The Competency of Public Opinion

It was Walter Lippmann (22) who shortly after World War I dramatically called attention to the restrictions which inevitably are placed upon public opinion. He indicated that most people must be guided by "the pictures" in their heads which he called "stereotypes." These pictures are usually incomplete reflections of political, economic, and social reality. Men have little time and few opportunities, he argued, to become acquainted with their environment and with one another; it is, therefore, easier for them to be guided by a simplified and not necessarily accurate version of events. In addition, people have neither the interest nor the skill to interpret what is happening. Finally, Lippmann showed how the media of communication in modern society deliberately or unwittingly present only a limited and therefore distorted picture of events.

Lippmann's view of the limitations of public opinion requires no essential modification, in spite of the turbulent events which have occurred and the additional knowledge as well as the views of the immodest semanticists which have accumulated since he wrote his book. His conception of "stereotype" now seems a little too intellectual and to lack the emotional and unconscious components that most psychological processes—like rationalization and displacement—possess. Here a stereotype is considered as one of the internal responses—knowledge—which evokes an attitude. It is the attitude which has drive value and thus produces action. Stereotype, like knowledge, is an end product of learning and usually represents a form of simplified knowledge.

Two assumptions must be made before public opinion or any stereotype can be considered competent or incompetent. There is an assumption concerning the facts which someone —perhaps an expert—says are involved; if people's knowledge includes these facts, they may be called competent; if it does not, they are incompetent. Then on the basis of the facts or in their absence a conclusion is reached concerning the course of action to be pursued: if the action is in accord with somebody's notion of "the good," it is thought to be competent; if not, it is branded incompetent.

Some human judgments are obviously competent. People wish, for example, to avoid physical pain. A proposal that all the inhabitants of an area be knocked over the head each day with a large stone until they lose consciousness would be viewed with disapproval, no matter how great the reward or how prestigeful the depth of the faint would become. In short:

Fact:	the blow produces pain.
Value:	pain is not desirable.
Public opinion:	opposition to the proposal.
Competency:	complete.

People also wish to eat: public opinion can be in favor of food if an issue arises. The food, however, must be of a particular kind and prepared in a specialized manner: public opinion can be in favor of a rather specific cuisine. A generation ago Americans were not accustomed to drink some type of fruit or vegetable juice for breakfast: public opinion was neutral toward juice for the first meal of the day, perhaps mildly antagonistic. Certainly if people had been consulted concerning the desirability of adding juice to the breakfast menu, they would not have agreed to the change or at least there would have been disagreement. In reality, agreement was more or less reached on this issue as a result of various factors over which most Americans had no direct control. They learned about the relationship of vitamins to health. They were told that fruit and vegetable juices contain vitamins. They were subjected to powerful advertising campaigns which stressed the desirability of drinking a juice at breakfast. Modern methods of refrigeration and canning enabled them to secure the juices more rapidly and in better condition. Their attitudes were gradually changed; internal and external public opinion on the issue was altered or formed. It would have been futile to expect people in general to discover vitamins and the presence of the vitamins in juices, to convince themselves that orange or tomato juice improves breakfasts, or to develop an improved system of distributing agricultural products. People simply had to learn a number of things and they had to be psychologically prepared to accept the innovation. Gradually their stereotype of breakfast changed. In summary:

Facts:	vitamins are essential for health; fruit and vegetable juices contain certain vitamins; most Americans eat breakfast; the taste of juices is satisfactory or pleasant to Americans.
Values:	health and taste.
Public opinion:	general acceptance.
Competency:	high regarding need for breakfast, the taste of the juices, and the values involved; low regarding function of vitamins and vitamin content of juices.

In both of these illustrations the values require little or no debate. The promotion of health, for example, is considered desirable because good health is associated with the prolongation of life or at least with the diminution of pain. Life, it is felt, should almost always be prolonged and pain should almost always be avoided because—and here the reason is either obvious or unprovable.

The moment the value at stake has no biological overtones, controversy arises and the role of public opinion becomes less clear. Consider, for example, an American city of 100,000 which contemplates a change in its form of government. It has had a mayor and a municipal council which, according to public opinion, has functioned reasonably well. It is then proposed that the city-manager type of government be installed. The problem is submitted to the people in the form of a referendum. How do, how should people react? They do react in terms of how the issue is presented to them during the campaign and in terms of the experiences they have previously had with their present form of government. How they should react is difficult to say, inasmuch as the expertness of the specialist in municipal government is not nearly so complete as that of the dietitian concerned with juices—or at least it is a different kind of expertness. The dietitian can say, with some degree of certainty, that vitamins promote health and his task is discharged. The specialist in municipal government can state with less certainty that the overall and the specific consequences of one form of government rather than another will be such-and-such, but in addition he is still faced with the problem of helping people decide on the desirability or undesirability of those consequences. In fact, there is some doubt as to whether the specialist or the average citizen is better qualified to assay those consequences. Here, then, the situation is more complicated:

Facts:	ways in which the new form can be expected to function, some known, some partially known, others unknown.
Values:	phrased in terms of "efficient" or "good" government which in turn presumably affects individual citizens.
Public opinion:	depends on which facts are known and what values are ascribed to them.
Competency:	low.

Average people can be said to know the facts and make "sound" value judgments on only a limited number of issues. Most of these pertain to themselves: they know their likes and dislikes, and they reveal a certain competency in discharging particular economic and social roles in their society. Even here, however, they reveal limitations. They have no way of testing which type of cloth is most durable, and therefore they purchase their clothes on the basis of style, price, or label. They find themselves suddenly in a mild depression and cannot account for their mood: saying that they "got out of the wrong side of the bed" on a particular morning is an innocent but not very helpful verbalism. They are frequently perplexed by the problem of raising their own children, some of whose behavior remains unintelligible to them. They do not know many facts and sometimes they know that they do not know.

People who are neither morons nor masochists are or try to be experts when expertness is required. A good mechanic can repair a machine. A good dentist can fill cavities. A good farmer can raise crops. Or at least each of them attempts to perform his job well and efficiently. They learn the proper responses because the rewards are sufficiently alluring. Such activity is *central* within them.

People do not even attempt to be experts when there is no incentive to learn the requisite responses. The competent mechanic may leave grease spots on the dishes he occasionally washes for his wife, the competent dentist may not be able to park his car in a small space, and the competent farmer may spell incorrectly the simpler words of his native language. Such interests are *segmental* for them.

Many of the issues which arouse public opinion require a certain expertness. If the issue is central within a group of people, they are motivated to become acquainted with the facts, to seek certain values, and to respond, as it is said, "intelligently." But if the issue is segmental, their responses, it is also said, are "unintelligent" or "superficial": the facts are lacking and their value judgments are unclear or not intense. Many persons may, to be sure, be vitally interested in a problem—like war or inflation—without being expert merely because their way of life has never required that they become specialists on those subjects or because the facts are not easily accessible.

People cannot be expected to have central attitudes re-garding all the issues of their society. Life is short and social obligations require that it be led along specific lines. The clerk cannot know what a cabinet minister must know, nor can the minister master the details which are the re-sponsibility of his subordinate. For this very simple reason, therefore, it is foolish to expect wisdom from the masses all of the time.

If wisdom concerning facts and values cannot be expected from the masses, it does not follow that only experts have a monopoly on the kind of wisdom required to resolve the great problems of an age. It is false to argue, since experts are employed to repair cars, to fill cavities, and to grow crops, that only experts should be utilized to settle all the issues facing public opinion. In the first place, the experts on many issues, as has been indicated, are not completely expert. Political scientists differ concerning both general-ities and details even before they approach the key problem of what is good for a group of people. Economists differ concerning interpretations and prognoses even before they seek to decide—if they ever do—what is best along eco-nomic lines. Historians interpret the past differently and certainly do not agree on what is or should be learned from the past about the present and the future. Sociologists usu-ally do not agree on diagnoses. And psychologists have a marked tendency to count the trees and philosophers to in-tuit the forest. Only dictators are convinced that they have mastered both means and ends, and thus are able to view public opinion as a stumbling block to progress or as a lump of putty which they alone are gifted to mold.

Then, secondly, if the experts have their deficiencies, it is essential to recognize the complexity of the issues which in-volve public opinion. People, their drives, their society, their culture, the idea of the good or the just, social change, leaders, natural and artificial environment—these are some of the factors at work. No pat solution is possible: the variables are too numerous, the interactions too intricate, the final result too unpredictable. For all the juices which Americans now consume at breakfast there must be many more products whose health-giving properties, whose publicity campaigns, and whose methods of distributions could be just as excellent. People can be hit by almost anything, but they do not respond favorably to everything.

Under these circumstances, therefore, a certain amount of trial and error is both inevitable and desirable. Selfish and altruistic interests seek to alter public opinion and in fact, when subject to pressure, it is likely that people will change. But the change occurs only when people believe that thereby they secure more satisfaction—temporarily at the very least. The problem of the social good is too vast for any man or any small group of men to grasp. Somehow, as implied in a previous discussion of socialization (*cf.* *18*), men work out the society which best fits the needs of their personalities and then that society helps shape the personalities of each generation as it appears. The interaction between men and their institutions is continual and hence there is social change.

Public opinion, then, has its limitations. People can be stupid and they can be wise. Their reactions depend on their expertness, and their expertness depends on their drives and their knowledge. Experts can give better judgments about aspects of some problems, but experts cannot necessarily prescribe the good life. Over a long period of time people decide their own fate. There is no one who can or who should make this decision for them completely.

Politics in a Democracy

In a democratic country the people are supposed to be supreme. This presumably means that important decisions depend, if only ultimately, on public opinion and that the day-by-day activities of government in some way or other reflect that opinion. The lip-service paid to public opinion by statesmen and politicians needs to be taken seriously: as a bare minimum, leaders must pretend that they are sensitive to the demands of their constituents.

A few years ago, as indicated in a previous chapter, 58 out of the 197 members of the New York State legislature were induced to respond to a questionnaire primarily on public opinion polls (*16*). One of the five questions was:

Do you consider it your public duty as a "representative" to reflect in official voting whatever preponderant sentiment your district displays on every issue, even if this is contrary to your personal conception of community welfare?

Significantly, 57 percent replied in the negative—39 percent were affirmative replies and the remaining 4 percent failed to reply at all or ran no risk by saying both "yes" and "no." Those who claimed they reflected the "preponderant sentiment" in their district were behaving—or so they asserted for the record—as they are popularly supposed to behave in a democracy. Those who stressed their "personal conception of community welfare" were expressing a somewhat conservative viewpoint reminiscent of the distrust the Founding Fathers felt toward the masses of people: the legislators considered themselves experts and capable of making a distinction between actual public opinion ("preponderant sentiment") and latent but enduring public opinion ("community welfare"). Such replies, though of questionable reliability and validity, at least revealed a divergence of opinion even on the crude level of a survey.

Then, when thirteen Congressmen were interviewed (*13*) and asked to state why they voted for or against the repeal of the Neutrality Act in 1939, twelve maintained that they were primarily exercising their own "independent judgment" and one gave as his reason the view of a public leader. These politicians, to be sure, must have been self-consciously talking for public consumption, but it is important to note that no one of them felt impelled to use "constituents' wishes" as his most prominent rationalization. Only seven in fact mentioned these "wishes" as a secondary reason. When the same investigator interviewed Congressional secretaries and newspaper correspondents concerning the reasons for the votes cast by ninety-six Congressmen on the same bill, "constituents' wishes" still ran a poor third after "independent judgment" and "party consideration." If these data are as "highly reliable" as the writer without proof says he "feels" they are, then public opinion in this instance was of relatively little importance to the law-makers.

According to a nationwide poll in 1944 (*15*), moreover, 77 percent of a sample *acquainted with public opinion polls* believed that "generally speaking . . . Congressmen should be guided by the thinking of a majority of the people in their districts on important questions." Twenty percent thought that "Congressmen should vote as they think best without regard to what a majority of the people feel." The re-maining 3 percent had no opinion on this question. But 31 percent of the very same people who had heard of polls claimed they would be influenced against a candidate if they knew that he "waited to see from polls what the majority of people thought before he expressed his own point of view on an issue." Only 11 percent would be influenced in his favor and the rest—58 percent—could not decide how or whether they would be influenced or maintained that they would not be affected one way or the other.

It would seem that public opinion is only one of the many factors determining political judgment. Government offi-cials, therefore, inevitably are—and, according to many citizens, should be—much more than what has been called (*25*) the "office boys" of their constituents. They do more than identify themselves with the people who have elected them. For they are human beings, and human beings are almost always variously motivated. There are political factors not directly related to public opinion: adherence to the principles of the party, sometimes regardless of their popularity at the moment; intelligent or blind opposition to the rival party or parties which perhaps only they as poli-ticians vent; or deference to influential rather than typical groups in the community. There may be social factors arising out of the voting situation: the crowd spirit which sometimes pervades the debate in a legislature; pressure from lobbyists or some vocal minority; the influence of a powerful leader. There may also be individual factors in addition to "the personal conception of community wel-fare": the attempt to secure publicity for other than political reasons; the influence of a friend, a wife, or a mistress; some form of a *quid pro quo,* including straight bribes; an idiosyncractic impulse arising from an aggressive streak, a mother-fixation, a poorly digested meal, etc.

Government officials sometimes claim that they can adequately represent and reflect public opinion because they are people "like the rest of us" and consequently their attitudes are the same as their constituents. Any man, however, can be typical of a group only in relatively few respects and then merely in terms of that group's average. A politician whose age is forty-two does represent a community whose average age is likewise forty-two so far as age is concerned; but even this is only statistical representativeness, inasmuch as some of his constituents are older and some younger. The laws which legislators make, moreover, affect all age ranges; and yet the constitution of the states or of the country prevents younger people from choosing one of their number by barring them from voting and requiring that prospective candidates attain some minimum age. If the most prominent occupation in a community is farming, then a politician who has been a farmer is typical. He is a farmer of a particular economic and social status, which may or may not be the average in the community and, in addition, he is definitely not occupationally representative of hired hands, shopkeepers, and professional men. As a matter of fact, the representatives of the people in the Congress of the United States tend to come from white-collar groups like lawyers (*17*) who are in the numerical minority. Since relatively few citizens have political ambitions, it follows that those who do must be unusual or not typical in respect to whatever psychological drives are reduced by being elected to public office. A representative can be slightly more representative on a particular issue involving public opinion if the attitudes of people are distributed in the form of a J-curve and if his own attitude conforms to that of the vast majority—in this case he represents everyone except the individuals whose non-conforming attitudes give rise to the J's tail.

The unavoidable unrepresentativeness of representatives

has at least two important political consequences. Firstly, it may mean that politicians have a degree of expertness higher than that of some, most, but not all of their constituents. They may be more intelligent or influential; they may be better educated or more economically secure. As a result, they can be in a more advantageous position to envision the results of political decisions—or they may simply conclude that they are. Sometimes, too, the representatives acquire expertness after being elected: members of Congressional committees in the United States, for example, learn procedures and facts which enable them to function more effectively. Then, secondly, the judgments of representatives are certain to be affected by their own unrepresentative personalities or by their own not necessarily typical social-class interests. It does not inevitably follow that such judgments are not "beneficial" to the majority of the people or even to groups and individuals whose status is different from that of their representative. Franklin D. Roosevelt's upper class status, for example, apparently did not prevent him from adopting a policy of aiding labor unions, although that status doubtless had a marked effect on his foreign policies, especially those relating to the British Empire. Representatives, in a word, represent not only public opinion *en masse* but also themselves and the specialized forces within the community.

Lippmann (*23*), having established the unstable grounds on which public opinion is formed, then suggests that people should be and in fact only are consulted when an issue has already produced its protagonists. This view appears to be a rather accurate description of the state of affairs in democratic society, but it could be debated on the level of political philosophy. Ordinarily it is recognized that in politics as in all other fields, men and women do not have, or cannot be made to have, central attitudes on every issue. A revision of the tax rate, for example, interests only those who are immediately affected, even though such a change in the government's fiscal policy may begin a trend which eventually involves almost everyone. A factual study of nonvoters in the United States (*5*)—and about one-third of

those eligible to vote do not go to the polls in a presidential
year—reveals that these individuals tend to have relatively
little formal education and to be economically less secure; to
be more satisfied than are voters with American politics,
with the established form of government, and in general
with the status quo; and perhaps to have less knowledge
about political affairs. Evidently there is some relation between non-voting on the one hand and interest and knowledge on the other.

In practice, each problem of government cannot be submitted to the people. There are day-by-day decisions which
have to be made with dispatch and there is simply no time
to consult public opinion. Only a few experts inside the
government possess the required technical knowledge concerning certain matters. Even the citizens of a democratic
country have few formal and established ways of expressing
themselves. Election day is one such way. In the United
States the practice of the initiative and the referendum exists in twenty states and that of recall in twelve; in theory
such machinery enables people to be consulted between elections and on a greater number of proposals at election time.
In England unscheduled elections, which occur when the
party in power feels it is no longer receiving the parliamen-
tary support it requires, give the electorate an opportunity
to pass judgment on the broad, general policies of the contending political parties. Before the last war there was
considerable agitation in the United States to have people
make the most crucial decision of all—whether or not to go
to war. The Ludlow Amendment which would have given
Americans that right, however, was killed in the House of
Representatives. Events after Pearl Harbor moved so
quickly that there was little time for public opinion to become articulately external.

Since a continuous series of referenda in a democracy is
obviously impractical and since people frequently demand to
be heard, public opinion expresses itself and representatives
become acquainted with public opinion in less formal ways.
The political party, it has been pointed out (*26*), arose in
the United States as a device for people to band together in

order to achieve their own self-appointed objectives. It continually offers the average citizen, who hesitates to see government officials, the opportunity to complain to someone—the ward boss, for example—whose recognized duty it is to listen to complaints and, if possible, to take appropriate action. Groups with money and power seek directly to influence the decisions of government by employing lobbyists whose function it is to exert direct pressure upon officials; or as an organization with some prestige they make known their desires to those officials with or without the implied threat of "do as we say or else we'll vote you out of office." Elected officials, moreover, deliberately talk informally with their constituents. American voters are supposed to avail themselves of the privilege of writing their Congressional representatives to make known their views on governmental activities. Then, in addition, ordinary people have some effect on the viewpoint expressed by the mass media of communication which in turn are consulted by officials interested in "the public reaction" to events. Finally and more recently, there are the public opinion polls whose status among legislators and administrators has been discussed in an earlier chapter.

There is some question, however, whether public opinion is really expressed through these informal devices. Results from polls may be truly representative in a sampling sense but, as has been indicated, instrument errors make those results misleading or at least ambiguous. According to a Gallup poll in the summer of 1946, only 14 percent of Americans had ever written their Congressmen or Senators, and 36 percent of these letter-writers claimed they communicated in this fashion because some other "person or organization suggested it." A study of a sample of mail received by all Congressmen on the issue of repealing the Neutrality Act in 1939 (*14*) and one of a sample of mail received by a small number of Congressmen on the issue of the Selective Service Bill in 1940 (*28*) revealed that the letters gave a very distorted impression of public opinion as measured by polls. In general, according to one study (*19*), these very letters from the public are considered by Con-

gressmen to rank first among ways open to them to determine the state of public opinion. Pressure groups by definition can represent only the organized and not public opinion
in general. The knowledge of public opinion that government officials possess, therefore, may be inaccurate, biased,
or inadequate.

It is in the voting procedure and in political parties where
the more important short- as well as long-run effects of
democratic public opinion must be sought. Why people
vote as they do is a question which fascinates both the candidate or politician and the voters themselves. Politics in
fact is the art of finding the devices which will gain the support of the electorate, that is, of public opinion or of important segments thereof. Stimuli are employed which will
arouse favorable responses in people who, consequently, will
vote for one individual or party rather than another. In a
democracy like England or the United States—and to a
lesser degree in all countries where free elections prevail—
one of the most effective stimuli is the party label. Between
1940 and 1946, Gallup polls in the United States reveal,
about 20 percent of the American people considered themselves "independents" at a given moment and probably their
preferences, therefore, determined the outcome of presidential elections. The rest, according to their own testimony, were Republicans, Democrats, or members of minority parties. Very few of the self-styled party members
actually participated in a party organization; nevertheless
they felt themselves favorably disposed toward one party
rather than another. Approximately half of a panel of
voters in Erie County, Ohio, had decided in May 1940 for
which party they would vote in November, even though at
the time neither of the two major presidential candidates
had been nominated (*21*).

Naturally party leaders seek to build up the prestige of
their labels by frequent references to past and present accomplishments and by the kind of petty but very significant
personal services rendered by the ward boss and others
higher up the line. This record may be exaggerated by the
politicians, it may be misinterpreted by the electorate, but

it nevertheless must be quite decisive in determining voting preferences Some individuals vote the party ticket because their families have done so for generations; or there may be regional traditions (as in the South and in many rural areas) from which few deviations occur. Yet the political complexion of an area or the country does change over a period of time, which means—aside from the important consideration of the merits or demerits of the particular candidates running for office—that the fluctuating rewards and punishments incurred from the domination of one party eventually have their effects upon the party labels. The differences between the major American parties may be of the tweedledum-and-tweedledee variety, as they tended to be in the era from the end of World War I to the time of Franklin D. Roosevelt, but eventually they impress themselves upon the electorate.

At a given moment the stimulus "Democratic party" or "Republican party" arouses a series of responses which leads to a favorable or unfavorable attitude. Consider, for example, the responses aroused by those labels in the month of February 1946—six months after the war against Japan had ended and ten months after Mr. Truman had succeeded Mr. Roosevelt. According to Gallup polls at that time:

1. Fourteen percent of Americans believed that the Democratic party was "most interested in persons of above average," 46 percent in those of "average income," and 61 percent in those of "below average income." The corresponding figures for the Republican party were, respectively, 57, 21, and 10 percent. These figures seem to show that the Republicans tended to be identified with the wealthy and the Democrats with the poor. Democrats in the polling sample agreed that Republicans were most interested in the wealthy and Republicans that the Democrats showed most concern for the poor. A larger percentage of Democrats than the Republicans, moreover, was convinced of its own party's interest in persons of average income.

2. Most Americans believed that the Democrats rather than the Republicans could handle the following problems: "dealing with world affairs," "keeping wages high," and "keeping farmers' income high." Conversely, more people had greater faith in the Republicans regarding: "encouraging new business to start," "keeping taxes from getting too high," and "keeping business profits high." Opinion was

almost evenly divided as to which party could cope more effectively with: "reducing strikes and labor troubles" and "running the government efficiently."

That the responses to these political labels vary with events is shown by the reactions of Americans to the one problem of "reducing strikes and labor troubles" over a short period of time. Asked by Gallup which Party had the advantage in dealing with the problem, successive samples responded as follows:

Party having advantage	Oct. '45	Feb. '46	Oct. '46
Democratic	41	38	23
Republican	31	36	46
Neither	28	26	31

In October of 1945 the great postwar strikes were just beginning, and so the Democrats' reputation in respect to reducing labor problems was still intact. Then as strikes continued during Mr. Truman's administration the Republican label gained in prestige.

The specific devices employed by politicians to impress the electorate are variations of general propaganda techniques and will be considered in later chapters as propaganda is analyzed. They range from the general promises of reward which the political platform offers to the kind of vague ego-satisfaction or identification which parents feel when their baby has been kissed by a candidate. They include the appeal to tradition and idealism as well as transporting the voter to the poll and purchasing his vote. They are based on the plea of love-me-because-I-love-you as well as on the cry of hate-him-because-he-means-only-misery. They vary from a voice on a national hook-up to one behind a soap box on a street corner. Politics is propaganda in the best and worst buckshot tradition.

Every politician and campaign manager knows, in addition, that he cannot trample upon public opinion in his effort to seduce people to vote as he wishes. He must keep his ear to the ground, his finger on the public pulse, his nose in the air, his eyes on the target, and so on until even his brain is aware of what people want and do not want. Patronage, the well-timed favor, and the political club room are employed to impress specific people in the hope that they will then spread the appropriate word to their friends. On a national scale in the United States, the climax of diagnosing the public comes in the formulation of the party platform. Here every effort is made to use the cliché-stimuli which will touch off the greatest number of responses favorable to one party and unfavorable to the other; to state the issues of the day in such general terms that almost all of the heterogeneous groups which compose the United States will somehow be vaguely pleased; to tailor the promises to the most promising candidates but to make them so unspecific that the party commits itself virtually only in favor of virtue and against sin; and to suggest with a rhetorical flourish that the victory of one party will mean a virtual state of Nirvana and its defeat the kind of chaos only otherwise produced by the explosion of an atomic bomb.

Public opinion in a democracy, moreover, may be contemptuously thought of as a kind of putty by fascists, but it cannot be considered quite so malleable when its effects on politics and politicians are observed. The representative of the people realizes constantly that he must be re-elected and, even when he has decided to retire or is ineligible for re-election, he knows he has an obligation to his friends and party; therefore he reminds himself again and again that ultimately he or his associates are dependent upon public opinion. If he favors one type of legislation rather than another, he cannot forget that his vote will be part of the public record and will influence people's attitudes toward him. Periodically while in office and permanently afterwards he must return to the community which has elected him. Privately he may view with great cynicism the letters from his constituents or the conversations he holds with some of them, but publicly he must show the greatest respect for their words. The party itself may be controlled by a small clique of bosses, but even their smoke-ridden conclaves must frequently be devoted to the problem of what people want. Since a party, moveover, is a social group with particular rules of organization, it is always possible for a collection of malcontents to bore from within and for the grassroots to smother the vermin.

The overall result of the political process in a democracy seems to be a kind of compromise. People seldom pick the candidates to be placed on the ballot, but they have an effect on the preliminary steps leading to the election. They seldom determine the precise nature of the platforms confronting them, but their needs are catered to as the documents are written. They are confronted with pre-established alternatives when they vote, but they have played some part in establishing the alternatives. The results of most elections are ambiguous because usually so many issues are involved, but even the most unscrupulous politician must make some effort to interpret what he calls "the mandate of public opinion" for the sake of his own future.

The dominant belief of democracy is that government exists for the people and that the people do not exist in order to serve the state. The available facts, however, indicate that public opinion is not the decisive factor in all situations and cannot be. In general, some people are listened to when they are determined to be heard, and all people are determined to be heard only when they feel that a crisis is at hand and that they themselves are personally involved. Government-by-public-opinion-only-in-a-crisis can be dangerous since it tends to relieve people and their representatives of important responsibilities. The people then have only a segmental interest in governmental affairs and their representatives have only a segmental concern for public opinion. Both await the crisis and may forget that most crises are the result of previous events whose impact in the preliminary stages is not always so striking. Democracy succeeds or fails as it manages to discover some point between government-by-public-opinion—which is not feasible and perhaps not desirable—and the crisis-approach.

To strive to reach such a point, the leaders and interested citizens place stress upon education. They believe that the electorate must become more completely aware of the issues which confront the country and should acquire as much of the relevant information as possible. What is discouraging about democracy in the modern world and what elsewhere has helped give rise to alternate forms of government is the increasing complexity of the affairs with which government must deal. If the forces of democracy have enabled information to be spread at an arithmetically increasing rate, it can be said without much exaggeration that technology and social changes have increased at a geometrical rate the amount of information which needs to be known for the electorate to be intelligent and reasonably expert.

Makeshift and ever-changing devices are employed to improve the relation between public opinion and government. Discussions and announcements of governmental decisions, for example, are placed on the public record, so that people will have an opportunity to pass judgment. Unfortunately some but not all of the most crucial decisions of government —those involving foreign relations and war itself—cannot be revealed for security or strategic reasons. Then efforts are made to equalize the unequal strength of the contending factions in a country by having citizens who are not members of organized groups testify before legislative committees; by requiring that all political candidates (including the small minority parties in the United States) be given an equal opportunity to use the radio; and by stimulating public forums at which everyone is encouraged to express himself.

Many Americans appear to display greater interest in a national campaign than they do in local politics and they are more likely to know the names of cabinet members than of the Congressmen from their own state or of the officials in their own county. This means many things. The popular media of communication give more publicity to cabinet members than to Congressmen. Americans are drawn to a contest: some of the attitudes aroused by national politics resemble those associated with prize-fighting and horse-racing. The interests of the electorate in state, county, or local government are segmental, whereas those involving national politics—while not central—at least can be more easily and more frequently aroused.

At the same time, when a community is small, well organized, and politically conscious, public opinion has a more direct effect upon politics. The American prototype of such a community is the small New England town where public opinion is vividly expressed at an annual meeting. There the problems requiring political action, the individuals who perform the action, and the electorate itself are so well known that the dividing line between public opinion and political policy becomes very thin. The issues to be decided are ones affecting people directly and usually include some in which almost everyone has a rather high degree of expertness. Should a garbage-disposal truck be purchased? Should a kindergarten be added to the local school? Should the tax rate on property be raised so that a new community center can be constructed? In like manner the skills and the defects of the candidates for local office are generally well known, though they may be misappraised as a result of people's prejudices. Such an ideal relation between knowledge and attitude of course cannot be achieved on a national scale, but it can be argued that only by approximating this condition can the long list of names and proposals confronting the voters in the voting booth become more intelligible. To expect a well-informed electorate on every issue or candidate is just as wishful a bit of thinking as it is to anticipate that a smart dictator can completely disregard the people he rules. Neither is possible. Perhaps governmental activities in a democracy can become more meaningful to greater numbers of people through decentralization along regional lines (*9*).

Foreign Policy

The foreign policy of a country consists of both the ultimate and immediate objectives regarding other nations which that country's government seeks to achieve or actually does achieve. The political and economic domination of the world, a continent, a number of nations, or a single nation has been the ultimate objective of some countries, notably the fascist ones. Security—which usually means or should mean the ability to ward off attacks by other nations with or without outside assistance or to carry on international trade under specified conditions—has been the ultimate objective of other countries, notably the democratic ones. Immediate objectives are usually considered to be means toward ultimate ones. A country seeks to conclude a non-aggression pact, to protect its merchants abroad, to agree on the exchange of cultural products like tourists or radio programs, or to sign a disarmament treaty when its foreign office believes that such an act will promote what it believes to be its destiny or welfare in the long run.

One of the principal sources of insecurity in the present world results from the fact that people in general do not know or cannot deduce with any degree of certainty either the ultimate or immediate objectives of many nations' foreign policies. Under such circumstances public opinion is bound to be either latent or, if actual, misinformed. Men and women in democratic countries wonder whether the Soviet Union is seeking ultimately to sovietize the entire world and whether therefore the swinging of an Eastern European country into the political or economic orbit of Russia represents a step in that direction. People in the Soviet Union or in Soviet-dominated countries are told that the United States and Great Britain wish ultimately to control the world economically in the tradition of nineteenth-century imperialism, and hence immediate proposals regarding international relations or trade are viewed with muttered suspicion. In addition, the inhabitants of a nation frequently believe they do not know what international goals their own country is seeking. Americans, for example, are not quite certain at any moment how far-reaching their country's agreements with Great Britain are and just what kind of relation with the Soviet Union is being sought. Sometimes people in general must conclude that the governmental officials charged with the responsibility of formulating and executing a foreign policy do not grasp too specifically what they themselves wish to achieve, or else that policies fluctuate with events.

The actual reasons for a nation's foreign policy are as diverse as the reasons for any complicated bit of behavior.

Geopoliticians like Spykman (27) emphasize that the country's economic resources and its geographical position vis-à-vis other countries are or should be decisive. Switzerland's foreign policy of peaceful cooperation with all countries is a function of its position within the heart of Europe, the difficulty of defending its frontiers which present no natural protection, and its dependence on foreign trade as a result of its own economic non-sufficiency. Other theorists and statesmen refer to less basic factors. There is historical tradition, such as that existing between the United States and Canada. There is the cultural bond, such as that existing between Great Britain and the United States or between Bulgaria and the Soviet Union. There is the determination of an individual, like Sir Cecil Rhodes or Adolf Hitler, or of a group, like soldiers or merchants, to have a country possess its places in the sun.

Usually public opinion does not play a direct part in the formulation of foreign policy. Democratic states have a group of experts like the Department of State in the United States or the Foreign Office in England who are charged with the responsibility of formulating and executing foreign policy. Major decisions, however, may originate elsewhere in the executive branch or in the legislative branch of the government, but they must eventually be approved by the latter. The leader of the country—the president or prime minister—may select an ultimate or an immediate objective and simply allocate the details to the foreign office. When Mr. Roosevelt signed the Atlantic Charter in 1940, he committed this country to a vaguely defined if gloriously sounding policy; then the Department of State was assigned in part the task of implementing that policy. The executives and legislators, moreover, are usually but not always guided by the experience of the foreign office when they concern themselves with foreign policy. That office is supposed to know the problems involved: it has more or less efficient intelligence-gathering facilities through which events and trends abroad are reported; it has had direct experience in the past in dealing with leaders and people of other nations; and hence in theory it is in the best position to predict what foreign reactions will be to a policy and how successful that policy is likely to be.

While the foreign office is called the servant of government and therefore of the people, it inevitably acquires a certain autonomy. Its experts have their prejudices for any number of reasons, and these prejudices are reflected both in the data and the advice concerning the area of their speciality which they present to their superiors. Its interpretation of policy at a given moment sometimes depends on the particular foreign-office official who is making the interpretation. During the last war, for example, the writer occasionally obtained different advice on the same psychological-warfare problem when he consulted various members of the Department of State. This was due not always to the absence of an official policy but to varying opinions concerning how that policy could be best implemented at a given moment through the information and propaganda disseminated in the name of the United States Government. Foreign policy, in short, functions through a bureaucracy and what emerges from most bureaucracies is usually affected by its passage through the individuals therein.

Public opinion may remain in the background as foreign policy is determined but it nevertheless exerts some pressure even under a dictatorship. The policy formulator at some point in his meditations attempts to calculate either what his own people wish or—at the very least—what they will tolerate. The concern for public opinion can function all down the line, from the leader of the country to the third clerk of the legation stationed in an unimportant nation. Whatever their motives at the time, both Mr. Roosevelt and Mr. Churchill must have considered how the statement of foreign policy embodied in the Atlantic Charter would appeal to the people of their own countries. Hitler could embark on a policy of aggressive diplomacy and action toward his neighbors only after the propaganda campaign he began in the early twenties had convinced enough Germans that their personal welfare was threatened by the Treaty of Versailles and the encircled position in which Germany allegedly found herself (*10*). Public officials, no matter what their personal conviction, hesitate to commit their country to a policy which has a strong possibility of leading only to war when they feel that people are not yet ready to sanction or engage in conflict. Public opinion, as it were, sits in judgment on foreign policy, and it occupies this important seat because people eventually must support or reject acts committed in their name.

When foreign policy seems to run counter to public opinion, policy is not necessarily changed or abandoned. Instead the officials may conceal their action until a more propitious time for its revelation arrives, until—in their opinion—public opinion is "ripe" to be informed. Before or after the revelation, moreover, an "educational" campaign—really propaganda—may be conducted to gain popular support or at least to rationalize what has occurred. A significant trend in democratic countries is for foreign offices to rely a little less on secrecy and a little more on their public relations divisions.

The precise effects which public opinion has on foreign policy varies with the circumstances. The circumstances include the country, its system of government, the issues involved, and the public opinion of varied groups within the country. The lobbyists for certain business enterprises in the United States helped determine American foreign policy as reflected in high protective tariffs for many decades : here the public opinion of one group proved decisive. Spain's support of Germany and Italy during the last war was evidently a decision made by Franco and his clique : here public opinion was unimportant, although in fact Spaniards had to be propagandized before suicidally inclined or money-motivated volunteers could be secured for the unheroic Blue Division which fought on the Eastern Front. It all depends —that is the aggravating observation which must be made about the relation between public opinion and foreign policy. And yet there are limits beyond which even the most astute and powerful policy-maker cannot persuade or propagandize his people to go. Hitler could not squelch all opposition to his regime. The military authorities of Japan, in spite of the traditional loyalty and devotion of the Japanese to their country and its Emperor, experienced great difficulty in maintaining the morale of their kamikaze pilots before the time arrived for the final, downward plunge (*12*). These are limits which become more apparent during a war than in peacetime.

It is probably true that in a democracy public opinion is generally more influential in affecting foreign policy than under a dictatorship. Democratic officials subscribe at least verbally to the conviction that they are the servants of the people and they, therefore, hold themselves in readiness, more or less, to be influenced by that opinion. They may adopt the timeworn shibboleth of pointing out that people are incapable of making sound decisions because they lack the relevant facts—and this may be true although the reason for people's ignorance can result from the failure of the foreign office to reveal the facts. At the same time they usually wish their actions to be popular or they feel an obligation to win popularity for themselves. Public outcry against a policy, public impatience with some diplomatic maneuvering, or public clamor for a change in strategy or tactics affects officials since they, too, are part of the public and they accord a certain amount of respect to the media through which the public partially expressed itself. Matters of foreign policy frequently enter into domestic political campaigns or, as in England, are discussed in party conferences.

Public opinion may even loom large in some of the foreign policies formulated by dictators. Here the effect of public opinion is quite indirect. The leaders may realize that internal public opinion is restive, perhaps because the food ration is low, perhaps because more political freedom is desired. A vigorous and carefully considered foreign policy may then be formulated and executed which distracts the people from their woes and enables them either to displace some of their aggression or to find a compensatory outlet. It has been said that a happy nation never wants to fight. Nor does an unhappy one, but it can be made to prefer fighting to misery and to displace its aggression upon an out-group (7).

Frequently diplomats are concerned with public opinion inside their own countries not simply because they wish to please their fellow countrymen for some conscientious, political, or necessary reason but because they seek to employ the fact of their popular support at home as a weapon in their own encounters with foreign diplomats. If they can say that the policy they are pursuing truly represents the will of their people—and offer proof thereof—they will be listened to more attentively than if their opponents know that their views are not representative or in fact unpopular. Foreign offices—including even the American State Department—maintain specialists in public relations whose responsibility it is to disseminate information concerning their own activities and objectives.

In addition, modern governments make more or less systematic efforts to win support for their policies not only at home but also abroad. The reasoning here seems involved but is really very simple: if friends in foreign countries are acquired, then those individuals sooner or later may be able to affect their own foreign offices or diplomats in a manner which can help the country they like or respect. Nowadays almost all nations, therefore, have established so-called "information offices" throughout the world which disseminate general information about themselves as well as specific information or propaganda in behalf of particular policies. Before the United States entered the war, for example, the Nazis were convinced that they could not convert officials of the American government to their point of view and therefore they made every effort to affect public opinion—by and large unsuccessfully—through shortwave radio, handouts about Germany and her enemies from the so-called German Library of Information, subsidies granted German-American and American sympathizers, and rumor-mongers. At the close of the last war, the United States felt that its policies were not reaching the peoples of Southeastern Europe because of local censorship. In an effort to break through that censorship and thus ultimately to create antagonism toward a Soviet-dominated foreign policy and enthusiasm for Anglo-American policies, radio broadcasts were beamed to those countries and information was distributed locally by American technicians stationed there. In at least one instance—that of Yugoslavia—the local "United States Information Service" office was ordered closed by the local authorities who apparently objected to the free flow of information. The American Department of State, moreover, increased its own prewar efforts, which had been largely insignificant, to reach people of other countries through "cultural relations" by taking over as many of the wartime informational activities of the Office of War Information in Europe, Africa, Australia, and Asia, and those of the Office of Inter-American Affairs in Latin America (*8, 20*) as Congressional appropriations permitted.

Many of the delegates to both the Security Council and the General Assembly of the United Nations have often not debated the issue at hand but have utilized their right to speak as a sounding board to express and secure world publicity for their own nations' particular viewpoints. The United Nations itself has been conscious of world public opinion almost from its very inception. It employs more and more media of communication to give people everywhere a knowledge of its problems and policies. Its general hope has been that a world organization can succeed only if people favor the ideal of global cooperation rather than that of national sovereignity.

Community Customs

The sentence, "public opinion is against it," or its equivalent is frequently expressed to indicate latent or actual disapproval of behavior within a community. In the United States, for example, public opinion on some issues can be expressed negatively:

A woman should not propose to a man.
Men should not tell women off-color jokes.
People should not have extra-marital sexual relations.
Parents should not neglect their children.
Children should not disobey their parents.

Laxatives should not be advertised on the radio.
Contraceptives should not be sold openly.
Nudity in the movies should not be permitted.
The press should not be censored.
Communists should not be allowed to teach school.
The church should not engage in politics.
A man should not be hit when he is down.
Men should not boast about their wealth.
The privacy of a man's home should not be invaded.

Almost all of these illustrative tabus in American life are customs which spring from the cultural heritage. Each has its own history and serves some function in modern-day society. Some are embodied in legal statutes or ordinances, while others are enforceable only through the pressure which public opinion can exert. That pressure can indeed be various. There is ostracism: people who do not follow the code are treated like strangers or with hostility, and they are prevented from participating socially in the community or in the social class whose edicts they have violated. In addition to other prerequisites, an appropriate set of manners is required of those who would rise in the social-class scale. These manners vary with the class into which the individual strives to climb; but no manners, no mobility (6).

There can be the threat of legal action. People are told that, unless they conform, they will be publicly prosecuted or a law is passed which enables such prosecution to occur. There is expulsion from the social group, such as being excommunicated from a religious sect for misbehavior as defined by that sect. There is remonstration: frequently even your best friend does tell you to be careful not merely about your bodily scent but about your general reputation among the respectable.

Internal and external opinion regarding a custom do not necessarily agree. People may really favor an innovation as they discuss the matter with themselves or their friends, but their public stand may be different for fear of being socially punished or of violating their own consciences acquired while they were being socialized in a particular atmosphere. A number of years ago, for example, 92 percent of the Methodists in an upper-New York state community stated in a rather formal interview that their Bishop, in selecting a minister for them each year, had "made a real effort in behalf of the community." When the "private" rather than the "public" attitudes were informally determined by investigators (*24*) who had won their confidence, only 31 percent of the same group gave the Bishop their unqualified endorsement.

Similarly people's actions can be different from their attitudes toward customs. During the uncomfortable days of prohibition in the United States, it used to be said that people voted dry and drank wet. It is quite clear why they drank wet, and it is reasonably certain that many of them voted dry in order to be in accord with what they considered to be actual public opinion. Other people, however, despised prohibition but never drank: their attitude toward obeying any law, they said, rather than their feelings about liquor governed their behavior.

The inhabitants of a community may be convinced that public opinion favors or opposes a current practice when actually only a strongly and effectively organized minority is managing to externalize its own and not the majority's attitudes. Such an invalid measure of public opinion can result from some process like projection: the respectable person wants everyone else to be equally respectable and hence he thinks that they are. Or it may be due to faulty perception facilitated by the minority's propaganda. A decade or more ago in the United States, for example, Dr. Townsend and his followers appeared to be gaining nation-wide support for a plan to tax all business transactions 2 percent; then every citizen over 59 years of age would receive a monthly pension of $200, provided he spent the full amount within thirty days. Townsendites spoke and wrote so loudly and continuously that 95 percent of Americans became aware of this proposal and some Congressmen began to feel that they would have to take action because of the pressure of public opinion. In the midst of the excitement, a Gallup poll calmly revealed that most groups—except those who would be directly benefited—were opposed to the plan (2).

Public opinion regarding customs appears to be like a sweet and innocent maiden waiting to be violated but fortified by the knowledge that men and women everywhere will spring to her defense. People have both favorable and unfavorable attitudes toward society, but usually the drive strength of the former is greater than that of the latter. Then they themselves help reinforce the favorable attitudes by imagining the dire consequences of non-conformity. What is imagined, however, springs from important drives, attitudes, and knowledge within themselves. Real or unreal, it serves a useful purpose and cannot be easily dissipated. Only rarely does a child appear with sufficient innocence to point out that the king, whose wondrous garments the population has been admiring, is really walking about naked. Or he says to the people who would defend the threatened maiden: don't defend her, she really wants an attack.

The Nature of Propaganda

━━━━━━━━━━━━━━━━━━━━━━━━━━━━━━━━

AN EFFECTIVE way in Anglo-Saxon so-
ciety to insult, belittle, or expose a man is to call him a
propagandist. Since a propagandist is an individual who
influences other individuals, apparently the influencing of
others is considered dishonorable. The situation, however,
is not quite so simple. For calling a man an educator reveals a respectful attitude toward him, except when he is
labelled a "professor," in which case attention is also being
called to his impracticality. But an educator is likewise an
individual who influences other individuals.

Why, then, is "propagandist" an epithet in our society?
Almost any other name sounds sweeter to most people. If
a man is not called an educator, he seems to prefer to be
known as a publicity agent, a public relations counsel or
officer, an advertising agent or account executive, a salesman,
a promoter, a barker, a preacher, a lecturer, or even a
politician. What was called propaganda acquired such unpleasant connotations during the 1920's and 1930's that the
word was avoided whenever possible when war began again
in 1939. Both in the United States and Great Britain, consequently, the home front, allies, and neutral countries were
provided not with "propaganda" but with "information."
In most instances even the enemy was not weakened by
"propaganda": Americans attacked him through the use of
"psychological warfare" and the British via "political war-

fare." Sometimes Americans concerned with propaganda to the enemy called themselves "psychological warriors," the British counterpart to which naturally became "political warriors." Consider, too, the very names of the American organizations charged with propaganda functions at various times during the war: Office of Facts and Figures, Office of Government Reports, Office of the Coordinator of Information, Office of the Coordinator of Inter-American Affairs, Office of War Information, Psychological Warfare Branch (or Division), etc. There was only one exception: an unimportant, publicity-shunning Propaganda Branch of Military Intelligence in Washington, D. C.

More than a matter of mere semantics is involved in the efforts to dodge the word "propaganda" or "propagandist." In other countries with different cultures the word is quite respectable or at least as respectable as any of the equivalents our ingenious language and our beleaguered propagandists have devised. Its derivation, moreover, is respectable: its Latin ancestor is the word "to propagate" or "to sow." Its currency increased during the seventeenth century for an equally respectable reason: it was part of the official titles of two Catholic organizations charged with the responsibility of "propagating the faith" through foreign missions and of training priests to become missionaries. Words in general, it seems, acquire unpleasant connotations for very good reasons. The tabooed words in our vocabulary, most of which relate directly or indirectly to religion, sex, and the eliminative processes, have been more or less outlawed because the behavior they represent is in fact also taboo or strictly regulated. Similarly the prejudice against "propaganda" must mean that people are hostile toward the activity they associate with propaganda. The inquiry into why propaganda is disliked must be searching and complete. Otherwise the nature of propaganda as well as the society in which it functions cannot be understood.

Education

The inquiry can best begin by considering education, that formal part of the process of socialization in which an older or more experienced individual influences other younger or less experienced individuals. Certainly one important aim of education is to increase knowledge. The knowledge may consist of the manipulation of numbers, called arithmetic; the accepted way to write sentences, called penmanship, spelling, syntax, or grammar; the best method of repairing an automobile, called physics, engineering, or mechanics; the duties and obligations of a citizen, called civics; the correct manner of behaving in social situations, called etiquette; or the desirable beliefs concerning God, the purpose of life, and the hereafter, called religion or philosophy. A man's education is said to be good or bad. It is good if he learns a great deal *and* if he learns the "right" kinds of things. It is bad if he learns too little *or* if he learns the "wrong" kinds of things. But what is "right" and what is "wrong"?

A question like this, though profound and puzzling, cannot be relegated to jesting Pilate or the reader's intuition or prejudice. Each person must be deliberately aware of what he considers right or wrong before he can pass judgment on education or distinguish education from propaganda. The problem of values cannot be avoided.

Any child from the age of one (or less) begins to acquire his parents' language. This knowledge is essential from the viewpoint of both the child and his parents. It facilitates, for example, communication between the two. The moron's limited knowledge of language is one of his principal handicaps. The language that is learned by the child may be imperfect: it may be a class-typed dialect which forever after will make it difficult for him to rise in the social scale; it may not be so efficient or considered by some to be so beautiful as another language; or it may not belong to the linguistic family from which as an adult the child will be compelled to learn another language. At any rate, by being forced to learn the language his parents speak, the child is both psychologically and physiologically prejudiced against other versions of that language and against other languages, as any English-speaking adult knows who has vainly attempted to learn the pronunciation, for example, of the letters *l* or *r* in German, French, or Spanish. The child, in acquiring the language of his parents, has been educated; but the education has been dictatorially if unconsciously imposed without his permission and has biased him against all other ways of talking.

The grade-school teacher is giving a spelling lesson. She tells the children that the correct spelling of "through" is "t-h-r-o-u-g-h." One boy, who is neither bright nor stupid, asks her why it is not spelled phonetically: "t-h-r-u." She tells him that only her version is the correct one and that his is unacceptable except to a few radicals and crackpots who advocate simplified spelling. Thereafter he always writes "t-h-r-o-u-g-h" and throughout his life is prejudiced against "t-h-r-u." Or the same teacher writes the word "itch" on the blackboard and then explains that other words in English containing the sound of "itch" are similarly spelled; for example, she jots down this word-family:

pitch
ditch
stitch
hitch
witch
bitch

She then may lose her job not because she is a poor teacher —after all, *rich, niche,* and *which* all contain the sound of *itch* although the letter *t* is absent—but because American children are not supposed to be taught to spell a word like *bitch.* "But, Mr. Superintendent, I was only illustrating what happens when a *b* is added to *itch,* and I was thinking of a type of dog, not of the filial expression you have in mind."

Another school teacher—and here an illustration will be constructed on the basis of one suggested by Freeman (5) —is planning an arithmetic lesson and wants to select an exercise from one of the following:

1. Divide 60 by 80.
2. A man wishes to borrow $80, but his friend lends him only $60. What percentage of the amount he wanted does he obtain?
3. Medical and health authorities agree that a family of four re-

quires a minimum wage of $80 per week. The John J. Jones Company in our town pays most of its workers only $60 per week. What percentage of a decent minimum wage do these workers receive?

4. If we do not use our atomic bombs against Russia within the near future, Russia will design her own atomic bomb to use against us. According to General John J. Jones, 60 out of every 80 people in a city struck by an atomic bomb are likely to be killed and the rest will be severely hurt. What percentage of people in our city will be killed by the atomic bomb which Russia will explode in our midst?

The identical arithmetical process is involved in all four exercises. The first is straight arithmetic. No teacher in the United States would hesitate to use the second because borrowing money is both frequent and respectable in American society. But the third raises a problem: even though the pupils only have to divide 60 by 80, there is the suggestion—which might more properly be expressed by union organizers or even communists—that the John J. Jones Company underpays most of its workers who therefore must be suffering from malnutrition and who certainly are not able to follow the good life. And the fourth illustration seems to possess an anti-Soviet undertone which has little to do with arithmetic; it might be more acceptable to some school boards than the third.

Spelling and arithmetic are ordinarily considered to be "pure" subjects which do not give rise to controversy. A child has to learn to spell and calculate, and that is that. Other subjects involving the child's or even the college student's social environment are recognized as problem-producing. They can be briefly illustrated by intercepting a few remarks which an American teacher or instructor might make in the classroom:

1. *History*: "You know that in the North where I was born and lived until I came here a few years ago that war is called the 'Civil War.' Personally I would much rather call it that than the 'War Between the States.' And I want you to. For it really was a civil war: the North wanted to prevent the South from seceding and from having slaves, and the South. . . ."

2. *Civics*: "What we really have been talking about is the way our city government is supposed to work according to the charter we have. In practice, though, the picture is quite different. Our councilmen don't vote as they wish or as the people they represent wish. They do what the political bosses tell them to do. Graft also is involved because. . . ."

3. *Geography*: "The capital of Puerto Rico is San Juan and the island has an area of 3,435 square miles. Most of the million and a half inhabitants are of Spanish or Negro origin and all of them have been helped in some way or other by the United States. In fact ever since we liberated Cuba from Spain and undertook to spread our civilization to Puerto Rico. . . ."

4. *Economics*: "We shall begin our study of economics by reading Karl Marx. Your first assignment is Chapters 1–3, inclusive, of his *Capital*, which I consider to be the most penetrating book ever written on our economic system. After you have understood Marx thoroughly, you will be in a better position to evaluate the classical economists who talk about supply and demand, the so-called law of diminishing returns. . . ."

Perhaps it is no longer necessary to belabor the point that the curriculum of formal education is permeated with value-judgments. It is tempting to do so, however, because it is not easy to stand off and detect those judgments: the individual's knowledge and attitudes make him frequently incapable of perceiving bias in his own thinking. The New Englander who shares the approach to the "Civil War" which the teacher from that area is using in a Southern classroom would think it right and proper to present the war from the Northern viewpoint; but the Southern parents of the children might call the teacher a "Northern propagandist." Few people would disagree that the formal functioning of municipal government should be explained in the school, but many might wonder whether a realistic approach to ward politics is a proper subject for immature minds which might thereby grow disillusioned. No one doubts that the capital of Puerto Rico is San Juan and that this United States possession contains so-and-so-many square miles; but readers of the *New Republic* and the *Nation* might disagree with the particular version of American colonial policy being taught. The illustration from eco-

nomics is not an imaginary one: it represents a more or
less accurate quotation from the introductory remarks of an
instructor in a foreign country whose approach to the subject shocked the writer completely since he had previously
studied economics as economics is taught in American
colleges.

Ultimately the values involved in what is called education
can be assayed by considering the effect of the teaching on
those who are taught. Sixty divided by 80 is .75 when the
operation is carried to two decimal points—this is a true
statement. But the effect of learning to carry on the operation can be a function of the example's context, whether that
context be a loan between friends, sub-standard wages, or
atomic warfare. That there was a conflict in the United
States which began in 1861 and ended in 1865 is a fact, but
the interpretation of that conflict being given by the Northern teacher is one which is not considered quite accurate by
historians (including those in the North) and any interpretation inevitably produces different responses in North-
ampton, Mass., from those which occur in Natchez, Miss.
Whether or not ward politicians control councilmen is a
question of fact which can be settled by investigation, but
teaching the fact—if it be one—may have the disillusioning
effect the advocates of idealism suggest or it may produce
more politically sophisticated citizens. Karl Marx—and
not Adam Smith, George Washington, or Winston Churchill—did write *Capital* which is therefore a book in economics
to be found in many civilized libraries, but the economic and
social views of a student who reads that book and no other
treatise in economics are likely to be quite different from
those held by a contemporary who has been assigned a text
written by a classical or neo-classical economist.

The implications of this discussion can best be summarized
by defining education as *the imparting of knowledge or skill
considered to be scientific or to have survival value in a
society at a particular time.* This definition, like most so-
called intensional or connotative definitions, does not resolve
perplexing problems but rather calls attention to their existence. In the first place, what is scientific knowledge? It is

knowledge which competent men in a society agree is correct
and which is therefore subject to verification. Water contains two molecules of hydrogen and one of oxygen, a fact
which chemists can verify in their laboratory and which
laymen, if they wish to achieve the competency of chemists,
can also verify. As of this moment and among us, therefore,
the teaching of this fact and its accompanying theoretical
structure is education. The parents in a primitive society
who tell their child that the sun is a large lake reflecting the
light from the earth are teaching him an alleged fact with
which the competent of their society—perhaps the priests—
presumably agree, but it is a pre-scientific fact which cannot
be verified. From our viewpoint, consequently, the parents
are not educators but from theirs they are.

The teaching of the belief about the sun, moreover, may
be absolutely essential in that particular society. The ado-
lescent who has not learned the "fact" will be debarred from
entering the religious society he must join if he is to be allowed to select a wife, to grow his own pigs, to win prestige
in inter-tribal warfare, etc. The knowledge possesses survival value in the society at the particular time. No
question of science or of verification is involved in calling
such knowledge part of the socialization process of this
group and hence education.

Scientific skill consists of a system of responses which are
best adapted to the problem at hand. The novice who is
told that to apply the foot brakes on an automobile it is
most efficient to lean down and press the right pedal with
his left hand is acquiring a rather foolish skill in terms of
both the construction of the car and his own body; he is not
being educated. The learning of the parental language, imperfect as it may be, is essential for the child; it is part of
his education and so considered by everybody, including even
this writer.

The foregoing definition of education is deliberately relativistic: whether knowledge or skill is to be called education
depends on the state of science at the time and on what is
broadly considered necessary for survival by the society or
particular sub-groups therein. A swift glance at any anthro-

pological treatise (*cf. 8*) is usually sufficient to convince the student of man that almost any type of behavior, including kinds which seem horrible or barbarous to people in our society, has been tolerated or encouraged somewhere or by people at some period in their development. Values in this sense are relativistic, as are the goals of socialization.

Science, too, is relativistic since what is considered or can be demonstrated to be true or false changes as men's knowledge accumulates. Until the acceptance of Galileo's conception of the universe, the well-educated man in European society had to subscribe to the Ptolemaic view that the earth is the center of the universe. Now the hypothesis is thought to be false or inadequate, and it has been discarded from all modern educational systems except those advocated by certain religious sects. At this point there arises again a troublesome difference between the natural and the social sciences. In the natural sciences facts and theories can be decisively if only eventually verified or disproved by the observation of the competent: there is a definite procedure to determine truth or falsity. In the social sciences, on the other hand, verification is much more difficult in almost all instances because observation of people is more complicated and hence the methods of ascertaining truth or falsity are less clear-cut (*3*). The well-educated Soviet economist, for example, is grounded in Marxism and his American counterpart in Adam Smith or one of Smith's modern successors; the difference here is a function not only of the social acceptability accorded the doctrines but also of their scientific character concerning which men of corresponding competency in both societies are unable to agree. Similarly there are historical facts, which means that there is convincing evidence at hand to show that certain events occurred in the past, but the interpretation of those events—the attempt, for example, to establish cause-and-effect sequences—gives rise to argument and leads to little or no agreement. Much of the content of social science, as a result, cannot be considered education in the present sense of the word. Frequently all that a social science has to offer as education is a scientific way of approach to the study of man, in addition to some facts and a few hypotheses which in all honesty ought always to be clearly labelled as tentative.

In short, the "right" kind of education consists of learning facts and theories which can be verified or of subscribing to points of view which are considered "good," "just," "beautiful," or "necessary" in the society. The "wrong" kind promotes unverified or unverifiable facts and theories as well as "bad," "unjust," "ugly," or "unnecessary" points of view. The educator has prestige in our society because it is presumed that he teaches what people want and need to be taught, in order to be socialized according to our standards. If he mixes radicalism with arithmetic or exposés with civics, he is branded a propagandist by the majority of people in the United States. If he mixes imperialism with geography or capitalism with economics, he is likewise angrily labeled a propagandist certainly not by the majority but by the radical-minded minority. Pick your science or the values you consider important in your society, and then you can decide what education is.

The Scope of Propaganda

Propaganda is not education as education has been here defined. Propaganda can be called *the attempt to affect the personalities and to control the behavior of individuals toward ends considered unscientific or of doubtful value in a society at a particular time.* What has been said of education applies to propaganda but in a reverse manner. The imparting knowledge which has not reached the scientific stage is propaganda, as is the teaching of a skill which is not adapted to the situation at hand. The dissemination of a viewpoint considered by a group to be "bad," "unjust," "ugly," or "unnecessary" is propaganda in terms of that group's standards.

This severe distinction between education and propaganda on the basis of science and survival value does not mean that the influence of an individual upon his contemporaries is clearly either one or the other. What almost always occurs is a combination of the two, or the influence can be variously appraised by observers with different conceptions of science and value. The learning of the parents' language by the child is education, for clearly it involves survival or the acquiring of a skill most suited to its particular environment. Not spelling "through" in simplified fashion is education, the majority of people in our society would say, but it is propaganda against simplified spelling, according to the advocates of this reform. The avoidance of the word "bitch" during the spelling lesson is an educational gesture by the teacher who knows that the use of this word in our society is maladaptive except among restricted groups of dog fanciers or among some individuals who feel impelled to make an unflattering reference to a male's maternal ancestry or a female's obnoxious characteristics. The rules and principles involved in arithmetical calculations are part of our educational process, but the illustrations employed for practising those calculations have an educational or a propaganda effect related not to arithmetic but to values considered important or unimportant, good or bad, etc. The social sciences as usually taught are mixtures of education and propaganda: to the extent that they teach verifiable facts or a scientific approach to a problem, they are education; to the extent that they rely upon dogmatism and obscurantism, they are propaganda from a scientific viewpoint but nevertheless also education in terms of the values possessed by special groups in a society.

To discriminate between education and propaganda, therefore, is not always easy. The individual attempting the discrimination must be aware of the state of scientific knowledge on a subject and must be conscious of the value judgments he is employing in his own thinking. It is tempting to say—as a popular cliché phrases it—that propaganda is what the other fellow is doing, but all that is being thereby expressed is disagreement with or antagonism toward the objectives that other fellow is seeking to attain. Individuals in Anglo-Saxon society do not like to be called "propagandists" because they recognize the hostility toward their scale of values which is thus implied. Propaganda is supposed to be underhanded or anti-social, but in fact

operates when there is no science or when people's values
are in conflict.

Propaganda acquired its bad reputation in this country
during the 1920's when countless writers and scholars exposed the lies which the propaganda machines of both sides
disseminated throughout World War I. In addition, "propaganda" is disliked in a democratic society because people
feel naively that their decisions should be made by themselves and not by someone else. The feeling is naive because
decisions result from past experiences, many of which are
usually culturally determined; but it is certainly in keeping
with the belief of our society that man, if he only will, can
shape his own destiny.

Admittedly the conception of propaganda here outlined
is broad and, it may be said, includes phenomena which
ordinarily are not so classified. It is felt, however, that no
sharp distinction can be made between the propaganda and
educational implications of most social processes and that
by focusing upon the science and values which they contain a
more useful insight into their nature can be obtained. Other
attempts to distinguish between education and propaganda,
moreover, seem to be relatively sterile or unincisive.

Toward the close of the debunking 1920's when the word
"propaganda" was particularly unpopular, Martin (*10*)
stated a point of view which continues to be widespread:

. . . Education aims at independence of judgment. Propaganda offers ready-made opinions for the unthinking herd. Education and
propaganda are directly opposed both in aim and method.

The educator aims at a slow process of development; the propagandist, at quick results. The educator tries to tell people *how* to think;
the propagandist, *what* to think. The educator strives to develop individual responsibility; the propagandist, mass effects. The educator
fails unless he achieves an open mind; the propagandist unless he
achieves a closed mind.

Martin's is the credo of a thinker in a democracy who wishes
to praise education and decry propaganda. But his phrases
are too general. Certainly the label "poison" on a bottle of
rubbing alcohol offers a "ready-made" opinion which should
not be disregarded; there can be nothing "slow" about the

"process of development" through which individuals must go if they are to profit from the warning; "what" should be the nature of thoughts people have concerning the contents of the bottle is scarcely left in doubt; and it would be foolhardy for anyone to question the label on his own "individual responsibility" in order thus to demonstrate that he has "an open mind" on the subject. It is, consequently, a purely verbal matter whether the label is called a propaganda or an educational attempt to affect people's behavior regarding the contents of the bottle. In addition, it is not possible to learn "how to think" unless the thinker thinks about something. That something may have propaganda implications, just as the exercise of a purely arithmetical principle may affect the individual's attitude toward certain social practices of his society.

Efforts have also been made to characterize propaganda in terms of the characteristic method which it allegedly employs. Lumley (*9*), for example, considers propaganda a form of "veiled" promotion and thus identifies certain activities which he chooses to attack. This crucial adjective, however, is vague; "veiled" from whose point of view it is legitmate to ask. More recently Henderson (*6*) has surveyed the definitions of propaganda which have wide currency and has decided that the essence of propaganda is the propagandist's effort to limit the "freedom of choice" available to the propagandees. It is true that propagandists do seek to restrict the responses which the propagandees can make, but educators likewise desire to eliminate responses from their students' repertoire—the false or the incorrect ones. The writer (*2*) once attempted to establish a sharp psychological distinction between education and propaganda: he maintained that education employs "suggestion" and propaganda does not. The difficulty here, he now realizes, is that he sought to dodge the problem of value and faced only the problem of science. To say, as he did, that what is learned in propaganda depends on the method of learning (*i.e.,* on suggestion) is to assume that only questions of fact are involved; but, since the customs prevalent in a society are also learned with or without the kind of learning he chose to call suggestion, the distinction has only a limited applicability.

The conclusion may be drawn that education and propaganda are special cases of learning which are evaluated in terms of certain specified or unspecified criteria. If the criteria are disregarded in making the analysis, then a distinction between education and propaganda need not be made. Both can be subsumed under some neutral concept like learning, tuition, instruction, presentation, expression, inducement, transmission, diffusion, or communication. It would be, perhaps, more efficient to use any one of these innocuous words which do not arouse violent or abusive emotions. Such a semantic manipulation, however, has one important shortcoming: the neutralization of terminology avoids even raising the problems of truth and goodness. After the explosion of the first few atomic bombs, many modern physicists no longer confined their thoughts to the description, prediction, and production of atomic energy—their traditional role in connection with any problem in physics—but of necessity began to make proposals concerning the control of this tremendous force. Both the work of the chairman of an adult forum studying a modern social problem and the deeds of a fifth columnist before the outbreak of a war are indeed illustrations of simple or complex "communication" and both involve suggestion or learning; but the problem of deciding what proportion of education and propaganda each communicates remains, if their efforts are to be fully evaluated. The words "education" and "propaganda," then, should be retained but with some misgiving because of the social connotations they have come to possess and because they are too frequently used as epithets.

It must be fully recognized, moreover, that propaganda is being employed here in a neutral sense to describe the influence of one person upon other persons when scientific knowledge and survival values are uncertain. From this viewpoint, propaganda is absolutely inevitable and cannot be exorcised by calling it evil-sounding names. All knowledge has not reached a scientific stage, and men who are thought to be competent do not always agree as to what is a scientific fact or theory even in our society. In the realm of social, political, and economic values, there is even less agreement and more prejudice. The faith of a free society is in its varied systems of values, each seeking expression and survival. At a given moment, none but a fool or a prophet will state which ultimately is true or untrue, which good or bad. Man's struggle to conquer his environment, to control himself, and to regulate his relations with his fellows is waged with half-truths which emotionally convince some and leave others unmoved, which fluctuate from generation to generation, and which cannot be eternally experienced or expressed. Only a complete dictatorship is free from propaganda, for then there is a single "truth" to be promoted and that "truth" must be considered true and good within the society. But those who by living in another country are not crushed by this dictator or who within the country have their own internal attitudes refer in shouts or whispers to the "propaganda" on which the regime is founded and subsists.

The last two sentences are a mixture of education and propaganda. They are educational to the extent that their characterization of dictatorship is accurate and would find agreement among those competent to judge. They are propaganda, too, since their mode of expression casts aspersions upon dictatorship and thus seeks to prejudice the reader still more against this form of government. The writer believes that dictatorship is "bad," but he cannot prove this belief in the sense that a chemist can demonstrate the distribution of hydrogen and oxygen in water. Even without completely convincing proof, however, he prefers to retain the belief and to propagandize in its behalf.

The Propagandist's Intention

There is an obvious but important difference between the individual who deliberately attempts to influence other people and the individual who unwittingly has a similar effect upon them. The advertising agent wants to promote the sale of a particular product, but the housewife who spontaneously praises the product in the presence of a friend is working toward the same end. The school teacher who has recently been converted to communism or vegetarianism prepares her lessons self-consciously and seeks an opportunity to score a point in favor of her new philosophy; but the spinster, who teaches her pupils after the gospel of the Republican party and other respectable doctrines which are prevalent in an American community and to which she herself subscribes, almost automatically absorbs and transmits these views of society. The enemy agent is paid to spread demoralizing stories, but the rumor-monger helps diffuse the tales not because he wishes to do so but because he thereby relieves some of his own personal anxiety. The advertising agent, the communist or the vegetarian school teacher, and the enemy agent are aware of a propaganda objective; whereas the housewife, the Republican and respectable school teacher, and the rumor-monger are rather blissfully unaware of the propaganda objectives their respective activities nevertheless achieve. The first group can be called intentional and the second unintentional propagandists. Intentional propagandists *deliberately* attempt to affect or control the behavior of a group of individuals, unintentional propagandists *unwittingly* do so.

Ordinarily the term "propagandist" refers only to an intentional propagandist whose efforts, when they are known, clearly represent an attempt to change people and their society. The unintentional propagandist, on the other hand, frequently is seeking to maintain the status quo, and hence his efforts are considered praise-worthy and educational. In addition, he does not or cannot appreciate the consequences of what he is doing and is usually horrified to be called a propagandist. Often the intentional propagandist can function more effectively than the unintentional propagandist because he can systematically vary the techniques he is employing to achieve his chosen objectives. But this advantage does not always exist. The unintentional propagandist occupies a position in society which enables him to have greater access to the media of communication. He behaves "naturally" and hence his propagandees have no reason to suspect his motives: "he may be prejudiced but he means well. . . ."

A propagandist can almost never anticipate the complete consequences of his own propaganda and therefore it must be said that some of those consequences are achieved unintentionally. One investigator (*11*), for example, produced attitude changes in American high school children on a variety of issues (such as capital punishment and the agricultural policies of the Roosevelt administration) by presenting them with clearcut points of view on the subjects. The average changes were in the direction of the propaganda materials. When "no conscious attempt" was made to change attitudes on the issue of divorce, no appreciable changes occurred. These changes, therefore, were in harmony with the propagandist's intentions and they tended to persist over a period of six months. Propaganda concerning labor unions made students, on the average, less favorably disposed toward these organizations, and, in addition, "sharply divided the group into two opposing tents." This last effect apparently was unforeseen; it was not observed in connection with the other issues; it must be called unintentional. Similarly, Chen (*1*) in the early thirties manipulated the attitudes of various groups of American college students toward the Sino-Japanese conflict over Manchuria by having them listen to intentionally pro-Chinese or Pro-Japanese "propaganda" speeches. What he considered in one instance to be "neutral material"—because it presented only the so-called "facts"—actually and to his own surprise made the students less pro-Chinese.

A group of investigators (*4*) who studied the effects which orientation films had on men in the United States Army during the last war discovered that sometimes changes in attitude would occur which were not desired or intended by the producers. The Soviet Union was not mentioned, for example, in a motion picture on "The Battle of Britain." After seeing the film, however, slightly fewer men thought that Russia "will keep on fighting until the end" of the war against Germany and that "if Germany is beaten before Japan, the Russians will probably help us fight the Japanese"; and slightly fewer disagreed with the statement that "after we help Russia beat the Germans the Russians are liable to turn around and start fighting us." According to the investigators, "the presentation of Britain's outstanding effort in holding off the Nazis" resulted in "a release of the men's former suspicions of Russian integrity that had been inhibited by their respect and obligation to Russia since she had currently been doing the bulk of the fighting."

Many intentional propagandists eventually admit that they are surprised by some of the results of their own propaganda. James A. Farley, for example, was Mr. Roosevelt's first campaign manager. He strove mightily to have Mr. Roosevelt elected and then re-elected a second time. Apparently, as he realized later, he himself had not appreciated in advance all the consequences of the New Deal. He did not and perhaps he could not guess that one of the effects of his successful propaganda would be to produce reforms and policies with which he would disagree, especially after his personal relations with the President had deteriorated and after he himself had acquired the ambition to become President.

There have been objections to a distinction between intentional and unintentional propaganda by those who would restrict the term "propaganda" to the intentional variety. Some critics have contended that, if unintentional propaganda be included in a discussion of propaganda, then the concept embraces too wide a field. It is true that the meaning or referent of the word is thus extended, but extension is legitimate since the phenomena included thereunder are identical with respect to psychological methods and social consequences and differ only in regard to the motivation of the propagandist. Others have maintained that the distinction is difficult to make unless the personality of the propagandist is known. This criticism is certainly correct, for the most effective propagandists of our time have not allowed themselves to be subjected to prolonged interviewing or to psychoanalysis. The inaccessibility of propagandists, however, does not mean that the problem of analyzing them and their motives should be completely neglected. Frequently

on the basis of scanty information it is possible to formulate
rather sagacious hypotheses concerning them. The analyst
who is unacquainted with the intimacies of an advertiser's
motives need not despair and block himself from concluding
that the man supervises the writing of copy to increase sales.
Such a conclusion is sufficient from a propaganda viewpoint,
even though psychologically his real motive may be to compensate for the strict cleanliness training he received as a
child.

Lasswell (7) "rejects the category of 'unintentional
propaganda' " once proposed by this writer. He says that
the "unintentional circulation of Communist symbols is not
propaganda, but may be a result of propaganda." Yes, but
such circulation may have no relation whatsoever to previous propaganda: it can be the consequence of social or
economic events in which intentional propaganda has played
little or no part. By making "manipulation" or "premedi-
tation" the keystone in his conceptualization of propaganda,
Lasswell restricts the term to instances in which the propagandist is conscious of his objectives. Certainly he knows
that the dividing line between the conscious and the unconscious is frequently most difficult to discern.

Sometimes it appears useful for practical or administrative purposes to call one kind of propaganda "education" or
"information" and another kind "propaganda," but the utility of the distinction should lead no one to believe that it is
an absolute one. During the last war, for example, overall
policy for England's propaganda to neutral and allied countries came from the Ministry of Information and to her
enemies from the Political Warfare Executive. The "information" from the M. of I. tended to contain more facts
on any standard than the "propaganda" of the P.W.E., although at times their radio programs were indistinguish-
able. The objectives of the two agencies, however, were
different: the M. of I. sought to reinforce Britain's reputation over a period of time extending beyond the war and
hence had to be more "truthful," whereas the P.W.E. was
necessarily interested in short-range effects directly related
to the war effort and hence was less "truthful." Since the

objectives were different, different types of propagandists
and of propaganda techniques were employed by each organization.   In the United States, the Office of the Coordinator of Inter-American Affairs prevented itself from becoming a part of the Office of Strategic Services and then of
the Office of War Information by maintaining with a false
grin on a not very competent face that its propaganda to
Latin America was "informational" and therefore should
not be contaminated with "propaganda" or "psychological
warfare."   Within the Office of War Information, which
was for the United States the equivalent of both the M. of I.
and the P.W.E., the distinction was maintained on an organ-
izational basis.   Such semantic and political considerations,
in fact, led one of the O.W.I.'s propagandists (*13*) to write
after the war that "information is one thing—propaganda
quite another," in support of which he could repeat only the
trite and psychologically meaningless dichotomy between
"reason" and "emotion."

Types of Propaganda

A classification of phenomena into types is usually a makeshift arrangement that is evolved for some practical reason.
Women may be called vaguely or precisely "tall" or "short"
in order to indicate which size coat they should buy or which
size man they should love or marry.   When a particular
woman is so classified, obviously only her height is being
considered and not the thousand-and-one other characteristics she possesses.

Innumerable schemes are available which can serve as the
basis for classifying propaganda campaigns.   All of them
are arbitrary and hence the selection of one rather than another is a function of which aspect of propaganda is being
emphasized at a given moment.   Types of propaganda,
then, may refer to the motive of the propagandist; the
methods he employs; the recognition or non-recognition of
his objectives by the propagandees; or the consequences of
his propaganda.

A classification of the basis of the propagandist's motives

has already been suggested: propaganda may be intentional or unintentional. This distinction refers only to the propagandist's awareness of what he is doing: is he deliberately or unwittingly attempting to influence other people? It does not take into account all the other ways in which propaganda may be characterized, nor should it be required to.

It is difficult to classify propaganda on the basis of methods because those methods are so diverse. A dichotomy may be derived from a moral judgment and then propaganda can be called "honest" or "dishonest." Or propaganda may be labelled with reference to a particular method: there is "repetitious" and "non-repetitious" propaganda. Propaganda may also be characterized in terms of the media of communication employed: "newspaper," "radio," "motion-picture," "magazine," "leaflet," and "rumor" propaganda are the principal categories. Each of these schemes has its merits and each, consequently, should be employed as the occasion demands.

An extremely useful criterion for classifying propaganda is to refer to the propagandees' recognition or non-recognition of the propagandist's objectives. Every normal adult in American society, for example, knows that the goal of an advertisement is to increase sales: the presence of the propaganda is thus appreciated and variously evaluated. The praise lavished upon the product by a housewife may be considered quite disinterested and objective, as indeed it is if she is merely an unintentional propagandist. Conceivably, however, she may be an intentional propagandist who is simply not revealing her interested motive to the propagandee: she or her husband may own stock in the company manufacturing the product or she may be paid to recommend the product as part of the company's promotion campaign. Regardless of her conscious intention, she is affecting the person with whom she is talking, and that person is not aware of the fact that he is being propagandized. Propaganda, consequently, may be *revealed, concealed,* or concealed at first and then revealed (*delayed revealed*).

Propaganda is revealed when the propagandees are aware of the fact that propaganda is affecting them. Voters during a campaign never or seldom forget that the candidates' immediate objective is to be elected. Concealed propaganda, in contrast, affects people even though they do not know that someone else—intentionally or unintentionally—is seeking to control their reactions. Fifth columnists pose as sincere patriots and try to prevent people from learning that they are being paid and directed by some outside power.

The division between revealed and concealed propaganda cannot be clearcut for two reasons. In the first place, the nature of the propaganda may be concealed at first but then later—because the propagandist makes the decision or is forced to make it or because the propagandees secure additional insight—it is revealed. The shrewd street-corner speaker does not reveal his purpose until he has attracted a crowd and aroused their interest; then he names his party or nostrum. Then, secondly, propagandees differ in their reactions to the propaganda which is affecting them: some may and others may not know what is happening to them. The same item on a radio newscast, for example, is revealed propaganda for the few who appreciate its origin and social implications, but it is concealed propaganda for the greater number who consider it an objective, important presentation of the "facts." Since minute analyses of propagandees are usually impossible and since, consequently, their own appraisal of the propagandist's objective cannot be obtained, any classification of propaganda into one of the three types must always be somewhat arbitrary. Sometimes a sample of the propagandees can be interviewed or otherwise observed, but the representativeness of the sample may remain open to question. More frequently it is possible to make reasonably probable inferences about the propagandees' reactions from the stimuli which constitute the propaganda. No investigation is required to decide that a political speech is a form of revealed propaganda for American adults, but one is necessary to determine whether members of a radio audience are able to recognize that a "news" item about a candidate has been smuggled into the press association's file.

Propaganda may also be classified in terms of its objectives. It may be called "good" or "bad" on the basis of some social, philosophical, or simply prejudiced criteria. The most obvious and distinguishing characteristic to single out is the field of human activity which the propaganda is attempting to affect. Common sense suggests types such as commercial propaganda, political propaganda, war propaganda, anti-semitic propaganda, communist propaganda, etc.

Sometimes it is useful to refer to the effort of one individual to influence others as *counter-propaganda*. This term emphasizes the negative objective of weakening customary responses which people make or of preventing responses desired by an opponent from occurring or being reinforced. In a sense, however, all propaganda involves some counter-propaganda, inasmuch as the drive strength of pre-existing competing responses must be weakened before learning can occur. The manufacturer may have a monopoly and therefore he is not forced to carry on counter-propaganda against a competitor, but he nevertheless is competing with other interests possessed by the propagandees. The term "counter-propaganda," therefore, has little psychological significance and should be employed only when it is necessary to indicate that a propagandist is seeking, intentionally or unintentionally, to counteract a competing propaganda which has been previously, is concurrently, or may eventually begin operating.

Persuasion

The analysis of education and propaganda so far has been made on the assumption that a group of individuals is being affected. The relation is that of one-to-many. In many situations, however, the educator or the propagandist is dealing with only one other person. When the student or the propagandee is a single individual (or perhaps an extremely small group like a family), the communication may be distinguished from propaganda by calling it "persuasion."

Education and propaganda cannot be completely adapted to public opinion because the people involved differ from one another and hence react variously to the stimuli that are presented to them. Usually the teacher and the propagandist have to employ a kind of buckshot approach: they scatter their shots to increase the probability of striking each individual with something. There is economy in this procedure since one set of stimuli potentially can affect many people. But education and propaganda are sometimes wasteful: the stimuli are so general that they fall along the gradients of no one individual and consequently do not produce the desired effects.

In persuasion, on the other hand, the educator or the propagandist concentrates upon one individual. The circle of people who can be convinced is thereby decreased, but the probability of actually affecting the fewer individuals who are reached usually increases. In the give-and-take of a face-to-face situation the approach can be quickly varied; arguments can be more easily adapted to an attitude expressed through the slightest wrinkle of the brow. All of the techniques of education and propaganda may be employed, but their potentiality can be more accurately calculated in advance and their effectiveness more easily and quickly observed. The skillful speaker at a public gathering concentrates on persuasion rather than propaganda: the aural stimuli he offers produce responses in his audience; he observes and is affected by these responses; he then alters or continues the themes eliciting an interested or a favorable response, etc.

Persuasion may depend upon previous education or propaganda. The prospective customer who has already been affected by a national advertising campaign is more susceptible to the arguments employed by the fast-talking salesman. The speaker can arouse his audience with greater ease if their very presence at the meeting is an indication of an interest they have in him or his subject. The habits already exist: the persuader's task is to find the subtle or crude stimuli which will elicit them.

Propaganda may also depend upon persuasion. Prominent people with prestige are persuaded to agree with the propagandist and then their agreement is exploited in the propaganda campaign. One of the functions of the testimonial in modern advertising is to convince people that a product is good because a prominent person likes or uses it. His alleged approbation has been obtained in the first place by offering him a fee for the use of his name or by attracting him with promises of publicity. Political candidates in the United States certainly believe that the expressed support of the President assists them in conducting their campaigns.

It is idle to attempt to decide whether propaganda or persuasion in general is more effective. So much depends on the particular situation and upon the objective to be achieved. A propaganda campaign, for example, is usually required to amend the Constitution of the United States, but a major or minor change in the administration of the federal government can frequently be obtained by persuading one man—perhaps the President or a Cabinet official—that the innovation is essential or desirable. During the last war, combat propaganda from the United Nations sought to weaken the morale of German soldiers and directly or indirectly to have them surrender; occasionally allied agents used almost every possible device to persuade individual German leaders or generals to cease fighting and surrender the armies under their command.

The Analysis of Propaganda

There are two groups of people interested in the functioning of propaganda. One consists of intentional propagandists who seek to discover and employ new devices or tricks to affect public opinion more effectively: they wish to improve their techniques. The other group includes propagandees who desire to know how and why propaganda affects people. The motives of the latter are various. They may be academic individuals who consider propaganda a worthy object of study, just as some of their colleagues carry on investigations in physics, biology, philology, or industrial design. They may be wideawake citizens who take delight in detecting some of the forces which seek to affect them. They may be students in school or college who are being given a "realistic" appraisal of the important influences in their society. Or they may be cocky individuals who have an ambition to outsmart those who wish to outsmart them. The unintentional propagandist does not fall easily into either group. He may be interested in the functioning of propaganda as an idle pastime, but he is not likely to make a deliberate or conscious effort to use whatever knowledge he gains from his observations.

The difference between the propagandist's and propagandee's interest in propaganda can lead to somewhat contrasting approaches, just as the artist who plans a painting necessarily follows a procedure different from the art-lover who views the finished product. The propagandist wishes to affect people to attain his ends; the propagandee seeks to understand how the propagandist is functioning to attain those ends—and he may first have to discover what the ends are. Typically the situation is like this:

Propagandist	*Propagandee*
I want to sell more of my product and to do so I must convince people that they will look lovelier, and attract and hold better mates if they use it.	This advertisement claims that I will look lovelier and have a happier marriage if I buy the product. Obviously the manufacturer wants to get my money; I wonder whether what he says is true.
I want to be re-elected and so I had better claim that I am in favor of virtue and opposed to sin. Now let me see: which virtues and which sins would it be best to mention?	He wants me to vote for him and he is using his record in the past and his promises for the future to win my approval. Just what do his words mean?

It is possible, however, to adopt a third approach which includes the interests of both the propagandist and the propagandee. This approach seeks to analyze propaganda at every point in its production and consumption. The results of the analysis can then be utilized either to plan or to understand propaganda. The writer will attempt to place the reader and himself on such a broad, middle road in the chapters that follow.

Propaganda involves many stages. There is the propagandist himself who initiates the campaign. There is the medium of communication which he employs. There is the content of the propaganda itself. And there are the immediate and far-flung reactions of the propagandees to the propaganda stimuli. The process of analyzing propaganda has been summarized (*12*) in the form of a slogan: *"who* says *what,* through what *channels* (media) of communication, to *whom"* and with what *"results"?*

Of course propaganda sometimes proceeds in a flash. The hungry individual in search of a restaurant suddenly perceives a sign announcing that, a few feet from where he is standing, steaks and lobsters can be ordered; he observes the shiny façade of the building; he concludes that he would like a steak and that this particular place will be suitable since its appearance attracts him; he enters the restaurant; he orders a meal, eats it, and he pays for it. Such commonplace behavior is relatively simple at first glance and requires no lengthy explanation or analysis. It must be conceded, however, that much must be telescoped before the behavior can be described so glibly: there are cultural factors involved in the individual's liking for steaks, lobsters, and shiny façades, and there are psychological factors embedded in his ability to perceive the sign, his very presence on a street instead of in a home when hungry, etc. It seems to be worthless to examine the separate steps until it is remembered that many individuals must be involved in this simple propaganda situation if the restaurant itself is to be a success. The owner must decide what kind of a façade his building should have, which types of food he should feature in various displays, how superior the food he serves should be, etc.

Other propaganda extends even for the individual over time. A whole generation of young men and women in the United States who called themselves pacifists in the early 1930's was not suddenly changed by Pearl Harbor or America's declarations of war in 1941. For years their pacifism had been affected by events and by the ways in which those events had been portrayed. They had become psychologically prepared to cooperate with the war effort even before they themselves realized that their pacifism had evaporated. Here there can be no question that analysis is necessary.

The situations in which propaganda functions are so diverse that at first glance each of them may appear to be unique. Entering a restaurant seems quite different from entering a war. Common to any situation, however, is a human being or a group of human beings. Their reactions spring from them and must possess a kind of unity. That unity can be perceived amid the diversity only when the underlying processes have been brought to light. It is the aim of propaganda analysis to indicate the nature of those processes.

A complete analysis of propaganda which is oriented from a psychological viewpoint, therefore, must follow propaganda from the time it is a vague thought in the propagandist's mind to the final effect which it has upon the propagandees. The sequence is long and tedious, but cannot be avoided. In outline, it involves these steps:

1. The propagandist
2. The content of the propaganda
3. The perception of the propaganda.
4. The initial response of the propagandees.
5. The changes produced within the propagandees.
6. The actions of the propagandees.

A separate chapter will now be devoted to each of these six stages.

CHAPTER 12

The Propagandist

I T IS always intriguing to wonder why an individual has adopted a particular trade or profession. Sometimes the explanation at first glance seems quite simple: he is following the example of his father; he was offered the opportunity by a friend; he was originally driven through desperation to accept the only work available. Further thought, however, usually reveals complexities which the simple explanation does not take into account. Why has he followed the example of his father when relations between the two have never been satisfactory and when he has deliberately sought to be different from his parent in all other respects? Why did he find himself in a desperate situation and why has he then refused to change his position when he was able to do so? The choice of a trade or profession, it appears, depends upon the individual's personality and innumerable factors present or absent in his society.

A shy person seeks and finds a position requiring only infrequent contact with people. Since he then meets or speaks to people infrequently, his shyness continues and perhaps increases. It is not inconceivable that his associates have been drawn to the same work because they too are shy. Regardless of his and their original drives, there is a strong tendency for all of them to be more or less singularly affected by their work and hence subsequently to possess more or less similar personality characteristics. Men tend to become what they do and, when they do things together, they grow to resemble one another. Most occupational groups have their standardized jargon which only the initiated use correctly and easily, but which outsiders try to imitate sometimes with and more usually without success.

At least three important admissions must be made before the profession of the propagandist is discussed. In the first place, the number of occupations involving propaganda and the number of individuals in those occupations is so great that any generalization inevitably cannot be true of, or applicable to, every single propagandist. What will be said refers only to average or central tendencies which appear to be discernible. Tremendous variability, then, is admitted from the outset.

The intentional rather than the unintentional propagandist, moreover, is being almost exclusively scrutinized. The intentional propagandist is more provocative: he is deliberately carrying on propaganda and there is at least the presumption that his very deliberateness makes him somewhat distinctive. In contrast, the unintentional propagandist knows not what he does, and hence an analysis of him would have to go far afield into the realm of social relations in general. Everyone during some moment of the day unintentionally kicks the propaganda ball, but only the intentional propagandist consciously devotes many hours to propelling it backwards or forwards.

In addition, there are few systematic data available even concerning intentional propagandists. As a group or as a specialized sub-group they have not been studied extensively. They seem to intrigue not social scientists but novelists who are more concerned with the dramatic peculiarities of the individual case than they are with prosaic generalizations. Whatever basis exists for this chapter, consequently, is largely the not unlimited experiences which the writer has had with propagandists. Here there will be no reference to

the formula of $\sqrt{\dfrac{p \times q}{n}}$ or to any other formula. Here no weighty psychological principles will be invoked. The writer is simply relaxing a bit and—quite frankly—expressing his intuitions. Let the reader be tolerant but extremely skeptical.

Propaganda Opportunities

The values and policies of modern society are unstable and therefore social conflicts are numerous. Social conflicts are almost always accompanied by propaganda. For this reason there are innumerable positions requiring the services of a propagandist.

The exact number of propagandists in the United States cannot be stated because there are no reliable figures at hand and because many of the professions and occupations related to propaganda—like teaching and acting—contain individuals whose functions are not exclusively propagandistic in nature. The 1940 United States Census, for example, indicated that 58,253 men and women were employed as editors and reporters; 33,712 were advertising agents; and 11,806 claimed to be authors. For obvious reasons it did not suggest how many of the 1,019,760 teachers below the college level or of the 33,701 photographers were carrying on intentional or unintentional propaganda. Nor did it present data for such categories as lobbyists, public relations counsels, politicians, group leaders, etc. According to the Federal Communications Commission, 10,750 of the 20,452 employees of the American radio industry in 1944 might be classified as propagandists—provided one arbitrarily excludes as propagandists those in a general managerial, administrative, technical, clerical, or "miscellaneous" capacity (2). Figures for trade associations, moreover, are incomplete. Although the slice of the nation's work devoted to propaganda cannot be estimated, in short, it is certain that number is sufficiently large to attract attention.

All of the professions and occupations involving propaganda belong in the so-called "white-collar" category and therefore possess at least middle-class status in the United States. Reporters, for example, tend to come from such a background (7) as did most of the prominent heads of state and their propaganda ministers during the last war (*11*). Since a similar or lower status is occupied by a majority of Americans, it follows that propaganda positions if not the title of propagandist have prestige. Propagandists such as advertisers receive sneers from certain groups like intellectuals and journalists, but the size of their incomes commands respect from others.

An equally important fact about propaganda occupations is that, beyond the costs of education, they involve no or in any case a small investment of capital. The owner of the newspaper of course must be a man of wealth or one with the ability to borrow money, but his reporters are wage-earners in almost the same sense that a ditch-digger or a machinist is. Propagandists progress or fail largely as a result of the talent they possess. The occupation of propaganda, therefore, is likely to attract individuals with distinctive talents and with a desire to employ those talents to become socially mobile.

Propaganda Proclivities

Lawyers, physicians, and propagandists concentrate on people rather than objects. The lawyer is constantly in contact with clients, the physician with patients, and the propagandist directly or indirectly with propagandees. Sometimes of course the contact with the persons involved is very indirect: the lawyer may specialize in preparing briefs, the physician in conducting research, and the propagandist in writing copy or scripts. To a certain extent, each wishes to influence people either to follow his advice and each, consequently, must be partially motivated by a drive to secure power over others by helping them.

In law and medicine, however, this drive is usually expressed only when people wish to be dominated for reasons that they themselves have more or less voluntarily selected. The lawyer's client desires to win a suit, to avoid a fine or a jail sentence, to have the suspected criminal prosecuted, or to draw up a correct deed or will; therefore he and not the lawyer establishes the initial contact. The patient wants to recover from or prevent an illness or injury; therefore he or some authority consults a competent physician. Most propagandees, in contrast, do not consciously wish to be dominated by propaganda or at least they do not deliberately place themselves in a position where they can be affected. The individual generally reads a newspaper or listens to a radio program not to be propagandized but to be informed or entertained. The student goes to school not to be given a biased version of the facts but to be educated —or his parents send him for that reason. The citizen in a democratic country who attends a political rally may do so because he would come to a decision concerning the rival candidates, but he must choose between men who have already elected to seek his support. Propagandists are usually self-appointed messiahs or leaders who strive to become important determinants of public opinion.

There is no recognized professional training which most propagandists are supposed to receive. The lawyer and the physicians must be graduates of a professional school and pass examinations conducted by civil authorities or their professions. Of the decidedly propagandistic professions, only teaching usually demands a more or less prescribed educational background, but little direct or indirect training in the techniques of propaganda is given. Relatively few reporters in the United States are graduates of journalism schools or have had college courses dealing with the subject (*cf. 8*). Only an extremely small number of American colleges and universities offers courses in "public relations," and their content as well as that of other courses which budding public relations counsels take is almost completely unstandardized and unsystematic (*6*). None of the most important political propagandists of our time received a formal education which prepared them directly for their careers; instead practical experience in politics and journalism apparently gave them the necessary skills (*12*). The qualifications of the successful propagandist seem rather to be various and vague: an average or above average IQ, a likable and perhaps extraverted personality, an interest in other people, imagination, resourcefulness, and above all actual experience with a propaganda medium or with propaganda in general. Some propaganda technicians like the artists who are employed by advertising agencies require, in addition, specialized abilities which may or may not have been developed formally in school or college.

Most of the qualifications of the propagandists are so unspecialized that innumerable individuals believe they either possess or can acquire them. Many American college graduates, who are repelled at the thought of another three or four years of intensive study at a law or a medical school and who much prefer to begin gaining their economic independence immediately, conclude that it is easier to achieve semi-professional status by becoming propagandists. The manipulation of people through words appears more attractive than controlling them through the standardized procedures of other professions. Besides what they do not know or cannot do now they can acquire with dispatch when they begin to function, for example, as advertising agents. In addition, they have before them outstanding examples of men and women who live by their wits and indeed live handsomely. A propaganda career, in short, seems to be the quick route to the stars; the simple way to realize the American Dream; the great opportunity for the middle-class college graduate to follow in the hallowed tradition of Horatio Alger and attain wealth, prestige, and a beautiful wife. The American pioneer spirit, together with the self-reliance and ambition it has always inspired, is still alive, but the geographical goal is no longer the fertile lands or the gold mines of the West but the City of New York.

There is nothing healthy or unhealthy, normal or abnormal, about the propagandist's drive to dominate other people. Men must be motivated by more than bread, butter, children, and automobiles when they select their careers and it little matters, socially or psychologically, whether they are also compensating for feelings of inferiority, rebelling against parental rules, or sublimating an impulse to masturbate in public. Propagandists have their internal problems too, but they are probably no different from those of propagandees and hence of all human beings. Maybe they are, to quote Lasswell's unsubstantiated hypothesis (*3*), "men and women who have broken away from their family tradition, which is suggestive of early emotional difficulty"; or maybe they are following the intellectual or professional interests of their fathers as did almost all the prominent leaders and propaganda ministers during the last war (*13*). Maybe they like people a little more and hence want to see and to help them; or maybe they like people a little less and hence want to sneer inwardly or outwardly as they meet and exploit them. Maybe they are idealists, or maybe they are realists—whatever it is those words mean. Maybe they are adjusted to the problems which face them and then become advertising agents, politicians, teachers, or journalists; or maybe they are maladjusted and therefore want to save the world through communism, the abolition of sin, the getting out of the vote, or the re-establishment— perish the thought—of prohibition. Propagandists merit no more admiration or pity than the rest of mankind.

The Propaganda Idea

Among intentional propagandists the Idea is worshipped above all else. A new Idea is greeted by its creator and sometimes by his associates as if it were the first-born child of the greatest lovers in history, a profound revision of Einstein's formula of relativity, or an eleventh commandment suddenly produced from the clouds. For intentional propagandists are convinced that it is Ideas which make the world go round and which therefore are peculiarly a symptom of their own genius.

The Idea has many names. It may simply be called a brain child or—if the propagandist is resolved not to be trite even in his moments of greatest creativity or if he would display his pseudo-knowledge of modern science—a brain wave. It may be dubbed a new campaign, a new angle, a new trick, a new line, a new approach, a new twist, or some equally hair-raising phrase containing the suggestion of novelty. It may even be labelled a thought.

The Idea of the intentional propagandist may be positive or negative, but in either case it is defended with enthusiasm and dogmatism. If it be positive, it is represented as the solution to all propaganda problems. If it be negative, then the Idea of someone else is criticized in the restrained language employed by a father whose daughter announces that she wishes to be seduced by the boy next door. Good or bad, the Idea of the propagandist is momentous—at least in the opinion of its progenitor.

Ideas are worshipped because original ones are not plentiful. It is difficult to find a new appeal to sell soap, cigarettes, or sanitary napkins. Hundreds of other account executives are similarly racking and raking their own brains or having brain waves. Ideas from advertising campaigns in the present and the past are so numerous that it truly looks as though there were nothing new under the sun. Different ways of demoralizing or deceiving the enemy in wartime cannot be discovered without much travail when the propaganda machine is already functioning, when undeniable situations exist, and when military security and political policy circumscribe the frame of reference in which imagination is allowed to function. The individual who has the Idea, consequently, believes in its wondrous characteristics because he wishes to do so; and the individual who accepts or rejects the Idea of another person brings credit to himself by demonstrating his own capacity for appreciating its virtues or unmasking its vices.

Professional Pride

In the midst of meetings on American propaganda policy during the last war, the writer would occasionally lean back and listen to the ways in which the participating propagandists defended or rejected the Ideas to be included or excluded from propaganda output. Quite impolitely but most objectively, he sometimes jotted down on the same piece of paper which received his sleep-inhibiting doodlings the rationalizing phrases they uttered. Here are some of those which were phrased positively:

"This is good propaganda."

"This is sound propaganda."

"This is good propagandistically."

"This will throw Goebbels into a panic."

"Our audience will be interested in knowing that . . ."

"That is exactly what the Japanese want."

"This will be good for the morale of the French."

"In itself it isn't terribly bad propaganda."

"This shows a good propaganda sense."

"Intelligence reveals that this is good propaganda."

"This is good propaganda doctrine."

"This is good psychology."

". . . from a practical propaganda point of view."

"If there is one thing I know about propaganda, it is . . ."

"This follows a fundamental rule of propaganda."

"I know these people and this will appeal to them."

These sentences were repeated with little or no modification as the argument demanded. They were spoken by men whose ordinary peacetime occupations had been in journalism, art, architecture, drama, poetry, business, advertising, public relations, teaching, administration, publishing, the Army, the Navy, the Department of State, the Department of Commerce, law, medicine, labor relations, and foreign missionary work—and it is literally true that men and women from these diverse occupations became "expert" propagandists. They were used by the young and by the old, by men and by women, by native- and by foreign-born, and by the intelligent and by the stupid. More often than not—especially when propaganda to enemy countries was being discussed—no factual basis existed for the sentence because really valid and reliable information concerning public opinion was missing (*1*) ; and there was seldom any rule or guide either from experience, intuition, or social science which automatically made one Idea "good" or "bad." What the propagandist was really saying when he uttered one of these clichés was: "I like the Idea" or—if a negative phrasing were used—"I don't like the Idea." But he had to translate personal preference or prejudice into more impressive words before he could sound convincing either to his associates or to himself.

Almost every propagandist, regardless of his medium or field of work, is convinced that his Ideas are sanctified by experience, science, or some divine being including, in some instances, his own superego. For to think otherwise and to qualify the thought with "maybe's," "possibly's," or "if's" is to give expression to one's own insecurity, to admit a lack of expertness, or to appear otherwise less impressive. A self-styled expert who acknowledges fallibility casts aspersions on his own expertness and thus disqualifies himself— and propagandists can all blithely consider themselves experts because nobody knows completely or convincingly what the criteria of expertness are.

The propagandist displays pride in his Ideas and way of approach most dramatically when he expands his chest in front of people who do not belong to his particular guild. Any profession of course is somewhat ethnocentric regarding outsiders. Many physicians, for example, rightly or wrongly assume that the communication of medical knowledge and especially of their diagnoses is an exceedingly dangerous practice; and sometimes they invoke "medical ethics" to keep laymen unnecessarily ignorant. Similarly some lawyers make their own activities sound complicated and mysterious by employing polysyllabic vocabularies which have been derived from Latin and have undergone alterations in meaning and pronounciation; thus subtly or directly they indicate to their clients that only an expert trained in the tradition of the law and wise in the ways of the courts can possibly find his way through the labyrinth. The propagandist's pride in his work is no different from that of the physician or the lawyer. He likes to "talk shop" with members of his profession and, when he has achieved status in his chosen field, he is amazed that simple laymen question his judgment or have Ideas of their own. He also seeks from outsiders the same kind of respect accorded members of the so-called learned professions and, being a specialist in propaganda, he propagandizes in his own behalf to increase that respect. He tells the world that he belongs to a profession. He surrounds himself with swank. He calls almost every clerk in his advertising office a vice-president because that title is supposed to impress clients. In fact he soon begins to believe that he is a member of the élite responsible for the salt of the earth.

Esprit de corps tends to be high among propagandists. They look upon one another as men with Ideas, and the respect they hold for the Ideas they transfer to the men who have them. If it is comforting, as everyone is told, to whistle in the dark, then the sense of comfort must be much, much greater as the number of people whistling there together increases. Propagandists who have misgivings concerning their own activities feel kindly toward their partners-in-crime and thereby reassure themselves that their guilt is at least shared with others.

Each propagandist feels that he "knows his way around." Such knowledge may include almost anything, such as access to the "right" people or the ability to write a radio script which lasts twelve and three-quarters minutes, no less and no more. Most teachers are devotees of their own teaching techniques and hence tend to resist innovations. Advertising agents say—and who can doubt what an advertising agent says?—that their campaigns promote sales but that, when sales drop, only the benighted place the responsibility upon the campaign. Many politicians in the United States without hesitation can point out the difference between "smart politics" and "bad politics" both in a general and in a specific situation. When a man calls himself a public relations counsel, he is not only seeking to attract customers through a fancy title, but he is also indicating to himself and to others that he has reached the height of psychological wisdom. From such a summit he knows that no task is beyond his ability, provided the fee is large enough or what he considers fame is not long in coming. He may even write books or articles telling people to return to religion, to speak up for democracy, and to restore public confidence in business and finance. He thus expresses avocationally what Lasswell (*4*) calls the propagandists' "exhibitionistic" urge resulting from "the necessity of operating from behind the scenes in their vocation." An American public relations counsel who almost always employed concealed propaganda in behalf of his clients once purchased a full-page advertisement in two metropolitan newspapers to present the modest claims that he had "charted the principles and methods of the profession" and that "his books are the authoritative texts used in universities." The same blurb contained the equally self-effacing and unbiased statement that "by using the objective, independent judgment of the modern technician in social sciences, the public relations counsel, who is qualified by education, professional training and experience to apply science to practical problems" can make American industry "run much more smoothly." Maybe yes, maybe no.

The American journalist deserves to be dissected at length for many reasons. He at least has a specific skill, the ability to write a story. He is everywhere in the world where he is permitted by his employers and foreign governments to go. Nothing is so sacred that it cannot be sliced by the sharp sword of the reporter. He has an itch to affect events either by creating news or by exerting a backstage influence on important people (*cf. 9*). If he tires of journalism, he may enter another propaganda field like publicity or politics which is already well stocked with ex-reporters (*5*). He usually believes in himself and considers that he is making an important contribution to mankind, as indeed he sometimes is. And he tends to be a snob.

He tends to be a snob because he is absolutely convinced that only the methods of American journalism represent a sure-fire path to absolute, ultimate truth. The facts, he says, speak for themselves, provided they are reported accurately and in the best traditions of his craft; his job is to get those facts and to get them quickly. Of course, as any school girl knows, facts do not speak for themselves: the people who perceive the facts do the talking and what they say depends on the facts which are presented, the way in which they are presented, and their own ongoing responses at the time when the facts are perceived. Only a journalist, moreover, is credited by journalists with the ability to gather facts—a journalist is a gifted person "with newspaper experience" and by newspaper is not meant a weekly published in a secondary school.

Without question almost every journalist makes a more or less conscientious effort to obtain the facts he considers relevant to the story he is writing, and he may exercise both ingenuity and skill in their pursuit. More frequently than not his quest is successful. When he himself realizes, however, that he has not been able to accumulate all or enough of facts, he may adopt one of three procedures. He may decide to "kill" the story, in which case he does not even submit it to his editor; but thereby he has failed to carry out the assignment he has been given or has imposed upon himself—and a rival reporter may be more successful than he. For these reasons, he is sorely tempted to submit the story anyhow. Since some of the facts are missing or incomplete, he may try to hedge as he writes his report. The favorite qualifiers of journalism usually begin with the same two words:

> According to official sources
> According to unofficial sources
> According to usually reliable sources
> According to well-informed sources
> According to unconfirmed reports
> According to reports reaching here
> According to best available information

Or sometimes Mr. Ubiquitous It is given as the authority:

> It was learned
> It appears
> It is reported
> It is unconfirmed
> It is known
> It is suspected
> It is thought

Some of these phrases not only indicate that laudable precautions are being taken by the reporter to point out the limitations of his story, but they may also reflect an effort on his part to protect his sources (and thus to keep open his "pipelines" to exclusive information) or an attempt by the source to obtain free publicity or to set out a trial balloon without assuming responsibility therefor. The headline that is placed on the story when it appears, nevertheless, may be quite extravagant, and the casual reader will perceive in the text only the alleged facts without the qualifications. Or, in the third place, the journalist may run the risk of writing up whatever facts he has without qualifying them, because he is under pressure from the home office to meet a deadline or because he has the kind of hunch which only a newspaper man with his "nose for news" would trust.

The nature of his profession, consequently, requires the journalist to state the facts even when all of them are not available and to generalize from those facts. With his peculiar kind of a nose, he is confident that he can get "the dope" on short notice, whether that dope involves the state of public opinion or the sex life of a dictator. The newspaper man, therefore, is unabashedly in his own terms "a wise guy" who can press one button and produce an exotic fact or another and reveal what is going to happen tomorrow or a year from now. The simple-minded laymen may lack the courage, the foolhardiness, the ability, or the experience to react like a reporter: he may not know the fact or he may be unwilling to hazard the guess. Unless he is tagged an expert by the reporter, what he calls a fact may be considered false and what he predicts will receive a sneer simply because he never covered the police court in Santa Fe, New Mexico. The journalist, in a word, is not a humble person; he always believes that he alone knows who is sleeping with whom.

Nor is the American journalist humble about journalistic style which he considers to be the finest and clearest method of writing yet devised by mortal man in any language. Other writing that does not come from a professional newspaper man, he believes, tends to be either unintelligible or literary: he is tempted to give it a good scrubbing or to have it blue-pencilled by a re-write man. He may enjoy the prose of non-newspaper men as he does a glass of beer, but he calls such writing wasteful because it does not present "the guts" of the matter in the first sentence or paragraph. Besides, long sentences or paragraphs waste newspaper space and run up high telegraph, wireless, or radio tolls. Good "re-write" men are born, not made—which is perhaps the highest (though patently inaccurate) compliment a journalist can pay to the individual who can whip a story into the kind of journalese created by an all-powerful deity and the American newspaper profession.

Many American reporters, however, admit privately that their profession's guiding spirit is not always the Goddess of Truth. In one investigation (*10*), forty-two out of seventy Washington correspondents willing to express themselves admitted that they were aware of a "definite, fixed 'policy'" of the papers they represented, and the same number agreed that they could "'sense policy' and are psychologically driven to slant" their stories accordingly. The candor of these men represents reporting at its best, but they were also making the assumption that journalists alone could report the facts and all the facts if only they could free themselves from the shackles of their publishers and managing editors.

A certain amount of personal conceit characterizes many American reporters. They feel they can write, a contention usually substantiated by their stories which do appear. They take special pride, too, in that nose of theirs. As a result, they are prone among themselves—after the doors have been locked and the pedigrees of those present carefully examined—to pour slanderous contempt upon their rivals. Included in their store of facts are tales concerning journalists who have by-lines because they are related to the owner, of others who learn what is happening in the foreign office of the country where they are stationed from reading the local newspapers in a cafe or coffee house, of others who are reliable prophets only for those readers who have learned through experience to expect exactly the reverse of what they predict, and of still others who do not know even how to write. Simultaneously the same group of gossiping journalists will pay high and tear-jerking tribute to some of their associates or rivals who are considered by them to be a credit to the journalistic profession. The tribute is usually justified.

Dogmatism

There is a strong tendency for every workman to respect his tools. For without them he would be unable to achieve his objective or at least he would achieve it less efficiently; and with them life is easier and considered better. The respect for tools is sometimes so great that people look on them as an extension of their own bodies: hurt my tools, hurt me.

The tools of the propagandist are of course Ideas and the words which express Ideas. The propagandist's veneration of the Idea has already been suggested. The words themselves are held in similar awe.

Propagandists tend to believe that words can accomplish anything, including miracles. People cannot eat, sleep upon, or have sexual intercourse with words, it is perfectly true, but words can make food taste better, beds appear more comfortable, and sexual intercourse—well, no doubt words can do something about that too. The belief in words leads to a corollary belief: it is merely necessary to find the right verbal combination to make propaganda successful. Somewhere, in someone, there is that right combination—maybe it is a slogan, maybe a new way of saying old things—and, if it can be found, there'll be pie in the sky and the propagandist at any rate will be very, very happy. This kind of delusion flourishes especially during war time. Then both officials and well-intentioned individuals who write letters to officials search for and sometimes believe they find a quick way to end the war by using a particular propaganda appeal. War propagandists in fact occasionally forget that the war is being waged with bullets and not with words. Their enthusiasm for verbal tools should not be criticized too severely: it motivates them to work a little harder and each group—whether it be the air corps, the infantry, the navy, the scientists, or the miners—feels similarly convinced that without its own contribution the entire cooperative effort would fail.

Propagandists not suffering from verbal compulsions usually do not like words in general, but are addicted to particular combinations. Those combinations have brought them or someone else success in one situation in the past, and they confidently anticipate similar rewards in different situations in the future. Old-fashioned political oratory in- and outside the United States Congress, for example, once represented the most effective style to win legislative support and votes; some Congressmen, therefore, continue to orate in this manner even though they are frequently not so effective as their less long-winded colleagues. During the last war, advertising executives who were employed as propagandists by the United States Government had difficulty in adapting themselves to a kind of task rather different from that to which they had been accustomed. Many of them imagined that it was necessary only to solve the perceptual problem of propaganda and then the perception of the magical words would result in the appropriate action. Thus at one point a slogan, "The Americas United, United We Conquer," was expected to be able to persuade the masses of Latin America, who by and large remained more or less feudalistically enslaved and politically indifferent, that their personal welfare was intimately linked with the Good Neighbor Policy. Considerable effort was expended to make this slogan popular: it was employed on shortwave, relayed, and ordinary longwave radio programs; American companies in Latin America agreed to include it in their advertising copy; sound trucks which invaded remote Indian villages to sell the drugs of a particular company blasted it out; and it was incorporated into a song which was plugged whenever possible. The seeing, hearing, and learning of the slogan, it was hoped, would counteract suspicion toward the Colossus of the North; would serve as a substitute for food and freedom; and, with or without United States pressure upon and subtle bribes to the ruling cliques, would eventually result in a declaration of war against the Axis by all of the twenty countries including Argentina.

By and large American journalists employed as war propagandists throughout the last conflict behaved less dogmatically than might have been anticipated. Most of them realized that propaganda had to be geared to the public opinion existing in the particular country to which their words were directed and therefore, for the most part, they were willing to be guided by what they considered to be or were told was expert advice. If a reporter, however, had once visited or filed reports from a given country, he then seldom questioned his own expertness in formulating propaganda policy or in executing that policy. The I-am-a-wise-guy-because-I-am-a-reporter attitude permeated his thinking. A division of one of the propaganda agencies was dominated by a ruthlessly ambitious and deliberately suave journalist who attributed omniscient propaganda powers to himself because he had held a responsible position with one of the press agencies and had received some national recognition for a journalistic scoop concerning a famous crime. Although he admittedly knew absolutely nothing about the propagandees whom his organization was attempting to influence, he imagined that propaganda success depended completely on the number of stories written in the American journalistic idiom which could be pumped into the areas concerned. He used to be more concerned, therefore, with the quantity and the length of stories his office produced each week than with the quality of their contents, their distribution, their suitability, and the reactions of the readers who might or might not eventually see and be affected by them. Luckily this particular individual was not typical and, aside from wasting government funds, caused relatively little short-run damage, since his propaganda was directed toward a section of the world that was far removed from all military activity.

A strange custom existed inside the Overseas Branch of the Office of War Information during the war: directives frequently required that operators report something "for the record." That something was usually an unpleasant fact which was then mentioned briefly in a story or broadcast. If it were very unpleasant, the story would be brief and the broadcast one not destined to have a large audience either because it was transmitted at a poor listening hour or because it was not relayed by stations close to the audience. But why report anything unpleasant? Well, American propagandists believed that theirs was a "strategy of truth," and truth means the unpleasant as well as the pleasant. The painful words, therefore, had to be written for the benefit of—for whose benefit was never quite clear, although sometimes it was either a Congressman or the Goddess of Propaganda (doubtless Calliope) who presumably jotted down this bit of verbal chicanery in his or her record book. Actually this custom probably helped to enhance the credibility of American propaganda.

The lot of the researcher associated with a propaganda enterprise tends in general to be an unhappy one. The propagandist has more faith in his own verbal formulas than he has in the nasty little data of public-opinion surveys or audience-reaction studies which conceivably could check the accuracy or desirability of his procedures. Sometimes the bitterness that tears the breasts of the investigator when no one will listen to him or read his reports conceals in reality a lurking ambition to abandon research and to become a propagandist. At other times the investigator naively believes that his research should be the sole determinant of propaganda policy, although in fact research can provide only the general setting in which policy is formulated and executed and within which other factors ranging from budgetary matters to sheer ingenuity must operate. The complaint of the investigator, nevertheless, is frequently justified, especially when the propagandist completely ignores really relevant data and hence grinds out propaganda which fails or which is not so successful as it might have been. The humble research director may then come to believe that his proposal has been rejected because the propagandist or his client is dominated by an indecent impulse, such as his love for some blonds whose voice has been shown to have a statistically reliable, most unattractive effect on the radio audience.

The investigator is not heeded and the propagandist dogmatically worships his own words for the same reason: propaganda frequently is unpredictably a success or failure. The poor prediction may in fact be made because research is neglected, but it is so much simpler to place the responsibility upon the Idea. Many propagandists are like primitive savages seeing demons everywhere in an environment whose vagaries and caprice they cannot or will not try to understand.

Sincerity

Individuals are considered sincere when there is little or no discrepancy between the goals they seek and those they claim to be seeking. The good, respected family physician, according to traditional folklore, is more interested in helping his patients than he is in the fees he occasionally collects from them. He would be called insincere if he expressed this interest in their welfare only to have them pay the fees. Deeper probing of sincerity can doubtless make the concept almost psychologically meaningless, inasmuch as the individual's desire to disguise his goals may often be traced to unconscious impulses of which he himself is not necessarily aware; still the concept has social or ethical significance.

Intentional propagandists are popularly viewed as insincere individuals who will barter their souls for propaganda profit. They are thought to be ready and eager to promote any cause, regardless of their own private misgivings, just as the law expects even the most despicable criminal to be defended vigorously by his counsel. They are supposed to adopt any means to achieve their end and, more especially, to resort frequently to subterfuge and fabrication. It is little wonder, then, that people do not like to be called propagandists.

On the whole such a conception of the propagandist as an inevitably insincere person is probably incorrect. Certainly the unintentional propagandist can immediately be absolved of the charge. By definition he devoutly believes in what he is doing and, in fact, is unable even to recognize the propaganda role he discharges. He may possess a sense of self-righteousness which stems either from a desire to conform to his milieu or from his failure to appreciate the good or bad consequences of his actions. Like the missionary, he may resort to trickery or employ subtly misleading devices to obtain converts, but God and his conscience approve.

The zealous crusader whose aim is to reform the world or a portion thereof through the organization in whose behalf he functions may also be sincere as far as his conscious motives are concerned. He may truly believe that he alone can provide the panacea, whether his propaganda objective is to censor or eliminate materials he considers pornographic and immoral; to have people abandon smoking; to win additional rights and privileges for Negroes, other minority groups, or labor; or to gain support for communism, nudism, atheism, or growing gardenias. The opponent of vice obtains secret joy from viewing the materials he condemns, but it is a secret he seldom if ever admits even to himself. The member of the Communist party really wants the reform or the revolution he makes so many personal sacrifices to achieve, even though as a personality he is able to secure satisfaction only by making these sacrifices. The nudist actually does believe that people also shed their unhealthy philosophies as they slip out of their clothes, regardless of the exhibitionistic, sexual, aggressive gratifications he himself simultaneously experiences amid his disrobing metaphysics. In our society so many institutions combine their socializing efforts to prevent people from becoming two-faced that duplicity and insincerity represent modes of adjustment not so easy to attain as is commonly thought. Good spies and good poker players are rare, as are insincere propagandists.

But certainly, it will be said, advertising agents cannot believe the hokum and the bunkum their copy contains. Certainly politicians are quite aware of their showmanship and their "appeals to blind emotions." Certainly Dr. Goebbels knew he was deceiving the German people when he blamed all their miseries on the Jews and when he invented atrocity stories in the interest of anti-Semitism. Undoubtedly such contentions are true, but it should be equally apparent that their validity can be conclusively established only by making a detailed psychological examination of the advertising agents, the politicians, and Dr. Goebbels. Such an examination has not been conducted and therefore the evidence at hand is piecemeal. There are, however, unreliable indications which the writer has frequently sensed that the propagandist is quite inclined to become his own propagandee. At first the advertising agent may be skeptical of the virtues of the product manufactured by the new account; or the politician, when he runs for office for the first time, may consider some of his behavior dishonorable and in fact in a class with other acts he fears may debar him from the pearly gates; or even Dr. Goebbels may have had low moments with his own conscience as he considered the inhuman consequences of his policies. Eventually, though, as the propaganda becomes successful and brings to the propagandist fame, money, success, or whatever it is he seeks, he becomes less suspicious of the intrinsic merits of these instrumental acts. His propaganda is so rewarding that he repeats it to bring himself additional satisfactions. He also mitigates any conflict he may experience between those satisfactions and the suspicion that his gains have been dishonorably obtained either by repressing or forgetting the suspicion or by setting up stronger, competing responses. In a word, the propagandist can achieve sincerity by consciously or unconsciously rationalizing his behavior.

The rationalization may assume various forms which are frequently expressed in such platitudinous fashion as the following:

"I might as well cut myself in on the gravy."

"A man has to earn a living."

"The paper is no worse than any other."

"In my spare time I write as I please and some day I'll publish something really decent."

"After all, I really like the stuff."

"In the long run we'll all be dead and then it won't matter."

"But remember I don't do anything; I did turn down that other account."

"Only the good survive."

"You can't sell anything people don't want."

"That's my contribution to the free flow of ideas."

"If I don't, someone else will."

"But don't you believe in freedom of speech?"

"It's just a racket, but so is anything else."

"When in Rome. . . ."

"No one is altogether free."

"Who are you to hurl the first rock?"

"You never know when you're doing good."

"But they asked me to do it."

These thoughts can be uttered and believed a little more readily in the presence of people who are liked and who also utter and perhaps believe in their validity. And the propagandist is usually surrounded by members of his occupation toward whom he feels kindly, even as most prolonged contacts promote friendliness. These associates of his are obviously good people, and good people do not have bad consciences. Maybe, consequently, they are right and the disbelieving individual is wrong. Maybe, he tells himself, it would be better for me to fall in line and to say and think what they do. It is these social pressures which conspire to rid the propagandist of whatever hypocritical feelings he has and which enable him to convince himself that he is an honest person, a decent citizen, or a sincere man.

Even the propagandist who intentionally employs concealed propaganda does not necessarily consider himself immoral or deceitful. He too has a stock of rationalizations at his disposal, all of which are equivalent to the oldest and most fallacious contention of them all, *viz.*, that the end justifies the means. As a dictator he may have contempt for the masses, while at the same time he believes that his propaganda is in their best interests if only they were wise enough to understand those interests. As a war propagandist he feels that he is saving lives by shortening the war. As a public relations counsel he maintains that he is hastening the inevitable and the desirable. In some such way he seeks to find peace for himself.

There are propagandists who do not resort to a convenient rationalization regarding their sincerity. They may admit their own insincerity and yet keep their propaganda zeal undiminished by separating their work from the ideals they consider important. Such men are like lawyers who derive their revenue from a conventional practice and then contribute their services without remuneration to causes they consider worthy. Then there are the rare propagandists for whom the rewards of success are spoiled by conscience pangs to such an extent that they actually modify their own behavior.   They may refuse to carry on propaganda toward ends they do not like.   There are public relations counsels, for example, who promote only educational, scientific, and medical enterprises.   The most drastic step of all is to abandon the career of being an intentional propagandist. In our society, however, there is little danger of a stampede out of the propaganda profession.

CHAPTER 13

The Content of Propaganda

WHEN it is necessary to know what a well-publicized liquid contains, there is a scientific procedure available that provides definitive and reliable information. Simple discussion, although provocative and interesting, is likely to prove futile and dangerous. A minister or a politician is not consulted because neither is thought to be an expert on liquids. The advertising agent is not questioned: his report would be somewhat biased. What is done, of course, is to have a chemist make the analysis on the basis of available facts or of experimentation. His intellectual competency is assumed: he must know how to conduct an experiment, he must have access to what has been thought and written in chemistry, and his report must be derived from the facts and be uninfluenced by what he thinks the liquid theoretically should contain or by his private philosophy of life.

There is no similarly standardized procedure to follow when the contents of a communication are to be analyzed. No one in our society has the recognized competency in this field that the chemist has in his. No profession of propaganda analysis exists. Certainly there are individuals who analyze propaganda content, but their professional, academic, or guild affiliations are diverse. Their methods of analysis are different even when their previous training has been almost identical. It is as though the person interested in the contents of a liquid would have to choose his analyst not from among chemists but from among ministers, politicians, horticulturists, physicists, novelists, and street cleaners.

Who, for example, should analyze the content of Nazi propaganda before, during, and perhaps after the last war? The journalist would have something to say: he might identify the principal propagandists, indicate which communication media were utilized, quote juicy sections, and report the propaganda results in an impressionistic fashion. The historian might contend that a journalist lacks perspective: he ascertains neither the historical background nor the permanent effects of the propaganda on the subsequent development of events. The sociologist would not be satisfied with the historian's contribution; he would prefer to stress in greater detail the connection between the propaganda and the society or societies involved, the reflection of the culture in the communication, and the relation of the propaganda to social change. The political scientist or the jurist would feature the role of government and the law in determining and regulating the propaganda. The psychologist would concentrate upon the propaganda devices employed and study, if he could, the ways in which individuals reacted to those devices.

In practice, it must be immediately added, journalists, historians, sociologists, political scientists, jurists, and psychologists never adhere strictly to their fields when they describe or analyze propaganda content. They may claim that they are employing a particular approach in order, perhaps, to demonstrate their own respectability and purity to their professional colleagues, but they willingly recognize that propaganda is a phenomenon which cuts across the formal and traditional fields of learning. Lumley (*27*), who is a sociologist, for example, has secured some of his data from journalists; Lasswell (*18*), who is a political scientist, has written a definitive history of propaganda in World War I and in his other numerous writings (*e.g., 22*) interprets propaganda as psychoanalytically as his data permit; and Kris

(*14*), who is a psychoanalyst, also provides sociological interpretations and generalizations. Propaganda cannot be strait jacketed.

Each of these approaches, it is significant to note, does more than analyze the content of propaganda: it wanders through all stages of the propaganda from the propagandist to the propagandee. The chemist can conduct his content analysis without paying attention to the producer of the liquid or to its probable effects upon animate or inanimate objects. The analyst of propaganda content, it will be seen, is in fact more like the industrial chemist or the biochemist, who must also consider the problems of production or human consumption.

The Institute for Propaganda Analysis

The Institute for Propaganda Analysis in the United States was financed in large part by the philanthropist Edward A. Filene, was sponsored and directed by various individuals attached to academic institutions (including this writer), and was operated largely by journalists. It began functioning in October 1937, and disappeared deliberately right before this country entered the last war. Its subscribers received a monthly bulletin which analyzed a contemporary propaganda campaign such as "Mr. Roosevelt's Foreign Policy" or "Communist Propaganda, U. S. A., 1939 Model." It organized courses on propaganda analysis especially in secondary schools. It supplied teachers with a "Manual" which outlined a method for analyzing propaganda and provided a bibliography. For a while it conducted a speakers' bureau for adult groups interested in propaganda and its detection. The bias of its sponsors and editors in general was slightly toward the left, but it did not hesitate to dissect the left as well as the right.

Throughout most of its existence the Institute analyzed propaganda in terms of seven "devices" which it sometimes called the "ABC's of Propaganda Analysis." These devices have been conveniently summarized in an Institute publication called *The Fine Art of Propaganda* (*24*):

Name Calling—giving an idea a bad label—is used to make us reject and condemn the idea without examining the evidence.

Glittering Generality—associating something with a "virtue word"—is used to make us accept and approve the thing without examining the evidence.

Transfer carries the authority, sanction, and prestige of something respected and revered over to something else in order to make the latter acceptable; or it carries authority, sanction, and disapproval to cause us to reject and disapprove something the propagandist would have us reject and disapprove.

Testimonial consists in having some respected or hated person say that a given idea or program or product or person is good or bad.

Plain Folks is the method by which a speaker attempts to convince his audience that he and his ideas are good because they are "of the people," the "plain folks."

Card Stacking involves the selection and use of facts or falsehoods, illustrations or distractions, and logical or illogical statements in order to give the best or the worst possible case for an idea, program, person, or product.

Band Wagon has as its theme, "Everybody—at least all of *us*—is doing it"; with it, the propagandist attempts to convince us that all members of a group to which we belong are accepting his program and that we *must therefore* follow our crowd and "jump on the band wagon."

In this particular publication each device is represented by a visual symbol which, like the title of the device itself, can be easily memorized. "Glittering Generality," for example, is "symbolized by a glittering gem that may or may not have its apparent value," and "Plain Folks" by "that traditional analogue for an old friend, an old shoe."

The book itself concerns the public utterances of Father Charles E. Coughlin, a priest whose fascist-sounding broadcasts attracted wide attention in the United States during the late 1930's. It demonstrates that he employed each of the devices. It refutes and debunks many of his assertions. It reproduces and simultaneously "analyzes" sections of his addresses by inserting after each word or phrase the symbol standing for the propaganda "device" he is said to have "used." The final paragraph from one of Coughlin's speeches on February 26, 1939, was as follows:

Ours must be a moral platform from which there is preached policy based upon the principles of religion and of patriotism.   For God and country, for Christ and the flag—that is our motto as we prepare for action, for Christian American action, which is neither anti-German, anti-Italian, nor anti-Semitic.   Any negative policy is destined to failure.   Only a positive policy can hope to succeed.   Unified action on a common program for God and country is more necessary now than at any other period in the history of our civilization.

The Institute's analysts seized this paragraph and sprinkled it with the visual symbols.   Here in place of the symbols, the names of the devices are italicized in parentheses:

Ours (*Plain Folks*) must be a moral (*Glittering Generality*) platform from which there is preached (*Transfer*) a positive (*Glittering Generality*) policy based upon the principles of religion (*Glittering Generality, Transfer*) and of patriotism (*Glittering Generality*).   For God (*Transfer*) and country (*Transfer, Glittering Generality*), for Christ (*Transfer*) and the flag (*Transfer, Glittering Generality*) —that is our motto as we prepare for action, for Christian American (*Transfer, Glittering Generality*) action, which is neither anti-German, anti-Italian, nor anti-Semitic (*Card Stacking*).   Any negative (*Name Calling*) policy is destined to failure.   Only a positive policy (*Glittering Generality*) can hope to succeed.   Unified (*Band Wagon*) action on a common (*Band Wagon*) program for God (*Transfer*) and country is more necessary now than at any other period in the history of our civilization (*Card Stacking*) (*25*).

In this single paragraph of five sentences, it can be seen, Coughlin made use of six of the seven devices—he omitted to drag in a Testimonial—and, moreover, he employed those six a grand total of twenty-two times.

This technique of analyzing propaganda content is open to several criticisms.   In the first place, the allocation of a device to a word or phrase is a purely subjective procedure. There is no guarantee that other analysts would scatter the devices amidst the propaganda in precisely the same way. Conceivably, for example, the first word "Ours" in the above paragraph might be listed under "Band Wagon" rather than "Plain Folks"; the next four words, "must be a moral," under "Transfer" rather than "Glittering Generality"; etc.   In fact, another analyst might not consider the use of "Ours" a propaganda device or he could assert that the word "platform" in the first sentence demonstrates that Coughlin was resorting to "Transfer." Then, secondly, no attempt was made in this or in any of the Institute publications to indicate the frequency with which the various devices were employed in a given propaganda campaign. The chemist is not content when he merely identifies the elements of a liquid: he also measures the quantity of each.

Nor is it clear, in the third place, exactly what part of the propaganda is being analyzed. The propagandist is said to "use" a given device. Does this mean that he deliberately selects the device because he believes it will promote his cause or does he intuitively and spontaneously employ it? Is reference being made to the ways in which the propagandees can be expected to respond or have actually responded to the propaganda? To choose between the first pair of questions would require an examination of the propagandist, and to choose between the second pair would lead to an investigation of the propagandees, neither one of which was made before Coughlin's or any propaganda was analyzed in terms of the seven devices. Finally, the scheme makes no formal provision for such items as the propagandist's intention, his position in society, or his organization; for the media of communication employed; for the effects upon propagandees either in the short- or the longrun; or for the evaluation of the facts or pseudo-facts being communicated. These subjects, it might be said, need not be included in an analysis of propaganda content as such, but some or all of them had to be mentioned journalistically and unsystematically in each of the Institute's reports.

Both the strength and the weakness of the Institute's approach to propaganda can be traced to its announced purpose of analyzing propaganda in order to help its subscribers detect the forces affecting them. After describing the seven devices, for example, the analysts of Coughlin consider the following sentence so important that they have italicized it: "Once we know that a speaker or writer is using one of these propaganda devices in an attempt to convince us of an idea, we can separate the device from the idea and see what the idea amounts to on its own merits" (*26*). This laudable purpose required that the analysis be simple and easily comprehended by high school students or, as some members of the Institute's Board used to say to one another, by taxicab drivers. The analysis had to be based upon a limited number of "devices" which could be understood and memorized with no great difficulty. But the need to oversimplify also gave rise to the elimination of crucial problems or to an informal treatment of them which depended on the ability and bias of the particular journalist who was writing the report.

The procedure of the Institute for Propaganda Analysis, nevertheless, was less literary and impressionistic than most of the other reports on propaganda which were being published at the time. At least there were the seven devices—and later eleven additional ones which were almost never used—and at least there was a more or less stereotyped format in all the publications. The Institute's investigatory activities, moreover, were limited by a budget which remained precarious, and therefore it generally had to confine its analyses only to an examination of the most accessible data, the printed or spoken words of the propagandist.

The Need for Quantification

Systematic efforts have been made to analyze the content of communications and propaganda in a very refined and quantitative manner. Lasswell (*e.g., 20*), who has been one of the most prodigious workers in the field, has sought to discover what the propagandist wishes to bring to "the focus of attention" of the propagandees. The research sophistication of people who quantify the content of communication has been far greater than that of the Institute for Propaganda Analysis and therefore their contribution will undoubtedly be more permanent.

Since almost everyone has an aversion toward numbers and their mathematical manipulation, it is necessary to ask why quantification of propaganda content is necessary. The answer is the same as that which must be given to justify any kind of quantification: greater accuracy and economy. The day is divided arbitrarily into twenty-four hours, the hour into sixty minutes, and the minute into sixty seconds not to make life more difficult but to simplify it. It is much easier for two people to arrange a meeting at 2:30 in the afternoon than it is simply to agree to meet "some time in the early part of the afternoon." In this instance it would be useless to mention the precise second at which the meeting is to occur, but the second becomes an important quantitative unit when a decision must be made concerning the length of time the film in a camera should be exposed by the opening of the shutter.

Very often propaganda materials are so voluminous that their contents cannot be grasped at a glance. In the month of March 1942, for example, the journalists and technicians employed by the Coordinator of Inter-American Affairs sent three so-called "Newsletters" to influential individuals in Latin America; distributed hundreds of news items to short-wave broadcasting stations for use in their Latin American programs; sent innumerable photographs, cartoons, and—by airmail—feature stories to Latin American editors; and published a picture magazine called *En Guardia*. The real purpose of this propaganda was to prevent Latin American countries from entering the Axis camp and to have them co-operate with the foreign and economic policy of the United States, but it was phrased as a sincere desire to improve relations among the twenty-one American Republics and to promote the "Good Neighbor Policy." It was difficult or impossible to know just which themes the propaganda was stressing at a given moment: so much had been produced and one individual, even if he had had the time and linguistic ability to read everything, would have emerged with only an impressionistic account of what had been featured and what had been neglected. In order, therefore, to check on the propaganda output, a group of analysts under the supervision of the writer read all the propaganda, analyzed and quantified it, and was then able to emerge with Table 1 which gave a concise summary of the propaganda content during that month. In addition, for each of the media a detailed breakdown was provided. At a glance, for example, the second column in Table 1—the one for news stories distributed to shortwave broadcasting stations—could be made more meaningful by consulting Table 2. Such an analysis, moreover, was continued month after month and hence the trend of the propaganda's content

TABLE 1

OVER-ALL PERCENTAGE OF WEIGHTED OR UNWEIGHTED MATERIAL
DEVOTED TO PROPAGANDA THEMES: MARCH, 1942

Theme	*A*	*B*	*C*	*D*	*E*	*F*
Factors contributing to United Nations' victory	68	18.5	58	44	70	28
Peace aims of the United Nations	2	2.5	1	0	0	7
Description of U. S. institutions	0	2	10	2	0	8
Condemnation of Axis policies in Europe and Asia	0	13	3	10	0	4
Menace of Axis to the Americas	0	6	0	5	0	0
United Hemisphere actions against the Axis	30	32	13	18	27	23
Common cultural interests of the Americas	0	25	15	21	3	30
Miscellaneous	0	1	0	0	0	0
Total	100	100	100	100	100	100

Columns: *A.* Three Newsletters; *B.* Stories for shortwave radio; *C.* Pictures and cartoons; *D.* Feature stories; *E.* Sixth issue of *En Guardia*; *F.* Airmail feature service.

TABLE 2

Percentage of Weighted Space Devoted to Propaganda Themes in Stories Distributed to Shortwave Stations: March, 1942

Factors contributing to United Nations' victory		18.5
Actual military successes	6	
Strength of U. S. industry and agriculture	2	
Progress in war production	2	
Civilian morale	3	
Cooperation of United Nations	2	
Other	3.5	
Peace aims of the United Nations		2.5
Description of U. S. institutions		2
Condemnation of Axis policies in Europe and Asia		13
Religious persecution	2	
Exploitation of oppressed nations	3	
Propaganda methods	2	
"Atrocity story"	3	
Other	3	
Menace of Axis to the Americas		6
Criticism of propaganda activity in Latin America	2	
Plans for conquest in Latin America	1	
Other	3	
United Hemisphere actions against the Axis		32
Significant cooperation	7	
Anti-Axis measures in Latin America	4	
Joint military collaboration	6	
Mutual economic assistance	12	
Other	3	
Common cultural interests of the Americas		25
Art	2	
Medicine and health	2	
Music	1	
Education	3	
Economic institutions	4	
Political institutions	2	
Society notes	4	
Other	7	
Miscellaneous		1
Total		100

could be observed. From quantitative breakdowns of this type, the journalists could discover to what extent they were implementing the policies of the United States Government.

Through similar quantitative methods various media of communication in- and outside the United States have been examined, their contents categorized, and statements made concerning the implications of the results from various viewpoints. In the early 1920's, for example, one survey of country newspapers in the state of Connecticut (*31*) showed that those papers were giving less news about their own areas and using more boilerplate as time passed; a little later, not dissimilar quantitative conclusions (*29*) were published concerning the weeklies in Nebraska. Another quantitative analysis of forty carefully selected and representative evening newspapers in the United States (*32*) revealed, for example, that only 5 or 6 percent of their news was devoted to foreign affairs and that those in New York City printed more of such news than papers elsewhere in the country. At the end of that decade a group of quantitatively inclined analysts as Bryn Mawr College (*13*) ran various American newspapers through their statistical mill and emerged with historically limited generalizations concerning the number of sensational and serious headlines that were employed; and concerning the amount of space allocated to the controversial issues of the day.

As World War II broke out in Europe, the frequency with which the United States was mentioned favorably or unfavorably—or mentioned at all—in headlines of German, British, Mexican, and Hongkong newspapers was tabulated (*19, 23*). In general, analysts tended to concentrate upon radio propaganda because the monitoring of broadcasts produced a voluminous collection of heterogeneous materials which invited analysis. The British Broadcasting Corporation organized an extensive monitoring and analysis section at Caversham not far from London. The Rockefeller Foundation in the fall of 1940 subsidized the Princeton Listening Center and an experimental group at Leland Stanford University.

Later, in the summer of 1941, the Federal Communications Commission established what was subsequently called the Foreign Broadcast Intelligence Service. Until the end of the war, this organization circulated daily digests of broadcasts from the most important radio stations of the world as well as weekly analyses of radio and (to a lesser degree) press materials. The weekly analyses were permeated with shrewd and naive interpretations of the propaganda and occasionally contained quantitative breakdowns. The use of this method to "measure" public opinion in Germany has already been suggested in a previous chapter. Once a simple graph revealed the rapid decline of Mussolini's political fortunes after he had been "rescued" from Allied forces by German paratroopers: right after the rescue in July 1943, the Nazi-controlled Radio Rome referred to him, on the average, over four times each day, but by the end of that year he was mentioned, on the average, only once every other day. The varying amount of time Hitler devoted to affixing war guilt, attacking the Jews, praising himself, etc., as he addressed the German people was quantitatively revealed; thus, a comparison of his beerhall-putsch-anniversary declarations of 1942 and 1943 indicated a marked tendency for him to devote proportionately less time to the increasingly unpleasant present and more to exhortations about the future.

During the war, too, Harold D. Lasswell's Experimental Division for the Study of War Time Communications, which was located in the Library of Congress, studied methodological problems of content analysis and also made outdated quantitative analyses of Nazi newsreels, the German press, etc. Under completely private auspices a group of scholars at the New School for Social Research concentrated on quantitative as well as qualitative analyses of German broadcasts which were obtained from the admittedly incomplete daily digests of the B. B. C.'s monitoring service. Their results were eventually published in various mimeographed memoranda and in a book on the domestic radio propaganda of the Nazis (*15*).

In addition to the research which has been done on the press and radio and to comparisons between these media

(*12*), there have been content analyses of communications as diverse as motion pictures (*10*), the language of the sane and the insane (*4, 28*), popular books (*30*), sermons delivered by Protestant ministers from 1929 to 1940 (*7*), the "major propositions of Freud's theory of the dream" that were discussed in American textbooks on abnormal psychology (*8*), the mail received by certain senators during the debate on the Selective Service Bill in 1940 (*33*), case histories of social workers in terms of the tension detected in their clients (*2*), and—as indicated in a previous chapter—letters intercepted by censorship authorities during the last war.

A precise analysis of propaganda content is not necessarily better than the commonsense method employed by the Institute for Propaganda Analysis merely because the data are quantified. For any analysis is only as good as the techniques which underlie it and as the technicians who conduct it. The technical problems which all content analyses must meet and resolve, consequently, must be examined in some detail. For illustrative purposes, the newspaper will be employed, but it should be clear that the analysis of any other medium or communication raises the same questions.

The Measurement Unit

The selection of a measurement unit usually involves both a sampling problem and a decision concerning the purpose of the analysis. Only infrequently are all the newspapers of a country analyzed—it may be necessary to choose only particular issues of each paper. When the analyst has one issue in front of him, he must decide which pages will be examined. Stories on the selected page or pages must be chosen. The unit of measurement is applied within a story, but perhaps only after part or parts have been singled out for examination. Finally, it may be thought desirable or necessary to weight the separate parts of the story.

Suppose, for example, the analyst wishes to study trends in the Bulgarian press over a period of ten years. Unless he has a corps of assistants and considerable money at his disposal, he will be compelled to select a sample of the newspapers appearing during that interval. His sample, like the pollster's, must be representative in respect to the known attributes of Bulgarian papers. These attributes undoubtedly include factors like the place at which a paper is published, the type of owner, the social or economic class of the readers, the circulation, etc. An attempt is thus made to choose a few papers which reflect those attributes and which, therefore, are representative of all the papers that are not examined.

When the analyst has chosen his sample of the press, he may find that he must confine his analysis to a sub-sample of each paper for reasons of economy or effort. This sub-sample must also be representative of all the issues of the paper. If he selects every seventh issue of a paper that appears seven days a week, then he will be confining his analysis, for example, to Tuesday papers—and Tuesday editions are likely to be different from those published on other days. Every sixth or eighth issue would result in better randomization. If a longer interval is necessary, then perhaps the analysis can be confined to the issues appearing on the first and fifteenth or just the first of each month—but then it is necessary to determine that there is nothing unrepresentative about Bulgarian papers which are published on those dates.

After specific issues of particular papers have been selected, the analyst must choose the page or pages that are to be sent through his statistical machine. Obviously this selection cannot be made at random since no one or two pages of a paper are at all representative of the rest. If only the first or the most important page is examined, then all the other pages which may be of greater significance to some readers are disregarded. On a given page, it is also necessary to decide which stories will be read.

Finally the story to be analyzed confronts the analyst, but his decisions are not yet at an end. Shall he read the headline or the entire story? If the headline is the unit, then only that which is guessed to be at the "focus of attention" is being measured and the text of the story is neglected.

Or perhaps the lead sentence or paragraph is used. If the story is the unit, then its headline, length, position on the page and within the paper, and the accompanying illustration or picture (if there be one) may or may not be taken into account. If the idea within the story is the unit, a decision must be reached concerning the vehicle which expresses the idea: will it be the paragraph, the sentence, the clause, the phrase, or the word? If it is, for example, the paragraph, what should the analyst do about a particular paragraph that contains more than one propaganda theme? Should all themes therein be scored or should only the dominant one? If only the dominant one, then some kind of definition of dominance must be provided.

Unless the analyst is interested in everything printed by the press of a country, he finds that he can make some of these numerous decisions by referring to the purpose of his investigation. An interest in the editorials of Bulgarian papers, for example, immediately indicates which page and which articles thereon must be analyzed. Similarly concern for stories about Greece which appear in the Bulgarian press results in the selection of only those stories which mention that country. Frequently, moreover, the sampling and sub-sampling problems are simplified when the analyst is considering not a ten-year period but a shorter period of time like a week or a month; then a proportionately large sample can be utilized and the problem of selecting that sample becomes less acute.

In any case, the selection of an analysis unit ultimately involves a number of psychological assumptions which may or may not be true. Lasswell and his students, for example, have made their press analyses manageable by concentrating upon the headlines of the most important page. No doubt they are correct in believing that these headlines are at the "focus of attention," but their belief requires empirical verification. It may very well be that what people remember is affected not only by the headline but by the opening paragraph which in many countries contains the essence of the story. It is equally clear, if the entire text of the story as well as its headline and lead paragraph are to be analyzed, that a paragraph buried somewhere toward the end of the story is probably less important than the headline or the lead. But how much less important? Should the headline be given a score of five and the buried section a score of one? If this is done, it must be assumed that the former is five times more important than the latter: does this mean that five times as many people will read the headline, that five times as many will remember that headline, or that the editor considers the thought in the headline five times more significant than the idea of the paragraph? Similarly an assumption is made when a theme is weighted directly in terms of its length. If one thought occupies twice as much space as another and hence the first is scored two and the second one, it does not necessarily follow that the "attention value," the memory value, or the adequacy of treatment proceeds in the same ratio.

What is done in practice, therefore, is to use an arbitrary but carefully reasoned system of scoring when content is being analyzed in detail. In the two tables concerning Latin America which have been reproduced in this chapter, for example, each photograph and cartoon was given equal weight regardless of size, because no assumptions could be made concerning which ones would be printed and, if printed, how prominently they would be displayed. The magazine, *En Guardia,* on the other hand, was a finished product and was therefore distributed to its readers in that form. The pictures on its front and rear covers as well as photographs in color were weighted more than those placed elsewhere in the publication or printed simply in black-and-white because it was assumed that prominent position and color would attract more readers.

The Selection of Categories

Measurement units are selected so that each of them can be thrown into one or more categories. When this has been done, it is possible to tabulate the frequency with which the categories appear in the propaganda whose content is being analyzed. The analyst, for example, may be interested in the references Bulgarian newspapers make to the Soviet Union. He has already made these decisions concerning the measurement unit:

1. To analyze every eighth issue of ten representative newspapers over a specified period of time.
2. To examine every story mentioning a country outside of Bulgaria in its headline or opening paragraph.
3. Not to weight the story in terms of the page on which it appears or its position thereon.
4. To use as measurement units the headline, the sub-head, and each of the sentences in the opening paragraph; to disregard the remainder of the story.
5. To follow the arbitrary rule of assigning one score to a category each time it appears in one of the above units, regardless of how many units each story contains and how frequently the category appears.

The simplest procedure then would be to count the number of times the actual words "Soviet Union" appear in the units of stories about foreign countries. But the Soviet Union can be referred to in different ways: it may be called Russia, the U.S.S.R., the Land of the Soviets, our neighbor to the East, etc. These too might be specified and counted. The final tabulation, however, would reveal relatively little concerning the actual treatment accorded that country by the Bulgarian press. It would merely indicate the frequency of reference, not the type of reference.

At this point the analysis could be expanded. Each reference to the Soviet Union might be classified as "favorable," "unfavorable," "neutral," or "ambiguous" from some specified viewpoint such as the reporter's attitude toward that country or the attitude which, it is assumed, he is attempting to have his readers adopt. The final tabulation would reveal to what extent Bulgarian reporters approve or disapprove or wish their readers to approve or disapprove of Russia, but it would not suggest the specific points concerning which they are expressing their attitudes or concerngin which they wish to affect their readers' attitudes. Both of the following statements, which are quite different in respect to subject matter, might be classified as "unfavorable":

"The standard of living in the Soviet Union has shown no steep rise in recent years comparable to that observed in capitalistic countries with similar natural resources."

"The foreign policy of the Soviet Union is based upon the doctrine of the permanent revolution which ruthlessly seeks to establish communism in every country of the world."

To differentiate between two statements like these in the final tabulation, it would be necessary to have a system of categories much more elaborate than the four which suggest the reporter's attitude or the attitude he seeks to promote. The analysis could be kept small and manageable by having general categories such as "domestic affairs," "foreign affairs," "Communist Party," etc. Even these categories, however, remain abstract and do not catch the concrete flavor of the statements that are placed thereunder. Thus the following two statements might be classified under "domestic affairs" and subclassified further under "disapproval," although their specific references are certainly not identical:

"Consumer goods in the Soviet Union remain scarce because the economy is mismanaged."

"Soviet citizens do not express their opinions for fear they will be liquidated."

Since no two statements are ever completely identical, it follows that a system of categories, no matter how detailed, cannot reflect all the nuances which each statement contains.

Again the purpose of the analysis and the analyst's resources must be the factors which determine how detailed the classification can be. A simple four-category scheme of favorable-unfavorable-neutral-ambiguous will be sufficient if all that is needed is the direction of the reference and not its content. It may be the only feasible scheme, moreover, if the analyst must work alone and has only limited time at his disposal: the greater the number of categories, the longer it takes to conduct the analysis. The same sentence, it must be emphasized, can be analyzed with completely different sets of categories, depending on the analyst's interests. A sentence like "the foreign policy of the Soviet Union is the only realistic one in the world today" can be scored as "declarative sentence, positive, unqualified" by the analyst concerned with the type of sentence employed by a propagandist; or as "Soviet Union, foreign policy, approval" by the analyst interested in the probable intention of the propagandist or the possible effect of such a stimulus upon the readers. Regardless of categories, it must be reluctantly concluded, a content analysis of propaganda makes an assumption concerning the propagandist or the propagandee. Certainly the number of words or references to a particular subject in a communication can be counted without further assumptions; but the counting stems from some purpose, and the meaning of the words and the tabulation itself become clear only when the reaction of a human being—the propagandist or the propagandee—is taken into account.

A system of categories can be designed to reveal both the attitudes expressed by the propagandist or the one he presumably wishes to evoke or create in his audience as well as the content of the attitude. The analyst may be required either to make two separate judgments for content and attitude or to choose from among categories which already indicate both. The first method would include categories like "Soviet foreign policy," "Soviet domestic policy," and "Soviet cultural traditions," each of which can be classified as "favorable," "unfavorable," or "neutral." The second would be based on categories like "praise of Soviet foreign policy" and "condemnation of Soviet foreign policy," each of which specifies the content and the attitude. In addition, other dimensions may be added such as adequacy of treatment or type of style.

Considerable time and energy are saved in the long run if the analyst carefully samples the propaganda to be analyzed before he sets down his categories and proceeds to quantify the statements. Only in this way can he be reasonably certain that all or almost all of the statements can be fitted into his scheme. The addition or the changing of a category or sub-category after the analysis has once begun usually means that the previous analysis must be repeated. Thus, with a simple system in which items are classified only in respect to attitude as "favorable," "unfavorable," and "neutral," the analyst may proceed without an "ambiguous" category until he comes upon a statement which cannot be classified under one of these three headings; then, if he adds "ambiguous" as a fourth category, he must examine each of the statements which he has previously classified to determine, for example, whether a statement he has called "neutral" ought now to be included among the "ambiguous" ones. It is especially difficult to choose inclusive categories when all the propaganda to be analyzed is not at hand, as when a current analysis of a medium is made. Government analysts were faced with this kind of situation during the last war when they were called upon to make up-to-the-minute analyses of enemy radio propaganda. There is no real solution to the problem. The new category may be added or the old one changed without redoing previous analyses by simply altering the tabulation at the point where the change occurs; but this procedure spoils whatever trends have been worked out. The addition or alteration, however, becomes less serious when the category involved is a sub-category or a sub-sub one, inasmuch as the higher category remains unchanged. A new category may be added without a re-tabulation if the analyst feels convinced that the communication has not already contained statements which would have been included thereunder and if the logic of his scheme permits expansion.

It is always tempting to have a miscellaneous category into which novel or different themes can be thrown. Such a category, however, discards part of the propaganda and is really only an index of the analyst's laziness. It should be employed, if at all, only very rarely.

The categories which were utilized to analyze United States propaganda to Latin America have been previously suggested in Tables 1 and 2. The seven main categories were deliberately selected because they were the principal points which the "information program" sought to make clear to Latin Americans. These were the intentions of the propagandist as they were communicated to the writer in the midst of the hurly-burly of a somewhat disorganized war agency. The sub-categories, on the other hand, represented the themes which were actually employed to implement the seven points and which the propagandee might "reasonably" be expected to learn. The system, therefore, sought to combine known intentions and guessed reactions.

The Reliability of the Analysis

Reliability is being employed here in about the same sense as it has been applied to polls and other methods of measuring public opinion. Reference is made to the degree to which two or more analysts classify the segments of the communication or propaganda under the same categories or the degree to which one analyst agrees with his earlier decisions when he repeats the analysis. The statement, "the Soviet Union always lives up to its agreements," might be classified by one analyst under "Soviet Union, foreign affairs, approval" and by another or by the same analyst subsequently under "Soviet Union, generality, ambiguous." The system of analysis would be considered in this instance to be reliable with respect to the category of "Soviet Union" but unreliable in regard to the other two categories. The various statistical procedures employed to determine reliability cannot be described here; they measure the relationship between two sets of data secured from an initial analysis and from a repetition of that analysis by one or more analysts or subsequently by the same analyst. Any measurement of reliability seeks to determine how dependent the analysis is upon the particular analyst. Approximately identical results are obtained no matter which competent chemist undertakes the analysis of a liquid. Propaganda analysis is always much less reliable, inasmuch as subjective elements creep into the judgments which must be made before a statement can be classified under one category rather than another.

Some of the factors determining reliability have been tentatively if inconclusively established (*5, 9, 11*) and, on the basis of this research and of experience in conducting analyses, certain precautions can be indicated which help eliminate as far as possible the subjectivity of the analysts.

At the very beginning, each category is carefully defined, and illustrations from the propaganda are given to demonstrate to which types of statements it is applicable. In the scheme employed in the office of the Coordinator of Inter-American Affairs, for example, the following definition was given in connection with the first main category, "Factors Contributing to United Nations' Victory":

These factors are directly related to the winning of the war. Of course anything that happens in the present world is related to the war in some way, but here we are concerned only with those events affecting the struggle in a very immediate sense.

Under this main category was one sub-category headed "Actual Military Successes"; these were the accompanying instructions:

Actual military successes means fighting and nothing else: it refers to specific bombings, specific attacks, specific battles, etc. The only abstract statement to be included is a reference to military strategy. Include discussion of Axis defeats and United Nations' successes.

Then the chief investigator carefully instructs each analyst and checks his preliminary attempts to apply the system of categories. If there is only one analyst, he repeats his own work after sufficient time has elapsed for him to forget his first judgments. In theory two or more analysts should always analyze the same propaganda, but in practice this is seldom desirable since thereby the labor is correspondingly increased. As a compromise it is necessary to conduct occasional trial-runs during the analysis in order to determine the reliability of each analyst, to correct the inevitable departures from the stipulated definitions which occur, and in general to prevent the analysts from succumbing to boredom.

There tends to be, unfortunately, an inverse relationship between the number of categories employed in an analysis and their reliability: the greater the number of categories, the less the reliability most generally will be. Equally unfortunate is a similar inverse relationship between the amount of initiative the analyst is permitted to exercise in applying the categories and the reliability. Both of these relationships are considered unfortunate because a system of classification with many categories which can be applied less rigidly almost always brings results that are more significant, but it does so at the expense of reliability. The use of only five categories means that through sheer chance the probability is one out of five that two analysts will agree with each other, whereas the use of ninety reduces the chance probability to one out of ninety. Practice also reveals that some categories have greater reliability than others for reasons virtually beyond the control of the analyst and his subordinates: those with relatively concrete referents and those which must be employed frequently because they appear again and again in the communication tend to be more reliable than abstract categories or ones resorted to infrequently. There is no hard-and-fast rule to assist the analyst in determining whether he should sacrifice the significance of his results in order to increase reliability or whether he should increase their significance while decreasing their reliability. Again some kind of compromise is generally necessary. It is always desirable, furthermore, to have analysts who have had extensive analytical experience and who are highly motivated to perform their tasks efficiently. Their judgments are likely to be more reliable than those given by a relatively inexperienced, poorly motivated group; hence the number and complexity of the categories they may be trusted to employ can be greater. It must be added that turnover among analysts on a large project tends to be great because the work is unbelievably tedious.

The same question of reliability must be raised concerning the units which are being identified. For practical purposes, perfect or near-perfect reliability can be assumed for clear-cut units such as words, sentences, or paragraphs—here simple counting is involved. The analyst who must decide whether a set of categories is applicable to part of a sentence may not agree with another analyst or, later, with himself concerning which parts should be isolated. It has been shown (3) that, while reliability concerning number of units may be relatively low, overall reliability concerning content may be much higher if only three categories are employed and if the results are expressed in terms of a ratio involving two of these categories.

The Validity of the Conclusions

After all of the units of the communication have been assigned to categories and after the number or proportion in each category has been tabulated, the analyst then emerges with his final results whose reliability he has previously determined. The question of the validity of these results then arises: are they an accurate measure of the content which has been analyzed? The validity of a chemical analysis is relatively easy to test: after the chemist has determined the ingredients of a liquid, he can check the accuracy of the analysis by securing each of the separate ingredients, by combining them under specified conditions, and then by observing whether the resulting combination resembles the original product.

Very rarely can the results of a content analysis be rigorously tested through the use of some independent criterion. The main categories employed to analyze United States propaganda to Latin America, for example, could not be validated by asking the propagandists themselves how much space or time they had been devoting or wished to devote to each theme: their own judgments were subjective and, besides, the system was devised in the first place to give them a systematic account of what they were doing. Nor could the validity of the sub-categories be determined by surveying the propagandees in Latin America: such a survey was not feasible under wartime conditions and with the budget at the writer's disposal. In fact a survey would have been impractical even under ideal conditions that never exist on this earth: no Latin American presumably was actually affected by all of the propaganda. The reactions of the propagandees who did perceive the propaganda, furthermore, would also have had to be thrown into a system of categories.

Approximate tests of the validity of content analyses have sometimes been made. In 1942, for example, certain individuals were suspected of being Nazi agents in the United States. During their trial, Lasswell and others (*21*) presented content analyses which demonstrated that parallel themes had been simultaneously utilized by the defendants and by official Nazi propaganda. The identities thus revealed might have been coincidental, but independent evidence from other witnesses and later from documents captured in Germany substantiated the fact that some of these individuals had actually been subsidized by the Nazis. Similarly during the presidential campaign of 1940 in the United States, one investigator (*1*) first analyzed the themes stressed by rival newspapers and radio stations and then he asked a sample of informants whether they had seen or heard the themes. The fact that some of his sample reported that they had "come across" the arguments gives an indication of the validity of the analysis.

Efforts to make inferences concerning the propagandist from a quantitative analysis of his propaganda have not proven in general to be astonishingly successful. Government analysts during the last war sought to infer the propaganda directives of Dr. Goebbels from the propaganda his organization emitted, and a few directives which subsequently were captured indicated that their inferences were reasonably accurate. No systematic attempt, however, was ever made by American authorities after the war to check the validity of the inferences concerning public opinion or morale that had been made by intelligence experts on the basis of propaganda materials.

Nowhere in their somewhat exhaustive study of domestic German radio propaganda do Kris and Speier (*16*) give one bit of evidence to substantiate their assertion that "propaganda analysis has in the past been helpful in detecting the enemies' intentions." What they show with admirable hindsight is that the Nazis had the propaganda tasks of preparing the German people for impending military or diplomatic actions and of confusing the outside world concerning such events, and that Goebbels and his associates accomplished or tried to accomplish these tasks in many different ways (*17*). Their propaganda techniques, however, varied so much from situation to situation that no inductive guide to the future could be obtained. Prior to the Norwegian campaign, for example, the Nazis stated that the British were preparing to invade that country. Prior to the campaign in the Low Countries and France, they claimed that the British were preparing to invade the Balkans. Prior to the Russian campaign, they said nothing: they simply kept quiet about invasions. How, in the writers' words, "one learns to read between the lines of German propaganda" *before* an event and then deduces that event is not demonstrated. Reading between the lines in this case, moreover, involved an additional hazard: there may not have been complete coordination between the propaganda and the military machines of the Nazis.

A common reaction to a quantitative analysis of propaganda is to assert with some disgust that the elaborate procedure simply demonstrates what any individual could grasp merely by casually examining the propaganda. This assertion is much too broad, for the frailties of common sense or simple observation are quite obvious, especially when the materials are voluminous. It is fairer to charge that so much quantification is scarcely worth the effort involved when the results are never completely reliable and when their validity can seldom be adequately determined. In reply it must be said that high reliability is better than unknown reliability—and the reliability of the simple observer generally is unknown, as was indicated in connection with the procedures employed by the Institute for Propaganda Analysis. The problem of validity, moreover, persists even when the observer pays no attention to it; at least many propaganda analysts are usually aware of its existence.

A more serious charge against content analysis is this: there is little or no uniformity in the procedures employed. As a result, it is almost impossible to compare studies which have been made even in comparable fields because the methods of analysis are so different. This intellectual anarchy results in part from rivalry among analysts: another man's concept or statistical formula, as Max Weber (6) once said in a similar context, is viewed "as if it were his toothbrush" which may not be employed unless the lender happens to have been the borrower's teacher or bureau chief. But more of it is due to the fact that different analysts have varying interests which induce them to make their analyses in the first place, and therefore their conceptual tools as well as their methods are almost certain to be different. The outlook for standardization is indeed bleak.

CHAPTER 14

The Perception of Propaganda

T HE individual is perpetually reacting to stimuli in the external and internal environment. Light reaches his eyes, sounds strike his ears, odors drift into his nose, air currents touch his skin, pangs contract his stomach, urine distends his bladder, substances have contact with his tongue, glandular secretions pour into his blood stream, and even thoughts occasionally affect him. In any case these stimuli innervate nerve endings which then produce action within the corresponding nerves. Many but not all of the nervous impulses reach the higher centers of the brain and at this point, it might be added, they may become conscious. When these physiological changes are disregarded, the first response to a stimulus can be said to be the perception of that stimulus. Thereafter changes may occur and learning can begin.

The perceptual response, however, is neither strictly mechanical nor passive. Even a camera cannot be said to record the environment in undistorted fashion. What this instrument reproduces depends not only on the object in front of the lens, but also on the nature of the lens, the aperture and speed of the shutter, the distance of the lens from the film, and the type of film in the camera. Physiologists and psychologists have long noted discrepancies between what the individual consciously perceives and what is known to be the nature of the stimulus in the environment. Railway tracks appear to converge as they approach the horizon— and no amount of hard thinking and no amount of training can prevent this illusion from occurring. Similarly a motion picture does not move and, if the projecting machine is functioning properly, not even the most perverted member of the audience can perceive the light upon the screen as a discrete series of motionless exposures which differ slightly from one another. The nature, then, of the stimulus and sense organ which mediates the energy from that stimulus affects the perceptual response. The sense organ's nature, moreover, may be temporarily affected by immediately preceding experiences. It is difficult to perceive much of a darkened environment after emerging from a brightly lighted room; eventually, as the eyes become adapted, many more perceptual responses can be made. Or, to recall the trite but pointed illustration, the same pail of water at medium temperature, into which two hands are dipped, is perceived as hot when the right hand has been previously submerged in water of low temperature and simultaneously is perceived as cold when the left hand has been in water of high temperature.

The perceptual response may also be markedly affected by other responses which the individual is making simultaneously and which therefore may cause him to fail to make that response, to distort or simplify it, or to project his own personality upon it. The pain from a toothache is less likely to be perceived when the unfortunate person, for example, is engaged in an interesting conversation than when he is attempting to fall asleep. The paranoid person, filled with anxiety for reasons not clear to himself and not infrequently unknown to his psychiatrist, reacts with suspicion and fright to an innocent greeting. The identical criticism of a political institution may be considered an illustration of the functioning of democracy in peacetime and an act of treason during a war. There is, therefore, no one-to-one relation between a perceptual response and its stimulus: perception is a response of the individual to a stimulus that is transmitted by particular sense organs.

The factors determining each perceptual response are variously weighted. No matter how brightly illuminated a visual stimulus is and no matter how determined the individual is to perceive it clearly, his perception may be vague or blurred if he is almost but not completely blind. No matter how distinct the sound is to other people and no matter how perfect his sense of hearing is, the individual may not perceive that sound if at the moment he is thoroughly engrossed in some other activity like reading a book. And no matter how hard the individual tries to perceive a part of a stimulus situation and no matter how keen his eyesight, he may not perceive that part of the stimulus if—like a needle in a hay stack or, better, the figure of an animal concealed in a puzzle picture—it is embedded in a confusing or complicated context.

From the interrelationship and interaction of these factors two guiding principles emerge. In the first place, the perceptual response depends to a greater extent on the sense organs and on past habits when the stimulus is not part of a previous gradient, *i.e.,* when it is unstructured. A stimulus like "PFXEY" is vague and undifferentiated. Similarly the type of ink-blot employed in a modern Rorschach test to measure personality characteristics is deliberately unstructured; it cannot easily be discriminated as part of one gradient rather than another; for this reason, the report of what the subject says he perceives is thought to be symptomatic of drives functioning within him. In contrast, other stimuli are so well structured that variability in perception is reduced to a minimum. A drop of ink on a white handkerchief is immediately visible, regardless of the other responses that ensue thereafter.

Then, secondly, the ongoing response which affects perception is an internal response with drive properties. If reinforced, it becomes a habit and subsequently functions the way any other habit does. After being evoked by a stimulus falling along its gradient, for example, it is likely to be decisive in determining perception. Cattle-breeders perceive steers not as romantic creatures but as reproductive organisms of particular capabilities.

Propaganda must be perceived before it can possibly have any effect. The advertiser must reach people with his message, or else they may never know of the existence of the product. The politician must speak to his constituents or have his own acts and promises portrayed by others or in the press if he is ever to win an election. The biased school teacher must have students to teach if his or her point of view is to be transmitted. The war propagandist seeks desperately to break through the perceptual barriers which the enemy erects to prevent the home and fighting fronts from hearing or seeing anything which might be demoralizing. The propagandist who does not reach his prospective audience is a failure from the outset.

In any society there is always a host of stimuli to which the individual can respond. Even the blessed savage of folklore fame who is supposed to lead a simple life is faced with a variety of stimuli: as he stands under the blue sky, cool breezes stroke his face, flowers give forth their scent, animals bestir themselves, and his family speaks to him in words of love and understanding. The lonely hermit may not perceive the bird on the tree because he has an itch or he may not scratch his skin because he is watching the bird. Stimuli, as it were, continually compete with one another to be perceived by people.

In modern society stimuli bombard the individual on all sides. From the physical environment come lights and scenery. From the internal environment come aches and drives and feelings. From the social environment come competing advertisements, competing political plans, competing social philosophies, and in general competing pressures. In the midst of all these stimuli appears some propaganda which therefore may not automatically be perceived. Means must be devised to have prospective propagandees perceive that propaganda stimulus.

The Size of the Audience

The most primitive and available medium of propaganda is the human voice and its accompanying gestures of face and body. For the voice can express the thought to be propagated and it can be perceived by someone else. This medium by itself is employed when only persuasion is involved or when a speaker is addressing an audience. More usually, however, some form of amplification is employed.

The amplification may consist merely of a public-address system which relays the sound of the voice to the far corners of the hall or beyond the fringes of the outdoor crowd. Or it may involve a national hookup of radio stations which potentially can transmit the sound in a form perceptible to millions of people. Obviously other media may be substituted for the voice. The propaganda may be printed in a Sunday supplement to a newspaper, a leaflet, or an annual report. It may appear in still or motion pictures accompanied or unaccompanied by captions or sound. The propaganda medium may be as permanent as a sign in sombre bronze or as impermanent as writing in the sky.

The choice of medium from a perceptual viewpoint depends on two considerations. In the first place, it is clear that the propagandist can utilize only those media which are available to him. A radio station must be functioning in the society or the country before there can be radio propaganda. Even if there is a station, the propagandist may be barred from employing its facilities: no time may be free for the program, certain types of propaganda may be banned from the radio, or radio may simply be an unsuitable medium for the propaganda. A billboard is considered to be an effective medium by American advertisers, but billboards have been outlawed from some important highways.

The war propagandist who seeks to reach as many of the enemy as possible usually commandeers all conceivable media of communication, but he is limited by very important physical and geographical factors. In the last war the radio was employed extensively since electrical waves respect neither boundary lines nor fortifications. The transmission of a program, however, by no means guaranteed that the target audience would perceive it. Reception from particular areas even under ideal atmospheric conditions is sometimes uncertain, unintelligible, or at least difficult. American broadcasts to the Orient, for example, were made on one wavelength during one half of the year and on another during the remaining months for purely technical reasons relating to optimal reception. Sometimes shortwave radio signals, such as those beamed to Albania from New York, were too weak to be perceived by any except the most powerful sets. Frequently radio waves reached the country for which they were intended, but the audience was more or less effectively prevented from hearing them: listening to foreign broadcasts was a capital offense in Germany; many German and Japanese radio sets were not equipped to receive any but local broadcasts; in most of the Soviet Union sets were confiscated at the outbreak of the war and were replaced with instruments which could receive only the "wired wireless" transmitted over telephone lines by the official Soviet stations; or the authorities "jammed" broadcasts which they considered dangerous. Printed communications also served as important propaganda media, but here again perception by the enemy was never certain. Considerable research was carried on to devise the best type of shell and the most efficient method of dropping printed matter from airplanes, so that leaflets and abbreviated newspapers would reach the maximum number of civilians or soldiers. Otherwise an unfavorable wind or a limited dispersion would have prevented the material from being perceived. Only nationals living abroad in neutral countries could ever be reached by books, newspaper articles, or motion pictures.

Ordinarily, unless he is a member of an unpopular minority group, the propagandist in a democracy is not faced with the physical or geographical obstacles that exist during a war. What limits him is a second factor which is almost exclusively economic. Propaganda costs time and money. The advertiser, for example, never has an unrestricted budget at his disposal and therefore, although it is perfectly obvious to him that he could be more successful if he were able to have more people perceive his appeals, he must allocate his funds judiciously.

The purely perceptual factor determining the choice of

propaganda medium and to a certain extent the content of the propaganda is the potential number of people who can be expected to perceive that medium.   An advertiser certainly selects the magazine with the largest circulation, *provided* its rates are no higher than its competitors and provided, as will be indicated in the next chapter, the subscribers include those people who are likely to be attracted to his product.   His decision will be based on budgetary considerations alone if he must choose between two magazines reaching approximately the same type of reader and if the one which charges twice as much as the other also has double the circulation.   Similarly his budget will determine whether he selects an advertisement of a certain size which costs $500 and is perceived by 40,000 people or one of a larger size which costs $2,000 and is perceived by 80,000 people.   Both experimentation and empirical investigation seem to reveal no one-to-one relation between the size of a printed message and the number of people who perceive it.   Instead the "attention value" of copy has been found to be *very* roughly proportional to the square root of its size: to double the number of people perceiving the propaganda in a given medium, its size must be not doubled but more or less quadrupled (*2*).

Stimulus Intensity

The more intense a stimulus is, the more likely it is to be perceived.   Intense stimuli are able to stimulate the appropriate sense organs to a maximum and, when this occurs, the stimulation for the time being may be stronger than any coming from other sources.   The structure of the outside world rather than the mental set of people is the decisive factor.

The sudden sound of a cannon close by is heard by everyone except the deaf, even when their previous preoccupations and their perceptual habits have been quite different.   During the last war, combat propaganda teams employed powerful loudspeakers in order to point out to enemy troops the futility of continuing the struggle and the desirability of surrendering. Obviously, good equipment could enable the amplified voice to traverse long distances and to compete successfully with other sounds on the battlefield.

The intensity of visual propaganda can be increased through alterations in size or color and that of aural propaganda through changes in loudness or duration. Other attitudes with the propagandees being equal or inoperative, a large or a colored headline is more likely to be seen than one that is smaller or conventionally black. Under similar psychological conditions, a commercial plug on the radio is more likely to be heard if it is spoken clearly and loudly or if it is long than if it is mumbled, whispered, or brief. Intensity, however, is seldom the crucial factor in determining the perception of propaganda. Unlike the enemy soldier who is surrounded by his opponents and their loudspeaker, most people are being stimulated by competing propagandas and are able, more or less, to change the stimuli affecting them by moving into other situations. Successful propaganda requires more than a boom.

Perceptual Repetition

Many people worship at the altar of repetition when they think of human learning or of propaganda. They have observed that apparently repetition can accomplish psychological miracles and hence they deify the process by ascribing to it sole efficacy in determining behavior. Repetition in truth is important, but its importance should not be exaggerated or misunderstood.

Habits, for example, are thought to be strengthened by mere repetition. A man drives his car along one route rather than another, it is said, "through force of habit," and the more frequently he does so the less likely he is to modify the routine. Actually closer analysis always reveals that a habit is strengthened through repetition only when it leads to a goal response. The man will quickly abandon his chosen route, no matter how often he has previously transversed it, when he becomes convinced that another is shorter or pleasanter and when he does not fear that some minor or major disaster will thereby befall him.

Similarly it is not true that repetition will enable any kind of propaganda to be successful. It would be difficult and impossible in most instances to stage a successful propaganda campaign whose objective was mass suicide; even the Japanese system of indoctrination regarding this face-saving method was not completely successful when put to the test after crucial battles in which the soldiers of the Emperor had been defeated. A brand of cigarettes, no matter how heavily advertised, will not be purchased by many people if the odor of its smoke is distasteful or if inhalation leads to serious illness or discomfort.

Repetition of propaganda serves various psychological functions, but in this connection only its contribution to perception will be mentioned. The principle involved is very simple: the more frequently a stimulus is repeated, the more likely it is to be perceived. Again and again, from 1939 or 1941 to 1945, for example, allied propagandists told the Germans and Japanese that their leaders were responsible for the war and that its continuation would bring only greater disaster. Other psychological considerations aside, a single statement of these arguments could not possibly have been effective. Many Germans and Japanese would not have perceived them if they had been given only a single opportunity to do so. Similarly more people can be expected to see an advertisement which appears in identical form and in approximately the same position in two issues of a magazine than when it is run only once. As is true of size, the number of people perceiving propaganda lags behind the number of repetitions: when all other facts in the stimulus situation are controlled as they seldom can be, quadrupling the number of times a message is presented induces only approximately twice as many people to perceive or remember it (3).

Stimulus Context

As a stimulus affects a perceptual response, it is seldom isolated from other stimuli. These other stimuli can be

thought of as the context of the stimulus and they in turn
can influence the ensuing perception. Against a black background, a grey-colored square looks very white but against
a white background the same square appears much darker.
A more refined analysis would show that the effect of con-
texual stimuli upon perception is probably in turn dependent
on the sense organs and concurrent psychological processes,
but for practical purposes the structure of the stimulus
situation can be considered decisive.

The importance of context in propaganda can be most
easily illustrated in the field of advertising. A magazine
advertisement measuring 2″ x 4″ has a better chance of
being perceived when it is the only announcement on the
page (the rest being solid text) or when it is alongside an
article of some interest to the reader than when it must
compete with other and perhaps larger advertisements on
the same page. The advertisement on the rear cover of a
magazine, regardless of the absolute size of the page, is
perceived by more people than one appearing elsewhere in
the magazine; it is almost impossible to avoid seeing the
cover. Generally it is rather useless to know that there is
a tendency for the left-hand side of the page, the upper part
of the page, and the right page to be perceived more readily
than, respectively, the right-hand side, the lower part, and
the left page (*4*) because—while these tendencies result
from reading and manipulating habits and in some instances
(*14*) merely from advertising folklore which then has affected readers—other factors usually prove more decisive
in determining perception.

Layout or contextual factors also interact with readers'
habits in determining which parts of a newspaper are perceived. There is no question that a large headline or the
placing of a story on the first rather than on some other
page of an American newspaper aids perception. The most
important story, moreover, traditionally appears under the
largest headline and in the extreme right-hand column of the
first page. The uniform practice of having the largest headlines over that column and of printing many newsworthy
stories there has established an arbitrary habit among Amer-

ican readers who therefore have come to believe that a story in this position must be important. A syndicated column, in contrast, is quickly perceived by its devotees not for any contextual reason but as a result of their interest in the columnist—they may even employ the paper's index to locate it.

The selection of the most effective stimulus context involves technical knowledge of the medium's subtleties which only experts possess but which laymen intuit. In advertising the layout specialist knows through experience, market surveys, or his own skill how to arrange copy so that its most cogent points are in a context enabling them to be perceived. Any good photographer is able to emphasize or de-emphasize the foreground of a picture by shifting the position of his camera or adjusting its focus.

Merchandise is usually displayed so as to take advantage of the contextual factor in perception. Department store managers, for example, assume that the decision to purchase hardware and other durable household goods has been made by most people before they enter the store. For this reason the perceptual problem is considered unimportant, and such articles are generally buried at the rear of the store or on another floor. More frivolous articles, like cosmetics and candy, on the other hand, are displayed prominently near the entrance, for it is hoped that the mere perception of them while en route to another part of the store will by itself arouse attitudes leading to actual sales.

Auxiliary Responses

Most propagandees do not seek or are unwilling to be propagandized. The propagandist's message, consequently, is not automatically perceived when it is intense, when it is repeated, or when it stands out among other competing stimuli. People must, as it were, be seduced into perceiving propaganda. They must be offered bait before they will even notice the hook. That bait evokes habits within them which then determine what they will see or hear.

The previous attitude which leads to the perception of

propaganda can be called an *auxiliary response* because its psychological function is to produce not the learning required by the propaganda but only the perception at the basis of the learning. The radio listener hears a particular program because he has discovered that it will feature an orchestra or an individual he likes. Beforehand he may not know who the sponsor is or even what he sells. While listening, he unavoidably is made to perceive the plug and may be so impressed by the appeal that immediately or eventually he purchases the product. His purchase results not from the responses leading to and accompanying the program, but from the propaganda he has heard and from other attitudes within him. The responses facilitating perception have been merely auxiliary though absolutely necessary for the final behavior.

Auxiliary responses, in addition to their perceptual function, can also affect the learning of the response in line with the propaganda objective. One of the reasons—though not the decisive one—why the listener purchases the product may be a conviction that his patronage will help ensure the continuation of the program. Here the auxiliary response itself has acquired drive value and helps mediate the response of interest to the propagandist.

Auxiliary responses, such as an interest in music, usually can be more easily aroused than other responses more directly connected with the propaganda, such as those pertaining to the merits of a product. They are well-established habits which have been so heavily reinforced that they invariably appear whenever an appropriate stimulus—or some similar stimulus along a gradient of generalization—is at hand. Or else they are elicited since the individual already has tension which can be reduced by projection, identification, or displacement.

Printed advertising in the United States and many other countries makes extensive use of auxiliary responses to solve the perceptual problem. Themes and illustrations remotely or directly connected with the sexual drive in its broadest sense permeate advertising copy. The photograph of an attractive woman, within or not within the embrace of an

equally attractive man, may be perceived at first for reasons
connected with stimulus intensity or layout, but these factors
by themselves do not account for the longer glance bestowed
upon her.   To males she may offer some kind of substitute
gratification, especially when their own sexual adjustments
are imperfect: she enables them to imagine that she belongs
to them or she inspires them to wonder what they would do
if she were really theirs.   To females she may be an alluring
object with which to identify: she enables them to imagine
how they would feel if they were as beautiful as she, which
most of them of course are not.   Superficially at least she
may give members of either sex what is called an esthetic
thrill, a delightful term which can refer to innumerable attitudes.   People stare at her, in short, because in the past
the photograph of an attractive woman has brought satisfaction and because they rightly assume that this stimulus,
too, will bring them a similar reward.   Then, as they respond to her, they unwittingly perceive the remainder of the
copy for which she is the lure.   Their responses to her may
remain purely auxiliary.   Sometimes even the copy-writer
does not expect such responses to be related to the final
response he is seeking for his clients.   A glamorous model
stands in front of the photograph of an automobile not to
suggest to men that such a woman is one of the standard
accessories which comes with the car like the rear bumper,
nor that the car and its owner will be deluged with alluring
women.   And women no doubt are not supposed to conclude
that their appearance and figure will improve the moment
they buy the automobile.   At other times, however, the advertiser may endeavor to connect the auxiliary response with
the learning process he is promoting.   His copy, for example, may assert that a man can attract such a wonderful
woman or a woman can become so wonderful merely by
purchasing and then using the product or service being advertised.

There are innumerable auxiliary responses beside those associated with sex which the advertiser or any propagandist
can arouse to have his propaganda perceived.   Advertisers
use striking, novel, or provoking illustrations and headlines.

They embody their copy in comic strips because they know that many people are addicted to this type of soporific entertainment; they sometimes hire an artist whose strip is already widely syndicated in order to attract for their purposes many of his regular devotees. Over the radio almost any interest which listeners already have can be employed as the basis of the program which emits the plug. As a result, there are commercial sponsors for symphony orchestras, soap operas, precocious and impudent children, original and unoriginal comedians, and even United States Government weather reports. On the streets in many American cities electric bulbs and neon lights not only strive to be intense and outstanding through the wattage they consume and the color they reveal but also to be sufficiently spectacular so that they will be perceived as interesting or beautiful objects. That ancient spectre, the rugged individualist, can point with doubtful pride to Times Square in New York City as an example of how competition encourages initiative and ingenuity, since there the conglomeration of signs has led advertisers to find original and bizarre displays to pierce the night in the interests of perception and propaganda.

Merchants frequently resort to various devices to have people enter their stores. They publicize "leaders" which are products offered for sale at a low price or even at a loss. They provide extra services to their patrons, such as a post-office sub-station, a telephone booth, a rest room, or entertainment during a holiday season. Some refuse to accept mail or telephone orders for certain desirable products. Consumers whose auxiliary attitudes are evoked by one of these attractions place themselves in a position where they are likely to perceive at least some of the store's merchandise.

The publicity agent and the public relations counsel solve the perceptual problem of their clients when they are able to have propaganda items reported in the regular news columns or in newscasts. Their propagandees are interested in the news, an auxiliary responds itself that has been previously evoked. While reducing this drive, they must also perceive as news the publicity or the handout which, if it had appeared as an advertisement or a plug, they may never have noticed.

The propagandist in war time must first arouse auxiliary responses if his propaganda is to be perceived by the enemy. For people in enemy countries, except for sympathizers in the underground, do not willingly perceive materials which they can readily appreciate are biased against them. Only the loudspeaker barrage across the battlefield has to be heard, whereas there must be some incentive to read a leaflet or listen to a broadcast sponsored by the very group which is attempting to defeat the homeland. In the last war, Japanese propagandists sought to attract American soldiers by printing pornographic pictures on one side of the leaflets they distributed across our lines and by confining the propaganda appeals to the other side. The Russians and Germans also employed the bait of sex, and the perceptual device was sometimes directly linked with the propaganda theme. On one German leaflet which showed a soldier caressing a rather completely disrobed and very voluptuous woman, the English soldier fighting on the continent was warned against American forces stationed in England who, it was asserted, were seducing English women while their husbands and sweethearts were being needlessly slaughtered in France.

Even when the technical problems related to perception were solved, it was extremely difficult for war propagandists to attract and then hold the interest of enemy radio audiences over a period of years. At one time or another all of them aped radio practice in the United States: they tried to entertain their listeners especially with music and inserted their propaganda like a commercial plug. Such programs seemed to have scored some success with troops who felt the need for any kind of relaxation, but they were much less attractive to civilians who could tune in on domestic broadcasts to hear music or comedy. Englishmen, however, listened in great numbers to William Joyce, the renegade Irishman who as Lord Haw Haw broadcast from Germany to England and who after the war was hanged as a traitor. Joyce was serious at first but, after his audience found him funny and ridiculous, he deliberately assumed the role into which he had been fitted until his became one of the most popular programs in all England. According to an unconfirmed but fairly convincing rumor prevalent in government circles during the war, British authorities considered him such a menace that they once contemplated wasting one of their own stations to jam him—but decided not to do so. Other Axis minions like Tokyo Rose and Axis Sally solved their perceptual problem by ensnaring troop audiences with double and not always subtle entendres involving sex, with rather good imitations of American forms of entertainment, and with inside information concerning Allied operations which sometimes proved to be amazingly accurate.

In general, American and British propagandists sought to have propaganda perceived in the midst of news. They assumed that many enemy nationals would occasionally suspect or grow weary of their own side's propaganda and version of the news and that they would turn to their radio sets both to discover how the news was being reported by their enemies and also to become acquainted with other events not described in their own press or over their own radio. Many American critics of the broadcasts made to Germany, Japan, and other Axis satellites—and these were individuals both inside and outside the Congress and academic circles—used to moan that the taxpayers' money was being spent to provide the enemy with a free news service. Such criticism simply ignored the very simple fact that propaganda has to be perceived before it can affect people and that news programs served the function of evoking the necessary auxiliary responses.

Each side also attempted to attract an audience to hear its propaganda by broadcasting the one item of news which in war time has probably the greatest and most pathetic drawing-power among the enemy: the names of captured prisoners, of soldiers found dead on the battlefield, or of sailors whose bodies have been washed ashore or discovered at sea. These names were often inserted into newscasts or straight propaganda talks. During 1942, for example, when Americans were eager for any scrap of news, Radio Tokyo employed this device in an attempt to trap an audience. In fact, some listeners on the West Coast turned their short-wave listening hobby into a racket by offering to furnish families with news of their loved ones after payment of a fee. There were also so many others who listened and then transmitted the Japanese information as a patriotic gesture that government authorities were compelled to outlaw the practice. Instead they themselves telegraphed excerpts from the broadcasts to the families with the warning that the source was the enemy radio. The supreme mating of sex and morbidity was achieved by the American and British operators of Radio Luxembourg after that station had fallen into Allied hands. In a program titled "Letters Which You Do Not Receive" a lush, erotic female voice read to the German audience excerpts from love letters taken from the bodies of German soldiers killed in battle, and she named names. For the sake of the record, it must be added that this program was rather hastily abandoned not in the interest of effective propaganda but of good taste.

The arousal of auxiliary responses requires a knowledge of latent and actual public opinion. For the propagandist must know which responses can be evoked and which stimuli can evoke them. The advertiser can assume that people have their sexual problems and are therefore seeking substitute satisfactions. He also need be no genius to know that neo-nudity of females is an effective stimulus for males or that certain types of amalgamated beauty (which are vapid rather than distinctly ethnic in appearance) have their allure. Ideally, for example, he likes to have both a blonde and a brunette in the same copy—and sometimes even red hair makes its simultaneous appearance. The obvious, however, sometimes palls or is an effective stimulus for too small a group: not even every male will look at a picture of a woman's figure in brazen contours. Systematic knowledge concerning auxiliary attitudes can be obtained while other facts about propagandees are being collected; for this reason, general research methods for both will be considered together in the next chapter.

One specific brand of commercial research, however, is

designed almost exclusively to measure the types and strength of auxiliary attitudes: the vast number of surveys conducted by the American radio industry which determine program popularity. A program "rating" indicates how many people are making auxiliary responses and reducing the tensions of their various drives by listening. The broad outlines of this type of investigation can be given relatively briefly.

Those who wish to measure program popularity are confronted with the same sampling problem as the pollster must face. They attempt, therefore, to reduce biasing and chance sampling errors and have been relatively successful in securing representative and sufficiently large samples. The more difficult problem to meet in radio research, however, involves instrument errors: through what devices can reliable and valid data be obtained? Certain techniques, therefore, have been evolved, as Chappell and Hooper (7) concisely and blatantly express radio's prevailing ideology, "to furnish people with the programs they prefer, and not with programs which some advertiser or company executive *believes* they prefer, nor yet with those some reformer asserts they *ought* to prefer":

1. *The face-to-face interview*: a representative sample is asked a series of questions pertaining to radio. Besides noting whether or not the radio is coincidentally in operation at the start of the interview, the investigator asks the respondent to recall the programs he has heard during a previous time period and, perhaps, to indicate why he likes some programs and ignores others. Slips of memory—which can be affected by the program's age, length, popularity, prestige, etc. (*8*)—and the desire to please the interviewer may falsify the results. It is claimed (*13*), however, that providing informants with lists of programs that have been broadcast during the quarter-hour intervals of a day—the so-called "Roster Rating"—eliminates some of the inaccuracies of unaided recall; yet it may also promote falsification. This method is employed, for example, by The Pulse, Inc., to survey radio audiences in the metropolitan areas of New York and Philadelphia.

2. *The delayed telephone interview*: by telephone a sample of individuals is asked which programs they have heard during a preceding period of time like two or six hours. Only the number at

home is used in calculating the percentages listening to the programs that have been on the air (*6*). The final rating given a program is the percentage obtained after dividing the number listening to it either by the total calls made or by the total number listening to any program at the time. Little information concerning preferences for particular sections of the programs can ordinarily be obtained. The sample is also biased since it includes only those able to afford a telephone.

3. *The coincidental interview*: by telephone a random sample from over thirty cities where programs from all four networks may be heard and where therefore the popularity of a program in the face of competition may be judged is disturbed at regular intervals like twice a month (*11, 12*). The person who answers the telephone is asked whether the radio in the house is turned on. If it is, he is requested to indicate the program and station to which he is listening; the product being advertised; and the number of men, women, and children in the household who are actually listening. The ratio between the calls made in a given city and the total sample is the same as that between the city's size and the total population. Inquiries concerning programs broadcast after 10:30 P.M. are made the next day and concerning those broadcast before 8 A.M. later the same day—even commercial research must draw some line and dares not inconvenience people when they are asleep. Homes which do not answer after six rings are classified among the non-listeners; the homes giving a busy signal may be divided, in accordance with the known facts about the number of party lines and the population's general habits, between the listening and non-listening categories. To rate a given program, three percentages must be obtained: the proportion of those who are at home and who therefore constitute the available radio audience; the proportion of the available audience actually listening to the radio; and the proportion of those listening to the radio who are hearing the program in question. The final report carefully indicates that it is based only on telephone subscribers in urban areas. Excluded from the sample are people who do not have telephones or who are listening to programs outdoors either on automobile or portable radio sets. With this approach slips of memory are unlikely, and the investigator can easily determine which respondents are answering truthfully since he knows what programs are being broadcast at that time. It is possible, too, to rate the popularity of a program during each five minutes of its transmission simply by having the interviewers note the exact time at which they put through their calls. The method that has been described here is employed in the United States by C. E. Hooper, Inc. (which modestly calls its final figure

for programs a "Hooperating") ; it was also used by Hooper's only serious rival, the Cooperative Analysis of Broadcasting, Inc., before that company was dissolved in September, 1946. The technique itself may be combined with other approaches, for example, to estimate the size of the listening audience in other cities or in homes without telephones (*9*) ; or, conceivably, to obtain qualitative information about radio habits by conducting face-to-face interviews.

4. *The panel*: a representative sample of listeners is paid to record its listening habits, frequently in the form of a "diary" (*1*). Sometimes a sponsor asks for detailed reactions only to his particular program. Results obtained in this fashion are said to parallel closely those from other methods and to cost less when a survey is extended over a period of time. Listeners, however, may grow self-conscious and thus introduce an instrument error if they remain members of the panel too long. For this reason, the diary method is usually employed for only a short period of time like a week. In addition, the respondents may record or recall their habits and preferences with varying degrees of conscientiousness. Mechanical gadgets called "Audimeters" can be attached to the radio sets of panel members: these automatically and mechanically record the precise times at which the sets are tuned to particular stations. This method which provides American broadcasters with a so-called Nielsen Index must assume a close correspondence between sets in operation and listening, and also between listening and a favorable reaction. The results, however, can be employed as the basis for asking questions in a face-to-face interview with listeners, and thus an effort can be made to understand both their qualitative reactions and the reasons therefor (*10*).

5. *Fan mail*: the quantity and content of mail which is sent spontaneously by listeners to broadcasters is tabulated and analyzed. Sometimes inferences concerning the letter-writers are made on the basis of the stationery they employ, their command of the language, their addresses, etc. It is quite unlikely that writers of fan letters represent a typical cross-section of the listening audience.

A good deal of propaganda must be perceived again and again if it is to be effective over a period of time. Often the fate of the auxiliary responses which induce or facilitate perception, consequently, cannot be disregarded, which means psychologically that the drives associated with these responses must be partially or completely reduced. A commercially sponsored radio program in the United States, which begins with a fanfare concerning the entertainment it offers, must actually fulfill its promise, or else people will not tune in again and thus effectively isolate themselves from perceiving the commercial announcements. Over the stations which were officially designated as "The Voice of America" and "The British Broadcasting Corporation," allied propagandists during the last war made every effort to transmit spot news as soon as possible after it was received. The enemy audience and friendly listeners in occupied countries were told that they would always be given "the latest news" and therefore, since they did receive prompt service, their listening habits were presumably reinforced. The British were especially astute in their European broadcasts, for during the dreary days of 1940 and 1941 they frankly reported the news which indicated an almost unbroken, monotonous string of Axis victories. Their listeners, therefore, learned that by and large they were hearing "news" and not "propaganda." The urge to learn how the enemy was reporting events was satisfied and the appropriate listening habits were established and strengthened. Many of them continued to tune in on the B.B.C. when, beginning with the Anglo-American campaign in North Africa and the epically successful defense of Stalingrad by the Soviet forces, the tide was reversed. During an allied landing or invasion, whether in Africa, Europe, or the Pacific, it used to be an agonizing experience for American and British propagandists to preserve an initial silence in the interests of military or naval security, especially when they could hear their propaganda opponents—who were not bound by security since their forces were on the defensive—reporting their own version of what was occurring and when they themselves had been secretly alerted for the event which they therefore knew was actually taking place.

Perceptual Variation

It is quite clear that, while people like the comfort of habitual modes of behavior, they also frequently seek novelty and variation. Only the proper mixture of oxygen and other elements is satisfactory for human breathing, but there are some individuals who like the sensation of being "out of breath." Americans may require coffee for breakfast and drink it at approximately the same temperature and with or without cream and/or sugar day after day; yet they usually demand variation in their diet at other meals, as every American soldier from the last war can testify who under combat conditions had to eat the same kind of canned food for long periods. The pleasure derived from an enjoyable motion picture a second or third time is usually less than the delight it initially evoked.

There is no easy explanation of the fact that a drive cannot always be reduced by the same goal response. In some instances too much of the reward is obtained and hence punishment results. The individual who craves a somewhat exotic dish like fried clams, for example, surfeits himself so thoroughly that he feels physically uncomfortable; then he is likely not to select this food again until some time has passed. In other instances repetition of the stimuli evokes dissimilar responses which do not serve adequately to reduce the drive. The initial experience of seeing a motion picture may be pleasurable because many of the details in the plot cannot be anticipated; thereafter the suspense that is so important to the entertainment disappears. The quest for variation, moreover, is not always present: people vote, plow fields, belong to churches, wear neckties, etc., because their fathers did and because not to do so is to court social punishment.

Variation of stimuli can promote the perception of propaganda. A brightly illuminated sign may be perceived at first because it constitutes an intense stimulus. Presently people become "adapted" to it, which means that looking at it is no longer rewarding since they see nothing new. Its contents, consequently, are changed at regular or irregular intervals. The over-all pattern of radio programs is repeated again and again when that pattern has been able to attract an audience. The anticipation of the expected proves to be rewarding and the comedian, for example, always acts "in character." Within the pattern, there must be variation. The comedian, who is thought funny because he is always the naïve butt of more aggressive characters even when he tries to assert himself, manages to become embroiled in a slightly different situation at each performance.

The stimulus in propaganda is varied not only to reduce the tension of auxiliary responses among the same people over a period of time, but also to arouse similar responses in people who have not been affected by a previous presentation. The snob, for example, may never notice or at least perceive the details of a cigarette advertisement when its illustration features the container in which the product is marketed, the famous men and women who allegedly smoke the brand, or the tobacco leaves which are its principal ingredients. His glance, nevertheless, may be arrested by the reproduction of a painting by a modern artist which depicts something about tobacco, as a result of his previous interest in art which is tapped by that painting. One man's stimulus is not another man's.

Stimulus Simplification

Psychologists have sometimes pointed out that what they call an individual's span or range of attention or apprehension is limited. If separate digits or letters are exposed for a fraction of a second by means of a very fast-moving shutter, it is found that the average person can correctly perceive and correctly recall three or four. When the digits are arranged in the form of a common combination such as "1948–1949–1950" and the letters in the form of well-known words, a greater number can be grasped. There is, however, the possibility of making a false interpretation of the combined units—"cheat" may be reported when the letters were actually "chaet." The perceiving and learning of more complicated material depend also upon the drive functioning within the individual: the more numerous the items, the more difficult both processes become *unless* the individual is highly motivated to perceive the stimulus and to learn the new response.

Since the motivation may not be intense, propaganda stimuli tend to be simplified or to be made unambiguous so that they more certainly will fall within the propagandees' generalization gradients. Modern science, for example, possesses prestige and hence many propagandists for commercial products and social panaceas seek to identify their propaganda with what they call science. The average propagandee for reasons beyond his control, however, does not usually have the intellectual background to understand the intricacies either of the scientific approach or of scientific findings. In propaganda, therefore, merely the word "science" may be employed; or an accepted symbol of science—like a test-tube, a stethoscope, a laboratory, or just a white coat—is portrayed; or there is a quotation from an anonymous or specified individual who is explicitly called a scientist.

Propaganda is simplified to evoke either the auxiliary responses producing the perception or the other responses that facilitate learning. During the last war, the Office of War Information adopted the commercial practice of identifying its overseas radio programs through the use of a standardized and easily perceived musical signature, the first few bars of Yankee Doodle. When this melody was heard, therefore, the listener knew that his radio was tuned to an American station and, it was hoped, an appropriate or favorable attitude would be aroused. In this case, incidentally, simplification promoted perception not only among listeners but also among the snooping Gestapo and other stool pigeons who thereby learned that the owner of the set was engaging in illegal listening. The advertiser repeats a slogan or displays his trademark again and again because they can be quickly grasped and remembered. Successful political propagandists, including those in fascist countries (5), have employed visual symbols such as swastikas or slogans and clichés which can be easily perceived and which serve frequently to elicit desired responses.

Public opinion on many issues is simplified not only because people like to reduce complex events to manageable form but also because their knowledge about those events has been derived from stimuli which propagandists have intentionally or unintentionally simplified. People perceive what they want or are able to grasp, and propaganda both caters to and reinforces these tendencies. In still simpler terms: people help determine propaganda, and propaganda helps determine people.

CHAPTER 15

Personality and Propaganda

THE analysis of propaganda is now progressing in easy stages. The propagandist, it is assumed, is deliberately or unwittingly using some vehicle of communication to reach a group of prospective propagandees. The content of his propaganda has been planned. The propagandees have perceived the propaganda. They are no longer hesitating to look at the advertisement, to tune in on the radio program, or to attend the political rally. Instead they are glancing at the copy, being stimulated or bored by the radio commercial, and listening to the candidate for public office. They are in a position to be affected.

Propagandees at this point are like the schoolboy whose parents have induced or compelled him to attend school for the first time. He is too young to realize why he is there: he does not know that in school he is supposed to learn a host of things which presumably will make him a useful and maybe even a happy citizen. As he enters the room, he cannot even decide whether or not he likes the place. Before he learns the initial lesson—before, in fact, he responds in any fashion—a drive must be evoked within him; he must be motivated to become a student. Naturally he does not face this crisis without some prior knowledge concerning what he may expect and hence some drives have already been activated. His parents and playmates have undoubtedly communicated to him an explanation of what is about to occur, and he may be filled with emotions ranging from anxiety to eagerness.

After perceiving the propaganda, the propagandees can then make a variety of responses. They may do the very thing the propagandist wishes them not to do: they turn over the page to another advertisement, tune out the program, or leave the meeting. When this happens, the propagandist has lost his battle even after winning the preliminary, perceptual round. Or the propagandees may respond in ways that are relevant or irrelevant to the propaganda objective. During his speech the political orator makes a flourishing reference to "the American home" that he is determined to protect from something or other. Relevant and irrelevant response series by different people might be these:

Individual A	*Individual B*
1. This man is talking about the American home.	1. This man is talking about the American home.
2. I like my home.	2. I like my home.
3. This man is going to protect my home.	3. My house requires new shingles on its roof.
4. Therefore I like what he is saying.	4. I wonder whether I can afford to buy new shingles right now.
5. I also like him—now what is that man saying?	5. I don't think so—now what is that man saying?

Responses #1 and #2 are identical for both individuals; #1 shows that perception has occurred, #2 is in turn a response to the perceptual response which thus has stimulus properties. The third response of Individual A is also a perceptual one which, with the aid of #2, leads syllogistically to the relevant response of #4, and #4 in turn elicits #5. The third response of Individual B, on the other hand, has been aroused by #2 and leads to #4 and #5 which are irrelevant to the propaganda he is hearing.

Among the relevant responses, moreover, there must be one with drive value or one which eventually evokes a drive. Otherwise propagandees respond without learning, like the schoolboy who watches and listens to the teacher without remembering or being influenced by what she says. For propaganda, it is recalled, requires learning, and learning occurs only when some drive is active.

The relevant or irrelevant responses evoked by the propaganda stimulus after it has been perceived are completely dependent upon the past experiences of the propagandee. They are learned responses or habits which the propaganda is capable of evoking. They are part of the propagandees' personalities and for this reason all propaganda is so intimately connected with personality. They may be in fact called *personality responses.*

The Composition of the Audience

Only rarely are there propagandists who realistically seek to affect every one in society. Naturally most intentional propagandists would like to convert as many propagandees as possible, but it is quite clear that some cannot be influenced or can be influenced only by an uneconomical expenditure of time and energy or by being knocked over their heads with a stout club. Republicans in the United States have no objection to winning votes from the Deep South, but in general that region's stubborn and traditional adherence to the Democratic party has made their propaganda efforts there quite desultory. The manufacturer of a very expensive automobile ordinarily does not advertise in one of the "pulp" magazines which circulate largely among people who cannot possibly afford that make of car; instead his advertisements appear in "quality" or in "slick" publications whose subscribers are better able to purchase luxuries. Only the war propagandist with almost unlimited funds at his disposal seeks to propagandize all groups and individuals among the enemy. After all, propaganda is usually cheaper than bullets, and there is always at least the possibility that even the most psychologically resistant among the enemy may under certain circumstances be swayed. But the war propagandist does make every effort to confine particular appeals to the groups likely to be affected by them and thus he too selects his audience.

Medium choice usually and automatically results in audience choice. It is necessary, therefore, for the propagandist to have certain information about the past and future patronage enjoyed by the various media. A propagandist who desires to employ a given medium or the owner of a medium who seeks propaganda patronage uses some measuring device to determine the kind of people attracted by the medium. All of the techniques available to measure public opinion—which have been described in previous chapters—can be utilized to conduct what is called in this connection not a poll but a market survey. Instead of determining people's attitudes toward the issues of the day, the interviewer seeks to know which media they read or hear and to collect census-type data concerning their income, forms of recreation, buying habits, place of residence, etc. Under certain conditions such data can be obtained with almost equal validity and perhaps at less expense through a questionnaire submitted to a representative sample by mail (*1, 8*), inasmuch as people are willing to answer flat questions of this kind without prodding from an interviewer especially if their replies are collected anonymously. It is often extremely useful to combine a market survey relating to media habits with a poll of people's attitudes bearing on the product in question. Even without this additional information, the survey's results are relevant both to the perceptual problem, since they include the number of people patronizing the medium, as well as to the personality problem, since they reveal who the propagandees are.

When the United States Government even before its entry into the last war began indirectly to broadcast shortwave programs to Latin America, it was necessary to ascertain through a survey how many Latin Americans had shortwave receiving sets, how many of them listened to particular programs at specified times of the day and night, and in general to what class of society the shortwave audience belonged. Many magazine editors in the United States possess data (which they publicize only when they wish to impress advertisers) concerning the percentage and type of people who read the various features or sections of their publications.

Intentional propagandists sometimes deliberately select a medium with a clientele which at the moment appears unresponsive to their propaganda. A solid gold pen or pencil is advertised in a "pulp" magazine not because the manufacturer believes that many of the readers are likely to purchase the article but because he wishes his brand name to be associated with a luxury product and hence to cast its prestige upon the cheaper pen or pencil that he also sells. The combat propagandist distributes safe-conduct passes to enemy troops even when he knows those troops are in no mood to surrender. He wants them at least to consider the idea of surrendering so that eventually, when and if their military situation worsens, they may actually do so.

The propagandist frequently tailors a medium to a prospective audience instead of accepting the audience of an existing medium. Once again this is done to increase the number of the people who are psychologically disposed to perceive and react favorably to the propaganda. In the wake of the astonishing success of the *Reader's Digest* in the United States, there has been a flood of new magazines imitating the format and the content of that deceptive periodical. A few older magazines have also followed the same trend by reducing their size. The wide circulation of the *Digest,* in a word, indicated to publishers and editors that many Americans favor such a magazine and hence they, too, have sought to appeal to the same and to other people with similar habits. During the last war, the Office of War Information stockpiled printed materials to be distributed to the peoples of liberated and conquered countries throughout the world. In the field of magazines, it was difficult to decide in advance how "slick" a publication should be. The reasoning in either direction sounded plausible: an expensive-looking magazine might be resented because people needed food and clothing, not propaganda or "information"; but it might also be admired as an indication that "our side" and not just the Germans or the Japanese was able and could afford to produce an attractive product. Here there was no conceivable way of coming to a decision since experts, refugees, and even a panel inside the country could only guess how people would feel as the allied armies approached under unforeseeable circumstances.

Related Responses

The repertoire of responses that a civilized man is able to make under appropriate circumstances is extremely large. He is ready to sneeze when the mucus membranes of his nose are irritated or to say that he prefers Mozart to Bach when he is asked to choose between those two composers. Among all the responses of which his personality is capable, the propagandist seeks to arouse only those that are or can be related to the propaganda objective. A response may be called *related* when it is instrumental in achieving a goal response or when it mediates such a response (6). Definitely related to reaching shore safely from an overturned boat are the responses involving swimming and not those associated with driving an automobile. An individual will not learn to swim in the first place if the stimulus of water makes him overwhelmingly anxious: anxiety is not related to nor is it compatible with learning this skill. In the case of propaganda, the goal response to which a personality response is related or unrelated is the propaganda objective.

Before related responses can be evoked, they must pre-exist within the personalities of propagandees and the stimulus must be found that can evoke them. The propagandist who drifts with the tide is gearing his propaganda to actual public opinion. Through a poll or introspection he is acquainted with the responses which people are making as well as with the goals which they seek and have not yet attained. The speaker can be certain that an approving reference to religion will find acceptance in a group of churchmen and he therefore attempts to link his propaganda to this theme. Stereotyped words and phrases play an important role in propaganda because there is a strong, habit bond between these simplified stimuli and the more or less uniform and simplified responses which, when they have been evoked, can then affect the learning process.

Advertisers (*e.g.*, *5*), psychologists (*e.g.*, *3*, *13*), and others (*e.g.,* *12*) are fond of listing the so-called "appeals" employed by modern advertising. By an appeal is meant the kind of personality responses (variously called "desires" and "motives") which the advertiser can arouse to achieve his objective. Lucas and Benson (*10*), for example, divide their appeals into three categories of "individual," "social," and "objective"; and then catalogue them as follows:

Individual	Social	Objective
appetite-taste	popularity	quality-size
success-power	sex-mating-parental	beauty-appearance
possession	rivalry	price
wealth-independence	domination-submission	prestige-age of busi-
beauty	conformity and dis-	ness
cleanliness	tinction	recommendations
health	sociability-hospitality	and testimonials
comfort	cooperative or altruistic	
play		
fear-avoidance		

In spite of the authors' warning that this list "is by no means complete and like many classifications should be used only as a convenient device," the impression may be gained that the advertiser has at his disposal a series of buttons, any one of which he can arbitrarily push to achieve his ends.

Almost all of the items on any list of appeals are ambiguous when they are applied to a particular piece of copy. Does the picture of a beautiful girl appeal to beauty, cleanliness, health, sex-mating-parental, or domination-submission? The question is dodged if the reply is given in terms of the accompanying text which, though it may reduce the number of categories on the list that are obviously applicable, nevertheless offers no guarantee that the propagandees are responding in ways describable by one category rather than another. All that can be said is that the advertiser or the artist who plans the layout thinks he is employing such-and-such an appeal, but which personality response his copy actually arouses is an empirical question requiring further investigation. Nor can it be argued that the nature of the product determines the advertising "appeal" to be employed. Soap, that commodity which has lent its name to the most primitive form of radio dramatization and which flowed through the veins of the principal characters of Wakeman's huckstering characters (*15*), by no means requires that its sale be promoted only through the appeal of "cleanliness," the one and really exclusive function of soap. Conceivably, if American advertisers were not inhibited by the Federal Trade Commission and by their own self-imposed ethics, soap could be boosted through the use of every single appeal on the list given above. The "personal appeals," for example, might be sloganized as follows:

appetite-taste:	"stimulates the blood like a springtime flood."
success-power:	"triples people's respect for you."
possession:	"makes you want to buy a case."
wealth-independence:	"gives you a toss that will gladden your boss."
beauty:	"brings out the Venus in you."
cleanliness:	"gets under your skin and over."
health:	"kills all germs by atomic action."
comfort:	"cools you in summer, warms you in winter."
play:	"is the only retort to the odors of sport."
fear-avoidance:	"purifies P. A.—perspiring armpits."

With a paper and pencil and with an absolute minimum of thought, the reader can design equally brilliant slogans for the "social" and "objective" appeals of soap.

A list of appeals, then, is a rule-of-thumb guide to propaganda but little more. Human behavior even for advertising purposes cannot be easily catalogued. At the same time it is conceivable that the rewards desired by most people in a society can be specified in most abstract fashion. It may be that by and large Americans want these rewards:

1. economic security
2. satisfactory family and interpersonal relations
3. social-class status
4. relaxation and health
5. esthetic and spiritual gratifications
6. self-understanding
7. understanding of others and society

Like every other list, this one is ambiguous in many respects. It indicates only the most general goal responses Americans seek to make. It neglects such secondary drives or dynamic processes as displacement, compensation, identification, projection, etc., which, though they might be subsumed under one of the seven headings, possess at a given moment unique attributes. It fails to specify the strength of the corresponding drives in various sub-groups at a given time. Most important of all, it deals with only half of the propaganda or psychological problem: it does not and it cannot suggest the stimulus gradients which are capable of evoking the responses. Perhaps it deserves faint praise only because it is brief.

From another viewpoint, personality responses can be classified as positive or negative. On the one hand people seek positive gratification: they want something which at the moment they do not possess. A hungry man requires food, a poor one money, an unhappy one happiness. On the other hand, they seek relief from something unpleasant like frustration or anxiety. Such a dichotomy, however, is by no means absolute. The hungry man can also be considered to desire not food but relief from hunger; and the anxious individual consciously wants not only to be rid of his negative fears but also to attain something positive such as a wife or an income. The distinction, nevertheless, has its practical side. There is, for example, not an absolute but still a vast difference between a positive and a negative appeal in advertising toothpaste: one stresses that the concoction produces beautiful teeth and the other claims that it will prevent the teeth from looking pale, yellow, or otherwise unattractive.

Instead of worrying about catalogues of appeals, it is usually wiser for the advertiser to make some kind of an investigation of consumer attitudes regarding the product about to be advertised; then the personality responses that can be aroused and related to the objective will be known with a fair degree of certainty. This research may be oriented in various ways (cf. *9*). It may seek to determine which attitudes a new product will arouse, which ones an established product has been arousing, or which ones exist without having been aroused by existing products. It may pertain not only to advertising copy but also to the methods of marketing which are being employed. It may be concerned with a competitor's product or type of advertising. Such data can be gathered by surveying a representative sample of consumers likely to make the purchase; by interviewing a sample of customers and determining why they purchased the product; by obtaining a not necessarily representative sample of opinions from the answers given by people to a contest question like "Why I Like 'Poison Cigarettes'"; or by having salesclerks or professional eavesdroppers note the comments and requests of customers in a representative sample of stores.

The candidate for public office in a democracy likewise seeks to find the arguments which will evoke related responses among the voters. As has been previously pointed out, he keeps his "ear to the ground" by talking to people, by consulting the bosses whose responsibility it is to be in constant contact with voters, by studying the mass media of communication, and even by watching or actually employing a public opinion poll. American politicians like the southern demagogue determine their campaign program and govern their political actions by observing actual public opinion, whether it be external or internal. Others—the true innovators of their time like Franklin D. Roosevelt—are able to take the superficial facts gathered by the bosses and pollsters and interpret them correctly or cleverly as symptoms of latent public opinion.

The personality response related to the propagandist's objective, it has been said, is part of the propagandees' repertoire, but it may or may not be functioning at the moment of propaganda impact. In wartime almost everyone, including the greatest heroes and the best fighters, is anxious. For people recognize the proximity of death, injury, or some other loss. They know, too, that their best efforts may not enable them to avoid these calamities. Enemy propaganda, which seeks to increase their anxiety in order to diminish their will to fight or to cooperate with their leaders, can reach them when they are filled with such fears *or* when some more powerful drive is temporarily dominating their behavior. Thus the civilian may hear that the bombing of his country will increase as he worries about bombing or as he momentarily is preoccupied with his everyday obligations as a citizen.

It is very difficult to determine in advance whether personality responses will become related responses since the total reaction of propagandees depends not only on one response in their repertoire but also on their personalities. A specific illustration from the experimental work of United States Army investigators during the last war (4) can make this problem clear. Men were shown a documentary film on "The Battle of Britain." Such a film, it might have been anticipated, would immediately evoke a general attitude toward the British war effort and that attitude would be related to the final propaganda effect. The investigators actually did discover a relation between the men's attitudes before and after they had seen the film: the more favorable their prior attitude, the more they tended to be affected. It would seem that this personality response determined the amount of learning, although it is important to add that even those men least favorably disposed toward the British were also affected favorably by what they saw. For equally good and logical reasons, however, it might also have been anticipated that men in April 1945, who believed that the war against Japan was going to be protracted would learn more from a radio transcription cautioning against overoptimism than would men who envisioned a brief war. As a matter of fact, the men's initial judgment concerning the war's duration bore no relation to the gross changes produced by hearing the propaganda. Here the personality response by itself apparently failed to function as a related response; there was, as indicated in the next chapter, an interaction between this response and other personality responses evoked by the film which influenced the learning process. Empirical investigation or a detailed psychological analysis is required before the importance of a particular personality response can be forecast.

Sometimes successful propaganda requires related responses that are not already part of the propagandees' personalities. Before the attack on the Soviet Union in June 1941, for example, most Germans would have replied to the question, "Who is going to win the war?" by saying "Germany." Their armies were stationed in most of Europe and dominated the remainder of that continent. Their only opponents at that time were the British Empire, poorly organized underground forces, and—at a distance, half-heartedly, and informally—the United States. In this situation British propaganda could not demoralize the enemy by evoking a response to the effect that "we Germans shall lose this war." Germans had to be taught to make this response. Their mighty teacher, of course, was the flow of military and naval events beginning in the late autumn of 1942, although allied propaganda doubtless hastened and facilitated this learning process by explaining the significance of those events before their ultimate implications had been perceived. In the absence of the proper related responses, therefore, prior learning must take place. The propagandist adopts a limited objective which will serve his ultimate end. Such a propaganda effort can be called a *sub-propaganda campaign*.

Almost all propaganda in fact involves some sub-propaganda. For people seldom possess the precise personality responses required by successful propaganda. The crusader against vice must convince some people that society and especially its youth will decay and perish if too frank references to or displays of sexual or sexually suggestive behavior are tolerated before he can win support and obtain financial contributions to his cause. Even the advertiser who usually endeavors to deal with actual rather than latent public opinion must often, as he says, "educate" that public before his copy can increase sales. When his product is modestly or drastically modified, for example, he must stage a sub-propaganda campaign in behalf of the innovation that may not instantly appeal to people. Then or simultaneously he proceeds to assert that only his product has the feature.

Repetition and Variation

One of the most obvious but easily overlooked features of propaganda is the large number of psychological functions which many propaganda techniques simultaneously or eventually can perform. There is a tendency for propagandees to believe that they understand the nature of propaganda when they can say to themselves or to others that the propagandist is accomplishing such-and-such by employing a particular stimulus. It has already been pointed out, for example, that the Institute for Propaganda Analysis used to instruct its students and readers to watch out for a "Band Wagon" appeal (7) or, in the revised phrase of the Institute's guiding spirit (*11*), for the "Together" device. Any reference to the support a project is receiving could then be labelled "Band Wagon," "Together," or—to invent another startling and original variation—"Keeping Up with the Joneses" without further analysis or insight. But such label-plastering fails to indicate how and at what point propaganda is promoted by the use of this stimulus.

Repetition and variation of propaganda have been shown in the previous chapter to be important perceptual devices. Here their role in evoking related personality responses will be stressed. It is essential to realize that both functions can be discharged by the same stimulus.

When a propaganda stimulus is repeated, not only may it serve to arouse the auxiliary responses that induce perception to occur or recur, but it may also evoke the same personality responses. "This is the Voice of America, one of the United Nations" was the opening sentence of the O.W.I.'s overseas broadcasts during the war. Listeners, therefore, could expect to hear the American version of the news which may or may not have been an auxiliary response promoting their perception of the broadcast, and in addition whatever responses they associated with American membership in the United Nations were evoked. The United States sought to make the latter responses related to its overall propaganda objective of demonstrating unity both in a military and a postwar sense. Repetition of a stimulus can thus serve to strengthen the habit bond between the propaganda stimulus and the related response. A good slogan is one which is repeated so frequently that it invariably arouses a more or less identical response.

Propaganda stimuli must also be repeated because, even when they are perceived by the same propagandees, they will not always evoke the same responses. The foot-loose male will be unimpressed by advertisements for household equipment until he is about to be married. The contemplated acquisition of a wife and home changes him as a personality and produces the very response tendencies which the advertisements previously could not arouse. Since propagandees' personalities seldom remain stable, repetition is required in most propaganda. Lord Haw Haw, whose technique of carrying the Nazi line to English listeners has been previously mentioned, may have been ineffective for most people over long periods of time because they found him amusing. Then suddenly, perhaps after a particularly dreadful blitz or as England's wartime diet seemed especially bland and monotonous, the same old arguments may have hit their mark.

Again there is no magic in repetition. The connection between the propaganda stimulus and the related response is strengthened not because of repetition as such but because each presentation in some way or other proves to be rewarding and hence induces the propagandee to learn something new. He may obtain individual or social satisfaction from being able to respond "correctly." The consumer can repeat to himself or his friends the advertising slogan which is dinned into his ears, even though he never purchases the product. The response may be learned for a reason which leads to a goal response not desired by the propagandist. "Yes," Nazis may have said to themselves as they heard the O.W.I.'s signature, "America is one of the United Nations which want to liquidate Germany." The fact that the same stimulus evokes a related response on one occasion and does not do so later signifies a change within the propagandee's personality.

Old-time political bosses in the United States are supposed to have feared not bad publicity but no publicity at all. This cliché is really a meaningless play on the word "bad." Such politicians wanted their names repeated so that people would not forget them. An attack served at least to remind the constituents of their existence and their hope, therefore, was that such "bad" publicity would be "good" at least in this respect. If the publicity had been truly "bad" and had evoked not only perceptual responses but also unfavorable personality ones, they would eagerly have preferred obscurity. In addition, they wished their publicized "badness" to appeal to people, perhaps by suggesting that a "bad" leader is a man who is active in behalf of his supporters and is therefore "good."

The content of propaganda is varied not only to induce the same or different propagandees who are not attracted by one approach to perceive the propaganda, but also to arouse personality responses which the first approach does not arouse. A safe-conduct leaflet in combat propaganda, for example, has a limited number of arguments to employ: surrender is honorable when the battle is hopeless; surrender is necessary to avoid annihilation; surrender is desirable when higher officers are deserting their men for the comfort and safety of the rear lines; surrender means that the war will end more rapidly; and prisoners receive good care and excellent food. Concentrating on and repeating one of these appeals is justified if, according to the best available intelligence, enemy troops are likely to be making one and only one response. When a division has been smashed to pieces and when the remaining troops can perceive that they are cut off and hopelessly outnumbered, then the theme which stresses the honorable nature of surrender has, under these circumstances, a chance of proving efficacious. More commonly, however, the propaganda content must be varied to fit the situation and the accompanying psychological state that situation can be expected to generate in the soldiers. Troops whose position is not obviously hopeless may be moved by propaganda directed against their officers, especially if it is known that some of those officers have actually moved to a higher headquarters. The propagandist in any field often finds it inexpedient to lay down a barrage by using every trick in his bag: he may be wasting his resources, he may make his propaganda too complicated to be perceived and learned, or he may arouse suspicion because his approach sounds too masterful.

People change over a period of time, and at a given moment they also differ from one another. These differences may be peculiar to them as individuals—since each man's reactions to events remains more or less unique—or they may result from the varying attitudes acquired from membership in the heterogeneous groups making up society. The politician with or without scruples realizes that an argument which wins him applause from one group will draw jeers or silence from another. Even the persuasion involved in baby-kissing cannot be utilized promiscuously: there are some sophisticated individuals who have learned that this act springs not from a sweet, decent sentiment but from an urge to rub the parents' ego. The national platform at the time of a presidential election in the United States, as has been pointed out in a previous chapter, must by and large be all things to all men if it is to affect many voters; the regional and group differences in this country are so vast that only the buckshot approach can ever reach a majority of the citizens. When the candidate for public office speaks in his own behalf over the radio, he must vary his appeals within a single address. He tries to say something that will please everybody, but he thereby runs the risk of alienating one group by arguments he must utilize to attract another. A similar situation faces him when he knows that one of his speeches, whether broadcast or not, will be reported by and perhaps quoted in the press, inasmuch as the sociological and psychological characteristics of newspaper readers are almost as diverse as those of a radio audience.

A sub-propaganda campaign can be conducted only by varying the propaganda content. For sub-propaganda is necessary, it will be remembered, when the propagandees do not already possess the related personality responses and when, consequently, those responses must first be learned.

Such learning usually requires in turn a change of stimuli, just as an individual cannot memorize a poem unless he has an opportunity to perceive it. The propaganda of Communist parties in capitalist countries consists of techniques that vary from Marxian lectures and books by Marx and Stalin to pageants and banners: evidently the conversion to communism demands a whole array of intellectual and emotional responses that can be acquired only after stimulation by diverse stimuli.

Auxiliary-related Responses

The aim of the circus barker is to have as many people as possible perceive and then patronize the sideshow whose merits he flamboyantly extolls. He shouts and gesticulates to attract an audience since these antics are likely to arouse auxiliary responses even among individuals who are not in the mood to be entertained. His description of the wonders inside the tent holds people's attention, and at the same time induces some of them to purchase a ticket and enter the sanctum. Through one set of stimuli he elicits responses which promote both the perception and the acceptance of his propaganda. Such responses are called *auxiliary-related responses* to indicate concisely their dual psychological function.

The propagandist who can relate auxiliary responses to the final response he seeks is indeed fortunate. For it is almost always easier to have propagandees perceive propaganda than to respond to it. Most people usually find it simpler to "window-shop" than to patronize a store. A response once aroused may not cease to affect the individual until it is rewarded, and perception by itself may not constitute an adequate reward. A woman, for example, is pleased by what she sees in the store window, but her pleasure becomes infinitely greater, her budget permitting, when she actually purchases the articles that have attracted her eye in the first place.

Responses always occur within people whose personalities are more or less integrated. The individual who listens to a radio program because of his interest in classical music and who thus inadvertently hears a plug for a specified make of automobile may not purchase the car as a token of gratitude toward the sponsor—auxiliary responses can seldom be related to the propagandist's objectively quite so easily. His purchase, when it occurs, will result from many factors, one of which may conceivably be the auxiliary responses evoked by the orchestra. Among the responses aroused by the car as he enters the salesroom can be one which vaguely or clearly recalls that orchestra. The internal response of the orchestra in turn acts as a stimulus for another response involving some trace of the pleasure he has experienced while listening. This response, surreptitiously or otherwise, puts him in a good mood. The mood, finally, facilitates the purchase without necessarily being crucial in its determination.

It is not imperative, as some writers do (2), to emphasize the subtle or compelling character of the learning induced by auxiliary responses. Such learning simply explains how people are swayed by their so-called emotions when they are swayed—and they are not always swayed, or else emotions constitute only one of the responses compelling them to behave as they do. The picture of the very beautiful girl that causes people to perceive an advertisement for beer can arouse pleasurable responses, but the psychological story can end at this point. The consumer admires her without ever noticing the rest of the advertisement. Or he reads all of the copy without ever buying the beer. Or he buys the beer without being affected by the girl, not even deep down in his unconscious. Conditioning does not automatically occur when one stimulus precedes another: among other factors, all of the ongoing responses within the individual determine whether or not the new bond between the conditioned stimulus and the response that previously has been evoked only by the unconditioned stimulus will be established. Frequently only empirical investigation can determine whether auxiliary responses also function as related responses, and such investigation may or may not be worth the effort.

Propagandists and propagandees alike sometimes refer to a principle of appropriateness which in essence seems to suggest that all of the responses evoked by the propaganda, whether auxiliary or related, should be somewhat compatible. Undertakers confine their advertising to dignified and brief notices in newspapers or announcements over the radio. They could very well become better known by utilizing multi-colored advertisements, comic strips, or jazz bands, which stimuli certainly provoke more powerful auxiliary responses in a greater number of people than do the restrained stimuli carrying their messages. It is recognized, however, that such auxiliary responses might promote perception but undoubtedly would not be conducive to actual patronage. People would be shocked: the auxiliary responses—pleasurable as they are—would act in this context as stimuli to evoke other responses which are incompatible with those dominating people at the sad moment when they must make arrangements for a funeral. The entertaining extravagances of the barker, in contrast, are appreciated because the sideshow itself is also supposed to provide entertainment. Usually an auxiliary response is considered appropriate for purely cultural reasons. Printing types known technically as Circular Gothic, Type Slope, and Engravers' Roman are associated in our society with luxury and dignity rather than with economy and strength (*14*). They are employed, consequently, by advertisers in behalf of expensive and exclusive merchandise like perfume and jewelry.

CHAPTER 16

The Learning of Propaganda

PROPAGANDA is a form of communication requiring the learning of new responses. These responses can be learned only after the propaganda stimuli have been perceived and after personality responses that are related to the propaganda objective have been evoked. The learned responses are attitudes and, like all attitudes, predispose the propagandees to action. When attitudes are learned through propaganda, they may be referred to as *pre-action responses* to indicate their proximity to and yet their distance from an action response. The distinction between a pre-action and an action response is a crucial one in the analysis of propaganda. It suggests that propaganda can be learned without a corresponding change in overt behavior. People may agree with a propagandist and yet not do as he wishes.

The hazards of the propagandist increase as his propaganda approaches the pre-action stage. For propagandees may perceive propaganda and then internally respond to it in a way related to the propagandist's objective, but they will not necessarily be affected by what has happened to them or learn a new attitude. The spectator enters a motion picture palace to be entertained and, while there, he sees a feature film whose intended or unintended purpose is to make him less intolerant of aliens. Although for the

354

moment the picture produces sympathetic reactions, in the long run it may have no effect upon him. A few weeks later he is not able to recall the title of the picture or its principal actor. Neither a hypnotist nor a psychoanalyst would be able to demonstrate a subsequent change in attitude toward aliens.

Similarly, not even the most devout Nazis could avoid hearing and reacting to the acid comments of the "ghost voice" which Soviet propagandists managed to inject on occasion during the last war into regular German broadcasts. It is to be doubted whether the German audience learned favorable attitudes toward communism as a result of this tricky technique. Perhaps only a sub-propaganda campaign was involved. Germans might have acquired some tidbit of knowledge unfavorable to the Nazis. Or their anxiety level might have increased: an enemy which can interrupt a broadcast may eventually break up the regime.

The personality responses aroused by propaganda can fail to have the propagandee learn a new attitude for three reasons. In the first place, their drive strength may be weak. The exceptional housewife for whom washing dishes is no great chore has some desire to simplify this work, but that drive when evoked by an advertisement for an electric washing machine produces scarcely a ripple in her personality. The responses, secondly, may be unrelated to the propaganda goal. The listener to enemy broadcasts in war time tends to discredit what he hears because of the bias he correctly attributes to its source. Or, in the third place, the drive strength of other responses that have been previously aroused may be greater. The voter agrees with the platform and promises of one candidate but does not vote for him because he likes the appearance of the rival candidate or is indebted to the competing party for petty favors rendered. In contrast, successful propaganda arouses strong personality responses that are related to the final objective and that can compete effectively with other, preexisting responses. The propaganda devices employed to evoke such responses will be examined later in this chapter.

Throughout this book the relation between public opinion and propaganda is being stressed: propaganda is based on the actualities and latencies of public opinion, and public opinion is formed in part by propaganda. What the propagandist accomplishes is a direct consequence of the ways in which people behave, whether subject to propaganda or not. Propaganda changes the content and direction of behavior; it does not alter the fundamental processes at work, no matter how much or how little people learn.

The types of pre-action responses produced by learning propaganda, therefore, are no different from those which are learned under other circumstances. The difference between one man who wants to murder his sister's rapist and another who wants to kill enemy soldiers because propagandists have told him that the country he is fighting seeks to invade and dominate his native land (and then perhaps to rape his sister too) is great only as far as the origin of the drive-to-kill and the obvious social implications of the actions are concerned. Psychologically, however, rather similar processes are at work. The properties of pre-action responses are like those of public opinion because both are part of human behavior.

Response Strength

A patient who has such an intense pain that he cannot perform many if any of the normal tasks of living does not hesitate to follow his physician's prescription: he swallows the pill, goes to bed, or consents to a surgical operation. He obeys the man not only because he considers him competent but also because he is willing to do practically anything to secure relief from the pain. Strong personality responses have strong drive-value, motivate learning, and result in a strong pre-action response. The propagandist, intentionally or unintentionally, strives to have his propaganda resemble the physician's prescription: he seeks propagandees in whom the drive strength of the personality response and therefore of the pre-action response will be so great that satisfaction can come only by making the goal response he seeks.

Frequently, however, the nature of that goal response itself prevents the propagandist from arousing personality responses which are central within the personality and which can lead to a strong pre-action response. Only a fictitious character or an intensely neurotic individual, for example, can be profoundly stirred by an advertisement for a particular brand of shoe polish, since in no real or normal manner can this product be linked to one of the eternal verities or a complete philosophy of life. Or in other situations some propagandees simply react weakly for reasons best known or perhaps unknown to themselves. Thus the range of individual interest in a political campaign in a democracy is considerable: at one extreme is the completely apathetic person to whom the outcome is meaningless and at the other the conscientious citizen or the politician who is convinced that the central core of his personality will be markedly affected. Under most circumstances, nevertheless, the propagandist makes every effort to arouse strong responses.

The propagandist surveys his future audience for three psychological reasons. He must become acquainted with their auxiliary attitudes in order to have them perceive the propaganda. Then, he must discover which personality responses he can conceivably evoke in order to relate them to the learning process. And he must also seek to ascertain how strong those related responses are. One survey may bring in all three types of data. Sometimes, though, special modifications in investigatory techniques are introduced in an effort at least to rank the intensity of the personality responses and thus indirectly to measure their strength. Housewives are asked not only why they prefer one soap to another but also in what order they are willing to scale their preferences. If one woman buys the product because of its low price and shape, she then can specify, perhaps, which of these two factors she considers more important. The net result of effective research of this variety is additional insight into actual public opinion.

Besides investigating the propagandees' responses, the propagandist may also seek to pre-test his propaganda: is it likely to produce strong pre-action responses? It is tempting to judge propaganda unsystematically and for its author

merely to say: "This looks good—or bad—to me."   Such
a judgment may be shown later to be quite accurate, especially if the propagandist has had wide experience in his
field of activity; but it may be quite inaccurate since it is
based on the reaction of only one individual.   For this reason, the sample may be increased and made more representative of the public.   A panel or jury of propagandees,
for example, is carefully selected, shown samples of the
propaganda, and then asked questions such as:

> Which copy makes you feel like buying the product?
> Does this appeal sound reasonable to you?
> What do you think of when you read this?
> Why do you like that one?
> Would you tell me what you remember?

It will be noted that answers to questions which pre-test
propaganda can indicate only the approximate strength of
the responses that are evoked or learned; that they are given
under somewhat artificial conditions; and that, therefore,
they cannot designate precisely how those responses will
fare when competing responses of varying strength are
elicited in the real situation.   But knowledge of a sample of
actual and external public opinion is far better, usually, than
guesswork on the basis of latent or internal public opinion.
   The fervently publicized "Program Analyzer" is a
gadget which is employed to pre-test radio and motion picture propaganda in a slightly more realistic manner.   A
panel listens to or sees a preview.   During the performance
each individual depresses one button when he likes a particular section, another when he dislikes it, and no button at all
when he feels indifferent.   The button-depressing of each
participant is recorded on a continuously moving tape by
having both buttons electrically connected with mechanical
pencils.   The members of the panel, therefore, are required
to react to a program and simultaneously to register those
reactions, a rather unusual task which can affect the nature
of their reactions.   The recorded results usually serve as the
basis for an oral interview in which each observer is asked
to interpret or explain his reactions (*8*).

The strength of the learned attitude may also be tested by examining people's actions: do they react as the propagandists wish? Sales records, for example, are consulted to determine the effectiveness of an advertising campaign. The problem here is one of interpretation: the propaganda cannot be held solely responsible for people's actions since they are being simultaneously stimulated by other forces in the environment. A good experimental design, however, can make the interpretation less equivocal. If two comparable panels or populations are selected and if it is known that they are subjected to approximately the same environmental stimuli except that one is exposed to Type A propaganda and the other to Type B, then whatever differences in behavior appear can be tentatively attributed to the propaganda. Unfortunately it is difficult to equate two groups completely, and most propagandists cannot afford the costs of such an experiment.

Responses with great drive strength at the moment may possess diminished strength in the future or vice versa. No amount of intensive interviewing of a population in peacetime, for example, can reveal in detail how people will react in wartime. For one thing they themselves do not know. For another, their reactions will also depend on the impact which the war has upon them; and that impact, too, is largely unpredictable. In propaganda terms, however, it is possible to outline in advance the kinds of pre-action responses which it is desirable for one's own side and for the enemy to learn. The following schematic table presents these responses in verbalized form not because people necessarily make them in this way but because even vague and formless impulses can be expressed only in words. Responses are arbitrarily grouped into psychological categories:

Response	*Home side*	*Enemy*
Frustration	"Victory is worth the price of the misery I endure"; "this misery will disappear when we win"	"My present misery is unendurable and will disappear only when the war ends"

Response	Home side	Enemy
Aggression	"I hate the enemy and everything he stands for"	"I like or am indifferent toward the enemy and everything he stands for"
Anxiety	"I don't want us to lose"; "I'll suffer if I don't cooperate"; "I'm willing to have the war continue"	"I don't care if we lose"; "I have more to gain than to lose by not cooperating with the war effort"; "I'm afraid the war will continue"
Gratification	"I like my society and its leaders"	"I hate my society and its leaders"
Desire	"I want victory"	"I only want the war to end"
Expectation	"We shall win but we can lose"; "the war will last longer if I don't cooperate"	"We're going to lose"

Naturally the above schema can be employed only with elaborate precautions. It is, for example, not applicable in all details to professional soldiers and officers, if there be such any more, who like war—they presumably are not frustrated by engaging in their profession. The time factor, moreover, is important. When people grow overconfident, as the American people were prone to do in the last war after every major and even after a minor victory, the propagandist interested in their "expectation" must seek to have them believe that their side is actually losing the war, a much more emphatic response than the ones indicated in the table. There is also an apparently perverse element in human behavior which sometimes must be taken into account. Doubtless most German soldiers, after the Allies had crossed the Rhine and the Russians had stormed Berlin, realized that their cause was hopeless. They certainly knew that "we are going to lose" and so, if this one psychological factor be considered in isolation, their stubborn resistance in many sectors becomes unintelligible. What happened may never be determined in detail. On the basis of interrogating prisoners at the time and of later surveys it can be cautiously said that the conviction of the hopelessness of the struggle was less powerful than one or more of the following responses and drives: as a result of previous indoctrination, men preferred death to a Germany without the Nazis; they were convinced that they in particular and their country in general would be severely punished for the crimes they had committed or merely for losing the war; or they were held in check by pressure from their officers or by military discipline and therefore as individuals waited to surrender until their ranks were so decimated that they no longer perceived themselves to be part of a military organization.

The outline of the pre-action responses sought by the war propagandist, moreover, is based on at least two psychological assumptions. In the first place, as May (*12*) has indicated, the nature of war is such that men's morale is not automatically high. For every response or drive that strengthens their will to fight or cooperate with the war effort there is usually a contrary impulse which weakens that will. In May's language, for example, drives oriented toward "the promise of immediate rewards of social approval, approbation, honor, money, prestige, a share in the loot of conquest, and the like" may be in conflict with other drives involving even the bravest soldier's "fear of loss of life or permanent disability." Propaganda is designed to strengthen the positive impulses and to weaken the negative ones, so that each individual can more easily resolve his conflict in a manner which will facilitate rather than inhibit his contribution to the war.

Then, secondly, it is assumed that perceived events do not prevent the propagandist from arousing or producing the indicated responses. Frequently, though, events cannot be gainsaid. After the sweep of the allied armies across France in 1944, for example, it was extremely difficult for Goebbels to convince the German people that "we shall win but we can lose" or that "the war will last longer if I don't cooperate." The later progress of the allies on every front, except the Italian, and the incessant bombing of Germany produced responses stronger than any which Goebbels could arouse through his references to Germany's secret weapons or to the *Volkssturm,* that miserable and pathetic collection of youths and old men who were called up for military service.

Propaganda Recognition

Should the propagandist reveal his purpose? Should he conceal it? Or should he conceal it at first and then reveal it? Frequently he has his choice of propaganda types. When he does have this choice, then the decision may rest on the kind of response which a knowledge of his purpose is likely to produce. Revealed propaganda is employed when that knowledge promotes the learning of the new attitude or when concealment is impossible for practical reasons. Concealed propaganda is necessary when knowledge of the propagandist's purpose prevents the learning from occurring. Delayed revealed propaganda is required when concealed propaganda may be either desirable or possible (or both) at first but undesirable or impossible (or both) later on.

The response of recognizing a propagandist's efforts as propaganda, for example, can indeed prevent the learning of the pre-action response. "Oh, that's just propaganda" tends to be a devastating reaction among sophisticated and not too sophisticated people in democratic countries and elsewhere. The cliché suggests that they appreciate the biased nature of what they are seeing or hearing and that therefore they are determined not to be affected. They do not wish to help that other person attain objectives they consider selfish, deceptive, or of no interest to them. During the last war, American soldiers who believed the purpose of certain orientation films they saw was to influence their attitudes were less affected by the motion pictures than were those who considered them merely "informational" or who could not decide what their function was (*3*).

As American authorities began to control the media of communication in Germany in 1945, they gradually learned that the materials they produced for the German people— they naturally called them part of the "re-education" program—could not resemble in format, approach, or content the propaganda that Goebbels had been using before the downfall of the Nazis. Germans had been so saturated with blatant propaganda and Germany's defeat had sufficiently exposed the propaganda to which they had been subjected that they tended to discredit any medium resembling one from the immediate past. The writer once watched a small group of Germans respond to the cover of the first issue of an illustrated magazine named *Heute* (Today) which was written, edited, and published by British and American technicians. The editors had chosen a clearcut, pleasant photograph of a German youth to symbolize the reconstruction of the country. The picture, however, reminded these Germans of the type of propaganda which had been sprayed upon them by an organization like the Hitler Youth, and so they turned away in disgust.

During the last war, revealed propaganda was known among British and American officials as "white" propaganda and concealed as "black." "White" propaganda was presented in the name of the government concerned or else its source could be easily recognized. It tended to be truthful and to reflect by and large only official policies, policies which frequently were motivated to a greater extent by postwar considerations than by the more immediate objective of demoralizing the enemy. Such propaganda was suspect: the enemy audience had been warned by its own propaganda machine to "beware of enemy propaganda." It sought to increase its credibility by presenting failures and dark spots as well as successes and bright spots. This widely announced "strategy of truth" severely limited both the nature and content of Anglo-American propaganda and hence, in spite of democratic scruples against irresponsibility and falsehood even in war time, "black" propaganda also had to be employed. "Black" propaganda, in contrast, concealed its source and purpose in an effort to convince enemy troops and civilians that what they were hearing or seeing was genuine and unbiased. It often contained deliberate falsehoods, inasmuch as the governments assumed no direct responsibility for its content. Whenever possible, it gave the appearance of coming from local groups or individuals within the enemy or occupied country. It employed such devices as the so-called "clandestine" radio station which posed as a representative of the underground or opposition; the planting of untrue but plausible stories in the press of neutral countries; the spreading of rumors by agents dropped or stationed behind the enemy lines; the printing and distribution of bogus newspapers and books which impersonated the enemy's; and various other methods of deception. "White" and "black" propaganda occasionally cooperated to achieve an appointed end. In the autumn of 1944 and throughout the last winter and spring of the war, for example, "white" propaganda made an effort to inform Germans through "The Voice of America" and leaflets that many of their Nazi leaders either were deserting them by fleeing abroad or were contemplating desertion in the future by depositing their wealth in neutral countries. The evidence for this assertion came from inconclusive intelligence, most of which was classified as "secret" and hence—lest its source be jeopardized—could not be employed in propaganda which reached the enemy. "Black" propaganda at this point assisted "white" not only by sowing rumors which spread the idea that the Nazis were deserting their sinking ship, but also by planting appropriate stories in the newspapers of neutral countries. The latter were then quoted in "white" broadcasts to Germany with strict attribution to the secondary source. "White" could thus say "truthfully" that such-and-such a Swedish or Swiss journal was the authority for a statement without of course mentioning the original "black" source. A "clandestine" station undoubtedly furnished delayed revealed propaganda to some listeners: at first they may have believed in its authenticity and then later have come to the conclusion that it was enemy-operated.

This brief account of "black" propaganda must not leave

the impression that only the allies in the last war resorted to undercover methods when the revelation of their identity would have been psychologically embarrassing. Long before the British and American propaganda machines were constructed and functioning, Germans achieved notable successes through the use of subterfuge. One writer (*14*), for example, asserts without proof that Goebbels publicized the substitute or *ersatz* articles being manufactured in Germany before the war when in fact the Germans were well clothed and well fed—he wanted Germany's enemies to underestimate her strength. "Black" Nazi propaganda helped demoralize the French before and after their country was overrun (*22*). French editors and publishers were bribed to present the Nazi line as if they themselves believed it. Fifth columnists throughout France launched "whispering campaigns of great efficacy"; one attributed local egg shortages to purchases made by the British Army. Fishermen in Brittany found in their nets anonymous leaflets titled "Why Should Bretons Die for Poland?"; other Frenchmen received similar tracts in hand-addressed envelopes that were sent through the regular mail. It has also been shown (*6*) how the Nazi propaganda machine had "informed sources" suggest that Germany was preparing during the summer of 1941 for a winter campaign in Russia, so that America would not feel a sense of urgency in her role as "the arsenal of democracy." That machine planted stories in a Swedish newspaper under its control for the purpose of raising false hopes concerning British military assistance to Russia. In order to deceive the French and British, the German High Command managed to have gullible American correspondents spread the tale that the invasion of England and not of France would be the next objective of the German Armies after the Belgian campaign.

The Communist party in democratic countries frequently engages in concealed propaganda to attain not the revolution on the morrow but immediate objectives considered to be along the revolutionary route or to be temporarily expedient. For any official act in its name is likely, especially in the United States and England, to arouse such adverse responses that the pre-action responses it seeks have little or no chance of coming into existence. People are loath to accept suggestions or advice from individuals they dislike, even when the ideas on their merits have a positive appeal. For this reason the Communist party has a strong proclivity to go underground and, by boring from within another organization or by establishing a new one with a non-communist name and with seemingly non-communist functions, to struggle for its ends under misleading colors. This is not to say, as the various congressional committees investigating so-called "un-American activities" have recklessly maintained, that any group containing a few communist or communist sympathizers is automatically a front for the party. At the same time, it must be pointed out that communists by and large take their communism very seriously—they agree, for example, to subject themselves to the party's discipline and to work for its principles at all times—and therefore through conscientiousness and hard work they seek most deliberately to dominate every organization to which they belong.

Advertising uses revealed propaganda almost exclusively. In fact printed copy which might be confused with the publications' content is labelled "a-d-v-t." Sometimes, however, the format of an advertisement so closely resembles non-advertising material that the unwary reader may be trapped into reading it before he realizes its propaganda objective or before he notices the identifying label. In such delayed revealed propaganda, both perceptual and related responses can be aroused prior to possible interference from the response of recognizing the propaganda. Over a period of time the advertiser may also employ delayed revealed propaganda to build up an interest in or a demand for his product. A classical instance, cited by *Printers' Ink* (*15*), was the sub-propaganda campaign staged after World War I by cigarette manufacturers to make cigarette smoking respectable among American women: a picture of oriental women who did not look oriental and who had cigarettes in their mouths was soon followed by "a hosiery advertisement which showed a woman displaying the merchandise and also smoking" and these in turn gave way to "the 'Blow Some My Way' advertising done by Chesterfield when the young woman was shown smoking only in a decidedly second-hand way." From a long-range viewpoint much of modern advertising can be considered unintentional propaganda for a so-called higher and certainly more luxurious standard of living, an objective generally concealed from and unknown to most consumers.

For children even the most blatant advertising can be concealed propaganda. They are generally too unsophisticated to appreciate the commercial implications of an advertisement. To them the plug over the radio is like a parental injunction, or a beautiful advertisement in a magazine resembles the gospel they are taught in school. They are less able than adults to experience skepticism and doubt.

Commercial and other interests sometimes resort to publicity rather than to advertising not only to solve the perceptual problem and thus secure a wider audience but also to strike that audience when it is in a more receptive mood. An item about a company that appears in a news column or program is "good publicity" for both these reasons. The propagandee feels he is reading or listening to an objective version of the truth. He may know that there are such phenomena as publicity agents, but it is unlikely that he will be acquainted with their machinations at a given moment. A favorable criticism of a book by a reviewer is usually much more valuable in promoting its sale than many inches of advertisements stressing its magnificent style or its world-trembling ideas. Certainly reputable reviewers do not formulate their criticisms as a result of direct bribes from publishers and authors; but they may learn of the book's existence by reading a note from its publishers, and unavoidably they may feel friendly toward its author whom they meet at a cocktail party staged by the firm's publicity department.

Publicity agents cover the waterfront of American activities. Their principal task is to persuade an editor to print or broadcast "news" about their clients. They sometimes resort to bribery: they pay the editor for publishing their

story or for incorporating their point of view into an editorial, or they offer an advertisement or threaten to withdraw one unless their conditions are met. They may also
seek to exploit a personal friendship they have cultivated
with the reporter—"Come on, Bill, give me a break"—or
they may convince an editor on the basis of past performance that their material really is newsworthy. They may
concoct a "news service" which contains straight feature
news or photographs as well as biased items in behalf of
their clients. Or the service may provide only propaganda
material, in which case it frankly reveals its purpose or, less
frequently, it masquerades under a misleading title. A dry
organization in the United States, for example, has called
its sheet the "American Business Men's Research Foundation" which has the motto of "Let's Have the Truth About
Alcohol." The scientific nature of such truth-seeking is indicated by a quip from one issue: "All liquids seek the lowest
level; alcohol takes the drinker with it." Publicity agents,
finally, seek to create "news" about their clients: a fountain-
pen manufacturer is flown around the world, a man likes
sauerkraut so much that he is determined to be buried in a
cabbage patch with a cup of vinegar inside his coffin, a politician lifts a load of manure as the newsreel cameras crank,
etc. Editors, publishers, and broadcasters, however, are
super-sophisticated and blasé in respect to publicity agents:
they can usually smell them a mile away and so they are
prepared to dump their releases into the wastepaper basket
—or to leave them unopened. In fact, disapproval of publicity for commercial products and enterprises is sometimes
expressed by calling such activity "space-grabbing": publicity agents, the phrase suggests, are trying illegitimately to
grab space in news columns instead of paying for advertisements. Publicity agents, therefore, seldom dupe their protagonists; their not infrequent successes depend either on
the news merits of what they are peddling or on the *quid
pro quo* they are able to offer.

Much of what is printed or broadcast as "news"—and
which may belong in that category from the propagandees'
viewpoint—actually stems from publicity agents or from in-

terested individuals whose high-sounding and often misleading titles range from public relations counsel to executive
secretary. So-called "dope" stories about impending events
may originate in the minds of those who have an interest in
the events and who hope that their prognostications transmitted through a journalist will affect what is about to happen. By remaining anonymous and hiding behind an innocent report they do not produce the antagonism or disbelief
which a revelation of their identity would create.

The handouts of governmental, educational, and scientific groups that are written and distributed by publicity
agents perform a very useful function in American society:
they frequently contain facts which reporters can digest at
their leisure and then use or not use as they see fit in the
stories they write for their papers (20). Certainly the
agents concerned wish to have their releases creep into the
news columns, but they are not necessarily attempting to
deceive people through the use of concealed propaganda.
The organizations' activities may be so complex that an
accurate handout is more likely to result in an accurate newspaper story than an interview with someone who is naive in
the ways of publicity or than a private deduction or intuition
on the part of many reporters. Direct advertising for these
groups is a clumsy or inappropriate medium, and the only
vehicle they have for reaching people is through the news
columns. Usually they do not wish to have their identity
concealed and are not ashamed of the fact that they are
feeding material to the press. Such legitimate publicity
should not acquire some of the opprobrium associated with
the very biased releases from commercial, theatrical, and
special interest groups simply because the same type of dissemination is employed. Certainly there is some rather innocuous deception involving ulterior objectives or consequences that are not mentioned in the release. A scientific
discovery in a university or a government bureau is newsworthy, and the institution's prestige is thereby increased.
The alumnus of the university may be tempted to contribute
money to his alma mater's endowment and the citizen to
vote for the party in power as a result of this publicity, but

such responses are inevitable once the news is presented in any form. These handouts, on the other hand, are deliberately contrived and therefore do not contain information the group wishes to suppress. As Rosten (*21*) points out, "there are no handouts on the failures, scandals, dissensions, and inconsistencies of an administration" in Washington.

The intentional propagandist must sometimes reveal his identity not because he considers that giving such knowledge to propagandees will aid him but because he has no alternative except to do so. To obtain large-scale patronage, the merchant must advertise: editors refuse to accept the specific information he wants to convey to potential customers concerning a sale he is launching, and the announcements in his store windows are seen by relatively few people. Consumers, moreover, are on the lookout for bargains and therefore, instead of greeting the advertisement skeptically or derisively, they may feel the impulse to buy. If a propagandist's reputation is generally good, moreover, the revelation of his name can work to his advantage. The manufacturer who wishes to sell a product which he has not previously marketed, for example, eagerly reveals his sponsorship of an advertisement, for he assumes that the satisfaction resulting from using his other products in the past will be transferred to the new merchandise or service. The candidate running for public office has to employ revealed propaganda since people know what goal he seeks. He may, however, simultaneously employ some concealed propaganda by surreptitiously spreading unflattering tales concerning his opponent.

The unintentional propagandist does not deliberately select his type of propaganda because he is unaware of how he is affecting people or because he does not recognize himself as a propagandist. For the very same reason that he does not grasp the significance of what he is doing, his propagandees may also fail to appreciate his intentions. Unintentional propaganda, consequently, tends to be concealed propaganda. The conventionally distorted version of history taught by the grade school teacher fits so well into actual public opinion that only a professional historian or an extremely radical or reactionary individual—and certainly not she or her pupils—can unmask her propaganda function and objectives. The unintentional propagandist, moreover, is usually thought of as a sincere or a naive individual, as indeed he or she may very well be, and what is called sincerity or naïveté may not arouse the skepticism associated with an "evil," "calculating," or "shrewd" propagandist.

Prestige and Submission

The leader of a group possesses prestige when its members have discovered or believe that their drives can be satisfied by him and perhaps by him alone. As a result, they tend to identify themselves with him and to project their own impulses upon him. They listen to what he says or they read what he has written with respect and sometimes awe. They anticipate that he will be able to repeat his past successes for them. After the German armies had reached the English Channel in 1940 and controlled all of Western Europe from the tip of Norway to the Spanish frontier (and—to add an intentionally propagandistic footnote—really to Gibraltar since Franco never forgot the role the Nazis had played in enabling him to seize control of Spain), there were few Germans who did not worship Hitler and attribute to him the powers of a genius in military and political affairs. Many people outside Germany who had no love for him shared the same point of view at least intellectually. A message from him during this period was important news everywhere, and Germans in particular were psychologically unable and unwilling to respond critically to his propaganda.

A stimulus with prestige prevents the arousal of or weakens critical or incompatible responses that otherwise might block the learning of pre-action responses. When the patient is in a hypnotic trance, he responds both to the commands and the presence of the hypnotist. The relation between patient and hypnotist is momentarily so intimate that many but not all of the responses which the latter's words would evoke under normal conditions are repressed or otherwise weakened. The son has agreed to be affected by the

father, he remains passive while pre-existing and appropriate habit systems are evoked, and he is relatively submissive
and obedient until the relationship is altered by the termination of the trance.   In a strict sense, propagandists cannot
hypnotize their propagandees—although a skillful demagogue in the face-to-face situation of a meeting may come
close to doing so—but they frequently approximate the psychological state produced by a trance through the use of
various devices.

The propagandist himself may possess prestige because
of the position he occupies in society or because of his past
successes.   In this case, as has been indicated in the previous
section, he can employ revealed rather than concealed propaganda.   Or at least he reveals his own identity if not
the precise objectives he intentionally or unintentionally
seeks.

One of the shrewdest propaganda campaigns of the last
war was conducted by the Russians against the Germans
through the use of the so-called Free Germany Committee.
This group was composed not only of German communists
who had sought refuge in the Soviet Union but also of
German officers and enlisted men, many of whom had
been captured at Stalingrad.   These Germans knew their
countrymen better than the Russians did and therefore
used the propaganda themes best calculated to arouse
strong and related personality responses.   Through them
but without the assumption of responsibility Soviet propaganda made political promises which official propagandists
could or would not state on their own authority.   Most
important, German speakers—even German communists but
especially German military officials—possessed prestige
which no Russian speaker could ever have.

The propagandist may include among his propaganda
stimuli persons other than himself and objects which have
prestige.   The testimonial's function is to produce submission: doubt and skepticism are supposed to be weakened by
the revelation that experts, prominent personalities, or just
average men and women support the propagandist's contention.   During the last war, for example, allied propagan-

dists featured in their broadcasts to the enemy commentators like Lindley Fraser whose prestige was steadily enhanced by the reliability of their reporting or the validity of their predictions; or they employed speakers like Thomas Mann who already possessed varying degrees of eminence. The testimonial has been exploited so promiscuously by American advertisers that it has come to evoke skepticism rather than submission (2). Even so, the device at least brings about the perception of the propaganda, and it certainly helps publicize the individuals whose opinions or practices are mentioned in the copy.

The past is assumed by propagandists to have prestige and so they are always eager to demonstrate that their cause has the sanctity of antiquity. Advertisements point out that producers were the "original" or the "first" ones to introduce the product: the audience is supposed to be impressed by the experience which comes with age and not conclude that the producer may be employing out-dated manufacturing techniques. When communists quarrel among themselves, each side finds a quotation from Marx, Lenin, or Stalin to add luster to its argument. The Bible, the Talmud, the Koran, or some set of Holy Scriptures is invoked for the benefit of those who belong to religious orders. Often the appeal is made simply to history, as in these samples of wet and dry propaganda:

The ancient civilizations of Egypt knew beer by many names . . . Beer such as the Europeans knew came to America with the Pilgrim Fathers . . . Among the famous men of Colonial America who brewed beer themselves were William Penn and George Washington.

From the time of our most primitive past alcoholic beverages have been a scourge to human life and a problem to human society. A tomb of early Egypt bore the inscription, "His earthly tenement was shattered before it was called for." . . .

Sometimes the part of the propaganda stimulus with prestige has little or no logical connection with the pre-action response and hence serves merely to produce submission without evoking related responses. The patriotic or march music preceding the speaker stirs the audience and leaves people in a receptive mood. A discharge button on the propagandist's lapel or the title of "Dr." before his name bestows upon his opinions an element of conviction and confidence when in fact the special experience or skill signified by the symbol may be quite irrelevant to those opinions.

Submission can be evoked by people's desire to conform to public opinion, and conformity in turn frequently results from identification and projection. F. H. Allport has stressed the significant role played by what he calls the "impression of universality" in institutional life: "the individual reacts to stimuli which he actually receives *as if* they were coming from an enormously greater number of people" and he "imagines that the entire vast assembly is stimulating him in this fashion" (*1*). The propagandist, deliberately or not, seeks to strengthen such an impression. He demonstrates the popularity of his cause by referring to the great numbers already supporting him or about to do as he wishes. In advertising the slogan of "America's fastest selling brand" appears in various forms with or without supporting statistics. Logically the effect of such an appeal can be to convince the consumer that the brand's popularity proves its excellence, for otherwise so many people would not be customers. Psychologically the process may not be so clear-cut: the claim can merely produce a vaguely self-deprecating response which, if it were verbalized (as it probably seldom is), might express a feeling like who-am-I-miserable-creature-to-question-the-wisdom-of-the-great-American-people. Psychological warfare strives to create the impression of defeatism among the enemy before defeatism is actually widespread by finding or manufacturing evidence purporting to show that only the forces of evil prevent public opinion from externalizing the same sentiments which one or two individuals have already manifested. On election eve all American politicians predict that victory will be theirs on the morrow, and almost always their predictions turn out to be quantitatively biased in favor of their own side.

The propagandist thus produces submission because people wish to conform, but it is important to note that he exploits a pre-existing drive which he himself has not created. With or without propaganda there is this straining toward conformity. The élite in a society, for example, are models from which other individuals learn some of their ways of behaving, whether it be a way of pronouncing a word in the language, of wearing clothes, or of cooking spinach. Such "imitation" can occur "spontaneously," which is a glib way of saying that lower-status individuals copy those of higher status and thus, without additional stimulation, seek and maybe secure whatever rewards they imagine are theirs for conforming. The diffusion can be facilitated quite deliberately through intentional propaganda, as the rapid adoption of debutante clothing styles by working girls is encouraged in our society by clothing manufacturers and women's magazines.

Submission may also be produced through identification and projection without calling upon propagandees to conform to public opinion. The campaign manager releases human interest stories about his candidate which fit the picture people have of the way they themselves would be if they were in a similar position of prominence. Or the stories show quite bluntly that the politician or statesman is like them, that he is just a common man after all. Part of his public personality, moreover, is left vague so that voters can fill in additional details by projecting their own aspirations or habits upon him.

The general attitude evoked by the propaganda or the vehicle of communication may affect what is learned. When that attitude is favorable rather than unfavorable, propagandees are more highly motivated to perceive the propaganda and tend to feel more submissive toward what they are hearing or seeing. Less conflict, in a word, is likely to occur. It is for this reason that the propagandist seeks to have his audience enjoy or develop an interest in his propaganda and that a theme in an appealing context is learned more readily than the same theme in an unappealing one. Very preliminary evidence gathered during the last war (*3*) indicates that the attitudes of American soldiers who liked a particular propaganda film were more markedly affected than those of men who disliked it.

Counter-propaganda

Almost all propaganda evokes contrary responses which hinder the learning process, or else those responses occur as the propagandees perceive the propaganda. Only the very immature and the extremely anxious can respond to propaganda without experiencing some degree of conflict. The basic problem in counter-propaganda is whether to ignore competing responses or to attack them directly.

A direct attack is often extremely dangerous. The conflict between competing responses can be intensified, and conflicts are unpleasant. It is so much easier to make a decision when one is faced by an attractive and an unattractive alternative than when both alternatives are more or less equally attractive or unattractive (*13*). An attack on an individual's conviction is likely to be resented or interpreted as one directed against him personally. Then there is always the possibility that the antagonistic responses may not be evoked or that their drive strength will remain at a low ebb if their appropriate stimuli are not mentioned for purposes of attack. Criticism, finally, can boomerang by giving additional currency to the very viewpoints which are being criticized.

Contrary impulses can sometimes be ignored or rendered less effective through the arousal and strengthening of competing responses. If a market survey reveals to the advertiser that people consider his product too expensive, he does not say that it is not expensive, but he argues simply that it is cheap. He may proclaim, for example, that the price is "only $168" and hope that "only" will somehow temper the shock produced by the numerals themselves. He may reduce the price a couple of pennies—"$1.98"—to try to remove some of the sting associated with the round number. In addition, he can always stress the earth-shaking virtues of the product and then state or imply that they are worth the extra cost.

While it is true that every action involves a counter-action, it is equally true that many people respond differently to a positive suggestion than they do to a negative one. The injunction to "drive carefully" has the same referent as one saying "don't drive recklessly," but the positive warning directs attention to what one should do (and only by implication to what one should avoid), whereas the negative stricture seems to have a greater tendency to promote the commission of what is intended to be an omission. Sometimes during the last war allied broadcasters in Europe dealt directly but negatively with one of the impulses which inhibited the peoples of occupied countries from committing sabotage against the enemy: they were told that the risks were relatively slight if they carefully followed instructions. At other times sabotage was encouraged simply by reporting instances in which saboteurs had been successful. When the positive approach was employed, it was not assumed that patriots could be made to ignore the real perils involved: the facts of enemy occupation and surveillance were much too patent for this to occur. Instead it was hoped that the stress on success would result in a minimizing of the risk and a maximizing of the impulses to help destroy the enemy.

Frequently the frontal attack cannot be avoided. People must be told to keep off the grass, to be on their guard against false claims, to pay no attention to lies from the enemy, etc. The direct approach is necessary when the competing responses are too strong, when they will be evoked anyhow by the propaganda, or when through a sub-propaganda campaign they can be weakened before their strength increases.

The dynamics of counter-propaganda are illustrated by an experiment performed in the United States Army toward the end of the last war (4). In April of 1945 it was thought desirable to convince American soldiers that the war against Japan would be protracted even after the defeat of Germany. The problem arose as to whether the propaganda should simply present the arguments pointing toward a long struggle or whether, in addition, it should seek to refute views widely held at the time which suggested that our victory would be a speedy one. One group of soldiers was then presented with a radio transcription containing only arguments for a long war, and a comparable group heard the same arguments as well as refutations of the optimistic estimate. Both procedures proved to be equally effective from an overall viewpoint. When an analysis was made in terms of the views the men had held before they heard the program, however, the predictions of the investigators on the basis of psychological theory were vindicated: counter-propaganda was necessary to convert the unbelievers but provoked doubt among the believers. The presentation only of one side was more effective among men who already were convinced that the war would be long than it was among men who had been thinking that the war would be short. In contrast, the inclusion of direct counter-propaganda had a more marked effect on men estimating the war to be short than it had on men estimating it to be long.

The same study also suggests that, if some conflicting attitudes are directly attacked, then all of them must be subjected to the propaganda barrage. The counter-propaganda against the short war was unable for policy reasons to mention the role which the Soviet Union might conceivably play in defeating the Japanese—and this was the very argument many men advanced for believing in a speedy termination of the Pacific conflict. As a result, fewer men hearing the counter-propaganda version considered that the presentation contained all the important facts bearing on the issue than did the men hearing the version containing only positive propaganda. The failure to refer to Russia, in the words of the report, "seemed more glaring in the presentation that committed itself to covering both sides of the question."

By and large the Communist party in a democratic country like the United States is unsuccessful either in building up a large membership or in winning support for the specific measures it advocates. Violently hostile reactions occur when most Americans hear key communist terms like "class struggle," "proletariat," "revolution," and "communism" itself. These reactions are symptomatic of the conviction— reinforced unintentionally throughout socialization and further strengthened later both intentionally and unintentionally by the opponents of social change—that Americans have the opportunity to rise in the economic and social scale, the very scale which a communist revolution would abolish. The occasionally impressive evidence which the party employs in its propaganda to demonstrate that American workers (and special groups like Negroes, Jews, and members of unions) are oppressed by their employers is not always impressive to men and women who expect an increase in pay before they grow much older, who may be organized effectively to secure that increase, and who know beforehand more or less how the extra money will be spent. It is certainly true that the energy and initiative displayed by party members have solved the perceptual problem: few Americans nowadays are unaware of its existence, although their knowledge of its objectives may be vague or distorted. It is also true that many American workers have profited from communist propaganda and agitation within one of the organizations selected by the party as a front, while remaining unaware of the role the communists have played and retaining only a feeling of contempt for a party whose principal policies are said to be dictated by a foreign government. The antagonistic responses of Americans, in short, cannot be appreciably weakened by counter-propaganda alone.

Counter-propaganda can serve as a prophylactic to arrest the disease at an early stage. Dictators closely supervise the school system to extinguish immediately any hostile attitudes which children are likely to acquire. The supporters of democracy, on the other hand, have been slow to learn that fascism must be discredited from the outset before it has an opportunity to delude large numbers of people.

Reinforcement

Even as they are important at the perceptual and personality stages, the repetition and variation of propaganda can also affect pre-action responses. In this connection they serve to reinforce the learning which is occurring. Or they strengthen pre-action responses after they have once been made.

The propagandee hesitates or the new attitude he has learned is unstable. For the moment he has been convinced by the propaganda but a minute, an hour, a day, a month, a year, or a decade later the new response may grow weaker or be supplanted by a competing one. He wishes to purchase the product, vote for the candidate, or cooperate with the war effort—yet this tendency may be wrecked by competing propaganda or a different and stronger drive.

Repetition reinforces the strength of the connections between the appropriate stimuli and the response sequence which is evoked, a sequence involving perception, personality responses, and now the pre-action response itself. The radio listener who has heard the plug for a face powder and whose personality responses have been favorable, nevertheless, feels no impulse to buy the product until on a later occasion—when she is generally frustrated or specifically weary of the brand she has been using—the repetition of the advertisement induces her to try the advertised brand. The connection between the advertisement and the decision has been established not merely because the advertisement has been repeated but because it has been repeated after the listener has had different experiences in the meantime. Or hearing the advertisement in the past may have produced a weak decision to do as the propagandist advises at some indefinite date in the future; in this case repetition serves to strengthen the pre-action response by increasing its drive value through the addition of a component, for example, of curiosity concerning the merits of the product.

Variation can similarly strengthen the tendency to act by increasing its drive strength. In the commercial field, for example, one observer (*11*) points out that the "summer slump in the consumption of coffee was decreased when it was found that consumers could be persuaded to drink iced coffee." In October 1943 the president of a dry organization in the United States varied her usual propaganda approach with this very timely and logical statement: "We are fighting three enemies: Germany, Japan, and the liquor

power, and the most likely to defeat us is the liquor power."
As the United States entered the last war against Germany,
many Germans became slightly anxious as they unavoidably
recalled the defeat their country suffered nearly twenty-five
years ago after the previous American declaration. This
anxiety could not mount until events and propaganda added
other anxiety-reproducing responses—connected with military defeats, aerial bombing, food shortages, etc.—which
together led to demoralization. Likewise the variation of
propaganda in the interests of a sub-propaganda campaign
can strengthen the pre-action response.

Variation, moreover, serves an extremely important function as an antidote to repetition. Modern peoples, after
two wars within twenty years and after being continually
subjected to waves of commercial and political propaganda,
have grown both propaganda-conscious and propaganda-
weary. One of the ways to diminish some of the weariness
and hence to decrease their resistance is to vary the propaganda content. All that really needs to be said in war
propaganda is: "surrender now." But propagandees do not
respond to such a simple command: they require reasons for
following a recommended course of action and it is these
reasons which evoke varied personality responses. People
would not listen to a voice, and they would not read a leaflet
which merely repeated "surrender now." If the voice and
the leaflet, moreover, varied the arguments advanced for
this course of action, the net effect could be better and yet
not appreciably better from the propagandist's viewpoint.
Propagandees might learn a sentence to the effect that "the
enemy's line is to ask us to surrender now," but this sentence
would not be very action-compelling. For this reason the
perceptible content of war propaganda must be varied, even
though a simple, central theme is occasionally but unobtru-
sively repeated with or without much variation.

Since the propagandist frequently varies his propaganda
in order to evoke attitudes with greater drive strength, it is
necessary at this point to discuss briefly the problem of the
consistency of propaganda. In general, propaganda seems
to be called inconsistent when different appeals are made to

different groups—the technique utilized by Hitler to win the support of over 40 percent of the German people in the Weimar days—or when the appeals to the same groups are varied to suit the occasion—the technique of the advertiser who keeps his copy "in tune with the times." Sometimes propaganda is thought to be inconsistent only when different appeals are used simultaneously on the same group and when, from the viewpoint of some one of the sciences or of Aristotelian logic, the appeals are considered contradictory. A political platform promises an increase in expenditures for public works and the armed forces, a decrease in the number of civil servants, and no increase in the public debt or taxation. These promises are widely separated by rhetoric, poetry, and references to the great past and the greater future of both the party and its candidates. They might be considered by an expert in political science or public administration to be inconsistent, since the attainment of the first objective, for example, would probably exclude the attainment of the other two. The use of different appeals to different groups really means only that the propagandist himself is inconsistent. The use of different appeals to the same group over a period of time or at the same time, however, involves the propagandist as well as the propagandees whose consistency has already been discussed in Chapter 5. The propagandee who fails to recognize the objective inconsistency of three appeals in a political platform may simply be responding to each appeal separately. The three responses do not act as stimuli to elicit the additional, internal responses (called thinking or reasoning) which are necessary before conflict can occur. More important to him than the logical compatibility of the three appeals may be the satisfaction he has already secured from the political party in question.

Recency

Even though there is some historically limited evidence indicating that the majority of voters comes to a decision long before (*10*), candidates for public office in a democracy campaign up until the time the ballots are cast. They believe that they can still win converts at the very last moment and, in addition, they seek in this manner to reinforce favorable pre-action responses. Their propaganda, they hope, will be the last to affect people. Under certain circumstances, it is quite true that recently perceived stimuli possess at least two advantages.

A recent stimulus may arouse a response that is the same as, or different from, one previously evoked. The pre-action tendency, therefore, is reinforced simply by repetition or variation. Some advertisers, for example, first search for their customers in the press, in magazines, and over the radio; they follow them on to the streets with billboards; and then they finally pursue them into stores where they seek to have their merchandise prominently displayed or further publicized on posters. The displays and the posters represent one last attempt to evoke personality responses or to reinforce the drive-to-buy.

The factor of recency may also be important at an opportune moment. Either as a result of previous propaganda or of drives that are aroused and that have little or no connection with propaganda, the propagandee is psychologically ripe to be affected. He may be frustrated, for example, and seeking—consciously or unconsciously—some method of expressing his aggression. Along comes the propaganda and proposes a scapegoat.

It is possible, however, to exaggerate the importance of recency. For the recent stimulus is simply the last chain in a series of prior events which are just as necessary if the pre-action response is to occur. American reporters during the last war had a tendency to give credit to combat-propaganda teams for "capturing" thousands of German and Japanese prisoners through the use of loudspeakers. These teams contained very brave individuals who would be the first to recognize that the reporters were stretching a point in the interest of writing a good story. Enemy soldiers, before the surrender appeal went out, generally had already been somewhat demoralized by the flow of military events and, to a much lesser degree, by other allied propaganda.

Limitation

The fair-minded educator is an individual who traditionally gives both sides of a question. He presents the best facts at his disposal, criticizes those facts when in his opinion they deserve criticism, and in general is not supposed to bludgeon his students to accept his private view or one based exclusively on faith. Should a public utility be nationalized? The instructor lists the advantages and disadvantages of complete, partial, or no nationalization and makes a conscientious effort to point out what the consequences of each policy can reasonably be expected to be.

In contrast, the intentional propagandist may present only those stimuli which will evoke responses related to the action he seeks. He limits the situation confronting the propagandees. He stacks the cards. The moment he himself takes a stand on the issue *and* wishes to convince his audience that his stand and no other is the correct one, he is wasting his own time if he arouses the antagonistic responses which inevitably are evoked by presenting both sides of a question. Sometimes he may give the impression of being open-minded in order spuriously to strengthen his reputation as an impartial individual or effectively to counteract competing responses which must be refuted. Unless he is a fool from the propaganda viewpoint, however, he eventually must weight the facts or the conclusions to be drawn from them.

There is—as has been argued in a previous chapter—no sharp line between education and propaganda. The most sincere educator does not know all the facts, unless he is an exceptional man; and those which he knows he cannot adequately communicate to everyone. Each simplifies the stimuli he presents. The difference between the educator and the propagandist in this respect is quantitative and by no means absolute. The educator presents more of all sides and, consequently, tries to be scientific; the propagandist intentionally or unintentionally presents more of only one side and less of the others.

The propagandist limits the content of his propaganda

stimuli so that only predominantly favorable rather than unfavorable responses are evoked. In this way he sets up fewer conflicts within propagandees or less intense ones. It is usually easier for individuals to obey a command or to respond to black-white or simplified arguments than it is for them to weigh alternatives which have been offered on an almost completely untipped scale. Why should a propagandist court trouble?

The facts that are available concerning a situation may be limited by the propagandist in two ways: they may be suppressed or they may be distorted. A third method of limitation consists of fabricating pseudo-facts. Any one of these usually represents a stimulus simplification and therefore facilitates the perceptual response as well as the learning of the propaganda.

By suppression is meant, of course, the withholding of facts which from a scientific viewpoint are considered relevant. Advertising copy never provides a complete description of commonplace commodities like soap, pie, or electric vacuum cleaners, for example, in terms of their molecular and atomic structures. The advertiser is not concerned with scientific niceties which he views as oddities. His method is to portray the objects only in those arbitrarily selected respects which will arouse personality responses related to the pre-action response he seeks. The "purity" of the soap's ingredients is featured, not its precise derivation from the animal, vegetable, or inanimate kingdom. The "taste" of pie is mentioned, not its caloric content. The amount of "work" saved by running a vacuum cleaner is trumpeted, not its expected life span in comparison with competing brands. Advertising copy, being relatively brief, involves suppression.

In theory democratic countries are opposed to suppression of information, and suppression in this context is usually called censorship. The facts are supposed to be made available to everyone so that public opinion can be based upon adequate information. So repugnant is the idea of government censorship in the United States that even during the last war the authorities did not impose a censorship code upon the American press and radio, but instead sought and secured their cooperation on a voluntary basis by explaining the reasons for the relatively few restrictions which security required (*9*).

The exceptions to the belief in the free flow of ideas and facts, however, are both numerous and inevitable. The so-called facts of life, for example, are usually not communicated to children, for it is believed (though in a real sense unproven) that a knowledge of sexual intercourse or masturbation would be "bad" for the characters of the immature and have "bad" effects as the individuals mature. In the name of "national security," particularly but not exclusively in wartime, facts are withheld from people not because it is felt that the information would harm them directly but because actual and potential enemies of the country would benefit from their revelation. Political leaders are reluctant to reveal their plans in detail, lest their opponents profit from such insight. While it is said that the media of communication should possess "freedom of information," certain limitations on those media are also simultaneously recognized. The *New York Times* must interpret its famous slogan—"All the News That's Fit to Print"— and hence does not deliberately print news it considers to be slanderous or libelous, the opinions of people it believes incompetent and unimportant, or facts it feels may invade "personal privacy." The democratic stand on suppression of facts relating to controversial public issues does assume that certain facts will be suppressed, but it asserts that eventually truth will out if no official steps are taken to prevent its dissemination.

People in democratic nations, moreover, believe that truth in some spheres can be established only in the long run if at all, and that a practical policy requires the presentation of many, varying, if not all viewpoints. In contrast, the small cliques which run totalitarian nations are convinced that, since they themselves know what is true and good, only the version meeting their approval should be disseminated and the others suppressed. The editor of a technical journal in the natural sciences does not publish an article which he knows to be scientifically false, nor does the manager of a Sunday School paper print a point of view which he believes to be morally bad. Why, then, the totalitarians ask, should newspapers and radio stations be permitted to communicate equally false or immoral information? The difference between a relative and an absolute scale of values is seldom so clear and practically significant as it is when democratic and totalitarian practices regarding suppression are compared.

The second method of limiting a situation is to distort it. The distinction between distortion on the one hand and suppression or fabrication on the other is not a sharp one, inasmuch as the withholding or falsification of information automatically has a distorting effect. There are instances, however, in which facts are not suppressed or fabricated but instead are placed in misleading perspective. The information service of the United States Government which during the last war supplied news to foreign countries not adequately serviced by the regular commercial press agencies and which now largely confines its news-dissemination function to shortwave broadcasts is always faced with a delicate problem whenever a disgraceful event like a lynching occurs in this country. For friends and enemies alike report such an event quite truthfully by stating the fact of the lynching in the South and then by adding a small or large number of the lurid details. A report of this kind involves suppression, however, since it neglects to mention the indignation provoked by a lynching not only in the North but also in the South. The indignation likewise is a fact which needs to be mentioned if the story is to be complete. The intentional motive behind the distortion may be to discredit this country or simply to report those aspects of a newsworthy event which conform to the readers' stereotype concerning the United States. On the other hand, an American or British press agency's report sometimes includes a brief reference to public indignation, which, however, is underplayed in the account. This, too, is a distortion achieved not by suppressing facts but by emphasizing some facts at the expense of others. In terms of sheer news values, the procedure certainly is sensible: after all, the killing of an individual by a mob is more exciting than the protests and investigations which follow.

It might be argued that the official information service of a government can best achieve its objectives by not giving further currency to an unpleasant story. Suppressing the fact of the lynching, though, would be most unwise. The news cannot be confined to the United States and, therefore, editors and listeners to the service would grow suspicious as they noticed the significant omission. Under the circumstances, consequently, what is usually done is to report both the lynching and the indignation it produces and frequently also to describe and attempt to explain why lynchings occur. This is considered to be the "true" story of the event in a "correct" context. Whether it is in fact *truer,* whether its context is more *correct,* or whether its emphasis is more *fairly* placed are questions that cannot be glibly answered since the problem of what constitutes the, or an, adequate treatment of any event is so dependent upon the individual who passes judgment on the three italicized words.

Part of propaganda's evil reputation in Anglo-Saxon countries results from its association with fabrication which means simply the presentation of false information or straight lying. It is true that the line between truth and falsity cannot always be discovered with dispatch or without reference to metaphysical postulates; nevertheless a pragmatic distinction is usually possible. In the United States, for example, the Federal Trade Commission seeks to prevent manufacturers from misrepresenting their products. A producer is not permitted to assert that the contents of the bottle he sells will cure a disease when competent medical authorities agree that such is not the case; nor that the medicine includes a particular ingredient when, in fact, chemical analysis reveals its absence. Without actual fabrication, however, there can be a distortion not of the factual information but of the stimulus eliciting perceptual and personality responses. The label of the bottle does not assert that the disease can be cured, but it may leave that impression through the mere naming of the disease: the harassed layman cannot distinguish carefully between the statement on the label that the contents "aids in the relief of" or "brings comfort to people suffering from" the disease and the easy cure he seeks. The label may literally conform to the letter of the law by revealing the ingredients (including sometimes their actual percentages of the total), but the print is so small that it is overlooked in favor of the brand name which often stresses an ingredient present only in insignificant amounts.

Fabrication is one of the traditional concubines of war propaganda. During the first world war, Germans were accused of atrocities ranging from the amputation of women's breasts to the use of human corpses for soap. Most but not all of these tales were exposed afterwards both by Germans and members of allied countries (*16*), an exposure incidentally which helped produce initial skepticism concerning the authenticity of the atrocities actually committed by the Nazis from the time Von Hindenburg handed over Germany to them until their downfall in 1945. German officials in that war also employed atrocities as a propaganda weapon (*17*).

World War II produced a fine crop of lies. The Japanese were fond of manufacturing naval victories for their side when in fact they had been defeated or no engagements had occurred. In 1940 German agents in France spread false rumors concerning the advance of their armies, in order to create additional confusion in that country. Some American officials magnified the effects of the strategic bombing of Germany far beyond the facts as subsequently obtained and no doubt as partially known at the time. The British made a consistent effort to stress their own rather than the American contribution to the war front in Southeast Asia. In passing, it may be noted that official communiqués concerning the military and naval progress of the war—with the exceptions of those issued by Japan, China, and Italy— tended on the whole to contain few fabrications, but limited themselves to minor distortions, major suppressions, and overall résumés at opportune moments.

Why do falsehoods and atrocity stories flourish during war time? From one viewpoint, the truth as it is known

to the propagandists involves fewer risks, but often that
truth is not an effective stimulus to arouse the personality
responses necessary for successful propaganda. The propagandist who seeks to create hatred for the enemy among his
fellow countrymen and neutrals is sorely tempted to invent
a story which he feels will provoke hatred. He realizes,
too, that fabrications, especially during the turmoil of war,
are difficult to expose and, even if exposed, will probably
have already served their purpose. People, moreover, take
a pathological interest in atrocities which usually involve,
according to one student of the subject (*18*), massacre,
mutilation, or maltreatment: while being shocked and indignant, some of them secure private and secret gratification, perhaps because they themselves are not the victims,
maybe because sexual elements are frequently involved, and
even possibly because they have similar sadistic drives of
their own. The mood to accept and believe atrocity tales,
in short, is upon people before the tales themselves appear.

Statesmen sometimes need some whoopingly big lies to
justify to themselves and their followers' actions which they
contemplate. Thus Hitler in August 1939 was obsessed—
because consciously or unconsciously he wanted to be or because he himself may have been a psychological eunuch—
with reports he claimed to have received concerning the
castration of Germans by Poles. Sometimes fabrication is
necessary to deceive the enemy. The American and British
in the last war, for example, concealed their very risky
Torch Operation—the invasion of North Africa in 1942—
by spreading tales concerning an invasion of Norway, the
Channel Coast of Europe, Dakar, etc. Fabricated propaganda was employed by the Germans and Japanese to fish
for military information: a false statement would be deliberately made in the hope that a denial—which might be
required in order to allay domestic anxiety aroused by that
statement—would reveal the location of a ship or a fighting
unit (*7*). Often the explanation for a falsehood is simple
and mundane: an overzealous public relations officer wishes
or is instructed to increase the prestige of his commanding
officer or his branch of the service. In World War II, Anglo-

American propaganda tended to be based on fact because, as Warburg (*23*) succinctly says, "fact was usually on our side and could usually be demonstrated without too much trouble."

In spite of the bombast directed against propaganda's tendency to limit the facts, it remains true that propagandists can employ this technique because people—with or without propaganda—really like a simplified version of their world and its inhabitants. War propaganda which pays little or no attention to post-war considerations seeks to have the home front view the enemy as completely black, certainly not white and not even gray. If the propaganda is successful, then the consequence will be that people will possess this limited view—and limited it obviously is in the eyes of a social scientist or social philosopher who knows that the fact of individual differences punctures any simplified generalization concerning a group of people as large as a nation. People's morale, however, can be high only when the enemy is made into an ogre and hence they tend to feel uneasy and become less effective patriots when they remember that their opponents, after all, are also human.

The same point can be made somewhat differently by referring to the explanation of behavior propagandized by Hitler and his clique. They said in words and phrases every German and many non-Germans could easily understand that man's behavior is due to his racial, inherited blood; that blood differs in quality; that people with good blood are destined and deserve to rule; and that people with bad blood are doomed and should be dominated or annihilated. Such a theory demanded the suppressing of numerous cultural and scientific facts accepted everywhere by men of competence; the distortion of history, biology, and the social sciences; and the fabrication in their place of a mythological system of pseudo-facts which disturbed or were even recognized by too few Germans. With the perspective secured through a different kind of socialization and through the passing of time, it is easy for people in a democratic country to ridicule and see flaws in the Nazi philosophy of behavior and politics. It is not quite so easy for them,

nevertheless, to perceive the simplified versions of "reality"
which they themselves accept or which, if properly propagandized, they are psychologically ready to accept. In the
United States, non-southerners and innumerable so-called
southern liberals are able to recognize a similar simplicity
in the attitude traditional Southerners have toward the
Negro. They themselves, however, may be demonstrating
the same kind of simplified behavior when they sincerely
point out, without a trace of hesitancy or humility, the differences between the Republican and Democratic parties, between those parties and some liberal party, between the
C.I.O. and the N.A.M., between Jews and Gentiles, between
one brand of coffee and another, between a summer resort
and its rival, between Florida and California, between
blondes and brunettes, between criminals and non-criminals,
etc.

In short, the limitation produced by propaganda cannot
be charged exclusively to propagandists. Propagandees
themselves usually limit what they perceive and learn, even
in the absence of propaganda. Testimony, for example, is
notoriously unreliable, and it has been said—and demonstrated—again and again that "no one lies like an eye witness." People have their own limitations, but these are self-
imposed only after they have been socialized in a particular
way, after they have acquired their social status, after they
have begun participating in the groups of their society, and
after they have been affected by various propagandas.

Some but certainly not all of the atrocity tales circulating
during a war originate not in the official propaganda bureaus
but among patriotic soldiers and citizens who falsely perceive and react to stimuli in their immediate or far-flung
environment (*19*). The responsibility for a few exaggerated claims rests not with advertisers but with enthusiastic
customers who, for example, imagine they acquire social
prestige or at least express themselves by boasting how they
have solved an intricate problem through the use of a particular product. In like manner not all mud-slinging during
a political campaign stems from politicians or journalists;
voters too have a proclivity toward this type of invective.

Even the conscientious educator, moreover, can be misinterpreted by his students. He may make a tremendous effort to present the facts objectively and to present all of them. His peers as well as his superiors may consider his presentation to be on a scientific level or as close to that level as is possible with present-day knowledge. The minds of some of his students, nevertheless, may wander or be so biased that only a portion of what he says is perceived and then he, poor man or woman, is libelously labelled a propagandist.

Limitation in some form, therefore, is inevitable. The well-informed propagandee in his effort to understand how propaganda affects him must know not only the facts in the situation but also the ways those facts are limited by the propaganda *and* by himself. This assignment is of course an impossible one, but some knowledge along these lines is essential before propaganda can be adequately analyzed. The inevitability of limitation, furthermore, should not serve to justify intentional limitation in a propaganda campaign. An imperfect situation that can never be completely perfect may be improved, and it is not improved when its imperfections are reinforced.

Learning Ability

It has been shown again and again that what propagandees learn depends both on the propaganda and the responses which they themselves are capable of making. At a given moment people cannot be made to feel patriotic if the propaganda does not contain the stimuli which arouse patriotic responses and if they do not have personality responses related to patriotism. Either the stimuli must be altered or a sub-propaganda campaign must be waged to have them learn patriotic attitudes. In addition to the propaganda stimuli and the personality responses, the reactions of propagandees are affected by the skill with which they can learn propaganda or prevent themselves from doing so.

It is not possible to separate the component of knowledge or past experience from the innate ability involved in any skill. The score an individual receives on a conventional intelligence test usually represents a hopeless mixture of past experience, the drive functioning at the time, and his innate ability. Skill is simply a way of indicating present learning ability which can be measured only by an indirect index such as a test or the amount of education received.

It can be assumed that skill plays an important part in learning or not learning propaganda. If individuals differ in the speed with which they learn to play marbles or become botanists, then certainly they will learn propaganda at different rates and in different ways. There is, moreover, some experimental evidence at hand which indicates this relation between skill and the learning of propaganda. During the last war it was found (5) that American soldiers' reactions to certain propaganda films did not seem to be affected by their age, marital status, religion, home community, nationality background, or army rank. The only decisive factor was shown to be the amount of schooling they had had, and this in turn reflected to a certain extent intelligence-test scores. The more formal education the men had previously enjoyed, the more facts they learned from seeing a film. Superior educational status was especially helpful in learning facts which were obscure or difficult to apprehend and in not learning other facts which in terms of the film's objectives were "incorrect" but which closely resembled "correct" statements. If drive strength be considered equal, therefore, the skill represented by educational experience promotes the learning of propaganda knowledge.

Education also aided the learning of attitudes which these films sought to impart, but its influence was not nearly so marked as in the case of knowledge. After seeing films which purported to explain why the United States was participating in the war, more men who had been to college came to believe that "appeasement made things worse" in the Munich days before 1939 than did men who had been to high school, and more of the latter subscribed to this viewpoint than did those who had been only to grade school. Sometimes, however, education prevented men from learning attitudes. Grade-school men were more susceptible to the films than high-school men, and high-school more than college men, when an attitude was tested by asking whether the Germans, if victorious, would "try to control our country completely and force Americans to work as slaves." The ability to learn as indicated by educational background, the investigators found, tended to facilitate the learning of more reasonable attitudes—reasonable attitudes were defined as those which a greater percentage of men with superior rather than inferior education accepted *before* seeing the films, since it was presumed that a superior education had previously enabled them to draw "correct conclusion from the information" available at the time. Those with an educational advantage, these findings suggest, are able to learn attitudes more efficiently, but this ability is decisive only when the propaganda is convincing.

If these results are applicable to other situations, it would appear that among more skilful propagandees the propaganda stimuli are likely to evoke a variety of conflicting responses and that out of this conflict the attitude sought by the propagandist is less likely to emerge. In contrast, the same stimuli evoke in less skilful propagandees fewer conflicting responses and hence they are more likely to learn the new attitude. It must be remembered, however, that skill is only one of the factors affecting reactions to propaganda. An anxious genius may be more susceptible to some propaganda than a happy high-grade moron.

The more complicated reaction which people with superior skill make to propaganda is illustrated in another experiment of the War Department previously mentioned in this and the preceding chapter (*4*). It will be recalled that presenting the arguments in favor of a long war against Japan was more effective than presenting both sides only among those men who agreed with the viewpoint of the radio transcription before they had heard it. Clearcut differences between graduates and nongraduates of high school also emerged: the program with counter-propaganda was more influential among the graduates and that without counter-propaganda among the nongraduates. Regardless of previous attitude, moreover, more graduates were affected by the version with counter-propaganda. In fact only those nongraduates who had previously believed in a long war tended to be susceptible to the one-sided version.

Since propaganda always involves a group of people and since individuals inevitably differ in respect to their learning skills, any collection of propaganda stimuli is likely to be better adapted to some propagandees than to others. When numbers count, as they usually do, then successful propaganda is pitched at a level which suits the majority of the propagandees. Those at the extremes—the superior and inferior in respect to intelligence, experience, or education— may then be adversely affected or not affected at all. The superior will be capable of learning the propaganda but may grow skeptical. The inferior will find the propaganda beyond their mental reach. Again the psychological advantage of persuasion can be appreciated: here the communication's content is determined not by counting noses but by concentrating on the particular nose of the protagonist. Similarly if less dramatically, propaganda that is class- or group-typed is faced with a smaller spread of skills and therefore can score a higher percentage of successes.

CHAPTER 17

Propaganda and Action

THE objective of propaganda is action, not merely readiness to respond. External rather than internal public opinion is sought. The learned attitude—the pre-action response—must affect behavior. It must lead to what may be called an *action response*. The advertiser convinces people that his product is good and perhaps superior to all others, but he also induces them to buy it and perhaps to keep buying it. The politician seeks more than admiration and respect; actual votes count. The war propagandist wants the home front to believe in the righteousness of his cause and, as a result, to cooperate more effectively with the war effort. He wishes the enemy to feel the hopelessness of their cause so that they will fight or produce less vigorously and eventually surrender.

Under what circumstances do attitudes lead to action? Exactly the same question but in a slightly different form has had to be raised in connection with two other problems that have been previously considered. For what reasons, it was asked in the analysis of the behavior of public opinion, does internal public opinion become external public opinion? How can the validity of public opinion polls be established, it was said as those polls were being evaluated, when there is no one-to-one relation between the attitudes that the polls measure and the behavior that they seek to forecast? One principle has been observed which is useful in the analysis of propaganda: attitudes affect external behavior when their drive strength is so great that it can be reduced only by action. That strength, whether originally small or great, is increased when the individual feels that some action is necessary; when he is aware of what action he can take; and when he anticipates that the action will be rewarding. Some action may occur as a consequence of a pre-action response established through propaganda, but it may be different from that sought intentionally or unintentionally by the propagandist. In short, the achievement of the desired pre-action response is only the last in a series of preliminary stages which, though necessary for the final action, do not guarantee its occurrence.

The last chapter has outlined the devices employed in propaganda to have individuals learn pre-action responses of great drive strength. They will have such strength if they represent central drives within the personality. They are more likely to be stronger than competing responses when propagandees feel submissive. They will be stronger if they have been reinforced and if the reinforcement has occurred relatively recently. They will not be weakened in conflict with other drives if the content of the evoking stimuli has been limited through suppression, distortion, and fabrication. In this chapter the devices will be analyzed which increase the strength of a pre-action response that has already been established.

Urgency

"It is later than you think"—almost every propagandist tries to employ this slogan in a direct or indirect form during his propaganda campaign. The impression he wishes to create is that time is running out; he who hesitates is lost; the moment for action is now. The drive strength of the pre-action response becomes greater, it is hoped, when propagandees are convinced that the satisfaction they anticipate may not be obtained unless they act immediately.

The crudest expression of urgency occurs in advertising

when the copy asserts that a limited quantity is available, the sale will continue for a short time, the article will no longer be manufactured or stocked after the last one is sold, etc. The potential customer is then supposed to believe that he will be able to obtain the advertised advantage only by rushing to a store and pushing some money toward an indifferent clerk. Magazine publishers set their subscription rates below the total price of copies purchased individually at newsstands, and a subscription for two or three years further reduces the price of each copy. The action of subscribing is necessary to save this money over a period of time and also "to be certain that you don't miss a single issue." In psychological warfare, the enemy's civilian population can be made to clog the roads of his retreating armies through a rumor or threat to the effect that, if they remain where they are and do not seek out safer places farther from the fighting lines, they are likely to be killed or injured by shellfire or aerial bombardment. Usually a few well-placed bombs produce panic more effectively and efficiently than such verbal advice.

Sometimes the nature of the propaganda objective makes it difficult or impossible to give propagandees a sense of urgency. Political candidates cannot command immediate action at the beginning of a campaign since the action response they desire, voting, will not occur for many months or weeks. Substitute activity like wearing a campaign button or actively campaigning for a candidate can be proposed, not to release part of the drive-tension connected with the pre-action response, but to commit the propagandee to the action response by having him thus signify his ultimate intention both to others and himself. Many sub-propaganda campaigns are postulated on the assumption that final action must be postponed until the propagandees are psychologically prepared or find themselves in a situation which provides the appropriate stimuli. Institutional advertising that promotes a generally favorable attitude toward the advertiser rather than a desire for a specific product or service—such as a tribute to physicians or pharmacists by a manufacturer of drugs—strives to increase the habit strength between the stimulus of the manufacturer's name and some kind of a favorable response without having that response expressed immediately in action.

At other times the propagandees themselves may possess stronger drives which, though they do not prevent the pre-action response from occurring, may delay or inhibit action indefinitely:

> "Oh, I know, but there are so many more important things."
> "I agree, but I have to do something else first."
> "You are right, but I guess I'll think it over."
> "Certainly, but I have already committed myself."

These are vernacular samples of the discouraging sentences which propagandists hear after their propagandees have reached the pre-action stage. Every insurance agent knows how people like to procrastinate, and hence his task is to persuade the individual—without becoming too depressing —that the perils of delaying a decision are legion. One of the cardinal sins in a democratic society is the conviction that a propaganda or educational cause is just and right, but that the other fellow should take appropriate action.

The impulsive individual seems to be a potentially easy propagandee. He acts on his convictions but only when they are strong, only when they are not in direct conflict with other habits, or only when the conflict can be avoided by so acting. It must be realized, moreover, that his impulses can be expressed verbally without accompanying action and that he may refuse to do what the propagandist suggests after he has agreed with him verbally. Children seem to be impulsive individuals par excellence. They carry out their own ideas or else attempt to have their parents do as they wish. In comparison with adults, they have few conflicts which inhibit action. For this reason the cooperation of the child, when once it has been obtained, is frequently so wholehearted. He obeys to the letter the rules of the group which he joins. He may wish to rush right out of the house and purchase the product recommended to him by the voice on the radio which precedes, interrupts, and then follows the serial absorbing his attention.

Indicated Action

Ever since August 1945, when the President of the United States announced that the atomic bomb had been perfected and that one had been dropped upon the Japanese city of Hiroshima, propagandists and educators have been stating in various ways that this new form of energy and destruction has formidable consequences for international, national, and domestic relations and that therefore some kind of action must be taken. Occasionally specific proposals have been advocated. The net effect of such agitation and cogitation has been either to raise the anxiety level of people so that they crave some kind of action or else to drive them more desperately into other activities so that they can forget the perils which beset them. Both the facts of atomic energy and propaganda concerning it, therefore, have made most people learn that some kind of new controlling organization is needed, but the course of action which they as individuals should adopt has not been indicated to them. Their pre-action responses have been all set to go, but the writing of a letter to a Congressman, the reading of a book on the subject, or fuming concerning the veto power in the Security Council of the United Nations seems to be an inadequate expression of the anxious or escapist tendencies within them.

The propagandee in whom the desired pre-action responses are functioning but who does not know what to do is like a lover who would win his beloved's affection if he were but told what pleases her. The liberal in American society resembles that lover in many ways. He wants progress, justice, and morality because the propaganda organs he reads, his own experience, and some thought reveal to him that there are forces of evil besetting the land. He does not mount a horse and charge off in all directions at once because, besides suffering from the handicap of not knowing where he wishes to go, he seldom has a horse. He can criticize what he does not like and vaguely indicate what he wants, but he lacks the ability to select a steadfast set of means to achieve those ends. For this reason there is always an open season for propagandists who seek to close the liberal's open mind, provided that the proper bait is offered him: a definite course of action which seems to lead gently to utopia but from which he may deviate without notice.

People who join and contribute to propaganda organizations feel the need for some kind of action: they have signified their willingness to cooperate and they must do something if their enthusiasm is to persist. It is then proposed that they write letters to editors and their political representatives, that they campaign in favor of men who subscribe to the organization's viewpoint and against those who do not, or that they themselves strengthen the group by securing new members. If they later become convinced that their contribution has helped win some kind of a victory, their own convictions will be suitably reinforced. In the United States, for example, the leaders of anti-alcohol movements mobilize their followers whenever the voters of a community are called upon to decide whether the sale of liquor will be permitted. Afterwards they are all saddened or gladdened by the outcome.

Propagandists frequently issue unambiguous commands to indicate the action they seek. Propagandees are told to "buy bonds," "vote the straight Republican ticket," or "ask for Punk's Pills." The indicated action may be accompanied by detailed instructions when its precise method of execution is not common knowledge. A cigarette manufacturer in the United States does not have to tell people where they can purchase his product since cigarettes are sold in almost every building that is open to the public. The producer of a particular type of clothing, on the other hand, cannot always be content with merely stimulating a desire for his product or with indicating, in addition, that it is sold "at all the best stores," but he must include in his copy or announcement a specific list of stores where it can be obtained.

Sometimes indicating the path of action is unwise because the propaganda then becomes revealed rather than concealed or delayed revealed and, as a result, the propagandees may react negatively. During the last war, it was usually the policy of the British and American Chiefs of

Staff to encourage sabotage by underground patriots throughout Europe. Direct exhortations were therefore made occasionally from London by the British Broadcasting Corporation and the American Broadcasting System in Europe (ABSIE). Except in very rare instances, however, no such appeals were delivered on shortwave programs originating in the United States. For it was felt that patriots would resent advice leading to perilous activities when it came from individuals living safely and comfortably so far away from the battlefields. The B.B.C. and ABSIE, it was thought, would not evoke this antagonism, since they were broadcasting from London, a city neither safe nor comfortable as the audience knew. Instead "The Voice of America" cross-reported to an occupied country incidents involving sabotage which were occurring elsewhere in Europe. In this direct way the accomplishments of saboteurs were indicated, and indirectly—without saying so and without therefore assuming responsibility—the need for similar action by the radio audience was suggested. The reporting of sabotage back to the country of origin served the same purpose; in addition, the very kind of news which the Germans suppressed was thus disseminated and recognition of the patriots' accomplishments was given by an official American agency. The latter type of reporting, however, ran the risk of damaging the broadcaster's reputation for veracity, inasmuch as news concerning sabotage inside Hitler's "European Fortress" was never very reliable.

No action need be indicated in a sub-propaganda campaign, for here the aim is simply the learning of an attitude to facilitate the main propaganda itself. The politician's favor is not accompanied by a plea to re-elect him to office— all he seeks at the time is a favorable attitude toward himself. Then during the campaign he suggests clearly enough that this gratitude can be expressed most appropriately in the voting booth.

In concealed propaganda, the desired action frequently cannot be indicated and consequently this type of propaganda—for all the psychological advantages it possesses through concealing its objective—runs the risk of leading to

no or to irrelevant action. The astute public relations counsel boasts to his client, to himself, and sometimes later to the
general public that he is able to utilize people with prestige
to influence multitudes without revealing his goal; and yet
by his cleverness such a man may have lost the support of
some individuals who could have been dominated by a
straight-forward approach. The unintentional propagandist, moreover, can seldom indicate action since he frequently does not foresee all the consequences of what he is
doing and since his campaign is more likely to be based on
intuition than on conscious calculations.

The action indicated by the propaganda must naturally
be of a type which people are willing and able to perform.
Many individuals in the European underground during the
last war may have been convinced by allied propaganda of
the need to carry on sabotage against the Germans but
lacked the courage to do so. Similarly the advertiser's copy
may give many people an overwhelming urge to purchase
his product, but they may not become one of his customers
for prosaic but compelling financial reasons. Frequently
the propagandist fails at this crucial point and is unable to
affect the one, final change in the propagandees: courage
could not be supplied to the underground by radio and the
advertiser does not present people with cash. At other
times, however, the propagandist can overcome the stumbling block and induce action, initially at least, by tempting
his propagandees with a sample.

Sampling Actions

The passengers in a railway coach are looking out the
window, reading, thinking, talking, dozing, or are doing
nothing at all except to allow their bodies to be transported
by the train. The vender passes down the aisle and distributes to everyone, except those who are asleep, a small
sample of candy "absolutely free." Most people immediately tear off the wrapper and eat the candy. Many of
these, when the vender returns in a moment and offers for
sale a much larger piece, then pay money to be able to

consume a larger quantity of the same candy they have previously tasted. Through the technique of sampling the vender has increased the number of purchases, a fact which could be proven by having him offer the same candy for sale to a comparable group of passengers in another car without previously providing them with a sample. The illustration is simple but it reveals an important psychological point about the propaganda: propagandees will act more readily when the proposed action has already proven satisfactory to them. Before the sample is distributed, some of the passengers may or may not be hungry. The tasting of one piece arouses a hunger drive which is only partially if pleasantly reduced; many, therefore, seek a further reduction by eating more of the candy.

Advertising itself has been called by one anonymous advertising agent (*3*) "a substitute for sampling." Everyone connected with a piece of copy is advised by him to attempt to portray the article for sale as vividly as only a sample can. Naturally written or spoken words and even illustrations cannot by themselves duplicate precisely all the responses evoked by the indicated action, he admits, but an approximation is frequently feasible. In terms of the stimulus gradient, there is some but not necessarily a great deal of similarity between seeing an automobile in an advertisement and in a show room; thus the photograph is a good sample of the visual aspects of the car.

Sometimes advertising actually follows the direct and immediate approach of the vender on the railway train or of the circus barker whose exhibit arouses auxiliary and related responses. People are told to "write for a free sample," they are given a sample of food in stores, and they are offered a newly introduced product "free" or nearly free if they are willing to purchase an established one. Other devices have been evolved to induce initial action when it is uneconomical to offer a sample. Propagandees are invited to visit a store or an exhibition to see a demonstration. Merchants usually arrange their merchandise in attractive displays not only to solve the perceptual, personality, and pre-action problems—as has been indicated previously—but also to provide their customers with a visual sample of the delights which will be theirs if they care to become the proud owners of what they see.

Consumers may be induced to purchase a product and thus to sample it. They are offered a "guarantee" that they may have their "money back if not satisfied." Only a small down-payment is required or a "free trial" is proposed before payments begin. Such devices also increase the likelihood of action by weakening various personality responses arising as a result of skepticism or budgetary considerations and hence are employed by those advertisers—like correspondence schools—interested in one and only one sale. It is of course important to note that most Americans display considerable reluctance to return products with which they are dissatisfied, even though the advertiser has assured them at the outset that they are assuming no "responsibility" when they agree to make a trial run: they find it either inconvenient or embarrassing to do so. People are tempted to sample certain American magazines when a number of issues is offered to them at a cost which is proportionately lower than the annual subscription rate.

In almost all other fields of propaganda it is extremely difficult to discover a technique that induces propagandees to take further action as a result of satisfaction derived from a sample. The candidate for public office who is running for re-election continually refers to his past record which, he says, is an indication of the kind of man he is and of the principles for which he will continue to stand. Some of the voters may have experienced directly the effects of his tenure in office and they, consequently, are in a position to judge whether this past sample has proven rewarding or punishing. Others may not have been affected by him or have not been aware of the effects he has actually had; for them his campaign will be based not on a sample but exclusively on the personality responses his propaganda is able to arouse. The candidate seeking election for the first time to an office higher than the one he has previously held—like advancing from the governorship of one state to the Presidency of the United States or from the House of Representatives to the Senate—can offer the constituents of the smaller district he has previously represented a sample of his ability, but voters outside that district can be impressed only by references to his record. During the campaign, moreover, any candidate has an opportunity to give voters some direct sample of himself: he shows them what kind of a man he is by the way in which he manages that campaign (or, more frequently, by the way in which it is managed for him by his advisers), by the content of his utterances, and by his manner of speaking. Whether these samples of behavior are representative of the way he will behave in office is of course problematical.

After the repeal of prohibition in the United States, the liquor manufacturers have sought to prevent a repetition of this "noble experiment" by offering themselves as a sample of good behavior. The Annual Report for 1946 of the Distilled Spirits Institute expresses the objective in these words: "the Institute's creed in public relations is a quiet, persistent, never ending effort on the part of those connected with the industry to conduct themselves so as to warrant and deserve public confidence." Specifically this has meant curbing or eliminating the sale of liquor to minors, the prevention of what is euphemistically called "over-indulgence," the promotion of what is ambiguously termed "temperance," cooperation with civil authorities and clergymen, and participating in community drives for charity or "civic betterment." Members of the liquor industry, therefore, are exhorted again and again to be respectable and law-abiding. At the same time, these demonstrations of respectability and righteousness are supplemented by conventional propaganda which indicates how much money in taxes the government collects from the manufacture and sale of liquor, how many people are employed by the industry, how essential industrial alcohol is in time of war, etc. But the backbone of the wet effort is action, not words.

There is little direct sampling possible in war propaganda. During the last conflict, the Nazi propaganda machine referred to the fate of Germany after World War I for the benefit of the millions of Germans who, following their country's defeat, experienced a minor amount of occupation. This appeal, however, was not employed excessively either because the experiences may have seemed in retrospect to be less frustrating than the actualities of war itself or because "strength through fear" could be more efficiently promoted by lamentations concerning the treatment to be anticipated after the second defeat. The theme actually stressed by Goebbels was, no doubt, very convincing even to the retreating, beaten German armies and to bombed-out civilians who had also experienced personal grief: many Germans possessed a conscious or unconscious feeling of guilt resulting from the way in which they or their representatives had treated the inhabitants of occupied territories and innumerable Allied prisoners. Allied propaganda toward the end of the war employed a vicarious sample by reporting carefully limited versions of how their military government was functioning in the areas of Germany that had already been conquered. The studious and continuous attempt by American and British propagandists to have their propaganda as truthful as possible, aside from its function of building up and reinforcing credibility, also served, it was hoped, as a sample of the kind of honorable behavior Germans might anticipate from their conquerors.

Since the last war the technique of sampling has been regularly employed as an aid to international diplomacy in the following way:

1. The representative of a big power says that "world opinion" will be outraged if a particular measure is adopted.
2. Shortly thereafter, as the measure is being discussed in the United Nations or after it has been adopted, the press of his own country and of other countries cries out in anguished protest.
3. Proof is thereby offered that the measure is actually unpopular.

Between the first and second steps, however, there is usually some well-planned action by the representative's government. His own press is told to attack the measure, as are the papers of those countries which are under the influence of or in sympathy with his government. Demonstrations may be staged. His prediction, therefore, appears to be vindicated and the unpopularity of the measure to be demonstrated. He has increased his stature as a propagandist by providing a sample of his ability to prophesy events—which, in fact, is just another sample of his country's political power.

Drive Reduction

Just as a sample proves to be rewarding and thereby promotes the action response, so the action response itself can result in drive reduction and encourage a repetition of that response. "A satisfied customer is our best advertisement" is a trite truism applicable to propaganda which is not a one-shot affair like a bankruptcy sale but which requires the propagandees to repeat their behavior. Such a customer is likely not only to make additional purchases in the future but also intentionally or unintentionally to carry on concealed propaganda among his friends and acquaintances in behalf of the product. If any link in the propaganda can be singled out as the most important one, it is the reward or punishment associated with the propaganda which merits this distinction and consequently which requires a somewhat detailed analysis.

People who seek to and then do make the same goal responses may be quite differently motivated. Smoking a widely advertised brand of cigarettes proves satisfactory to smokers but for varying reasons: one smokes because he likes the taste and odor of burning tobacco, another because the nicotine stimulates his nervous system, another because he can blow smoke rings, another because he can dispose of excess nervous energy, and another because premature weaning makes him crave the tactual sensation on his lips which the cigarette can produce. In addition, it is rare for only one drive to be reduced in response to a collection of stimuli. A single individual, for example, may find smoking rewarding in two or three respects. Usually the drives reduced by any one propaganda campaign are similarly diverse.

The satisfaction associated with the action response can

arise after the occurrence of that response or in the course of the propaganda campaign. The individual who joins one of the numerous pressure groups seeking to affect Congressional action in the United States will not necessarily resign if the group's representatives in Washington fail to achieve their objectives. While such a success serves as one reward to reinforce his faith in the group, he may obtain additional satisfaction from participating socially with other people in the organization, from convincing himself that his self-interest coincides with the interests of the country, from securing status among his associates, etc., all or some of which may have been promised him by the group's propagandists or have been anticipated by him before he joined. The satisfactions of propagandees are indeed multitudinous, as multitudinous as the responses and drives of which people are capable.

It is almost literally true that the consumer smokes both the cigarette and the advertising which has induced him to buy the pack. Aside from the direct and indirect satisfactions smoking brings him, there may linger within him the personality responses leading to the purchase. He may feel smug that he has enough sense to smoke only those cigarettes which are made from the finest tobaccos, which are popular or fast-selling, which are used by statesmen and actresses, which are an aid to his health and happiness, or which allegedly do whatever it is the advertising campaign claims they do. As he smokes, the esthete within him may be pleased by the color scheme of the package containing the cigarettes or by the shape or tip of the article itself. One little puff involves more than the taste and the sight of the smoke.

Advertising in general and repetition in advertising in particular have been so successful in promoting sales partially because of these additional rewards which over time are made meaningful to the propagandees. There seems, in fact, to be a certain amount of prestige attached to the purchasing of a nationally advertised product: propagandees experience the satisfaction which comes to people when they feel they have taken advantage of the opportunities offered them or when they conform to public opinion. Sometimes the advertising copy advises them directly to be so sagacious or to win the praise from others which can come only from owning or consuming the product.

Basically, however, much of the success of advertising is due to the ignorance of consumers. In a complex society people are not given impartial instruction concerning the ingredients of a product as well as its immediate and far-reaching effects upon their bodies and minds. Or their other interests are such that they cannot teach themselves. Advertising, in short, is operating in a field where public opinion tends to be incompetent—and it is exploiting this incompetence. In accordance with a legal regulation, for example, the label may state that "preservatives" have been added to a widely advertised jar of food, but few laymen know what a preservative is, what it does—except of course that it "preserves" something or other—how it tastes, whether it is desirable to eat, etc. Their ignorance, nevertheless, does not prevent them from enjoying the product or its advertised claims. Similarly most consumers do not own or have access to scientific laboratories which might enable them to distinguish between an expensive and an inexpensive product. They are forced to assume, on the basis of some experience in the past and a conspicuous ideology of the culture, that price is a valid index of quality or durability. In some instances sales have increased among the unavoidably gullible by raising the price of an article and then selling it under another name and with the aid of different advertising themes.

The objectives of many advertising campaigns, moreover, involve only segmental and not central responses among propagandees. Most people, for example, will not lose face or grow corns if they buy one brand of shoes rather than another. Advertising, nevertheless, may convince them that their friends will not like them or that they will have to consult a chiropodist unless they purchase the advertised shoes and no others. In this manner propaganda can make shoe behavior much less segmental by connecting it to more central drives and by enabling those drives to be partially or completely reduced.   The individual may not be willing to run the risk of experimenting with a rival brand from which he anticipates less reward or even punishment.

If advertising can sell almost anything, as many advertisers believe and as some of them have demonstrated, then it must follow that buying habits can be readily established. For all the reasons mentioned, the perception of the product by the consumer who has been subjected to advertising is affected by the copy he has seen or heard in the past.   He may then think of the product's slogan and recall the various claims that have been made in its behalf.   His reaction to the product, whether favorable or unfavorable, is more likely to be vague and to depend on his familiarity with its name, the generalized way in which its advertising copy has previously affected him, or the reward he has associated with it as a result of past patronage.   Such a vague response is the culmination of learning to discriminate: responses which at the outset were evoked by a variety of stimuli are now evoked by one stimulus alone, the brand name, and those evoked personality responses in turn act as stimuli to produce the favorable or unfavorable pre-action response.

It is an empirical fact, however, that familiarity with a brand name can exist without actual patronage (*1*).   In the United States, for example, it may be that some people associate "shave" as well as the geographical area in Southeast Asia with the word "Burma" because of the unique method of highway advertising employed by the manufacturers of Burma Shave; yet relatively few actually use this product.   "Burma" as a stimulus has been made to produce one of the desired internal responses but that response does not necessarily lead to a sale.   From the company's viewpoint, people should be able to say "shave" when they hear or see "Burma": it is more important, though, for them to think of "Burma Shave" and as a result to make pre-action responses when they are on their way to or enter a store to purchase shaving soap.   Before "Burma" can become a response with these stimulus properties, more complicated learning must occur.   A drive can evoke the response of the brand name not through mere association with it, since such association results only in the evocation of the drive by the stimulus of "Burma Shave." For the reverse sequence to occur, the drive must first be reduced by rewarding behavior which simultaneously evokes the name. Thus the motorist purchases a jar or tube of Burma Shave out of sheer devilment because he has seen it so widely and amusingly advertised. As he uses the product, he is constantly aware of its name either because the label keeps reminding him of it or because the shave itself is sufficiently distinctive to do so. Then, if he likes the product, he will probably use it again. On his way to the store, he will think of its name which can then act as a stimulus to evoke whatever responses he has associated with it. In the meantime, moreover, he may have seen more signs with different appeals and hence the name, once he has thought of it as a result of his pleasant experience, will be able to elicit remnants of these additional responses. In the last analysis, consequently, what needs to be repeated in propaganda is the reward resulting from action.

When a brand name, then, acquires stimulus properties, only half the propaganda battle has been won. For children the word "camel" evokes the image of the desert animal, but advertising in the United States produces in many adults the response of "a brand of cigarettes" to the stimulus "Camel" or "Camels." Camel-devotees think of this brand when they run out of cigarettes or when asked which brand they smoke. Non-Camel-smokers, moreover, can mention the brand in response to the question, "What are the four most popular brands of cigarettes?" In such a sequence, although "Camel" has occurred as a response, that response will not lead to action, and it may or may not evoke other responses resulting from Camel advertising copy. If it does include responses originating in the copy, then Camel as a stimulus already has the properties desired by its manufacturers even without a sale. Individuals with such responses, therefore, are potential Camel customers: dissatisfaction with the brand they are smoking or the perception of Camels in a friend's hand may induce them to change. In this manner, advertising engages in a sub-propaganda campaign among the non-converted by reinforcing the stimulus value of its name. There is learning up to a point not because of the reward of consumption but because of less compelling rewards such as social approval for being well-informed, curiosity concerning the contents of an advertisement, or vicarious thrills from daydreaming when no purchase is contemplated. Then an actual rewarding experience can complete the process: "Camels" becomes a response to the smoking drive and as a stimulus helps elicit that drive as well as a host of pre-action responses.

There is one short-cut which advertisers sometimes seek to employ: instead of having the propagandees learn a connection between product and brand name through experience and reinforcement, they provide a sentence which they hope will facilitate the establishment of that connection. "When you want cheese, think of Chase's Chipper Cheese," they say in effect. Such a sentence can be remembered if it is easily perceived and even if a drive of weak strength is functioning at the time. Thereafter the stimulus of cheese in- or outside the individual is likely to evoke the snappy sentence because it falls along the latter's stimulus gradient, and the sentence in turn can evoke the other responses which have been learned as a result of the advertisement. Here again is an illustration of how verbal responses can accelerate the learning process.

The symbols, slogans, and clichés employed in propaganda other than advertising can also function more easily as a stimulus than they can as a response. In either role, however, they are effective because they can be perceived, remembered, and constantly reinforced. As the Allies moved into Germany in the last war, they removed all the swastikas in their path. For they knew how strongly identified these signs, both as stimuli and responses, had become with the Nazi way of life. Removing the swastikas, however, proved to be simpler than eradicating the responses which their promulgation had established in most Germans.

Many propagandists are faced with a difficult assignment when their clients tell them, in effect, "Here is the product I want to sell; now go design some propaganda which will increase sales." It may be true, as has been suggested above, that part of the reward from action depends on the propaganda which has brought about that action, but more important may be the satisfactions resulting directly from the action itself. No matter how alluring and extensive the advertising copy, it is difficult to imagine how a brand of coffee which tastes like disagreeable cough medicine could ever be successful. No matter how many surrender leaflets in time of war are sprinkled from the sky and no matter how the facts and pseudo-facts therein are limited, it is unlikely that many soldiers will surrender to an enemy whose actual maltreatment of prisoners has been substantiated and publicized by the International Red Cross. And no matter how much cake and propaganda and no matter how many circuses a dictator provides, undoubtedly his popularity will not increase appreciably when his people need bread and are otherwise suffering. Propaganda, in a word, cannot accomplish miracles in the face of competing responses evoked by frustration and dissatisfaction from behaving as the propagandist wishes.

The intentional propagandist whose objective brings punishment rather than reward—or not so much reward as a competing propaganda—consequently makes minor or fundamental changes in the product, service, or program that is offered. Or he advises his client to do so. For the propaganda to be successful, the manufacturer must improve the taste of his coffee; the military authorities must treat their prisoners decently (and perhaps resort to the age-old trick of allowing a few to escape without knowing that their escape has been permitted, so that unintentionally they will correct the existing impression among their compatriots); and the dictator must adopt measures which will make his people happier in more fundamental ways. In the commercial field, the real distinction between an advertising agent and a public relations counsel is that the former is more likely to promote the product and the client as he finds them, whereas the latter is more prone to study both and suggest changes which will be more rewarding to the propagandees. Either may propose that the color of the product or its wrapper be altered because an intuitive or systematic survey reveals an unfavorable reaction to the old color ("it's too gloomy") or a more favorable one to the new ("it's so very cheerful"), but the public relations expert usually advocates more basic changes and in fact is employed to do so. The company's labor policy may be liberalized to increase good will among employees and the potential customers they influence in their day-by-day contacts. Ivy Lee, perhaps the first of the self-styled public relations counsels in the United States, improved the reputation of the Standard Oil Company by having that company supply adequate information about itself to the press and by altering the public picture of John D. Rockefeller from that of "the striding, ruthless monopolist in high hat and long coat gripping his walking stick and entering a court house" to one of "a frail old man, playing golf with his neighbors, handing out dimes to children, distributing inspiration poems, and walking in peace amid his flowers" (*2*). Lee released stories not only concerning the hobbies of Mr. Rockefeller adopted in his later years but also concerning his notable and newsworthy contributions to charities, the sciences, medicine, and the humanities. It was presumably rewarding to receive a dime from a great man like Mr. Rockefeller or to benefit from his philanthropy and aid to human knowledge.

At first glance it might appear as though war propagandists are faced with the unalterable facts of military and political events and that therefore the role of psychological warfare is limited by the "product." It is true that the events represent inescapable facts, but they are not unalterable facts. What can be altered are the rewards and punishments which the events bring to people. For the facts of success and failure are always interpreted by those who experience them, and propaganda can affect the interpretation. When an army advances a few kilometers or inflicts heavy casualities on the enemy, its supporters ordinarily are cheered: some progress is better than no progress at all. But when they have anticipated a major victory, as many Germans did during the counter-offensive in the Ardennes toward the end of 1944, then the event produces no mild elation but a profound depression. Hopes which have been raised by propaganda and wishful thinking are then blasted by events. Even the complete victory over France in 1940 brought forth interpretations by Nazi propaganda, so that Germans would feel not only happy and triumphant but also grateful to Hitler and his clique for avenging the defeat of World War I (6). The propaganda drums at that time were also sounded in a way calculated to increase British anxiety. Similarly, when an army retreats or suffers casualties, its supporters ordinarily are depressed: retrogression is worse than no progress at all. But when they are convinced that the objective which is being lost is worthless, when they feel that their armies are not being forced back but are voluntarily altering their position, and when they believe that the new position will better enable the commanders to stage an offensive in the near future, then the event is no calamity but perhaps a source of pride and of confidence.

The defeat at Stalingrad was also a defeat of the Nazi propaganda machine—or at least it could not mitigate the punishment the repulse brought to the German people (7). For the importance of Stalingrad had already been emphasized to the German people, and therefore its loss could not be discounted even by exaggerating Russian casualties. In addition, Hitler himself had been predicting that the city would be captured, and at one time he also stated that his armies there had been victorious. Faced with these handicaps, Nazi propagandists could hope only to arouse another series of responses which would improve German morale. As German military authorities realized that the German position was becoming untenable, they began to prepare the German people for the disaster by having the military spokesman—General Dittmar—hint broadly that all was not well, by admitting the strength and power of the Russian forces, and by rather frankly announcing the German defeat at Velikie Luki. There were vague references to the future when the German armies would recapture the initiative, and half-hearted attempts were made to claim that German resistance at Stalingrad had disrupted Russian plans for a great offensive. Very heavy emphasis was placed upon the heroism of the German garrison at Stalingrad which was included in the company of Germany's legendary heroes in the past.

Then, when the Soviet forces drove the Germans out of Stalingrad and captured General Paulus' Sixth Army, Nazi propaganda sought to improve German morale by deliberately increasing anxiety concerning Russia, by directing aggression against that enemy, and by stimulating in-group solidarity through the sharing of a common grief. The great sacrifices were justified, for example, by reference to "the menace of Bolshevism" for all civilization. Three days of public mourning were officially proclaimed. Resorting to "strength through fear" in this fashion was a desperate propaganda measure, but it was one which could not be avoided especially in view of the fact that the "total mobilization" which immediately followed Stalingrad produced greater privation.

"Propaganda in times of lull," Kris and Speier (*8*) point out, "is a substitute for warfare and provides action." For during such a period the communication media are not crowded with reports from the battlefields and it is possible to interpret the flow of past events and to celebrate one's own military and cultural strength. More important, people are anxious concerning the future and, as a result, they are in a mood to discover something about the events that will soon occur. If they learn only the propagandist's version of those events, their present outlook will be affected and they may grow over-anxious or over-confident. Or else they will subsequently interpret the events themselves more or less in accordance with the propagandist's wishes and thus feel correspondingly rewarded or punished.

The war propagandist also seeks to influence the interpretation of events by peoples in neutral countries so that their drive tension will be raised or lowered. According to one observer (*4*), for example, the Nazis employed various stratagems at different times to diminish American aid to Great Britain and her Allies before the United States entered the war:

Nazi propaganda theme	*Interpretation sought*
Germany's opponent is very strong.	No aid is needed.
Germany's opponent is very weak.	All aid is fruitless.
Peace is about to be declared.	Any aid will arrive too late.
Germany controls the high seas.	The risks of sending aid are too great.

These themes were stressed in concealed rather than in revealed propaganda in order to increase their credibility.

Primacy

It is difficult and sometimes impossible to shake off past experience, especially when that experience has been intense or prolonged and when it has brought satisfaction. "As the twig . . ."—the principle in fact has become part of our folklore, and it is reluctantly admitted that young rather than old dogs are psychologically prepared to learn new skills. Similarly the mature adult may be unable to eliminate the prejudices he has acquired in his youth, even though he is intellectually convinced that those prejudices are unsound or unworthy. He continues to feel uncomfortable in the presence of Negroes, Japanese, Irish, or Portuguese in spite of his best efforts to treat every person as a human being.

The effects of culture upon the individual and upon public opinion have been mentioned again and again throughout this book. Many of the personality responses which people make to propaganda, consequently, they have learned as children when they were in no position to have themselves exposed to other modes of thinking and acting. The first habit or response-sequence is likely to endure because of the rewards which quickly become associated with this behavior. Children are impressionable principally for two reasons. They lack a "critical faculty," which means—as suggested earlier in this chapter—that the number of contradicting or competing responses aroused by most stimuli is limited. Then they fail to win approval and affection from their parents and associates unless they conform to the propagandas and philosophies flourishing in the family and the immediate milieu. Their dependent status tends to prevent them from seeking substitute satisfactions. If habits are firmly established, they are less likely to be disturbed by counteracting influences later; hence the best counter-propaganda against these influences is strong reinforcement during the crucial period of childhood.

Youth, therefore, is always a favorite propaganda target for political dictators who know that the perpetuation of their regime depends upon the support they receive from each generation as it matures. Some of the fanaticism displayed by younger Germans on the battlefields of the last war resulted from the rather thorough indoctrination to which they had been subjected by the various Nazi organizations from early childhood on. In the United States the ward boss begins to cultivate a following among the immature through the services he renders to the children's parents and hence to them too. Socialists and communists also have their youth groups, but the major parties through the so-called Young Republicans or Young Democrats reach a post-adolescent group of voting age.

Within any country tribute is paid to the principle of primacy whenever there is a struggle over the kind of textbook which is suitable for school children—and usually there is some kind of a battle in progress. School boards, parents, and other respectable members of the community frequently examine these books with great care and diligence lest they contain suggestions which run contrary to actual and latent public opinion. Because highly nationalistic countries present their children with an appropriately nationalistic version of history, it was to be expected that one of the first acts of Allied Military Government in the Axis countries during and after the last war was to shut down the schools and not reopen them until suitably purged textbooks and teachers could be found. In the United States patriotic groups like the American Legion have been especially anxious to have the proper kind of "Americanism" taught in the schools, and from time to time pressure groups, such as public utilities in the 1920's (*5, 9, 10*), have invaded the classroom from grade school to college by attempting to indoctrinate teachers and textbooks alike.

The advertiser in the United States has not overlooked the younger generation. The easiest way to arouse related responses among the immature is to offer a premium in return for a number of box tops or labels with or without a small sum of money allegedly to defray "postage" or "wrapping costs." The child really wishes to enjoy the cloth hat, the tin button, or the cardboard walkie-talkie and he therefore may eat the cereal or plague his parents until the box tops or the labels have been accumulated. The manufacturer presumably is less interested in the immediate sales produced by these tactics than he is in the possibility of having the guillible child develop a genuine liking for his product by sampling it at an early age. Perhaps the presence of the product in the household induces the unfortunate parents to consume it, in which case—especially when they find it satisfactory too—the propagandist has struck down two sets of customers with one propaganda campaign. Premiums are also employed to have adults sample a product, but—in comparison with children—their tastes are a little less likely to be changed and the duration of their patronage may be shorter.

The propagandist scores an initial advantage whenever his propaganda reaches people before that of his rivals. Newspapers compete with newspapers, radio stations compete with radio stations, and each medium competes with the other to be the first to present a news event or a forecast or analysis of that news. They do so because they believe their audiences are also infected with the "scoop" tradition infesting journalism in the United States and in many other countries. At the same time their readers or listeners are then biased to comprehend, forever after, the event as it has been initially portrayed to them. If they are told in a headline or a flash that the battle has been won, the criminal has been caught, or the bill is certain to pass the legislature, they will usually expect subsequent information to substantiate this first impression. When later facts prove otherwise, they may be loath to abandon what they believe to be true until, perhaps, the evidence becomes overwhelming. In the commercial field, the manufacturer has an enormous advantage over his competitors when his trade name is the first to enter the market or to grow popular and when, as a consequence, that name in lower case becomes the generic term for all products of approximately the same type. An ancient example of this phenomenon in the United States is the use of the copyrighted term "victrola" for any kind of phonograph or gramophone, and more recently "spam" has tended to mean any brand of canned pork.

CHAPTER 18

The Printed Media

An ANALYSIS of public opinion and propaganda requires an understanding of the communication media. Newspapers, magazines, photographs, drawings, cartoons, books, billboards, placards, sky-writing, pamphlets, leaflets, handbills, radio stations, public address systems, motion pictures, plays, meetings, rumors, and parades —these diverse media are among the important determinants of public opinion in modern society, and they in turn are influenced by public opinion. Both the propagandist and the propagandee, moreover, have a specific interest in the vehicles of propaganda, the propagandist because he must comprehend the nuances and peculiarities of the media he utilizes and the propagandee because propaganda reaches him only after it has become part of some medium.

By and large the newspapers and the radio are the principal media serving to acquaint people in modern society with events that they themselves have not witnessed. For most of them there is usually no other way to learn about science and fads, or about death from murder, war, and old age. This dependence tends to be overlooked, just as the importance of oxygen is assumed and forgotten until its absence calls attention to the vital role it plays in respiration. Without large headlines and special radio bulletins, the writer found it difficult to appreciate the significance of

Mr. Truman's first announcement concerning the atomic bomb: he was visiting the American-operated radio station in Luxemburg at the time and saw the news on a brief tele-typed note which merely reported what had happened in matter-of-fact fashion. The other media of communication, especially the motion picture and the magazine, influence people's knowledge of their own society and of other societies.

Greatest emphasis will be placed upon the newspaper, the radio, and the motion picture because these are the media which reach the largest numbers of people. Each will be examined with respect to its social background, its propaganda content, and its psychological techniques. The remaining media will be treated more briefly.

The Social Background of Newspapers

Historical accounts of the growth of modern journalism (*19*) reveal that what is considered in Western Europe and North America to be the primary function of the newspaper —the dissemination of news to all who will buy and read— is a fairly recent practice and one that is linked with the growth of democracy. Throughout most of its history, the newspaper or its predecessor was accessible only to the ruling clique in a society and then, when all men were permitted to purchase a paper, what they perceived was not news but the frank opinion of the editor. A quick and over-simplified dash backwards (*16*) reveals that:

The tablets of ancient Assyria and Babylonia which contained news of a kind were intended only for kings.

Julius Caesar condensed selected news items into bulletins, one version of which was posted in the Forum and another circulated "among members of the governing class."

The Catholic Church during the Middle Ages employed messengers to gather news for the higher clergy and secular rulers.

With the growth of nationalism, the principal function of a diplomat was to report events to the monarch who had dispatched him.

Bankers during the Renaissance had their private news sources to aid them in their own financial transactions.

The richer gentry in the early parliaments of England employed the precursor of the pollster to keep themselves abreast of public opinion.

During the first quarter of the nineteenth century, the English press consisted exclusively of journals of opinion which printed news in order to attract readers to the opinions. The actual results of the Battle of Waterloo, for example, were mentioned in a few lines. News itself in English papers became a source of revenue via the unsavory routes of blackmail and bribery: scandal was printed or else withheld for a price. It was, in fact, the advent of advertising that made newspapers honest and reasonably respectable, for this commercial form required a large circulation which was achieved through the relatively unbiased report of events. News was thus employed to evoke auxiliary responses which increased the likelihood that the advertisements would be perceived.

Although a free press was guaranteed in the Constitution of the United States and in most of the constitutions of the separate states, the first penny newspaper with a mass circulation and devoted almost exclusively to news rather than opinion, the *New York Sun,* was not established until 1833. By that time mechanical inventions enabled a paper to be printed quickly and cheaply, and the election of Andrew Jackson to the Presidency was symptomatic of a growing democratic wave in this country. Thereafter intense rivalry among American newspapers and additional technical improvements like the rotary press and the telegraph produced rapid developments in news gathering. News was printed as quickly as possible to score a "beat" on competing papers. To boost street-corner sales, the size of headlines grew larger. Correspondents were dispatched to foreign countries not only to find Livingstone but also to report home less dramatic but more significant items. The three press agencies were established and expanded so that newspapers with a low circulation had access to a variety of news. Sensational but not necessarily important news began to function as circulation bait. Feature material was added in order to compete with magazines.

As in England, the outstanding trend of the modern American press is to increase the concentration of power (*7, 9, 28*). No matter what phase of the newspaper business is examined, it appears that fewer individuals or groups of individuals control the contents of papers which more and more readers see:

1. Even though the population of the country has shown a steady increase and even though the estimated total circulation of daily newspapers likewise steadily increased except during the depression of the thirties, the number of these newspapers reached a high point in 1909 but has been on the decline ever since. Between 1918 and 1944, for example, the total number of daily newspapers decreased by 19 percent, but their circulation increased by 60 percent.

2. In recent times, fourteen individuals representing eighteen or about 1 percent of the daily newspapers have controlled approximately 24 percent of the total daily circulation; and on Sundays nineteen newspapers or about 3 percent of the total have accounted for almost one-half of the total circulation.

3. From 1910 until 1940 the percentage of towns and cities in the United States having one and only one daily newspaper increased from 43 to 87, but competition has tended to persist in those cities with a population of more than half a million.

4. The total number of newspapers controlled by chains as well as the total circulation represented by such papers rose phenomenally from the beginning of the century until 1932–33. Even though both figures significantly declined thereafter, six chains still controlled about one-fourth of the total circulation.

5. The number of newspapers dependent upon the press agencies has continued to increase. Ernst (*10*) stated in 1946 that "the 1,247 domestic subscribers to the Associated Press number 81 percent of the total daily papers and control 96 percent of the total daily circulation," a figure which is slightly misleading because some papers receive news from more than one press agency.

According to the public utterances of their owners, American newspapers are a form of public service. Actually they are a business enterprise which must show profit like any other business. The profit can be maintained or increased by attracting readers and advertisers. Although only from 10 to 35 percent of newspaper revenue comes directly from readers and the remainder from advertising, the advertising rates depend ultimately upon the number of people who read the paper. A large circulation is necessary, therefore, to take advantage of the decreasing costs per copy of the paper and to increase the volume of advertising.

Sometimes the advertiser seeks to affect news and editorials directly. At the end of the last war, for example, a press association which represented 4,000 small daily and weekly newspapers in the United States obtained a contract from the steel industry which stressed its explanation of a strike then in progress (*8*). After 1,400 publishers had been paid to carry these institutional advertisements, the association advanced the following suggestion in a written communication:

We are counting on you to give us all the support your judgment dictates. This is your chance to show the steel people what the rural press can do for them. Go to it, and pave the way for more national advertising.

It is estimated that about 15 percent of the publishers slanted their news and editorials as they had been requested. From time to time, advertisers tend to boycott a newspaper with a liberal editorial policy. In 1947, for example, some businessmen in a small North Dakota community objected to a publisher's attack on what he chose to call "monopoly capitalism" and his defense of Henry Wallace, cooperation, peace with Russia, and government regulation of business. Enough of them withdrew their advertising to force the man to sell his paper.

Such direct pressure, however, is relatively infrequent in modern times and is often wildly exaggerated by hostile critics of the American press. Well-established metropolitan dailies with large circulations, in fact, are able to reverse the procedure: they accept advertising only when it conforms to their own standards. In addition, the financial resources of such papers are so great that they cannot be intimidated by individual advertisers, even though their profits come from advertising as a whole.

The indirect influence of advertising upon the press, nev-

ertheless, remains great. To attract readers, the editor
consciously or unconsciously provides news and features
which people like. A comic strip is preferred to an economic
analysis, a sensational crime in the vicinity to a new peasant
movement in a foreign country, a dogmatic editorial to an
indecisive one. The interests of publishers and their advertisers in maintaining aspects of the status quo, moreover,
are usually sufficiently identical, so that there tends to be
very little discrepancy between the kind of editorial policy
that the publisher willingly adopts without outside pressure
and the one that the advertiser and his clients might be
willing to exert pressure to obtain. Advertising which promotes business is good for the business of the press.

In theory, then, the modern newspaper in a country like
the United States fearlessly presents the facts as it sees
them and it does so because objective reports are part of its
sacred credo. In practice, there is only limited competition
among newspapers as a result of increasing consolidation,
and the facts are presented within a general framework
which is affected by the press' status as a business enterprise.
In theory, too, the newspaper reader can read another sheet
or listen to news over the radio if the presentation of news
in his favorite paper displeases him or if he seeks another
version of events. But in practice there may not be a competing newspaper in the community. He can read out-of-
town newspapers, but these are likely to be more expensive,
to reach him a little later, and to neglect the local events,
issues, and advertising which interest him. The news he
hears on the radio may come from the same press agency
which supplies the paper he is accustomed to read. The
diversity of newspapers in the United States, therefore, may
give a misleading impression. When the press as a whole is
surveyed, it can be pointed out that almost every bias is
represented by at least one newspaper, whether it be the
communism frankly expounded by the *Daily Worker,* the
erratic liberalism displayed by *PM,* the considered conservatism and conscientiousness of the *New York Times,* or
the arch conservatism of the *Chicago Tribune* or any Hearst
paper. Nobody, however, except a professional journalist

or a clerk in a clipping bureau, ever has the patience or interest to run the gamut of viewpoints represented by different newspapers; and the number, circulation, and influence of papers to the right are much greater than those to the left.

Newspaper Propaganda

Some of the propaganda appearing in the regular columns of the press is unintentional. The general biases created by a newspaper's dependence both on advertising and on the kind of society which requires and permits advertising to function must be considered propaganda, but it is propaganda which has become "second nature" to the owner, publisher, and many of the editors and reporters to such a degree that they are likely to conceive of themselves as distributors of truth and the upholders of morality and justice—and certainly not as propagandists. The standards that each newspaper maintains and drills into its reporters may or may not be intentionally devised in the interest of a propaganda objective. The policy of some great papers to reprint in part or in full addresses by important men, for example, reflects their educational effort to present facts. Intentionally it also serves to increase their prestige among readers who are not satisfied by meager excerpts. The reprinting of an address containing thoughts contrary to the newspaper's policy—for example, the speeches of Hitler before and during the last war—can unintentionally affect some readers in a manner not desired by the editors. In contrast, the policy of the *Christian Science Monitor* to avoid reporting crimes and to feature stories in favor of its cult and opposed to alcohol and tobacco has been deliberately formulated.

Sometimes an editor instructs a reporter to file a type of story which is in accord with the viewpoint of the paper. More often, though, policy quirks are already known to reporters who—as Rosten (27) discovered when he carefully investigated 127 Washington correspondents in 1935 and 1936—are prone to further their own interests as employees by finding, featuring, or creating "news" which will be printed because it implements that policy. Forty out of the sixty-six reporters willing to reveal their attitude to Rosten agreed that their "orders are to be objective, but I *know* how my paper wants stories played." Half of those answering his questionnaire admitted that they had had the experience of seeing their stories "played down, cut, or killed for 'policy' reasons." A newspaper, when confronted with almost equally news-worthy stories about two political candidates, will undoubtedly give slightly better coverage and a slightly more prominent position to the report about the candidate who is approved by its own editorial page.

The largest part of propaganda in newspapers cannot be conclusively typed as intentional or unintentional. The facts about an event abroad, for example, must filter through a whole series of lenses before they are perceived by the reader of a paper: the biases and abilities of the individual reporter as well as the sources of his information, if he himself has not been an eye-witness; the journalistic style into which the facts are fitted; whatever censorship exists at the source (*29*); condensations to reduce cable tolls; the revisions of the re-write man; the headline and position allocated the story by the editor; and possibly some last-minute cuts if the story is too long for the space it has been assigned on the page. Each of these lenses may introduce some kind of change either deliberately or unwittingly. What emerges, therefore, is propaganda for something. The reporter may be intentionally expressing one of his pet biases, or his original perceptions may be unintentionally affected by the fact that he has been socialized as an American. He may be given the assignment in the first place because it is in accord with the paper's intentional policy to feature events which reveal the foreign country in a favorable or unfavorable light; or the assignment may result merely from the editor's wish to cover the news, regardless of the newspaper's own editorial policy.

The Nazis at the start of the last war showed great talent in creating newsworthy events which served their purpose. According to one journalist (*13*), American reporters in

Berlin before December 7, 1941, tended unintentionally to spread Nazi propaganda in the news columns of the American press. They cabled to their papers accounts of how the Nazi and the Nazi-dominated press was reacting to world events, reactions which may have been intentionally created by Goebbels because he knew they would be cabled to America and presented there as news. Early in the war, according to another reporter (*15*), a German White Book on Norway received worldwide publicity because its publication had been carefully staged. Correspondents were told that Foreign Minister von Ribbentrop was to make an important announcement, and they were instructed to appear in dark suits at his office to hear some momentous words. After such a build-up had been reported abroad, it was virtually impossible to ignore or play-down the disclosure which was, in fact, only routine propaganda attempting to prove that the British had planned to invade Norway.

The propaganda in newspapers, then, can be appraised either by discovering the intention of one of the individuals responsible for its appearance or by considering its probable or possible effects upon the readers. An item originating from a publicity agent who seeks to increase the popularity of a product, a motion picture star, or a diplomat is straightforward intentional propaganda. The description of a crime can be an "objective" treatment of what has occurred and may be carried because the event is considered newsworthy, but it can also produce a favorable or unfavorable reaction among readers toward law and crime in general, it can attract or repel them and hence induce them to continue or discontinue reading that paper, or it can crowd out other stories which would have had propaganda consequences in their own right if they had appeared.

Contrary to journalistic folklore, relatively few events are so newsworthy that they must be reported. Obviously it is true that editors of one country who have been schooled in a particular journalistic tradition frequently agree that certain events are newsworthy and that major newspapers quite independently feature the same stories on their front pages, but such judgments are almost identical because the judges have similar attitudes toward news and events. Let it be reliably reported that an ingenious individual has been able to compound an atomic bomb from fertilizer, whipped cream, and pure silk in the proper proportions—and of course every newspaper in the United States will print the story and give it a banner headline. Editors in the Soviet Union, however, might be instructed to withhold the tale until its authenticity has been checked, until Soviet officials have decided what their attitude toward the invention is going to be, or until the Soviet Government itself announces which counter-measures it will adopt. Conceivably, the story may never appear in any Russian newspaper. This illustration is not far-fetched just because fertilizer, cream, and silk—as well as the Soviet Union—are involved. It very definitely suggests that newsworthiness depends not only on the event but also on somebody's judgment about that event (*17*). That judgment in turn is affected by the policy of the paper, the tradition of the country, the fashion of the times, and other events at the moment.

Many events must be made newsworthy before they can appear in print, and hence reporters search for "angles." An "angle" is a way of writing a story so that it will presumably interest people. What interests people, American journalists believe, is the unusual, the exotic, the tense, the exciting, and the commonplace. For this reason so many newspaper accounts are pitched as examples of conflict, and thus readers' interest in this form of presentation is reinforced.

The reader who believes that he reads pure news and, by and large, little propaganda in his daily newspaper is strongly advised not to explore the deep caverns of his own mind before deciding whether the present analysis is correct or exaggerated. Instead he should subject himself to some very simple exercises that can be conducted at little cost in time, money, or energy. Let him compare, for example, the treatment accorded the same event in two or more different newspapers, or let him examine even in a casual manner two or more different newspapers which have appeared on the same day. The experience will be more vivid and perhaps exciting if he usually reads one of the papers and if the other is either a paper from another country or one in this country like the *Daily Worker* which has a leftist orientation (or a rightist slant if the reader per chance inclines toward the left). In comparing the treatment of the same event by different papers, it is well to make note of the following in each of the papers:

1. On what page and in which position does the story appear?
2. What is the size of the headline and what impression does it give?
3. What source is suggested for the story in the credit line and for the individual items in the text itself?
4. What impression does the lead—the first sentence or paragraph —give?
5. How long is the story?
6. What statements are presented as though they were uncontested facts?
7. From what phrases, if any, is it possible to deduce the bias or biases of the reporter or the editor?

As some of these questions are pointed at one version of the story, similar information should be secured for the other version or versions. In this manner it is possible to note how the same event can be reported quite differently in from one to seven respects.

An address by a public official is almost always summarized diversely in the American press even when copies of it have been distributed to reporters in advance. For questions like the following must be answered by reporters and editors before any kind of report is attempted:

1. Is this an important address or should it be considered important? This judgment determines the page on which the story appears, the position on the page, the size of the headline, the length of the summary, the number of verbatim quotations that are printed, and a descriptive sentence or two in the opening paragraph. If it is considered very important and the paper's policy as well as the flow of news on that day permits, the entire address may be reproduced in addition to a summarizing story.

2. What is the significant or newsworthy idea or ideas in the address? This judgment determines the thoughts expressed in the head-

line and lead as well as the particular sections that are quoted, summarized, or omitted altogether. It must be realized that the editor of a newspaper almost always must limit the number of quotations he gives from even an important address: every speech cannot be reprinted in full because there may be other and more important news or else advertising may demand space. In place of quoting the speech completely, only sections may be excerpted and the rest summarized or omitted. Incomplete quotations may be interrupted to add an opinion or observation of the reporter. The speech may be summarized without any direct quotations. Or—in the tradition of European journalism—the entire speech or parts therefrom may be quoted but slanted through the use of exclamation points, sub-heads, and varying sizes and kinds of type.

If an identical text is treated differently—and on a simpler level it is often amazing to observe how differently the same official government weather forecast is cryptically summarized on the front page—it is not surprising that a riot or a meeting gives rise to markedly dissimilar stories. The text of the address at least provides reporters with a common stimulus, but the stimuli from other events are variable and are differently perceived. Two different reporters may be watching a riot but from opposing vantage points. Even if they are standing on the same spot, they will see and hear different stimuli, since there is competition among the stimuli and since what they perceive is affected by their previous attitudes. An examination of how Boston newspapers reported the debate on the repeal of the Neutrality Act in September, 1939 (*1*), showed that with the passing of time each paper had a tendency to "skeletonize" or simplify the issues involved. The particular simplification which was employed varied with the paper, and the editors seemed to show more restraint than those readers whose letters they saw fit to print.

A casual analysis of two or more newspapers appearing on the same day is particularly illuminating. Usually observations like these can be made:

1. Unless some great event has occurred or unless papers of a similar type are examined, each newspaper makes a different decision concerning the one story which it considers the most important, and

that story is then given the largest headline on the first page. A scandal involving sex is more likely to occupy the leading position in a tabloid than it is in a conventional paper which tends to feature more serious events and to relegate sexual promiscuity or indiscretion to a headline in smaller type, to a back page, or to the trash heap.

2. Pictures or other types of illustrations usually arouse auxiliary attitudes and hence solve the perceptual problem of the stories they accompany. A photograph may be deliberately employed to promote perception, or it may be printed simply because it is available or newsworthy or because it adds variety to the page's make-up.

3. After glancing at three or four papers, it is possible to decide what events have actually occurred; then the reader can note the discrepancies between the different versions and he can observe which stories have been omitted from a given newspaper. Omissions result from editorial policy, failure to obtain or to give credence to the report, or simply lack of space.

4. The same story from the same press agency is treated differently by each paper. The editor must decide whether the story is newsworthy and where it should be placed. A headline must be composed. Sometimes the story is presented in full, but at other times sections of it are omitted.

5. The connection between the opinions of the paper as expressed on the editorial page and the news policy of the paper is usually difficult to establish from an examination of a single issue. It is necessary instead to observe the paper over an extended period of time before the small or large effect of its policy upon news selection and treatment can be detected. In the American press, moreover, there may be little or no correspondence between the opinions of the syndicated columnists and those of the editor—but, more frequently than not, a paper prints only the columns of those writers who by and large do not deviate from its own line.

6. Filler—material to round out the small sections of a page not occupied by news, features, or advertisements—almost always consists of exotic facts considered to be innocuous and entertaining, but may reveal the intentional or unintentional biases of the editor or his news service.

7. The comic strips reflect either some of society's minor problems in human relations or people's not necessarily unhealthy desires to escape from reality into a very crazy sphere of fantasy. Certainly they provide entertainment, but simultaneously they tend to strengthen or weaken—in most instances strengthen—prevailing habits of thought and action. A similar function is served by those feature

writers who display their sagacity for the benefit of the lovelorn or the mentally disturbed.

Sometimes a comparative analysis of the papers appearing on the same day reveals only trivial differences in the treatment of news. It should not be concluded from one attempt, however, that a continuing analysis would produce similar results. The existence of any differences, moreover, no matter how unimportant and unimpressive, is sufficient reason for suspecting differences all of the time. The analysis of papers, furthermore, is a more profitable exercise when the reader is acquainted with some of the individuals responsible for the news, whether they be the publishers, the individual reporters, or the press agencies.

Since with few exceptions American newspapers have become, as the dichotomy is phrased in French journalism, journals of information rather than journals of opinion, it follows that people buy and read newspapers not to discover the editor's opinion as expressed on the editorial page but to obtain the news and to be entertained. For this reason · the editorial page has declined in importance, although in recent years the syndicated columnist has sought to follow in the grand tradition of Tom Paine and the fighting editors of a generation or more ago. It has become fashionable, therefore, to assert that the influence of the press is on the wane just because fewer people read the editorial page. Time and time again, for example, it has been pointed out that Mr. Roosevelt was elected and then re-elected to office although the majority of the editorial writers and columnists opposed him. As a matter of fact, the same state of affairs tended to exist before Mr. Roosevelt's time. It has been estimated (*26*) that in the eight presidential campaigns between 1796 and 1824, when the popular vote was taken in less than three-quarters of the states, only three of the successful candidates had the support of the majority of the press; and that, in the twenty-six campaigns of the next hundred years before Mr. Roosevelt's first campaign, only fifteen of the successful candidates were backed editorially by the majority of the newspapers which openly declared their political positions. Mr. Roosevelt's ability and that of many of his predecessors to succeed in spite of the press, however, merely demonstrates the propaganda impotence of editorials and of columns, but it by no means proves that the newspapers themselves are ineffective vehicles of propaganda. While a newspaper damned Mr. Roosevelt on its editorial page and lustily printed the criticisms of columnists, it usually performed its function as a distributor of news by describing his campaign in its news columns and certainly, prior to the campaign, it reported both the accomplishments as well as the failures of his administration. And it was reports on his deeds and promises, as they appeared in relatively undistorted fashion even in those papers whose editors truly hated him or as they were reported too over the radio, which constituted one of the more important factors determining the reactions of voters to him. In fact, an adequate summary of one of Mr. Roosevelt's campaign speeches appearing in the *New York Herald Tribune* probably affected readers more—one way or the other—than the most brilliantly cogent criticism of that speech on the editorial page of this fair but conscientiously Republican paper.

There seems to be no conclusive evidence concerning the relation between editorial policy and readers' attitudes. Certainly partisan groups like communists or Christian Scientists read the official journals of their particular faith and thus, while demonstrating their loyalty, have that faith reinforced. At the same time they also read other papers with whose viewpoints they disagree in order to satisfy their interest in news as such or to be entertained by a feature. One study (*21*) in fact suggests that editorial policy is "a negligible factor" among those influencing most Americans to read one paper rather than another. No doubt this is so largely because editorials as such are unimportant and because few readers are conscious of the effect which a newspaper policy has upon its method of presenting the news. In one-newspaper communities, moreover, the men and women who disagree with the paper's viewpoint must read its columns anyhow if they are to remain informed concerning local events.

No over-all conclusion concerning the propaganda importance of the press need or should be drawn in absolute terms. The fact that the three outstanding revolutionary movements of our time—those headed by Lenin, Mussolini, and Hitler—were able to seize power in the face of strong opposition from the leading newspapers in their countries simply indicates the insignificant role of newspapers in modern revolutions. These men, moreover, did employ newspapers both to solidify the militant minority which propelled them into power and then, after the initial victory, to gain ever-increasing popular support or toleration. In other situations, for example, Pulitzer prizes are awarded newspapers whose fact-gathering talents and persistence have brought about the exposure of corrupt political practices, and usually the prizes really reflect the propaganda or educational accomplishment involved. All that needs to be said, therefore, is that the press is propagandistically important and that its precise importance depends on the factors operating in the given situation.

The radio of course has been responsible for whatever propaganda, educational, or informational ground the press has lost. Newspapers, for example, now receive a considerably smaller proportion of advertising than they did before radio established its effectiveness as an advertising medium (*3*). Certainly some but not all of the time people have come to spend in listening to news broadcasts used to be devoted to reading newspapers, and more probably fewer of them than formerly are either initially or permanently affected by the press' version of news. Evidence collected by Lazarsfeld (*18*), however, indicates that newspapers are more important than the radio in the lives of those Americans who probably exercise the greatest influence on the country's affairs. With the exception of women of low economic status in very small communities, more people claim they are "regular newspaper readers" than "regular radio news listeners." The higher the individual's economic status and the larger the community in which he lives, moreover, the more likely it is that he calls himself a "regular newspaper reader" and—perhaps more significantly—the greater the chances of his maintaining that he prefers to read "national and foreign news" in a newspaper rather than to hear it over the radio. This research, finally, suggests that those who prefer the newspaper have an older and a greater interest in the news than those who prefer the radio. The leaders in almost any field of activity, it can also be presumed, are more likely to read a newspaper than to hear a newscast because as busy people they can select the spare moment when they read, whereas they must conform to the broadcaster's schedule if they would listen.

During the first two weeks of July 1945, when the war against Japan had not yet been terminated, there was a strike of newspaper distributors in New York City. A survey organization conducted a poll at that time for the Bureau of Advertising of the American Newspaper Publishers Association (4). From 83 to 89 percent of a representative sample of New Yorkers said they were convinced that radio was not "completely fulfilling your need for news." In addition, 43, 32, and 25 percent believed they were missing, respectively, "most," an "important part," and "very little" of "the national and war news you usually get" from newspapers. Finally, 44, 24, and 32 percent stated they were missing, respectively, "most," an "important part," and "very little" of "the local news" the newspapers formerly gave them. These figures, though based on somewhat loaded questions and obtained for a not disinterested source, nevertheless, take on added significance when it is pointed out that many New Yorkers wished so ardently to read a newspaper that they were willing to go out of their way to purchase one. Over-the-counter sales rose from a little less than a quarter of a million on the first day of the strike to over a million and a quarter on the last day. Of course, newspapers were missed not necessarily as a source of news or opinion, but as a vehicle for features like death notices, stock market quotations, and local advertisements which cannot be transmitted efficiently by radio. This demand which is manifest whenever a strike prevents the newspapers of a community from appearing, in short, is another demonstration of the press' continuing strength: evidently its role is somewhat different from radio's.

Psychological Techniques of Newspapers

The content and propaganda of newspapers are perceived for a variety of reasons. Some kind of an auxiliary response occurs which predisposes the individual to buy or pick up the paper. He may wish to become informed about events, he may seek to be amused, he may even desire to look at the advertisements. The newspaper is an accepted medium to attain these ends and, moreover, it is always relatively inexpensive and accessible. A large headline on a newsstand can be a sufficiently intense stimulus to evoke the auxiliary response. Then, after the paper has been purchased or received, the reader is guided by auxiliary responses: he looks for additional information about the events of interest to him, he turns to the comic strips or the sport page, he searches for the advertisement of the local theater or department store, or he reads the details under the banner headline. What he thereafter perceives depends less on his reading habits than on certain technical factors in the make-up of the paper.

Headlines of course continue to elicit auxiliary responses which may or may not be related to learning or acting upon the propaganda content. As has been previously suggested in connection with advertising, other things being equal, the larger the relative size of the headline, the greater the chance that the reader will be oriented toward it. A large headline in a newspaper which customarily plasters its first and other pages with big type is less likely to arouse strong auxiliary responses because its readers have learned that there is little or no relationship between headline size and the event described thereunder. Headlines are important, as every newspaper man and almost every reader know. Besides being readily perceived, they are almost always the first part of the story to be perceived and hence the responses they produce in the reader are likely to affect his subsequent perception of and reaction to the story itself. They may give a concise but relatively accurate summary of the story that follows; a summary that is objectively inaccurate, as impartial judges would agree; the intentional or unintentional suggestion to evoke a response that would probably be evoked anyhow by the story itself or may never have been evoked. Many individuals, moreover, read only the headlines and therefore their entire impression of a story is derived from this not necessarily adequate source. On one occasion (*30*), careful research punctured an old journalistic belief to the effect that people are more likely to buy newspapers with pleasant than with unpleasant headlines: during a three month period in 1942 it was shown that the circulation of seven fairly representative American newspapers was not affected by the tone of the headline concerning the progress of the war.

A story may also be perceived as a result of the page on which it appears and of its own position on a particular page. The first page is always the most important one in the United States, but in many European papers the vital or last-minute news appears on a middle page or on the final one. While the top half of the page possesses a perceptual advantage over the bottom half—people begin to read from the top—factors in the layout can easily prove more decisive. A small story which is boxed in the middle or toward the bottom of a page, for example, is sometimes more readily perceived than a story with a much larger headline at the top of the page. Type which differs in size or kind from its surroundings or which is set off by unusual space arrangements is also likely to be seen. A photograph or any kind of an illustration on a page with no or few other pictorial devices serves to orient the reader toward the article it accompanies. Finally, the amount of space given a story helps determine not only its scope and the number and kind of responses that are evoked but also the readers' appraisal of its importance.

The personality responses aroused by a news story depend on the event, the previous attitudes of the readers, and the way in which the event itself is reported. The reporting may endeavor to be as objective as possible, in which case the reporter seeks only to describe what has occurred and to withhold his own private opinions of and reactions to the event. This journalistic ideal, as has already been suggested, is difficult if not impossible to realize: the facts have to be selected if only in accordance with the conventional standards of what is newsworthy and what is not; they usually have to be interpreted or else the story is dull or unintelligible; and the decision to report the event at all has propaganda consequences. The event, moreover, may be the expression of opinion by an important person or the assessed opinions of the little people in a country and hence may be an intentional or unintentional form of propaganda. Or it may be an incident deliberately staged by a publicity agent or a politician in order that it be reported and then affect people. The reporter, moreover, may intentionally include his own opinions as he describes the event. This practice of mixing "news" and "opinion" has been prevalent among continental European newspapers, notably those "journals of opinion" which seek also to present a certain amount of "information." It is a practice which in recent years has increased in American newspapers, too, and they are thus departing from their role as dispensers of pure information. The famous correspondent with a well-known byline is now expected to appraise and interpret the situation, for his appraisal and interpretation in themselves are considered a form of news. Many of the events in the modern world, furthermore, are so complex and swift-moving that the reader practically begs to be told not only what is taking place but also why it is taking place and "the meaning" behind the externalities.

The mixture of facts and opinion has certain advantages in promoting propaganda. It may be the news which evokes auxiliary responses but, to perceive this news, the reader unwittingly perceives the opinion; those responses solve the perceptual problem. As soon as he reads the news, moreover, he is told by the editor what position he should assume. The presentation of the facts may be and usually is arranged in support of the opinion, in order to create a consistent impression. From the reader's viewpoint, the propaganda may be clearly recognized, or his conviction that the news columns of a paper contain only news may prevent him from detecting the propaganda nature of the communication affecting him.

A daily newspaper can most effectively utilize repetition and variation to influence its readers. Day after day similar personality responses are evoked through the use of identical or slightly different stimuli. Events are usually so numerous that it is possible to select only those which are likely to elicit the desired responses without giving the impression that a propaganda campaign is being staged. Or only certain aspects of a developing event are featured and the remainder "played down" to gain the same effect.

There are newspaper readers who have a strong tendency to be submissive toward what they are reading. They are usually aware of the fact that hundreds or thousands of other people like themselves are or will be reading the same article and they may, therefore, feel appropriately humble. The printed word as such, moreover, possesses a certain amount of prestige. People appear to believe that the mere expenditure of time and energy which printing requires must be a measure of the content's significance. Such naive gullibility, however, has decreased somewhat in recent years as a result of unrewarding experiences which many Americans have had with printed words. They know that printed advertisements cannot be completely trusted, and some of them have learned—through the attacks that the press has levelled against itself and from amateur and professional critics whose number is not small—that newspapers are not always pure instruments of enlightenment. Most editors, however, seek to retain the prestige of their medium by being accurate. Local events, for example, are described as completely as possible, since most readers are more likely to be critical of details in such reports and since usually some have actually witnessed the events or have known people who did. Less caution need be exercised when news is reported from far away or inaccessible places: readers seldom have an opportunity to check the veracity of the version they must read. Journalists and especially columnists who predict future events diminish the peril to their reputations by phrasing their prognostications in general or ambiguous language. Then later they publicize their hits and ignore their misses.

Each paper possesses its own prestige which may be great or small. In every country, for example, there are newspapers—like the *New York Times* in the United States and the *Times* in England—which have the traditional reputation for presenting news more or less impartially. In Europe there are the so-called official or semi-official journals which are controlled or subsidized by the government in power: they are read avidly to gain insight into that government's viewpoint. Other papers which state frankly that they represent a minority or political group attract readers who are interested not in being affected by the propagandistic arrangement of the news and the editorial opinions but in discovering what the party line is at a given moment. A particular newspaper possesses prestige for innumerable reasons: the fame of its publisher, its editors, or its columnists; its inclusion in or exclusion from a chain; the press agency or agencies from which it secures a large part of its news; the crusades it has conducted in the past; the extent to which its views are quoted elsewhere in the country or in the world; the quantity or quality of its news and features; the emphasis given local, folksy news; etc. Many reporters have their own reputation for being accurate or inaccurate, and so their bylines become stimuli that can evoke submissive or derisive responses. In any case, the paper usually makes every effort to boost its own prestige by patting itself on the back editorially, by proclaiming its achievements and other claims to immortality and morality in advertisements inside and outside its own pages, and sometimes by sloganizing what it considers to be its distinctiveness on its first page or close to its masthead. During and after the last war, newspapers in Germany—including those at first published for the Germans by British and American authorities as well as those later published by Germans who had been granted a license to do so—were

not permitted to use the names of papers previously existing
in that country, since under the Nazis the names themselves
had become contaminated stimuli for certain types of responses. In this way another attempt was made to dissoci-
ate the new regime from Hitler's.

Either intentionally or unintentionally newspapers can resort to limitation most effectively. When news is suppressed
—because it is not considered newsworthy or to be in accord
with the paper's policy, because it runs contrary to governmental censorship regulations, or because it has been
crowded out by other stories—the reader usually is not
aware of the omission. Nothing is crossed or cut out.
There are no blank spaces. There is no stimulus, in short,
which can arouse suspicion. Unless the individual deliberately seeks to determine which story is not mentioned or
unless he has an opportunity to become acquainted with the
event through actual observation or through another paper
or medium, he is unable to evaluate the newspaper's contents. In wartime most civilians must follow the progress
of the fighting as it is reported in the press or over the radio.
They themselves cannot make a daily tour of the battlefields. Stories are more or less uniformly censored by representatives of the theater commander and by the authorities at home. The enlisted men and officers, who are the
eye-witnesses and who collate the actual reports from the
fighting zones, are inaccessible and under strict security regulations.

Photographs, Drawings, and Cartoons

A newspaper or any medium employing verbal language requires that words evoke responses concerning the situations
to which those words refer. Photographs, drawings, and
cartoons are based on another technique: they themselves
are more or less faithful reproductions of situations. They
belong, therefore, to the class of what Morris (25) calls
icons or iconic signs which possess many of the properties of
the situations they represent. There can be a vast difference
between the words "stormy sea" and a photograph or draw-

ing of the phenomenon. The words must first evoke a series of internal responses before their meaning is grasped, but the immediate, perceptual response to the visual presentation may itself be that meaning.

The pictorial media possess an initial perceptual advantage: they are almost always different from their surrounding verbal context and hence are quickly perceived. When a magazine or a book is devoted almost exclusively to photographs, however, this advantage is less pronounced and each photograph must compete with its surroundings. It is easier for most people to catch the point of a photograph or a drawing, and hence these visual media are understood by, and can be employed for the benefit of those whose educational level or reading ability is low. An American investigator (*14*) once estimated that "a pictured page in a newspaper will be read by a third more adults than anything on the front page."

Photographs have an element of prestige because many individuals assume that they are accurate reflections of reality. Like the reporter, however, the photographer must select some particular aspect of a situation. What he selects will depend upon what he considers newsworthy or worthwhile from some viewpoint. The viewpoint may be thought by him to be artistic, but the photograph that emerges most frequently reflects intentional or unintentional propaganda. The lens of a camera in this respect is no more objective than the lens of the human eye: the rays of light passing through it are regulated by the attitudes of the photographer. The way in which the film is developed, the technique of producing a positive from the negative, and the method of printing the photograph in the mass medium all contribute to the impression given the reader or the propagandee. Only authorized photographs of the British Royal family are distributed to the world's press, which means that this family is almost always displayed in regal and not in unconventional or undignified poses. In contrast, the readers of a newspaper expect a man accused of a dreadful crime to look like a dreadful criminal, and usually the photographer assigned to take his picture manages to find a pose or the editor to select the print which comes closest to justifying this expectation.

In addition, photography is such a highly developed skill that pictures can be retouched or faked without giving the casual reader the impression that they are anything more than informal snapshots. In contrast, a drawing and especially a cartoon are obviously the product of an artist, and therefore it is assumed that some degree of manipulation or distortion by him is involved. What they lose in respect to credibility, however, they can gain in clarity: reality can be arbitrarily arranged so that the evocation of the personality responses is practically guaranteed. The photographer may not be able to snap the pose which best suits his purpose, but the artist can erase a line or two and emerge with the facial expression he is seeking. Any one of these visual media, finally, may elicit a vivid response that is less likely to be forgotten than even the most purple prose.

A few cartoons and a small number of drawings and photographs are able by themselves to evoke the responses desired by the artist, photographer, or propagandist, but most require some verbal explanation in the form of a title or a caption. These written words elicit responses which influence the initial or subsequent perception of the illustration. The propaganda message, moreover, may be only within the text, in which case the illustration serves the perceptual function of directing the reader to that text. Many of the misleading photographs which circulate during a war are not necessarily retouched or deliberately posed, but falsely captioned. A not unbiased German authority (2) once tried to track down the source of various atrocity photographs employed during World War I. One photograph of two corpses being viewed by a saddened group in the background, for example, was published by a French newspaper in 1915 under the heading, "The Crimes of the German Hordes in Poland." The same photograph, the writer sought to show, was circulated on a postcard "by Russian Jews after the Odessa pogrom of 1905" under the caption "Mother and Child Cruelly Murdered in Odessa." Almost every day of the week it is possible to observe how captions distort the effect of pictures by examining the varied texts accompanying the identical picture from the same agency but appearing in different newspapers.

Magazines

There are perhaps 700 magazines published in the United States (*11*), and their variety is indeed staggering. On a single newsstand, periodicals are displayed which specialize in off- or on-color humor, the confessions of the frustrated and the anxious, women's styles and other whimsies, literary criticism, the motion picture, sophistication, photographs, liberalism, fiction, science, psychology, news, etc. In fact, almost all of the problems of modern life are reflected in and discussed by magazines during a given week or month. At the same time, the bulk of the advertising and circulation drifts toward only six publishers and it has been estimated (*23*) that from twelve to fifteen magazines control the mass circulation of the country.

If mechanical facilities permit, the immediate goal of every magazine is to increase circulation. Even editors who are more concerned with a cause rather than profit do not grow depressed by a rising circulation. They seek to please their present readers through the excellence of their product or its consistency. They try to attract new readers by an occasional publicity campaign which maintains that the magazine offers bountiful insight into our social, economic, and political system. For them, nevertheless, there is seldom a compromise between bait and the message; the message is more important than the bait.

Publishers interested in magazines as business enterprises, on the other hand, deliberately seek to increase their revenue from subscriptions and counter sales and thus to be able legitimately to raise advertising rates. The reader or public opinion is king. Most editorial decisions are made not in terms of what the editors consider good or bad either from a social or an artistic viewpoint, but on the basis of the known or assumed preferences of the public to which the magazine attempts to appeal. The "market," as the readers are sometimes accurately called, is therefore studied with some enthusiasm. Reader surveys are conducted by those large magazines which can afford them, in order to determine which type of article, photograph, illustration, or "stopper" is perceived with relative avidity; then future is-sues are more or less influenced by the results. The changes suggested by research, however, are introduced slowly (*20*). The magazine usually has contracts with authors and artists which cannot be abruptly changed. Readers have become accustomed to a particular format and, it is presumed, would feel uncomfortable if they were confronted with a completely different product. Editors will agree that the magazine could be improved, but may hesitate to alter a product which has been able to attract and hold its sub-scribers.

With or without a survey many—perhaps most—maga-zine editors dedicated primarily to increasing circulation be-lieve, in the grand tradition of the propagandist, that they and maybe one or two other people possess the divine gift of being able to predict what will interest or bore their pub-lic. The explanations they offer for their sagacity are usu-ally quite unchallangeable: "I just know this will have a great appeal" or "It's quite obvious that no one is interested in that right now." Sometimes their soothsaying is accom-panied by deeply convincing explanations: "I'm a woman and I know what women will say about this" or "I'm from the Middle West and I can tell you that this sort of thing won't be liked by the farmers of Kansas."

Naturally there is no sharp line between the policies of magazine editors interested only in intentional propaganda and those dedicated to large circulations and profits. Every editor is frequently tempted to adopt certain measures which he frankly recognizes as "compromises." The propa-gandistically inclined editor, for example, runs an article not because it appears to aid his propaganda program but merely as a device to attract readers who then are more likely to perceive the propaganda he wishes to have them perceive. Unless he is too rigid, such an editor may resort to "cheese-cake," fiction, or helpful household hints, no one of which has direct or indirect relevance to his propaganda objectives. Similarly the "ideals" of the profit-seeking editor lead him to include material which his reader survey or his superb intuition warns him will not increase the popularity of his publication. Serious analyses of a social problem do appear in picture magazines not because many readers have the patience, interest, or ability to examine them but because the editors like to work for publications which print serious material. As a result of such bravery, they are considered heroes by their wives, mistresses, or cocktail-party hostesses. Maybe in the long run—they openly believe— circulation will also be helped. There *are* some people who read a magazine containing serious articles, and this type of feature may also impress advertisers and producers who struggle with their own feelings of intellectual inferiority. It remains true, nevertheless, that the writer of penetrating analyses or fiction, no matter how influential his literary agent happens to be, is usually unable to find a market for his manuscripts among magazines with mass circulation (*24*).

Magazines that intentionally seek to please their readers are reinforcing responses associated with the status quo. The happy ending which most editors, like Hollywood producers, demand and obtain from their writers and which only the editors of magazines with very limited circulations usually avoid, is of course a distortion: reality relatively infrequently produces bliss without depressing or difficult problems. Aside from offering readers an escape into a very limited form of fantasy, this hackneyed but effective formula leaves them with the impression that God is in Heaven and that this Heaven will also be theirs—or could have been if they had been a little luckier, if they had shown a trifle more enterprise, or if they had come from a family of slightly higher social status. The advice pervading the women's magazines in the United States is dedicated to the expressed purpose of making life as it is lived in our society somewhat easier for the reader, whether that ease involves the menopause or baking cookies. In order to be different and thus to be microscopically ahead of their competitors,

in order to attract other people, or in order to express segments of their own liberal philosophy—and frequently for
all three reasons—some editors try to keep a quarter jump
ahead of what they know or believe to be what actual public
opinion will tolerate. The guide here is: be in the vanguard
but only if you can be absolutely certain that almost all of
your readers will catch up with you a few seconds later.
Thus if a word like "abortion" or "homosexuality" is confined to the vocabulary of impolite or restricted groups but
if it apparently is just about to diffuse to polite and less
restricted groups (included among which are the readers of
the publication), then it may be considered courageous,
original, and revolutionary to run a story dealing with the
subject.

According to one writer (22), *Collier's Magazine* published during the first eighteen months of the last war and
hence before America's entry a total of twenty-eight stories
containing pro-British themes. The magazine was consistently interventionist: it also published non-fiction "in favor
of the Lend-Lease bill and all its implications." One of its
rivals, the *Saturday Evening Post,* was opposed to interven-
tion and, consequently, its non-fiction attacked this policy.
Evidently, however, the *Post's* fiction had to respond to
public opinion, for during the same period it published only
one less pro-British story than had *Collier's.* The same
writer also points out that magazine policy regarding war
fiction was deliberately slanted; he quotes from an associate
editor writing before America's entry:

We are accepting pulp fiction dealing with the present European war.
The former ban on anti-German stories has been lifted. For *Air
Adventures* we would like air story writers to make their heroes English, French, or American adventurers. For *Fantastic Adventures*
and *Amazing Stories* we will welcome stories dealing with Nazi intrigue in the United States.

The slight risk which some editors are willing to incur as
they creep a little ahead of public opinion, however, represents a propaganda contribution to social change. At the
very least the change is accelerated. At the very most it is

realized—and it might not have occurred for a long time, even though the editor sensed its imminence. Individually, in short, magazines affect and reflect public opinion. Certainly the precise part they play cannot be easily disentangled from the other social forces that are operating simultaneously.

The most outstanding characteristic of magazines in the United States is their adaptation to the public opinion of almost every conceivable social group. The group may be extremely small and specialized like enthusiasts for miniature cameras; it may be limited roughly to one social class as many of the large monthly publications appeal to the middle class; or it may cut across two or more social classes like the weeklies which summarize the news or the digests which pretend to offer an easy route to wisdom. Instead of spreading their information and their intentional and unintentional propaganda thin in the manner of the motion pictures or many of the great metropolitan daily newspapers, they can, if they wish, respond to and then influence the particular group which is their target.

Magazines offer no new psychological problems that have not already been discussed in connection with advertising and newspapers. Like a newspaper, each magazine has a prestige peculiar to itself which predisposes the reader toward the propaganda therein. Most magazines, however, tend to have prestige as such: their dignified appearance, the more elaborate layout, the increased use of color, and their higher cost can produce greater submissiveness than the more ephemeral newspaper. The fact that magazines are published less frequently than newspapers usually prevents them from exploiting the factors of primacy and recency, but their relative freedom from pressing deadlines enables them to achieve greater perspective and to obtain a larger number of facts. A summary of news which makes the reader feel that for the first time he understands the rationale of events or a social analysis based upon a careful investigation which produces new facts not discovered by the press can have a more lasting effect than a headline, a bulletin, or a feature story in a newspaper.

Each magazine devotes some space to making subtle and unsubtle claims concerning its own virtues. The brief summary which precedes a story or article seeks to attract readers by heaping lavish praise upon its contents. Or the fancy of people is supposed to be tickled by this blurb and the illustration. The biographical sketches of the magazine's contributors are seldom phrased in modest terms. Features that will appear in future issues are mentioned in breath-taking language. Letters to the editor are reprinted for various reasons. They may be interesting on their merits. They may contain flattering evaluations of the magazine which the editor himself cannot make because of a sense of exquisite delicacy. They may criticize the magazine: reprinting of adverse comments indicates that the publication is broadminded and fair. They may point out inaccuracies which the editor acknowledges—and thus the impression is cultivated that the remainder of the magazine has been completely accurate.

Obviously the American magazine is one of the more important media for advertising. About the same amount of money spent in *national* advertising—30 percent—is allocated to magazines as to newspapers (5); and one survey (*12*) has shown that the average amount of space devoted to all advertising in the sixteen leading American magazines was 42 percent in 1940, with a range from 18 to 56 percent. In the so-called standard magazines, the advertising is confined exclusively to the series of pages at the beginning and at the end. The advertisements appearing on the back cover, on the inside of the back or front cover, or right before or after the reading material have a great perceptual advantage over those which are buried among competing advertisements (*6*)—great or specialized must be the drive of the reader who voluntarily plows through the advertising sections. Most American magazines of large circulation are of the flat type in which the advertising permeates every section except the one of varying size devoted exclusively to reading matter. The reader of such a magazine becomes interested in an article and then discovers that the article itself or a continuation of it is engulfed in columns or pages of advertising. Inadvertently he perceives the advertising unless he is overwhelmingly absorbed in the article. Then, since advertising often constitutes the bulk of many magazines, the advertiser tries to make his copy so attractive that readers will "read the ads" for their own sake.

Both deliberately and otherwise, furthermore, the magazine publisher and the advertiser assist each other. The magazine's prestige—as well as its revenue—is increased, for example, when a nationally known product advertises on one of its pages. Similarly a product may add to its own prestige by having an advertisement in its behalf accepted in a magazine with allegedly or actually strict advertising standards. The term "Good Housekeeping Seal of Approval" is bestowed upon advertisers and enables them thereafter to render propagandees a little more submissive by indicating that the magazine of the same name guarantees the validity of its statements; the printing of the Seal upon the product in turn advertises the magazine. Finally, it is well to point out that the way of life in our society fostered by the glib formulas for stories and articles in magazines of wide circulation is an almost exact reproduction of those conditions which must exist if most advertisers are to continue to produce and distribute their products or services. It is quite clear why no character in a magazine whose revenue comes from advertising ever pokes fun at advertising in any serious way which could conceivably affect people's fundamental attitudes toward that form of promotion. Nor is it difficult to understand why such a magazine —unless it is a news magazine—never prints articles which debunk or analyze advertising or which praise consumer cooperatives or other consumer groups whose aim is to give people objective facts about products. But it may not be quite so obvious that the happy-ending, the-boy-meets-and-marries-girl, the-poor-lad-becomes-rich, the-louse-gets-it-in-the-neck, or many of the other themes which saturate most of magazine fiction serve to reinforce the reader's drive to patronize the advertiser of consumer goods so that he too can find his salvation.

Books

Books symbolize some of the important achievements of a civilization. They are one of the principal means through which intellectual progress is recorded and transmitted from generation to generation. They reflect the literary and artistic tendencies of a people, and they summarize the problems which confront them. They are the foundation of education because they always affect the teacher and usually the students too. To burn or ban a book is almost always considered a step backwards, and to say that a man has "book learning" is to credit him with knowledge if not with experience. The presence of books in a home adds to the prestige of the inhabitants even when their exclusive function is decorative.

The responses evoked by books are almost as numerous and diverse as those which an individual makes to other people in a social situation. They can provide instruction and insight and thus elicit a whole series of actions whose reward is additional skill in solving problems. They can be satisfying in themselves by affording entertainment, escape from everyday difficulties, or emotional expression. They can also be propaganda vehicles.

As propaganda vehicles they can reflect or they can shape public opinion—and more usually they do both simultaneously. The textbooks of a school are pervaded with the prevailing beliefs and practices of the community, especially when an ambiguous subject like history is involved. A popular book like *Uncle Tom's Cabin,* whose effect in helping to bring on the Civil War in the United States is frequently dramatized and almost always exaggerated, summarized sentiment against slavery which already existed in the North but which was strengthened by being crystallized in the volume.

Like any writer, the author of a book may be carrying on intentional or unintentional propaganda. The books of Karl Marx certainly fomented revolution quite deliberately, but the effects his words have had upon modern communists and communist-baiters could not have been foreseen in detail by him in spite of the numerous predictions he made concerning the development of society. The objective of the detective yarn is to entertain and thereby to increase the profits of the publisher and the royalties of the writer, but at the same time a particular story may unintentiontally affect some readers' evaluations of the social groups and institutions which are described ostensibly only in the interest of the plot. The inspired author is popularly considered to be quite oblivious of his potential audience and to be merely unburdening his soul. Somewhere between the first chapter and the last, it may nevertheless be surmised, the thought occurs to him that he is enmeshed in the process of communication, and his output is influenced accordingly.

Books may have prestige in our society, but they are usually not willingly perceived. Only children and people whose livelihood depends on knowing their contents—like the members of professions—are highly motivated to seek them out and then to read them. For in comparison with all other media books are expensive, quite inaccessible, and certainly more time-consuming. Although between seven and ten thousand new books and new editions are published in the United States each year, relatively few people regularly purchase them. Book shops—as distinguished from the shelf or two of books in many drug stores—are poorly and inadequately distributed throughout the country. There are approximately 800 circulating libraries in the United States, but again only a small proportion of the total population actually uses them. In America, within recent times, the popularly priced reprint and the inexpensive but excellent paper-bound book have increased in numbers and have been distributed with almost as much enterprise as magazines; if this trend continues, as it probably will, the direct effects of books upon unprofessional adults will be greater.

In the meantime, however, it is not easy for publishers to elicit auxiliary responses which will cause people to purchase and then perceive a book. The publishing business, therefore, has had to develop specific propaganda methods to solve this problem. Urgency may be suggested by offering a discount on pre-publication sales. Direct advertisements are employed, especially on the book page or in the book section of newspapers and in specialized periodicals, on the sensible assumption that those who read about books or who have special interests are likely customers. There is a marked tendency for a publisher to advertise when a book first comes off the press and then not to allocate funds for additional advertising unless the book receives favorable reviews *and* is selling well. Some advertising is also done through the mails. The appeals employed are diverse and depend on the content of the book, but usually favorable reviews are quoted and, if the book sells, the number of copies or editions is featured. Publishing houses distribute releases to the press in the hope that something about the author or his book will strike the editor as sufficiently newsworthy for his regular columns or, if not, at least that a relevant item will be included among the news he prints about books. The banning of a book by a community like Boston usually results in a publicity bonanza: reports on the prudish action appear in newspapers and thus thousands of people learn of the book's existence and become convinced that they have a golden opportunity to secure vicarious sexual satisfaction. Almost any public figure in the United States—whether his fame derives from flagpole sitting, from commanding a victorious army or navy, or from having been the fourth assistant to the housekeeper of a competent or incompetent statesman—is persuaded by some publisher to write a book or have one ghostwritten on his experiences and philosophy. The publishers' confidence that a book by such an individual will be mentioned in the press and will also arouse a certain amount of curiosity is usually not misplaced.

Critics of course pass judgment on some of the complimentary copies which publishers eagerly send them. Their reviews—whose content varies from a digest of the book to utterly subjective evaluations or digressions into subjects which may not have the remotest connection with the book's theme—can affect the sale of the book. They themselves or their publication possesses prestige or, at the very least, their description or discussion of what they have idly or conscientiously read can give readers an impression of the book's content which tends to be more concrete than its title, author, or publicity. A sentence of praise from a popular radio commentator with a mammoth audience can sometimes sell thousands of copies and make the spirits and income of the book's author and publisher rise to the clouds.

Whenever a book first appears in another medium of communication, its existence is better known and the number of people who read or purchase it usually increases. Before some books are published, for example, the entire contents or sections therefrom are printed serially in a magazine whose readers then may or may not express their delight by purchasing copies for themselves or their friends. American publishers usually bring out new editions or publicize old ones when novels they have issued are selected to be filmed, however faithfully, by Hollywood producers: some movie patrons apparently are curious to discover how the books have been adapted or maladapted to the screen. A play which is produced before or after it has appeared in book form may be read by those who have been satisfied or dissatisfied by its presentation on the stage. There are some authors who seek to acquire prestige not only for themselves but also for the characters they have created or the points of view they advocate; a new book by them may be purchased on the basis of rewards previously acquired from the earlier books.

When the prospective reader actually enters a place where books are sold, the book itself seeks to carry on propaganda to promote a sale. Its jacket and blurb about the contents and author constitute a bit of last-minute advertising and hence capitalize especially on the factor of recency. The color of its cover, its typography, its illustrations, its size, its length, its thickness, etc., can be decisive factors. Sometimes its preface, table of contents or its opening paragraphs elicit related responses.

Like newspapers and magazines, books possess a prestige of their own which tends to make readers feel submissive toward their contents. Usually they are more dignified in appearance. Their higher price by itself may suggest greater wisdom and truth, since what costs more is thought to be worth more. Then books are so universally recognized as important cultural products: mere contact with a book constitutes for many people a direct approach to one of the eternal verities. Children especially respect textbooks which they consider a part of the classroom where presumably only "truth" is disseminated. This attitude has a tendency to persist into adult life, in spite of a lingering aversion toward "book learning." The very length of a book, moreover, enables the author to present his case both repeatedly and variously. The fact that readers must spend so much energy and time in reading a book may lead to the arousal of central rather than segmental responses, and hence their pre-action responses are more likely to be strong.

Miscellaneous Printed Media

The propagandist or the educator is not through with stimulating the eyes of men when he has printed and sought to distribute newspapers, illustrations, magazines, and books. Before creating sound waves to strike their ears, he has at his disposal innumerable other printed media through which he can communicate his intentions or thoughts. These can be given a somewhat cursory examination because they are only special adaptations of the printed materials which have already been considered.

There are various printed media whose principal propaganda function is to have the propagandee perceive the existence of the propagandist. A motorist cannot prevent himself from seeing the billboard which confronts him at a turn in the road, much as he opposes in principle the injection of advertising into the scenery he likes. A passenger in a crowded bus or street car is almost compelled to perceive the advertisement plastered right behind the strap or post to which he is clinging. The sandwich man is observed because he is the only individual on the street with one board fore and another aft and because his gait is usually slower than that of other pedestrians. The electric sign—whether it employs bulbs or neon lights, whether it is white or colored, whether it is animated or not—reaches at least the retina of the propagandee's eye since as a stimulus it is more intense than the competing stimuli in its vicinity. Almost involuntarily people look up to see the announcement trailing from an airplane or a dirigible, inasmuch as a hovering aircraft is a relatively uncommon sight; and sky writing of course is still more unusual. The theater-goer extracts tickets from an envelope which names and briefly proclaims the advantages of a restaurant located near the theater.

As a result of severe space limitations, these media tend to neglect stimuli which might arouse personality responses; they must rest content with the perception of their identity and a brief slogan. Many of them are linked to propaganda that is more fully developed in other media. The advertiser, for example, rents or owns a billboard to supplement his voluminous press, magazines, and radio campaign. It is not correct to conclude, however, that the media are ineffective merely because their messages are short. They may, in fact, appear at a crucial moment and exploit personality responses which have already been evoked. The motorist who happens to be in a traffic jam when the billboard tells him that he could ride in comfort by train or plane; the bus or street-car rider who is wondering how he shall spend his evening when he sees the sign displaying a picture of his favorite movie star; the pedestrian who is thirsty and searching for a bar when the sandwich man points the way to Elysian fields; the smoker who is about to enter a cigarette store when his attention is caught by glittering lights which ask him to try a particular brand just once; the woman who has forgotten her intention to purchase a fur coat next winter when she observes the name of a furrier drifting in smoke upon the summer sky; and the theater-goer who, before the beginning of the performance, is in a hurry to snatch some food when he reads a restaurant's invitation on the tickets' envelope—these individuals are psychologically vulnerable to the brief messages they are made to perceive.

Pamphlets, leaflets, and handbills are generally employed to reach a limited number of people as inexpensively as possible. Whether they are distributed free-of-charge or sold, they are almost always recognized by those who read them as propaganda and their authors are generally intentional propagandists. Through large or unusual print or through pictures and illustrations they seek to arouse auxiliary responses which will induce the passerby to perceive their contents. They can contain longer messages than some advertisements and hence may evoke a greater number of personality responses. Their space, however, is limited and, as a result, the action sought by the propagandist is usually stated explicitly.

Historically pamphlets have been extensively employed, for example, by Voltaire anonymously to arouse the French people against Louis XV, by Tom Paine to gain support for the American Revolution, and by Trotsky to keep the Bolshevik party united and later to reconcile the radical factions in Germany and Austria. Nowadays they are normally less important because they have been supplanted by other media like the radio which reach larger numbers of people and because—at least in the United States—they tend to be associated with fly-by-night, irresponsible propaganda. An index of their low prestige is the term "throwaway" which is sometimes applied to them. But in some situations they can be most effective. Toward the end of a political rally, a handbill may reinforce the speeches the voters have heard and help them remember the names of the candidates who spoke. Then, as has been previously pointed out, during a war leaflets may be the only medium which can reach enemy troops and civilians. The safe-conduct pledge they make on the battlefield can on occasion have important military consequences.

CHAPTER 19

Radio

W ITHIN a little over a decade the radio has grown from a plaything of amateurs into a giant industry and a most significant vehicle of communication. All surveys seem to agree that over 90 percent of American families have at least one receiving set in operating condition. Whereas the individual who was over fifteen years of age in 1925 had to make innumerable personal adjustments in his habits of entertainment and procuring news before radio listening could become part of his behavior repertoire, by the late 1930's a new generation of young people in a country like the United States had grown up with radio literally booming in its ears. During that latter period, for example, a group of over 3,000 more or less representative children between the ages of ten and thirteen in the metropolitan area of New York City was found to listen to the radio, on the average, slightly more than six hours per week (*10*). Over 71 percent of 1200 junior and senior high school students in Trenton, New Jersey (*45*) claimed they received most of their news from the radio, whereas smaller numbers simultaneously mentioned newspapers (58 percent), newsreels (26 percent), school (21 percent), conversation with family (19 percent), magazines (14 percent), and conversation with friends (13 percent). In spite of a ban on hard liquor commercials, between 1928 and

1944 radio's slice of national advertising in the United States rose from less than 1 percent to over 15 percent (*1*).

In World War I, radio was lackadaisically employed to reach a few key journalists and officials. In contrast, even before the second great conflict formally began, almost every country was spraying almost every other country with radio propaganda. Unlike the press, however, it cannot be said that radio has even approached maturity. Technical innovations continue to pour forth, like frequency modulation, television, facsimile broadcasting, more sensitive receiving sets, more economical methods of relaying programs, and more efficient transmission of short- and medium-wave programs. In addition, major social issues like the relation of radio to government or the international regulation not of wavelengths but of program content are far from settled. It is difficult, consequently, to foresee the social context of radio either in the near or far future.

In almost every country except the United States the government has closely supervised or directly controlled radio broadcasting (*38*). In Russia and Ireland the government has actually run the stations, a system which Nazi Germany also employed. In prewar Austria, Italy, and Czechoslovakia the government associated itself with a private monopoly by controlling the stock or by appointing the directors. In Great Britain and Canada, the government has set up a corporation which it oversees. In France and Australia government stations have competed with private ones. Revenue for broadcasting under all of these systems comes not from advertising but from mandatory listeners' fees; in fact, commercial advertising is generally prohibited. In a sense, then, broadcasting outside the United States resembles the earlier stage in the development of the democratic press or the press in non-democratic lands: the medium is the property of the ruling group. Unlike English and American newspapers two centuries ago, however, radio programs have been made available to anyone who can afford a set and the fee, and public opinion affects to a minor or major degree the content of broadcasts.

In the United States, on the other hand, radio has been

allowed approximately the same privileges as the present-day press: it has developed under private auspices and its principal objective has been not public service or intentional propaganda, as has been true elsewhere, but the profit of the owners. One technical factor, however, has compelled the federal government to assume a more active role in the regulation of radio than has ever been contemplated for the press. Until shortly after the last war, less than a thousand stations could be permitted to broadcast. There were only about one hundred regular wavelengths to be assigned (*14*), and therefore the power of two stations operating simultaneously from geographically separated points on the same wavelength was carefully controlled in order to avoid interference with reception. Then the judicious crowding of existing channels, the contemplated use of other channels for standard broadcasts, and the introduction of frequency modulation (*28*) permitted at least more than twice as many stations to operate. As a result, the number of stations soon exceeded the number of daily newspapers (*48*) and continued to increase.

If each station in the United States could select its own wavelength and power without regard for other stations, there would be the kind of chaos which existed in 1927 before Congress assigned the Federal Communications Commission (at first called the Federal Radio Commission) the task of regulating wavelengths and power through the distribution of licenses. The Commission's scope has gradually increased not because federal officials wish to exercise greater control over radio—of course there have been a few who have sought to do just that—but because some criteria have had to be found to justify the granting, renewal, and revoking of licenses for which the demand has always exceeded the supply. As a result, the F.C.C. has considered the "over-all program service in passing on applications" for licenses (*18*) and has sought to compel American stations to pay genuine rather than perfunctory attention to the contributions they make or fail to make to the common weal. Other principles of a democratic society have also been invoked to define "service" more specifically.

In accordance with the belief in freedom of speech, the theory if not the practice has prevailed that individuals with various viewpoints should be given an opportunity not only to express themselves over the air but also to own and operate broadcasting stations. In somewhat contradictory fashion, however, there has also been the conviction that government should be the custodian of people's morals and should outlaw corrupting influences; although that Commission is not authorized to censor broadcasts, it has prodded stations and some stations have prodded themselves into formulating codes in harmony with what anyone connected with American radio operations so frequently and ambiguously calls "good taste." The faith in free competition as a stimulant to improvement and a cure-all for the evils of monopoly has resulted in the curbing of large networks, notably the National Broadcasting Company which was compelled to lose one of its two chains and to be faced with another competitor in the form of the American Broadcasting Company. Thus the American radio which began as a child of private enterprise has been constantly under governmental surveillance and in some respects has been no "freer" than the government-owned stations elsewhere in the world.

The American listener, when he twirls his radio dials to select a station, may have the impression that he can choose from a wide variety of entertainment and education, but in fact his choice of programs is more limited than he thinks. For, as in the press, there has also been a sharp trend toward concentration of power in the radio industry in spite of the best efforts of the Federal Communications Commission which, it must be added, has always been handicapped by an inadequate budget (*49*). During and immediately after the last war, only 57 of the more than 900 commercial and non-commercial stations in the country were Class I stations of fifty kilowatt and operating on clear channels; of these 57 stations, 22 had exclusive nighttime channels and 4 were compelled to share time on two exclusive nighttime channels (*50*). The great majority of American stations, therefore, were permitted to broadcast at a much lower strength, shared their wavelengths with more than one station, and in some instances were permitted to broadcast only during specified hours of the day or night.   Then over 75 percent of the commercial stations were owned or affiliated with the four major networks, including 55 of the 57 Class I stations mentioned above (*51*).   Stations controlled by networks were obligated to transmit each day a certain number of network programs and were not permitted to accept programs from other networks. Gradually, however, the F.C.C. has sought to weaken these and other controls, although 48 percent of all radio time in January 1945 still came from the networks (*19*).

When radio was developing in the United States, newspaper owners and the press agencies at first fought this threat to their advertising revenue. Then, as networks began establishing their own newsgathering facilities, it was apparently decided that participation in the radio industry was more profitable than competing with it (*52*).   By the early 1940's about one-third of the stations in the country, therefore, were owned completely or in part by newspapers (*47*) and the press agencies derived an important portion of their revenue from selling news to broadcasters. Whatever uniformity exists in the press thus tends to be transferred to radio.   More than half of the radio stations have been the only stations in their communities, and of these about one-fourth have been associated with the only newspaper publisher (*15*). As of 1947, moreover, there were 5,575 American communities with a population of 1,000 or more without a local radio station and, of these, 136 were cities between 20,000 and 300,000 inhabitants (*53*).   Naturally most listeners live sufficiently close to neighboring communities or have sufficiently sensitive receiving sets so that they are able to hear programs other than those from local stations; but sometimes distant programs are not received so well and they usually reflect only the interests of and news from their own localities.   It must be said, too, that the existence of a local station is no guarantee that the radio audience will hear local issues discussed or local talent perform, since stations tend to prefer network programs which bring them greater revenue (*20*).

The high costs of broadcasting have also increased concentration. It is expensive to operate a radio station and therefore, unless there is a subsidy from a private organization like a university, the owner must depend on advertising for his income. Then it is estimated (*16*) that as of the early 1940's only approximately 300 companies could afford to advertise on a national network. The American radio, in fact, has been largely under the control of advertisers and especially of advertising agencies. In 1943, according to one writer (*17*), over 97 percent of *network* revenue came from 144 advertisers. In 1945, twelve advertisers accounted for 46 percent of one chain's total gross, seven for 38 percent of that of another, and four for 25 percent of that of a third (*54*). Newspapers derive about 70 percent of their advertising revenue from local advertisers and the rest from national and regional ones; the figures are reversed for radio (*17*). The power of the advertising agencies is still greater than that of their clients. When available figures for the three networks are examined (*55*), it is seen that as of 1945 between one third and almost one half of the total advertising revenue of each network was allocated by its five leading agencies—in fact, almost one fourth of the time on these networks was bought by only three agencies. Advertising agencies are so important not because they sell radio time, but because they rather than the broadcasters plan and produce their own radio programs and virtually decide at what times and in which cities their productions will be heard. As White has pointed out (*56*), these "advertising people" bring to radio "not only their language but also their mores and standards." To create better-balanced programs and to liberate themselves to a certain extent from advertisers, some stations and networks have been attempting to evolve a "package" program which they themselves construct and produce and which contains "spots" for commercials. These "spots" are then offered to advertisers on a take-it-or-leave-it basis.

In summary, then, it can be said—to the extent that these conditions still prevail in the United States—that many radio listeners are able to hear only a relatively small number of stations which are broadcasting. In most instances they have to select their program from among the three or four being transmitted by a national network. They are likely to be affected by a station whose policies are controlled or at any rate affected by the press. They may have to listen to one and only one station if they are interested in the affairs of their own community, and they may not have an opportunity to hear even one local station. They must almost always tune in on a station whose owners seek a return on their investment by broadcasting programs which are sponsored by advertisers. They hear network programs which are paid for by a relatively small number of advertisers and which are channeled to them by a still smaller number of advertising agencies. By 1947, however, a new kind of broadcaster began to play a more active role on the American radio. The Federal Communications Commission granted frequency-modulation licenses to labor unions, cooperatives, educational institutions, and other non-commercial groups which slowly sought to compete with the "standard" stations by offering programs not permeated with advertising ideology. As this book goes to press, the outcome of the competition is not clear; consequently, the present analysis of radio in the United States is largely based on the practices of the "standard" stations.

Every achievement of radio so far has been accompanied by failure, no matter what standard of judgment is applied. On the one hand, international shortwave broadcasts should enable the peoples of various countries to become better acquainted with one another or at least with some of their cultural products; on the other hand, this medium has been employed largely to disseminate chauvinistic propaganda. The international exchange of broadcasts could also promote such understanding; yet relatively few exchanges occur because it is expensive for stations to receive and then re-transmit programs from abroad. Even on-the-spot round-ups of news by radio reporters stationed in various countries are usually subject to local·censorship regulation and—at least in the United States—they tend to be exotic and entertaining more frequently than they are informative and original. Radio, which does not respect boundary lines, should be able to offer the people of one country the opportunity to hear directly what is occurring elsewhere in the world and thus to circumvent whatever governmental restrictions are placed upon their own media of communication; but this function of radio has been considerably curtailed in many countries by local regulations that prohibit listening to foreign countries, by the deliberate sale of sets that can receive only local programs (as in Nazi Germany), by the substitution of wired wireless for receiving sets (as in the Soviet Union during the war), and by wartime and sometimes even peacetime jamming. Besides, domestic programs can seldom be heard at great distances, few of these programs are ever transmitted simultaneously by shortwave, reception of shortwave broadcasts is generally unclear and unreliable, and linguistic barriers often intervene.

A paradoxical situation exists especially in the United States. More Americans for the first time have been able to hear and grow to like what people call "good music" as a result of radio, but—with the exception of those who have been to college—many more prefer to listen to popular or sentimental music and to stereotyped comedy (*29*). For every serious talk and discussion on the radio there are from one quarter to twenty times again as many soap operas and productions which entertain an audience through comedy and silly questions-and-answers (*57*). The news of the world is given quickly, frequently, and efficiently by radio, but many of the reports consist of little more than expanded headlines or serve as a vehicle through which commentators can editorialize or entertain their listeners. Notable services for the farmer are performed each day by stations which broadcast weather and crop reports, but with significant exceptions little sustained interest is shown in people who inhabit rural or sparsely settled areas since their purchasing power is relatively small.

Many if not all of the so-called "evils" of radio, however, cannot be partially or completely ascribed to this medium itself. The failures of international broadcasting, for example, are more numerous than its successes simply because radio has been abused in an era of intense nationalism that requires the suppression of almost all moral and legal standards. In the United States broadcasting has tended to adapt itself to commercial standards inasmuch as commerce and the advertising that aids commerce are an important part of our national life. No one compels Americans to listen to soap opera, dismal comedians, slapstick, amateur hours, or opinionated commentators. If the research facilities of broadcasting companies revealed that such programs were unpopular, they would soon be exterminated. By broadcasting such materials, of course, these stations do reinforce interest in one type of script rather than in another, but in theory the audience has the privilege of rebelling. Few educational institutions run radio stations in the United States not only because the F.C.C. has preferred to grant licenses to commercial groups, but also because, as White has shown (*58*), they themselves have demonstrated little tenacity or originality in this field. No, the culture which people have—including the media of communication—is usually the one they deserve since it is adapted to actual and latent public opinion.

Radio Propaganda

Most people listen to the radio to be entertained. Usually their set is located in the home, in an automobile, or in a public place where play and not work is their principal objective. The housewife who hears a program while performing her daily chores, the truck driver who turns on his set to relieve the monotony of a long drive, and the worker in the factory whose efficiency expert has proven that blasts from a radio will increase output are eking out some satisfaction in the midst of their more or less frustrating tasks. Newscasts in the United States are popular, provided their contents can be effortlessly absorbed. Serious features are of interest only "once in a while" (*30*).

Conceivably information and education rather than entertainment could have been stressed to a much greater degree as radio developed in the United States; if they had, perhaps the popularity of this medium would never have been so great. Radio's reputation, however, is now established and therefore listeners almost always demand that it remain in character. In any country, moreover, the audience ultimately decides whether it likes a program or not. While loudspeakers can be erected in public squares and the secret police of a totalitarian regime can track down illegal listeners, no practical method has been devised to compel people to turn on their radio and then to listen to a particular program.

Entertainment, in short, affects the propaganda objectives and content of all broadcasting. Even the dictator's propaganda ministry has to oscillate between music, comedy, or drama on the one hand and revealed propaganda on the other. Only an intense drive under rather unusual circumstances can induce people to listen to programs that are not entertaining. The radio becomes important to the inhabitants of a flooded area when it gives them information which can help them save their lives and property. Some enemy civilians and many underground patriots in Europe listened to the broadcasts of the United Nations during the last war, because they wished to know what was occurring outside Hitler's Fortress and how the voices of those nations were reacting to the events. School children in the United States and elsewhere cannot very well avoid hearing programs designed to increase their appreciation and knowledge of music, history, or geography when the radio is turned on in the classroom or when they are held responsible for the contents. Listening to news may not be a form of relaxation when more depressing rather than cheering events are described, but at least it is a less arduous method of being kept superficially informed than reading a newspaper.

Under a dictatorship the propaganda objective of radio is clear-cut: to foster the values considered important by the regime. No doubt Goebbels would have preferred to dedicate every minute of German broadcasting to his doctrines of hate and glory, were it not for the fact that even his audience would not have tolerated such outright preaching. He provided entertainment, therefore, but he made certain that the music had been composed only by men whose alleged racial stock, nationality, and style met his and Hitler's approval. Drama and comedy were also slanted along strictly Nazi lines. There were news programs galore, but the reports were distorted, fabricated, and suppressed until they conformed to the official version of the Wilhelmstrasse in Berlin. There seemed to be a consistent effort to keep entertainment at a minimum except when Nazi authorities believed that the German people required another outlet to escape temporarily from their everyday frustrations.

Radio propaganda is more difficult to detect when the stations are owned or supervised by a democratic government as in England or Canada. The directors of the radio monopoly operate under a charter which contains general phrases like "trustees of the national interest" and "a means of education and entertainment," but which assigns to them the specific task of planning and producing the programs, subject to periodic executive or legislative review. The precise programming which results depends upon the charter, public opinion, and the ways in which both of these are interpreted by the directors. The charter and the interpretations can override public opinion to a certain extent, since people are faced with the alternatives of either listening to the domestic programs, of attempting to tune in foreign stations, or of abandoning the radio as a form of amusement. Public opinion, however, cannot be overridden completely: listeners can protest to their representatives and perhaps change broadcasting policy. Many directors feel that they have a mission, which usually consists of raising what they consider to be the educational level and the artistic tastes of the vast majority. If people like light music—as most people do in one form or another—light music is played but not so frequently as the audience would wish; instead classical music is smuggled into the programs on the assumption that even an unwitting acquaintance with the compositions of dead masters and living innovators will eventually lead to real appreciation. If people want comedy —as most people do—they are given comedians and variety shows, but on occasion they are subjected to more serious drama. If people want news, then news is broadcast but less often and usually more calmly than in the United States. People, however, are not eager to be reformed even when they are told that what is being done to them is in their own self-interest—or eventually will be. The British Broadcasting Corporation, for example, is being constantly criticized by its audience for being dull, stuffy, and not sufficiently entertaining. Some English advertisers before the last war, consequently, decided to cater directly to English taste by broadcasting from radio stations in Ireland, France, and Luxemburg which could not be controlled by the B.B.C. And evidently many Englishmen tasted and reacted favorably during the war to the commercial American programs destined for American troops stationed in England and on the continent.

The owners of radio stations in the United States are also faced with the problems of their license from the F.C.C., public opinion, and their own interpretation of the license, but—since profit is their primary motive—they and the advertisers who exert such a powerful influence upon them devote considerably more attention to public opinion. With the exception of the few non-commercial stations owned and operated by universities and crusading groups and the one municipal station in New York City, the motto of American broadcasting is: the public be entertained. The radio and advertising industries, therefore, make every effort to provide entertainment of interest not to specialized groups whose purchasing power is small but to as many potential customers as possible. It is for this reason that a slightly novel type of program, if it proves successful, always gives rise to a host of imitators: the sponsor and the advertising agency want to invest their money in a program which almost certainly will attract a large audience and they prefer to leave experimentation and trail-blazing to someone else. The someone else may be another sponsor, but frequently it is a single radio station which is willing to run a risk involving less money and prestige in the hope that a successful program will eventually pay off by finding a sponsor. Spe-

cialized groups in the United States, however, represent
some purchasing power and, therefore, their entertainment
needs are not completely neglected. Classical music and
other serious types of programs are sponsored on national
networks, although the percentage of people if not the absolute number interested in them is relatively small. Almost
always, though, such a sponsor simultaneously employs other
radio programs and other media to carry his propaganda to
a much larger segment of the population. Foreign-language
groups are entertained on strictly local programs.

The requirements of the F.C.C. license and the broadcaster's conscience and scruples, moreover, affect the planning of American radio programs. Sustaining features are
sustained, that is, paid for, by the broadcaster so that he
can retain not his audience, but his license and his self-
respect. They consist of addresses by public officials, eye-
witness accounts of important events, novel plays, discussions
of public issues, music by symphony orchestras, courses in
instruction for schools, etc. They may also include almost
any kind of program for which the station or the network
has been unable to find a sponsor. Their function in the
over-all broadcast picture, according to the F.C.C. (*21*),
has been to help stations and networks achieve a "balanced"
schedule of programs, to enable them to present controversial issues and to carry on experimentation in programming, and to provide an outlet for minority groups and non-
profit organizations which cannot afford to pay for radio
time. In 1946, however, the Commission (*22*) discovered
to its horror that many stations had made solemn pledges
concerning sustaining and other public-service programs in
order to obtain a license and that they then had failed most
miserably to carry out their promises. Instead of broadcasting such features of their own or relaying them from
networks, they substituted regular commercial programs.
There has always been, moreover, a tendency for American
stations to relegate these features to the less popular and
hence less profitable morning, afternoon, and very late
evening hours.

American broadcasters have good reasons to avoid con-

troversial questions. If a controversy is aired on a commercially sponsored program, it is likely to antagonize some
members of the audience and thus to make them desert the
program or to feel less rather than more friendly toward
the sponsor and his product. If an issue is discussed or
dramatized on a sustaining program, the station or the network may become the target for similarly aggressive actions.
It is remotely possible that individuals who feel wrathfully
that the moral or political system of the country is being
wrecked by various radio programs may abandon listening
altogether. In addition, broadcasters are afraid to provoke
the influential people in the country who can exert pressure
upon the F.C.C. to revoke their licenses or otherwise regulate an industry that is opposed to governmental regulation.

The National Association of Broadcasters in 1939 established certain "Standards of Practice" concerning whose
section on "Controversial Public Issues" White somewhat
sardonically but accurately remarks: "In some three hundred and fifty of the most carefully weighed words in the
history of advertising double-talk the drafters made certain
that broadcasters would eschew controversy as a plague-
ridden orphan, feared by all, unwanted by the makers of
soap and cigarettes" (*59*). That Code maintained that
"time for the presentation of controversial issues shall not
be sold, except for political broadcasts." Since sustaining
programs provide no revenue and represent a financial loss,
broadcasters had little incentive to present the controversial
except when prodded by the F.C.C., pressure groups, or their
own sense of public responsibility. They were reluctant, in
accordance with the view that both or all sides of a controversy should be presented, to begin a discussion which
then entailed the allocation of more time to the various
viewpoints and hence the further curtailment of revenue.
The F.C.C. six years later ruled that "an absolute ban on the
sale of time for the discussion of public issues may under
certain circumstances not serve the public interest," but it
simultaneously agreed with the N.A.B. that "such broadcasts should be primarily of a sustaining nature" (*23*).

A new Code—proposed to the N.A.B. in the fall of 1947

but, because of opposition from the independent stations to its regulations regarding commercials, not submitted for final discussion and possible adoption until May of 1948— omits the requirement that controversy be presented only on sustaining programs, although it bans "dramatizations of controversial issues." The wording of its section on "Public and Controversial Issues" is much more liberal in tone:

Time for the presentation of public questions, including those of controversial nature, should be allotted with due regard to *all other elements of balanced program schedules,* and to *the degree of public interest in the questions to be presented.* A broadcaster in allotting such time should use his best efforts to insure fair presentation of those issues which concern *the welfare of the community.*

The italicized phrases offer an excuse to avoid the controversial in favor of the commercial. Certainly the meaning of "balanced program," "the degree of public interest," and "the welfare of the community" is both elastic and indefinite. The director of a station, if he so chooses, can decide that the broadcasting of a controversial issue will throw his program schedule off balance. Or he can maintain that most people have no interest in an issue which, consequently, concerns neither the community or its welfare.

Labor groups in particular have had to struggle to be heard over the radio. The Manual accompanying the 1939 Code specified that "discussion—or dramatization—of labor problems on the air is almost always of a controversial nature." "Even the so-called facts about labor," it stated rather ruefully, "are usually challenged" and hence "the presentation of a labor program usually calls for at least one other program because of the division in the ranks of organized labor." Then it added with a deep sigh: "the situation is further complicated by the fact that employers, as a rule, won't discuss their labor problems on the air and are inclined to frown on those stations, especially in smaller communities, which open their facilities to labor leaders." As labor's power increased during the early 1940's, however, more and more stations—including those belonging to the

N.A.B.—permitted labor problems to be discussed not only on sustaining programs but also on those for which labor paid the standard commercial fee (*60*).

There are relatively few labor programs on the air. Unions either are unable or unwilling to pay the costs and, in addition, such programs are not very popular. As a result, labor problems are usually mentioned only in news dispatches. People's attitudes toward these problems, it is clear, are affected not merely by a logical presentation of the issues involved but also by their general impression of the participants. And one side—management's—is frequently on the air in the role not of pleaders for its viewpoint but of sponsors for its products. Through the entertainment they offer, employers can attract an audience. On these programs they do not directly advocate their viewpoint regarding labor and they seldom if ever mention the conflicts and disagreements they have with unions, but they most certainly build up their own general prestige by extolling their products. Their listeners, therefore, are tempted to generalize from the excellence of the product and the radio entertainment to the excellence of whatever they do, including perhaps their labor policy. Some of the institutional commercials emitted by large manufacturers like the Ford Motor Company are devoted much less to their products than they are to heaping praise upon the overall wisdom of management, of private ownership, and of our present economic system (*24*). Labor leaders have no corresponding opportunity to exert an *indirect* influence on public opinion.

Such concealed or delayed revealed propaganda for a specific version of the status quo places any less powerful minority in the United States at a disadvantage in the field of radio. Commentators with liberal views are considered to be liabilities by most sponsors, and relatively few of them are employed on sustaining programs or, if employed, carried by the affiliated stations. Church services are broadcast by the score, but atheists and other free thinkers are seldom heard. Patriotic observances produce hymns of praise in behalf of our background, traditions, and ideals; but groups like the communists who advocate quite a different approach to past, present, and future events do not burst upon the radio audience on May Day or on an important anniversary of the Soviet Union. Many broadcasters, moreover, have adopted their private censorship codes because, they say, radio programs which enter the home and can be heard by all groups must be carefully scrutinized. Certain references to sexual matters are eliminated from songs, jokes, and important discussions in order not to corrupt the youth or any age group which, it is assumed, is waiting to be corrupted; but there are people in this society who consider that our sexual mores are too strict or who believe that a suggestive song, an off-color joke, or a serious and specific reference to sex can have only beneficial effects. All stations ban advertising by the manufacturers of hard liquor, again for reasons associated with morals; except for women living in rural areas, the majority of Americans—who certainly are not alcoholics or whiskey manufacturers—have no objection to this type of advertising (*31*).

It is definitely not being argued that radio stations should give equal opportunity to all minority groups. For practical reasons everybody cannot be granted the right to broadcast whenever he chooses to do so. Some line has to be drawn, but any line must be arbitrary and will penalize someone or some group. Many if not all American broadcasters may personally favor the perpetuation of the status quo which has proven so profitable to them. Their interest in the present system of radio, however, is itself no valid reason to make that system suspect or to alter it drastically unless the social and propaganda consequences of the change—and inevitably there will be consequences—seem more desirable. In defense of the broadcasters, moreover, it must be said that they make a conscientious effort to present an accurate and impartial summary of public controversies in many of their newscasts.

When once the listener appreciates the general propaganda biases of radio, he should have no difficulty in detecting and analyzing the particular programs he hears. News reports and commentaries can be subjected to approximately the same kind of analysis as that suggested for the press in the last chapter. The cryptic style of radio, it will be noted, leads to condensations that frequently result in serious distortions. The American listener is seldom told the source of the news in general or of specific items as he almost always is by his newspaper, and usually he is given only the highlights of a story which in the interest of entertainment may be accompanied by feature material. There are two relatively easy ways for the listener to check these limitations. In the first place, he can tune in on another newscast from a different station or network and note the varying content and emphases of the two programs. He will always discover that some events are mentioned on one program and not on the other, and he will almost always be able to discern how the alleged facts presented in connection with the same story differ. Such observations become more meaningful if he is acquainted with the news source upon which the newscaster depends; variations in the factual content of the same story, for example, are likely to be few if two newscasters rely on the same press agency. Listening to two popular commentators on the same evening provides insight into their tricks and may indicate with dispatch the motivating biases behind them. Then, secondly, a tedious but rewarding procedure is to compare a newscast and a newspaper of the same time period.

Straightforward entertainment is a little more difficult to analyze because the listener usually lacks certain crucial and relevant facts and because he is more eager to enjoy himself than to be critical. He may think, for example, that popular songs win public approval on their merits and that the one he hums or listens to on the record which he has consequently purchased is far superior to its competitors. In all probability, however, he likes the song because he has frequently heard it on the radio, and he has heard it broadcast frequently—more often than not—because its publisher many months before has decided to stage a deliberate campaign to make it not just another offering from Tin Pan Alley but a "hit." The song, for example, has been foistered upon entertainers through the wiles of professional "pluggers," it has been heralded as "the song you will all be singing soon," and it has been played to the point of satiation during one solid "drive week" or more (*44*). In general, music on the radio requires little or no analysis, except that in passing it is sometimes interesting to note the type and nationality of the classical composers whose works are played, the ethical assumptions and arguments contained in the lyrics of popular songs, or the extent to which the problems of the society and composer are reflected in the music he writes. The announcer's introduction and program notes can contain direct propaganda themes which may influence the listener's response to the composer as well as to the type of music and the particular selection about to be played or sung.

The radio comedian, like any comedian, requires more careful scrutiny because his comedy is likely to disarm his audience so gracefully that his intentional or unintentional propaganda remains concealed. Primarily he is interested in his own popularity—as measured by a market survey, letters from his audience, the laughter of the studio audience, and the praise he receives from his sponsor—because being funny is his life work. To be funny, though, he must release certain tensions within his audience which are already there or which he has evoked. Puns enable people to behave like children who suddenly realize that they are masters of the language they speak. Sometimes the tensions released in comedy reflect aggressive tendencies toward foreign countries, outlying communities, political and social leaders, wives and husbands, mothers-in-law, radio commercials, other radio programs, ethnic groups, and personality types such as the cocky, the miserly, the inhibited, or the socially ambitious individual. Other tensions involve unsatisfied or repressed drives, like those relating to sex, profanity, social mobility, the anal functions, etc. These are the principal but by no means the only psychological conditions promoting laughter in our society. Minority groups, for example, are the favorite butt of jokes because the guilt and aggression people feel toward their members has stimulated the learning of a series of internal responses that stand ready to be evoked and thus to bring the release and relaxation promoted by laughter. The comedian in the United States who manages to vary the old saw concerning the thriftiness of the Scots cannot be held responsible for establishing that group's reputation in the first place, but his use of this type of joke serves to reinforce the impression people have of those who inhabit or come from the Highlands and the Lowlands. He himself may have a high opinion of the Scots and he may intend to bring no harm or good to members of this ethnic group; yet in employing them as a source of innocent merriment he is helping to perpetuate the reputation. The listener interested in propaganda analysis, consequently, must perpetually ask himself why he laughs, and he will not reply satisfactorily until he learns something new about himself or his society.

Radio is important as an instrument of propaganda because of the vast audience it can reach. On each of ten occasions, for example, it has been estimated that Mr. Roosevelt addressed forty million people simultaneously; and the same writer (2) also points out that more people have listened to one Sunday afternoon broadcast of the New York Philharmonic Orchestra than have been present in its concert halls throughout its existence. An audience for an important event, moreover, can be attracted or increased by newspaper advertising or placards and by announcements which appear in newspapers or which are made over the radio. Ordinarily, the radio in the average American home is turned on about four hours each day (3, 32). Faced with a hypothetical but most dreadful question—"if you had to give up going to the movies or listening to the radio, which one would you give up?"—a mere 11 percent of a representative sample of Americans believed that they would abandon their sets; only 30 percent stated they would do likewise if they had to choose between "reading the newspapers or listening to the radio" (33). By and large, as compared with their attitudes toward churches, newspapers, schools, and local government, most Americans can be made to appear satisfied with radio's performance (34)—though of course they might not be so smug if they could possibly appreciate what radio fails to provide or how they would react to programs containing a different and perhaps improved type of news, information, or entertainment.

Except under unusual circumstances, there is in the United States an inverse relation between the cultural level of a group and its dependence on radio as a source of news and entertainment. Lazarsfeld, besides suggesting—as indicated in the last chapter—that influential Americans are more dependent on the newspaper than on the radio, has collected a number of additional facts concerning the radio audience. The lower the individual's economic or educational status, the more likely it is that he will have his radio turned on at any given hour of the day (*39*). Radio as an inexpensive and easily accessible form of passive entertainment is thus less important to wealthier and better educated individuals whose money and training enable them to enjoy more frequently, and to have developed greater interests in other forms of amusement. No doubt a complicated interaction is involved: on the whole radio programs are not adapted to the tastes of such individuals since they are not ardent radio listeners, and they are not ardent radio listeners because the programs on the whole are not adapted to them. At the same time, "people actually do less serious listening as the cultural level descends," Lazarsfeld points out (*40*), and "serious listening" includes classical music, opera, political speeches, discussions of public affairs, "educational" programs, newscasts, etc. Soap-opera addiction decreases as women ascend the educational ladder (*35*). The lower income or more poorly educated groups have their dependence on radio constantly reinforced by another complicated interaction: they prefer the radio because they do not read with facility, and their preference for radio partially prevents them from acquiring facility in reading; they are less interested in classical music because they have had fewer contacts with this type of music, and they continue to have fewer contacts because they listen to the station which tends to offer them the kind of music they want; or they know less about the issues of the day because they listen to fewer programs or read fewer articles about those issues, and serious programs or articles have less of an appeal to them because they do not possess the background which is necessary for an understanding of the issues. Lazarsfeld's most general conclusion is this: "If people have the choice between radio and print for fairly comparable subject matter, the higher their cultural level the more likely they will be to read rather than to listen" (*41*). It is not surprising, therefore, that the better educated people are much more critical of American broadcasting than those who have been unable to attend high school or college (*36*).

Statistical tendencies like the above, while suggesting that radio is the instrument for the masses rather than the élite, cannot be taken at their face value in appraising the propaganda importance of radio. By and large the more influential people themselves may be affected less by radio, but they in turn must always respond in some way to public opinion. Quantitatively at least, radio has great impact on the very people who constitute that public opinion and hence it can reach circuitously those who are not its devotees. Then any statistical generalization is an average. There are influential people who do not conform to the norm of their cultural group: they depend on the radio for the news rather than on the press. Mere listening, moreover, does not necessarily produce a change in response, especially when people are motivated in the first place to be entertained or to improve their health or status. Inconclusive studies of the effects of a serious program like the Town Hall Meeting of the Air (in which many sides of a question are rather freely discussed) have reached the tentative conclusion that people remain relatively unaffected by what they hear and instead search for and substantiate the views they have previously held (*43*).

Besides, Lazarsfeld's subjects had not grown up with radio as intimately as children in the next generation. When that latter generation has been examined, it has been found that their radio habits are different from those of adults. Perhaps these habits will persist when the children mature or perhaps they simply represent a phase of development and will be subsequently modified in the direction of their parents. In one study (*46*) it has been shown that radio rather than the press appears to introduce children to news but that, as they grow older and while they are still in school, they have a tendency to turn more and more to newspapers. For the group of children as a whole there was a slight tendency for those whose news source was predominately the newspaper to know more about the news—as measured by a paper-and-pencil questionnaire—than those who were predominately dependent on the radio, but this tendency was affected and sometimes reversed by the factors of age, sex, and intelligence. Economic or social status was found to have no effect on knowledge of news except at an early age and among the less intelligent. In another study of children (*11*) no relationship likewise was observed between economic status and amount of time spent listening to the radio. The crucial factor here seems to have been the population density of the child's neighborhood: the denser the neighborhood, the more numerous the recreational opportunities and hence the fewer radio programs that were heard.

Psychological Techniques

The radio propagandist seeks, first of all, to have his program broadcast. He must be permitted to use some station or he must be able to afford the fees involved. Only underground broadcasters can flout the rules of their society, but even they must assemble the necessary equipment and then transmit on one of the conventional wavelengths to which their audience is accustomed. In commercial radio, American stations and networks have the reverse problem to solve: they use every possible persuasive device to attract advertisers away from other media and from competitors within the radio industry itself. They carry on research which indicates the size of the "market" they are able to reach. "To all elements of the business community, these facts affirm that radio advertising today is a better investment, in terms of sales-per-dollar opportunities, than at any time in its history," one network stated at the end of a survey in 1947. Broadcasters also boastfully publicize their better-known programs to demonstrate the strength of the "market" they can offer advertisers. So much energy, in fact, is devoted to pursuing advertisers, as the Federal Communications Commission points out (25), that selling programs has become more important than writing them: "For every three writers employed by 834 broadcast stations in October, 1944, there were four salesmen employed" and "for every dollar paid to the average writer, the average salesman was paid $2.39."

After the radio propagandist has a program on the air, he is next interested in having that program perceived: propagandees must turn on their sets. To induce them to do this, certain auxiliary attitudes must be previously evoked. First and foremost is people's interest in radio as such, whether to be entertained, to hear the latest news, or otherwise to release tension. This interest of theirs, however, tends to fluctuate with the time of day, the day of the week, and the season of the year. It is known (7), for example, that in the United States fewest people listen early in the morning and that the listening peak is reached between 9 and 10 P.M. More Americans have their radio sets in operation early Sunday evening than at any other time. Evening audiences are smallest in the summer and largest in the winter.

The propagandist, however, wants people to listen to his program and to his alone. They may learn of this program's existence from friends, from a log or advertisement in the press, or from a prior announcement on some other radio program. They may then be attracted to it because of its content or performers—or because it is less unattractive than its competitors at the particular listening time. Frequently they turn on their sets merely to listen but not to a specific radio program. What they then perceive may be determined by the signal strength—for the stronger the signal of a "standard" station but *not* of one employing frequency modulation, the easier and pleasanter it usually is to listen. Otherwise their perception depends on the nature of the auxiliary response immediately evoked by whatever program they more or less fortuitously strike. The size of a program's audience is affected by the popularity of the programs which it immediately follows or precedes (*8*); in radio's parlance, the former is called an "inherited audience." In one of the studies previously mentioned (*12*) the children stated that they had found their favorite program in the following ways: recommendation by another child (42 percent), radio logs (29 percent), random dialing (24 percent), advertisements (4 percent), and advice from parents (1 percent).

In the field of printed advertising, it is relatively rare for propagandees to look for advertisements unless they have some specific incentive like discovering bargains or the name of the motion picture being exhibited at the neighborhood theater. The advertiser in newspapers or magazines, consequently, has to start almost from the very beginning each time his advertisement appears. The radio propagandist, on the other hand, can build up the prestige of his program or performers to a point where the listeners will be eagerly seated at their radio sets just before or just as the performance and its plugs begin. Then all that he must do to retain this purely perceptual advantage is to acquaint his audience with the time and station of the broadcast, a bit of learning he seeks to facilitate by keeping these conditions constant from week to week and, if possible, from season to season. He may also make every effort to attract a larger audience or the right kind of audience by having the program go on the air at a time of day and on a particular day when more people or the desired type of person is listening. After his "Hooperating" indicates that he has a popular program and has thus solved his perceptual problem, he can utilize the same program in behalf of other products he manufactures or distributes, instead of running the risk of presenting another program that must slowly build up its own following. The proposed 1947 Code of the N.A.B. recognizes and approves of this practice, but it bans the plugging of the other products through the use of "simulated spot announcements which are divorced from the program by preceding the introduction of the program itself ['cowcatchers'], or by following its apparent sign-off ['trailers' or 'hitch-hikers']."

The individual radio stations and the networks also carry on intentional propaganda in their own behalf, in order to convince listeners—and hence advertisers and advertising agents—that they and not their rivals provide the best and the greatest amount of entertainment and news. They reveal their identity and sometimes their wavelength at least twice every hour; although this information consumes only a few seconds, it is repeated so often and it is so essential for the listener to know that it is not easily forgotten. Both on the air and in the press they also advertise the features and performers to be heard and, in addition, they are not at all reluctant to add to their prestige by calling attention to their sustaining programs.

When the program has an audience, the task of the radio propagandist is then to arouse the personality responses related to his objective. People are likely to be affected when the drives associated with the auxiliary responses which causes them to listen can be reduced only by perceiving the propaganda itself. The listener who is interested in news must hear a newscast whose inevitable propaganda content can have a temporary or lasting effect upon him. The citizen who already knows how he will vote on election day but who nevertheless wants to hear the final radio appeals of both candidates can suddenly be convinced by an argument which has not previously impressed him and, as a result, he may come to a different decision. As pointed out elsewhere, the danger of enemy radio minions during the last war—like Axis Sally, Tokyo Rose, and Lord Haw Haw—was this: their chatter, innuendo, and information provided entertainment but at the same time they thus enticed their audiences to perceive the entire broadcast which in some listeners and under circumstances of extreme privation must have produced demoralizing results.

The commercial propagandist who employs bait to solve the perceptual problem frequently discovers that his audience enjoys consuming that bait but nevertheless escapes from his hook. Many, many more Americans eagerly listen to an orchestra or a comedian on a sponsored program for the purpose of being entertained than actually purchase the sponsor's product or, in fact, even listen attentively to his plug. The advertiser for his part realizes that he cannot affect everybody and is willing, for example, to entertain ten or even a hundred people in order that one of them may become a customer. He also knows, as the analysis of advertising has previously suggested, that mere acquaintance with the name of his product may not produce an immediate sale but in the long run can prove decisive.

The sponsor's plea, consequently, is inserted into the program in such a way that the listener cannot very well avoid perceiving it. The plug precedes, interrupts, and follows the program—the proposed 1947 Code of the N.A.B. abolished the obnoxious "middle commercial" only from those newscasts which are "less than fifteen minutes (14:30) in length." It may be regionalized when it is spoken by an announcer in the local station during the interruption of a network program. It may be worked into the body of the script so skilfully that it is perceived by the listener before he realizes that he is hearing propaganda of little or no interest to him. It may be spoken by an individual—like the star of the radio play—all of whose words, whether commercial or non-commercial, thrill or amuse his audience. It may be the butt of a joke, it may be presented amusingly, or it may be contained in—the writer apologizes even for mentioning this—the lyric of a jingle or a song. It may be part of a "chainbreak" which means that it is transmitted during the few seconds allocated for station identification. There are, in short, too many different methods to seduce the attention of the radio audience once it has agreed to listen.

In spite of the lure of the bait, the listener may, nevertheless, never even notice the hook, no less be caught by it. Many Americans appear to believe that the home radio playing in the background is as essential to their happiness as a roof over their heads. Whether their principal occupation at the moment is talking, reading, eating, studying, tinkering, cleaning, or even napping, they like to be dimly aware of music coming out of their receiving sets. Under these circumstances, the perception and learning of the sponsor's announcement are extremely unlikely. Even when there are no strongly competing responses—as when people listen with rapture to an opera or symphony orchestra, when they are thrilled by a soap opera or a play, when they roll with laughter over the comedian's jokes, or when they eagerly hear the latest news—listeners can still fail to hear or remember the commercial: at the crucial moment their thoughts may wander or they may discuss what they have been hearing. In a study of children (*13*), it was found that 84 percent of the group could recall correctly the hour at which programs heard the previous week had been broadcast, but only 74 percent could name the sponsor—and thus 26 percent of this juvenile audience had not even gone beyond the first or perceptual stage.

The sponsor's problems can be concisely stated in terms of three indices (*26*). He wants his "Hooperating" or "popularity index" to be high: the more people who listen, the greater are the chances that his message will be perceived. More important, he wants his "sponsor identification index" to be high: the more people who learn his message, the greater are the chances that action responses will occur. But most important of all, he wants a high "product use index": the more people who listen to his program *and* purchase his product (in comparison with those who do *not* listen), the more successful his propaganda has been.

In commercial broadcasting in the United States, moreover, there is one bit of evidence (*9*) which suggests that mere listening may increase sales. The number of people who said they used a given product was greater among those who listened to the sponsor's program than among those who did not; and it was also greater among those who listened frequently than among those who listened only occasionally. More people who listened to a program and could identify the sponsor's name, furthermore, said they used his product than was the case among those who listened but forgot his name. Surprising, however, is the fact that a greater percentage of customers was found among those who listened and forgot the sponsor's name than among those who did not listen at all.   This last finding, according to the guess of the writers, may indicate that "a program's effectiveness in influencing the behavior of listeners is quite independent of any 'conscious impression,'" but certainly the commercials must have been consciously perceived at some point during the broadcasts.   Learning took place, but evidently a stronger connection was eventually established between the sponsor's product and buying behavior than between the program and the product.   The initial purchase occurred either because the propaganda appeals on the radio had been effective or because those customers who prefer known brands experienced, as they saw the product on the shelf in a store, a vague and not necessarily "conscious" feeling of familiarity as a result of having heard the program.   This purchase then served to reinforce the bond between the product's name and buying, whereas that between the program and the product became weaker since it was not necessary to know the name of a sponsor in order to hear his program.   In addition, there may have been a selective factor at work which attracted potential or actual (if inattentive) customers to the program in the first place.   Finally the interview question concerning sponsorship may have been less capable of eliciting knowledge which existed than the one pertaining to brand patronage.

In the United States there are periodic outbursts against the length and the content of the commercial plug by listeners, by the F.C.C., and sometimes even by performers.   One of the greatest heroes of all radio time was probably an unsponsored newscaster of the American Broadcasting Company who for six months listened with profound disgust to the singing commercial which immediately preceded his program.   Then finally one morning, after enduring such a plug, he began his own report by stating: "The atrocity you have just heard is no part of this show."   The stations and the networks, therefore, are on the defensive.   They are fond of indicating that only a small fraction of the broadcast day is devoted to commercial announcements—as if a thorn in the flesh hurts less because it is in contact with only

a quantitatively small section of the skin. Somewhat ir-
relevantly and ambiguously they maintain that theirs is the
"freest" or the "best" radio system in the world. They
finance polls which purport to show by means of somewhat
biased questions that people really like to listen to advertising (*37*). Sometimes, too, with or without moral and
legal aid from the Federal Communications Commission,
they modify the regulations which they impose upon their
sponsors: they limit the amount of time devoted to commercials during a program of a given length at specified
hours of the broadcasting day or the number of commercials
permitted during a particular time period (*27*); or they
more carefully censor the content or techniques of plugs.
The N.A.B.'s proposed Code of 1947 issues the warning
that "broadcasters should take particular care in the production and presentation of commercials."

The widespread antagonism toward commercials can
have serious consequences for the radio as a propaganda instrument. The listener may deliberately refuse to listen to
commercials or he may even boycott the sponsors whose
pleas strike him as being particularly obnoxious. He may
cut down on his total listening time or perhaps, as has been
widely rumored without confirmation, throw his receiving
set out the window. He may listen only to those programs
or stations whose commercials consume a minimum of time
and whose content is not particularly offensive. In short,
the trickery employed by advertisers to solve the perceptual
problem may solve that problem for a moment or two, but
it can be so punishing that the antagonistic responses render
the propaganda unsuccessful.

Even American sponsors appreciate the fact that their
commercials are not popular. Whenever a most unusual
event occurs—and it has to be about as important as a wartime invasion, the death of a President, or Christmas Eve—
they somewhat obsequiously and with a guilty conscience
that pervades the kilocycles announce the omission of their
commercials; they thus indicate that even they possess a
sense of decorum and an acute awareness of public opinion.
Some national advertisers have responded to public criticism

and have made their announcements as brief and as dignified as the rare publicity paid for by a funeral parlor. A few have even allowed their programs to proceed without commercial interruption. Too many sympathetic tears, however, should not be shed for the poor, poor sponsor who, when he finally manages to have people perceive his propaganda, then discovers that his listeners, instead of being grateful for the entertainment he offers and for his contribution to keeping radio in private hands, resent the very message which he wants so much to deliver to them. Sponsors, let it be recalled, are willing to pay the enormous bills of broadcasting for the very obvious reason that advertising by radio pays off. It may be difficult to attract and hold a radio audience and plugs may be violently disliked, but people apparently are affected anyhow. If they were not affected, advertisers would get off the air. And there is no indication of any significant decline in the desire of business to employ radio as an advertising medium.

Some indirect evidence has been collected (6) which shows that the recall of a program two hours or less after it has been heard is promoted by factors which the broadcaster eventually can control: its length, its popularity, its age, and the network which carries it. Recalling a program is at least a first step in recalling a sponsor. Then, although an unfavorable attitude toward advertising seems to have an effect on individuals' reactions to all phases of radio and although only about one in five persons claims he really is "in favor of" radio advertisements, it seems fairly clear that most Americans, unlike this prejudiced writer, have adopted a grin-and-bear-it policy regarding commercials: they "don't particularly mind" them or they are willing to "put up" with them (37).

To evoke personality, pre-action, and action responses the commercial radio announcement resorts to techniques which do not differ appreciably from those employed in printed advertising. Similarly the methods of other forms of radio propaganda closely resemble their visual counterparts. But radio, since it is heard and not seen, has introduced a few variations of its own.

Just as an advertiser selects his printed medium on the basis of the type of reader it attracts, so the radio propagandist designs a program which can be expected to appeal to the greatest number of potential propagandees. A book or a book club is promoted on a program of recorded music. Those who like such music are undoubtedly the same people who buy serious or semi-serious books. The audience listening to a popular orchestra may also contain book-buyers, but in such smaller numbers that the cost per potential customer is greater. In addition, the serious-minded book-reading audience may be offended if a book is advertised on a program devoted to jazz, whereas the response to classical music is presumably compatible with and hence related to the pre-action response leading to book-buying. It seems that varied auxiliary responses can be evoked by any type of program but they must also function as related responses: fish in general may like many kinds of bait, but some fish are more discriminating.

The radio propagandist is able in some instances to have propagandees actually sample the action he seeks. His audience has the privilege of being able to hear the effervescence of ginger ale, the orchestra of a night club, the spontaneity of the columnist on a quiz program, the applause of the real audience, and—at least during the Bikini tests of 1946—the sound of an exploding atomic bomb. From these auditory perceptions inferences can be made concerning the similar rewards or punishments which may be anticipated from experiencing the real situation. Sometimes the inferences are validly derived (the case of the orchestra); they may be quite invalid (the ginger ale and the atomic bomb); and at other times their validity is not easy to determine (the columnist and the applauding audience). Many people are convinced that they can make innumerable deductions concerning the appearance and personality of a speaker from hearing his voice, a conviction which, when experimentally tested, turns out to be at least partially but not startlingly correct for some individuals (*4*).

Sampling on the radio has the advantage of enabling the

auxiliary responses which induced listening in the first place to function as related responses. The advertiser who wishes to attract customers to his nightclub by having an orchestra broadcast a sample of its style is in a psychologically more advantageous position than the manufacturer who explains the merit of his drug between numbers played by an orchestra. Whatever makes people like jazz may induce them to patronize a nightclub which employs a pleasant-sounding orchestra but will certainly not tempt them to buy one pill rather than another or to buy any pills at all.

The advertiser in a magazine does not beg his readers to "show your gratitude for the attractive color, the artistic illustration, and the brilliant message in this advertisement by purchasing my product." In his wildest fantasies, he does not expect his propagandees to be grateful to him for having aroused auxiliary responses; he can merely hope that those responses in some way or other will be related to the action he seeks. The advertiser on the American radio, on the other hand, sometimes blatantly asks his audience to show "your appreciation for this program by patronizing" whatever it is that is being plugged. Or the performer unblushingly asks his listeners to write him if they have enjoyed his program, and thus he reveals the kind of action he seeks in order to increase his prestige in the eyes of his station or sponsor. Frequently, the propagandist prays, it is not necessary to be quite so direct. The listener who enjoys or profits from a program day after day or week after week will involuntarily contract a kind of debt which can be discharged only by doing what the propagandist wishes. This obligation is incurred apart from the perceptual value of the program and the direct effectiveness of the plug or the appeal. Certainly some members of a radio audience must feel grateful when a program has been particularly good and express their gratitude other than by listening to the program again, praising it to others, or writing a fan letter. Patriots in the occupied countries of Europe stated at the end of the last war how deeply they appreciated the special news services supplied by the British and American stations during the occupation. Presumably an unknown number of them was thereby additionally motivated to engage in activity detrimental to the Nazis.

The reaction of the radio listener can be heightened or at least affected by others who are listening simultaneously. The others may be "present" in three forms. They may be next to the listener himself and their responses and comments can directly influence his behavior. Cantril, Gaudet, and Herzog (5), for example, have shown that some individuals believed that Orson Welles' broadcast in 1938 on "The Invasion from Mars" (which was thought by many Americans to be a genuine invasion of some sort) was merely a dramatic performance by that gifted actor until members of their families, who were seated beside them, interpreted the broadcast as a real invasion; then they were thrown into panic too. The others may be members of a studio audience whose laughter and applause may be infectious, puzzling, or just annoying. In any case, the sounds of a studio audience—whether spontaneous or controlled—can induce the listener to conform to this unrepresentative type of external public opinion. The effect increases when the sounds come not from a studio but from a real audience at a public event like a political gathering or football game that is being broadcast. The others who affect the listener, finally, may not be either visible or audible but may be the members of the radio audience whose presence the listener is able to imagine. For he realizes, in spite of the ingratiatingly personal tone some performers deliberately adopt, that he is not the sole recipient of radio's largesse. Printed media with mass circulations achieve the same effect but not quite so vividly because their readers seldom feel that the same sentence is being read by millions at precisely the same instant. When the leader of a country like the King of England or the President of the United States addresses his compatriots over a radio hook-up that reaches most of the far corners of the earth, the speaker's voice seems to possess an awesome quality: listeners know that it is being heard by so many people in so many different places.

A final psychological advantage of radio involves the

factor of primacy. News and views can be broadcast almost simultaneously, and the radio version is frequently the
first to reach large groups of people. There is evidence
from polls (*42*) which shows that at every level—including
even those at the top who ordinarily do not listen to news
over the radio—people turn to their radio sets for news
when there is an important crisis in international affairs.
Then later they may read a fuller newspaper account.

Public Address Systems

Public address systems are employed to reach people who
for various momentary reasons cannot or do not hear an
unamplified voice or a radio program. Loudspeakers are
installed at public meetings so that the speaker's words are
carried to all corners of the hall or to those congregating
outside the building. They are attached to posts on city
streets to transmit important announcements or to retrans-
mit radio programs. They are transported in trucks and
infrequently on airplanes; then some one talks through a
microphone or a record is played in order to make a brief
announcement. In peacetime political candidates sometimes
employ a mobile public address system to remind voters of
"your public duty" immediately before election day or to
prod them to attend political rallies during the campaign.
In war the equipment of many combat-propaganda teams
includes some method of voice-amplification which can reach
enemy troops at strategic moments and call upon them to
surrender.

The only unique characteristic of this propaganda medium is its method of solving the perceptual problem
through increasing the intensity of the stimulus. Intense
auditory stimuli are generally unusual, and hence people
have a strong tendency to orient themselves to the sounds.
In addition, the auxiliary responses evoked by music may
also be utilized in the interests of perception: a stirring
march is played by the mobile truck and then at regular
intervals the propaganda is emitted. The loudspeaker must
compete successfully with the ongoing responses being made

by the propagandee at the moment the sounds reach him.
He may be talking to a companion, he may listen to the
sounds just as automatically and unwillingly as he sometimes glances at a billboard, and then almost without pause
he can proceed with the conversation. Except at a public
meeting, the medium can carry only short appeals and hence
the action sought by the propagandist, if it occurs, usually
results from previously established attitudes which are
merely touched off by these auditory stimuli.

CHAPTER 20

The Media of Sight and Sound

LIKE the radio, motion pictures developed very rapidly into a mass medium of communication. They began as a curiosity in a sideshow and became within a quarter of a century a gigantic industry which in the United States alone is capitalized at over two billion dollars. Like the radio, too, they might have been employed exclusively as an educational device or in behalf of intentional propaganda, but instead they have been dedicated primarily to the promotion of entertainment. The addition of sound to the silent pictures in the late twenties served to increase their popularity (which, as a matter of fact, was showing a slight decline at the time in the United States) and hence their importance.

Many educated Americans tend to feel somewhat snobbish toward motion pictures. They and most cinema critics judge each picture in terms of their own somewhat rarefied social philosophy and esthetic standards, and they find the output of Hollywood deficient in almost all respects. Some of them are more devoted to foreign pictures either because only exceptional films are imported—the run-of-the-mill picture abroad is about as dreary as any Hollywood product— or because they demonstrate their own sophistication by claiming to appreciate the exotic. The medium, however, cannot be dismissed with a sneer: it is too powerful an instrument of education and propaganda.

During the period of the silent picture, Hollywood tended to dominate the world market. Foreign countries expressed little or no resentment because their own producers could not begin to satisfy the enormous demand for films. Then the introduction of talking pictures enabled these producers to compete with American films by offering dialogue and music in the local idiom (*37*). At the same time, politicians and educators outside the United States recognized that their peoples and those in other nations were securing an exclusively American version of entertainment. They became convinced that for purely nationalistic reasons it was necessary both to halt the flow from America and to have pictures produced at home. As a result, most major countries began to regulate or restrict their importations from Hollywood, so that at the start of the last war that flamboyant production center groaned under fifty-eight different legal restrictions pertaining to the exporting of films. In some countries, the government itself either produced or aided in the production of motion pictures, and thus the film was tied to the official propaganda machine. Right before and during the war, Hollywood had to face real competition from British companies not only throughout the British Empire but also, to a much lesser degree, in the United States. One of the first "cultural" steps undertaken by liberated European countries was to revive, if possible, their motion picture industries. The Soviet Union has consistently exported pictures which add to the glory of Russia and communism, and in general it has been willing to accept only those foreign pictures which provide escapist entertainment or illustrate some deficiency in the capitalist world.

In the United States the motion picture industry, like the press and radio, shows an increasing trend toward centralization (*19*). The bulk of the production has been controlled by five companies (Loew's or MGM, Paramount, RKO, Twentieth Century-Fox, and Warner Brothers) and three satellites (Columbia, Universal, and United Artists). These eight companies:

1. Produce ordinarily over 50 percent of all pictures and almost all of those expensive pictures which draw large audiences and are most profitable (*22*).

2. Have contracts with the most popular actors and actresses.

3. Own or control the theaters which attract the bulk of the box-office receipts.

4. Possess important interests in music publishers, recording companies, and radio stations. When television looked as a rival, they began to invest in this medium.

The control of the eight companies over the distribution of films has been exercised in various ways:

1. They have specified the theaters at which first-run pictures can be shown as well as the length of time which must elapse before such pictures can be exhibited elsewhere.

2. They have indicated the day of the week when the theater owner is permitted to show a specific picture. Such a regulation is important because, for example, almost 50 percent of movie attendance occurs on Saturdays and Sundays.

3. Before the practice of "block-booking" was outlawed by the courts in 1946, they compelled exhibitors to contract for a series of unproduced and sometimes unknown pictures; if the exhibitors refused to sign such a contract, they were cut off from the company's list or could not obtain other pictures they wished to present.

About 37 percent of the motion picture theaters have been in one-theater towns and hence have no local competition. Another 8 percent have been in two-theater communities, but it is estimated that about three-quarters of these are operated by the same individuals (*20*). There have been in the neighborhood of from sixty to seventy independent producers in the United States, most of whose products, however, are exhibited through the major companies. During and immediately after the last war, prominent motion picture stars established so-called independent companies with the consent of the executives for whom they had been working, in order to reduce federal taxes by having their profit classified as a capital gain rather than as personal income; but this practice was subsequently outlawed by the federal government whose anti-trust suit against the major companies reached the Supreme Court in 1948.

Potentially more important or at least as important as any Hollywood feature is the educational film. Such a film can be roughly defined as a motion picture which is exhibited by someone who calls himself an educator or an instructor in behalf of what he considers to be education or training; the exhibition, moreover, usually occurs inside a public building like a school and not in a commercial theater. Naturally this pragmatic definition is glib and inadequate, for films projected in theaters may also contain "education," and "educational" films may be entertaining. Within the last few decades there has been a marked increase in the number of educational films. They have as their objective the teaching of a particular skill, such as some of the extraordinarily excellent films employed by the United States Army during the last war to help men learn some of the details of soldiering. They impart specific knowledge which has reached a scientific stage, such as films on the physiology of the human organism which are shown in schools. They are documentaries which explain how a social institution functions or why a particular social problem exists; sometimes newsreels fall in this category. They are pictures with a socially approved objective, such as a series of animated cartoons by Disney on malaria control, vaccination, and other medical subjects which were distributed in Latin America during the last war. Or they are features or adaptations of features which are displayed in schools in order to provoke discussion on a social problem.

Both educational and propaganda objectives can also be attained through the use of film-strips. These are a series of still photographs or drawings which are projected without benefit of sound upon a screen in the manner of the old "magic lantern." The text can be provided on the film or the operator may say whatever he wishes. During the last war this medium was employed by American propagandists in foreign areas that lacked suitable movie equipment.

Motion Picture Propaganda

An analysis of motion picture propaganda immediately heads straight into the generalization which has been repeated so frequently throughout this book: motion pictures affect public opinion and public opinion affects motion pictures. Loose talk occurs whenever a critic, a student, or a producer focuses on one half of the generalization and neglects or forgets the other. It is said, for example, that Hollywood has given people outside the United States a false conception of this country: it has perpetuated innumerable myths involving Indians, gangsters, immorality, streets paved with gold, dollar-chasing, superficiality, poor taste, etc. Two careful observers like White and Leigh (*38*) do not present any evidence for their contention that "the consensus of Americans who lived and traveled abroad during the period between the wars seems to be that American movies have hindered more than furthered an understanding of us." This is the popular judgment, but it has never been substantiated. It neglects to mention that foreigners already had inaccurate ideas about the United States before they saw Hollywood films and that they have continued to receive such ideas from other sources, including books, their own press, emigrants, American tourists, etc. It fails to point out that Hollywood produced misleading films because people both at home and abroad liked them and hence expected the United States to be portrayed in one way and not in another.

In non-democratic countries, where the film industry has been under direct control of the state, motion pictures have been deliberately designed as propaganda vehicles with a thick sugar-coating of entertainment. Soviet pictures place great emphasis upon the glorification of Russia's past, especially that portion of her history which fits or can be made to fit into current communist theories concerning the reasons for her greatness. Events leading up to and including the seizure of power by the Communist party in 1917 have been dramatized again and again and always as world-shaking epics.

Before and during the last war Japanese pictures conformed to the prevailing ideology concerning the need for all good Japanese to cooperate with the Empire in its effort to establish the Greater East Asia Co-Prosperity Sphere and to make the necessary sacrifices in behalf of the emperor. Most of the films, which the writer at any rate had the opportunity to see, were not at all stirring to an occidental and sometimes produced among non-Japanese quite the reverse reaction intended by the producer. In one picture called *The Chocolate Wrapper,* for example, the hero was drafted away from his wife and children for whom he had only genuine and moving devotion; he then had to endure the miseries and hardships of military life; he was shipped to fight in China where his discomfort increased; the enemy was never mentioned nor pictured; the last glimpse of the hero before he was killed in battle showed him lonely and homesick; his wife and his oldest son broke into tears when news of his death reached them; and the only somewhat joyful event occurred at the end of the film when that oldest son's collection of chocolate wrappers which his father had been sending him from the battlefields won a candy manufacturer's prize. The picture seemed to the writer to be one of the most effective indictments of war which he has ever seen, for war—and not the Chinese—appeared to be the real villain of the story. Evidently a Japanese audience was expected to respond by feeling more grateful to its armed forces and more determined to sacrifice itself, if necessary, for the good of Japan and the emperor. Japanese newsreels, on the other hand, closely resembled those produced in any European country or in the United States, except of course for their pro-Japanese slant.

Nazi feature pictures were of two distinct types. On the one hand there were the straight propaganda films which paid tribute to the Nazi party and the German way of life. On the other hand, there was the comedy and musical-comedy picture which was devoid of political content and ideology and which might have been produced in Hollywood. The latter evidently was supposed to provide the entertainment which Germans sought when they went to the movies (but then the newsreel's blatant propaganda struck them as they awaited the feature) and was also exported to help the Nazis secure much needed financial credits abroad. There was almost never a mixture of the two types. German producers, moreover, developed the documentary and the newsreel as extremely effective instruments of psychological warfare. Films showing the march of the German armies across Poland, Norway, the Low Countries, and France, for example, were cleverly utilized to impress anxious and wavering neutrals with Germany's strength. These films were so dramatically and artistically constructed that they were able to create momentary terror even among Harvard University and Radcliffe College students who were safely seated in a theater in Cambridge, Massachusetts, in the early part of 1941 (*8*).

By and large, film producers in democratic countries have intentionally avoided pictures which can be labelled propagandistic because they have thought of their medium as a vehicle of entertainment. This means, in turn, that the propaganda content of pictures has been mostly unintentional. Producers swim with the tide of public opinion in order to attract as many customers as possible; Hollywood, Rosten (*31*) points out, is dedicated to "the proposition that maximum profits reward maximum innocuousness." American newsreel companies, for example, seem to believe that the most newsworthy events to photograph continuously are horse races, bathing beauty contests, and the exotic foibles of simple people. Evidently their market surveys suggest to them that such events—rather than the myriad of more socially significant occurrences—evoke the kind of response which audiences wish to experience while seeing a newsreel. In the United States both world wars stimulated the production of feature pictures which presented Germany and especially her leaders in an unfavorable light, and the iniquity of the Japanese was stressed during the second catastrophe. This intentional propaganda continued only as long as the films remained popular. Anti-Nazi pictures decreased in number the moment box-office receipts seemed to demonstrate to Hollywood that people wanted to escape from the frustrations and anxieties of the conflict and not to be given additional reasons for cooperating more vigorously with the war effort.

Competition is keen among producers and exhibitors,

and therefore the various Hollywood companies sometimes seek an advantage for themselves by producing slightly unusual pictures. There have been films lashing out against chain gangs, racketeers, antisemitism, the white slave trade, the use of drugs, etc.; and relatively undistorted biographies of historical characters have been screened. The producers of such films risk some money and a portion of their reputations because they hope that people will admire their pioneering, be entertained, and thus contribute anyway to the jackpot. The risk can never be too great, simply because feature pictures are very expensive to produce. The producers of documentary and educational films, on the other hand, have shown much more social courage: their capital investment is less.

The American motion picture industry is surrounded and surrounds itself with a long series of censorship regulations, the net effect of which is intentional and unintentional propaganda in behalf of what can be called prevailing standards of good taste or morality. Almost every organized group in the United States is set to pounce upon a picture and claim that its treatment of some theme, person, or symbol is unfair, inaccurate, or perilous. Hollywood apologists (*e.g.,* 36) are fond of recalling one particular incident to illustrate that almost any part of a film is likely to offend some group in American society. A number of years ago, the story goes, a comedian in a picture used the unbrilliant simile of "as thick as flies in a Greek restaurant." The very next day after the picture was shown in New York City, sixteen members of the American Society of Greek Restaurateurs called upon an official of the motion picture industry to protest formally against this reference to their popular reputation, a reputation they considered wholly unjustified and which, they said, they had been trying for years to change. Similarly, as Rosten (*32*) recalls, indignation was expressed by an association of silver fox breeders "because in one picture a Negress was seen wearing a silver fox." The owners of Greek restaurants and the breeders of silver fox, with all due respect to them and their products, are not an important group from Hollywood's viewpoint since their number is relatively small. But when organizations like the Legion of Decency, the Boy Scouts of America, and the General Federation of Women's Clubs begin to find fault with films, then Hollywood must begin to worry: too many movie patrons are involved.

The American motion picture industry, therefore, complains that almost any theme or scene or line in a film is likely to provoke what is called a "kick-back," and kickbacks can result in boycotts and diminished box-office receipts. Only bankers, physicians, and business men appear to show no serious concern about how their professions are portrayed in motion pictures and hence do not stand ready to cut into Hollywood's profits if a slur or an innuendo is cast in their direction. One official of the Motion Picture Association of America has written humorously but desperately:

> If we paid serious attention to one tenth of one percent of what looks like legitimate protest, it would be utterly impossible for us to make any pictures at all, or have any kind of villain unless he were a native born, white, American citizen, without a job and without political, social, religious, or fraternal affiliation of any kind (*23*).

Six important states—Kansas, Maryland, New York, Ohio, Pennsylvania, and Virginia—as well as seventeen major cities from Atlanta to Seattle have their own censorship boards which function regularly or sporadically. Massachusetts examines only those pictures which are shown on Sundays! At any moment, too, there is always the possibility that some other state or community will decide that a film or its promotion is immoral, corrupting, or subversive. As a result, the producer must try to be certain that he does not flaunt one or more of these red lights. Since films are distributed on a country-wide basis, regulations in any one state or city virtually affect the entire output.

There is another red light which a Hollywood producer cannot ignore: the foreign censor. Before the last war, some films with anti-fascists motifs were either drastically cut or eliminated altogether. The foreign governments concerned had filed protests that they were about to be maligned, or the producers themselves decided that the pictures would invite such protests or be banned abroad. Hollywood remains afraid of portraying characters or situations in a way which will offend its existing foreign market: why jeopardize a source of revenue?

American producers and directors attempt to anticipate "kick-backs" and censorship regulations by submitting each script before it is produced and each picture before it is exhibited to their own Motion Picture Association of America which was known first as the Hays and then as the Johnson Office. The film industry established this organization in 1922 at a time when its reputation was suffering from what were considered low-grade and immoral pictures. In addition, too many famous actors and actresses were receiving publicity by deviating from the sexual mores. The advance submission of the script prevents a wasteful expenditure of money, and advance censoring helps greatly to eliminate those sections that can produce public outcries. The Association in turn operates under an occasionally revised "Code to Govern the Making of Motion and Talking Pictures." This Code should be examined in some detail because its one section containing the regulations is also a precise summary of Hollywood's negative propaganda themes and because the other section supplying the "reasons" for those regulations dramatically suggests how the industry officially diagnoses American public opinion and customs. According to Inglis (*24*), although its original author was a Jesuit priest and although its chief enforcement officer has been a Catholic layman, the Code is "no more peculiarly Catholic than it is Baptist or Presbyterian or Jewish": it "represents a common denominator of all morally conservative points of view."

The Code begins with a Preamble, the first three paragraphs of which are quoted in full:

Motion picture producers recognize the high trust and confidence which have been placed in them by the people of the world and which have made motion pictures a universal form of entertainment.

They recognize their responsibility to the public because of this trust and because entertainment and art are important influences in the life of a nation.

Hence, though regarding motion pictures primarily as entertainment without any explicit purpose of teaching or propaganda, they know that the motion picture within its own field of entertainment may be directly responsibility for spiritual or moral progress, for higher types of social life, and for much correct thinking.

Here is frank recognition that a film can function not only as a source of entertainment but also as a propaganda and educational vehicle, although naturally the phrasing is very lofty. The "reasons" offered for this Preamble are many, and they seek to justify the need for censorship. Three points are made:

1. "Theatrical motion pictures . . . are primarily to be regarded as entertainment." "Entertainment," however, "can be of a character either helpful or harmful to the human race" and, consequently, "the moral importance of entertainment is something which has been universally recognized."

2. "Motion pictures are very important as art," but art like entertainment "can be morally good, lifting men to higher levels" or it "can be morally evil in its effects." "Morally evil" effects can be seen "clearly enough" in the case of "unclean art, indecent books, suggestive drama." Art is never "unmoral" for two reasons: it is "the product of some person's mind, and the intention of that mind was either good or bad morally when it produced the thing"; and it "has its effect upon those who come into contact with it." In particular, motion pictures "reproduce the morality of the men who use the pictures as a medium for the expression of their ideas and ideals" and "they affect the moral standards of those who, through the screen, take in these ideas and ideals."

3. For eight reasons, motion pictures have "special moral obligations" to the public. One: they appeal "at once to every class." Two: they reach "places unpenetrated by other forms of art." Three: "it is difficult to produce films intended for only certain classes of people." Four, five and six: they differ from "book material," "the newspaper," and "a play" in respect to their contents, their techniques of presentation, and the kind and size of the audience they reach. Seven: "Small communities, remote from sophistication and from the hardening process which often takes place in the ethical and moral standards of groups in larger cities, are easily and readily reached by any sort of film." And eight: "The grandeur of mass settings, large action, spectacular features, etc., affects and arouses more intensely the emotional side of the audience."

The main body of the Code is introduced by three "General Principles" which are vague and really general enough to inhibit even the most crusading of Hollywood producers:

1. No picture shall be produced which will lower the moral standards of those who see it. Hence the sympathy of the audience shall never be thrown to the side of crime, wrong-doing, evil or sin.

2. Correct standards of life, subject only to the requirements of drama and entertainment, shall be presented.

3. Law, natural or human, shall not be ridiculed, nor shall sympathy be created for its violation.

"Particular Applications" of the principles then follow. These are the subjects covered: "Crimes Against the Law," "Sex," "Vulgarity," "Obscenity," "Profanity," "Costume," "Dances," "Religion," "Locations" ("The treatment of bedrooms must be governed by good taste and delicacy"), "National Feelings," "Titles" (which shall not be "salacious, indecent, or obscene"), and seven "Repellent Subjects"—ranging from "third degree methods" to "the sale of women"—which "must be treated within the careful limits of good taste." A few scattered and fairly typical quotations from the "Reasons" section of the Code reveal how difficult it is to rationalize the restrictions:

By natural law is understood the law which is written in the hearts of all mankind, the great underlying principles of right and justice dictated by conscience.

Even within the limits of pure love, certain facts have been universally regarded by lawmakers as outside the limits of safe presentation.

The effect of nudity or semi-nudity upon the normal man or woman, and much more upon the young and upon immature persons, has been honestly recognized by all lawmakers and moralists.

The reason why ministers of religion may not be comic characters or villains is simply because the attitude taken toward them may easily become the attitude taken toward religion in general.

The just rights, history, and feelings of any nation are entitled to most careful consideration and respectful treatment.

The Code is not easy to interpret. Certain matters directly related to sex—"scenes of passion," "seduction or rape," and "undressing scenes"—for example, are not permitted "save where essential to the plot." What does "essential" mean? It is conceivable that one of these subjects can be considered "essential" to a particular plot; but why, it is legitimate to ask, was it necessary to select that plot in the first place especially when one of its ingredients, according to the Code, will shake the very foundation of society? What is striking psychologically about the Code is that almost all of the subjects declared taboo or to be accorded careful treatment are the very ones which attract people in our society. The attraction they may not acknowledge even to themselves, or it may represent a drive in deadly conflict with other drives, but it is present in some form. Virtually every producer knows that this is so and hence is always tempted to break the Code or come as close to breaking it as the Association, the censorship boards, various social groups, and his own conscience will permit. A picture which is daring in terms of the Code's standards is likely to be a box-office success. The Code, then, seeks to express the conventional standards of our society; the productions reflect the Code but not too faithfully.

When an American producer begins work on a picture, therefore, he is faced with certain restrictions but within those restrictions he can select a relatively wide variety of plots and themes. He must make a diagnosis of what the public reaction is going to be to a particular story. This reaction he can estimate on the basis of his experience and intuition, or he can have it studied systematically through a survey organization like Gallup's Audience Research Institute. He may also pay relatively little attention to the story as such because he feels confident that the reputation of the featured actor or actress, the lavishness of the production, or the fame of the story (whether from the Bible, a best seller, or a topical event) will almost guarantee a sufficient return on his investment.

The few published analyses which have been made of American feature pictures reveal that Hollywood indeed is portraying an unrepresentative sample of American people and of the situations which normally confront the general population. Jones (*26*), for example, examined 100 Hollywood features of all types which were released between April, 1941, and February, 1942:

Of the 188 major characters in these pictures, 126 were males. Three out of five were "independent adults" who were "economically established, free of parental influence, and with definitely established social and economic responsibilities." In addition, 46 percent were wealthy or well-to-do, 32 percent had moderate wealth, 17 percent were poor or destitute, and 5 percent could not be classified. In respect to marital status, 70 percent were single, 19 percent married, 5 percent were divorced or separated or widowed, and 6 percent were "single with a promise of marriage throughout most of the story." Eighty-one percent were Americans.

This sample of character types certainly does not reflect the American population as it is known to the Bureau of the Census, whose function, however, no one ever imagines Hollywood is assuming. These figures are significant not so much because they represent distortions of American life but because they indicate the kinds of individuals with whom the audience wishes and is able to identify itself. Most Americans derive satisfaction from seeing wealthy characters portrayed on the screen.

Mrs. Jones in the same study also attempted to discover the dominating drives within the 188 major characters and, sure enough, "love" led all the rest. Almost 80 percent of the females and 64 percent of the males—an over-all average of 68 percent—craved love, and about 95 percent of them wanted that love for themselves. One-third of the women and less than 12 percent of the men, moreover, were depicted as being dominated by love alone and by no other drive. The remaining drives were classified as follows: fame, reputation, prestige (26 percent); health, bodily integrity, safety of life (16 percent); way of life (14 percent); money or material goods (10 percent); and devotion to duty (9 percent). Hollywood's addiction to the "happy ending" is shown by the fact that 61 percent of the characters had their drives reduced by being able to make the goal response they were depicted as seeking; 10 percent were frustrated; 14 percent experienced gratification of some drives and frustration of others; and in 5 percent of the cases the investigator could not decide whether the characters relaxed or remained tense, or it seemed as though they had begun to strive toward other goals. Again neither the motivation ascribed to the characters nor their success at achieving what they wished is typical of the vast majority of Americans, but it is probably true that Hollywood is portraying a way of life which Americans like to observe because so few of them can follow it.

The great themes of the American motion pictures are those which pay tribute to the activities and people preferred by most Americans. They may be summarized, with minor loans from those already formulated by Dale (*17*) and Rosten (*33*), as follows:

Love

Love conquers all, including the individual's background, past history, and misunderstanding.

Love is noble and what is done in the name of love deserves respect or at least sympathy.

Mother love is sacred and so is the family.

A mother is a man's or a woman's best friend, but a mother-in-law is not.

First love is a wonderful thing.

Sex and saintliness don't mix.

Usually marriage solves all problems because marriages should be based on love; but sometimes the problems remain unsolved for a spell until they are solved.

Human nature

Wars are caused by bad people and these bad people should be punished.

Optimism is better than pessimism.

People are either good or bad.

There's a spark of good in every man.

Comedians have their serious side; they, too, are human like you and me.

Men like to be flattered; so do women; so do children; so do animals—the cravings of plants and inanimate objects cannot be so easily specified even in Hollywood.

People are always consistent, or at least consistently inconsistent.

Wisdom is apt to come from the mouths of babes or old men or from anyone who is not expected to be wise.

It's the individual who makes the world go round.

Men commit crimes because they are bad; they are responsible for the crimes; they deserve to be punished; but sometimes criminals have admirable qualities.

Social goals

A go-getter can rise in the economic and social scale if he perseveres; perhaps he needs a little luck too.

Luck, virtue, and good will are more important virtues than skill, intelligence, or talent.

Self-sacrifice is rewarded, selfishness is punished—and they jolly well should be.

The wages of sin are punishment.

The luxuries of life are most desirable, but money can't buy everything.

The evil that men do should be forgotten when they die.

The best man and the most beautiful and/or decent woman always win.

A man can live by his wits, but he should not forget his obligations to society.

A college education isn't necessary to be a success in polite or almost any kind of society.

Revenge is justified, provided it is honorable.

History

It must have been wonderful to be alive in pioneer days.

The history of America is glorious and without blemish.

Great men were human after all.

History is made and changed by great men and little incidents.

Ethnic groups

America is unquestionably the greatest country in the world in every conceivable respect; everyone except bad people or stupid foreigners agrees that this is so.

Foreigners are either very dangerous or very stupid; or they are very harmless or very smart; or at least whatever they are they are very strange.

Negro men are almost always servants and almost always funny and lazy; Negro women are always good cooks.

Swedes in America are either sailors or janitors.

Occupational groups

Policemen tend to be stupid, but detectives are very bright.

Artists are queer ducks.

Professors are impractical.

Scientists can produce miracles overnight.

Physicians and ministers do only good in the world.

The reader is invited to add to this incomplete list or to formulate one of his own. Such a task is both interesting and rewarding for at least two reasons. In the first place, insight is obtained into a vague but important aspect of public opinion which frequently is ignored because the thoughts appear vague or untrue. In 1935, for example, the Lynds re-examined sociologically the midwestern city in the United States they had called Middletown on their first visit ten years before. One of the useful tasks they performed was to assemble the prevailing ideologies of the inhabitants (*30*). There is a striking parallel between many of the ideologies they noted and the dominant themes of the motion pictures. What people believe they wish to see in the movies and what they see in the movies they come to believe. These beliefs are part fantasy, part fact; each man in his way secures comfort from them; and the movies increase their own revenue by reinforcing them.

The detection of the central themes in motion pictures, moreover, constitutes the first important step in the analysis of film propaganda. Details of each plot of course vary (or otherwise Hollywood productions would in fact be about as identical as they sometimes appear to be), but the underlying motifs do not change appreciably. When there are changes, it may be that public opinion itself is undergoing a modification which is momentary or enduring. By teasing the underlying themes out of the pictures, the analyst is in a position to proceed and determine how a particular picture seeks, intentionally or unintentionally, to carry on its propaganda.

There is no question that motion pictures constitute an important propaganda vehicle in modern society. In the United States, for example, it is estimated (*25*) that there are approximately sixty-five million paid admissions each week—other sources (*9*) place the figure closer to a hundred million. This does not mean that a similar number of people sees a picture each week since the figures include many who go more than once a week. Of those not too young, old, or sick to enter a motion picture house, about 70 percent attend "once in three weeks or oftener" (*25*). Attendance also fluctuates with the individual's social group. Probably those at the extreme ends of the social-class ladder go less frequently, the lower class because they cannot afford to and the upper class because they have many alternate forms of entertainment at their disposal. People in rural areas are not so devoted to movies as those in urban areas: they have fewer theaters near them and generally travel to town only once a week or so. In the late 1930's when Mr. Will Hays was "czar" of the motion picture industry, he bemoaned the fact that "we are far from the saturation point in movie attendance" (*35*). For those who do go regularly, however, the "habit" may begin between the ages of five and eight and is fairly firmly established even before adolescence (*18*). It is thought (*9*) that two-thirds of motion picture patrons are below the age of 30.

The precise effects of motion pictures are not completely known, because research has been inadequate and because it is almost impossible to disentangle this medium from all other media and social forces which simultaneously affect a population. Right before the movies acquired sound, the Payne Fund in the United States conducted a series of studies which aimed to estimate the influence of motion pictures on children. The dozen monographs published in 1933 have been conveniently and competently summarized by Charters (*10*) and therefore references are made only to that summary. In brief, the research suggested that motion pictures have effects upon knowledge, attitudes, emotions, and behavior but not in an unequivocal fashion:

1. *Knowledge*

By the time children reached the age of 15 or 16, they tended to remember about 90 percent of the details of a picture recalled by superior adults, and they tended only slowly to forget what they had seen. Whereas younger children were prone to remember items involving sports, conversation, crime, and fighting, adolescents concentrated on beauty hints, clothes, mannerisms, and love techniques (*11*). Motion pictures, therefore, can be a source of information and misinformation and what is remembered depends to a certain extent on the interests of the audience.

2. *Attitude*

Children who were regular patrons of the movies had a greater tendency to admire cowboys, popular actors, dancers, and chorus girls. The irregular patrons were more interested in serious individuals like medical students and college professors. There were no significant differences in the two groups' judgments concerning, for example, athletes, Chinese, robbers, gangsters, marriage, and sex (*12*). In addition, the attitudes of children toward Germans, Chinese, war, prohibition, gambling, capital punishment, etc., were measured before and after they saw films dealing with those subjects. Changes in attitude were recorded. Two or more pictures on the same subject, furthermore, had a greater effect than one, and the effect persisted in some children over an eighteen-month period (*13*). Motion pictures, therefore, can change some attitudes, but leave others unaffected; and some individuals are influenced, while others are not.

3. *Emotions*

Not unexpectedly, motion pictures produced emotional responses as measured by changes in heart and respiratory rate and the functioning of the autonomic nervous system; by what the children themselves reported; and by an increase in subsequent movements during sleep. Most of the effects, however, were not dramatic. Boys between the ages of six and nineteen, for example, showed an increase in sleep movements after seeing a motion picture approximately equivalent for some of them to those occurring after going to bed at midnight rather than at 9 o'clock or after drinking a cup of coffee before bed time (*14*). Motion pictures, therefore, produce emotional responses, but so do a great many other social stimuli.

4. *Behavior*

Children who attended motion pictures from four to five times per week were lower in deportment, poorer in school work, less emotionally stable, and more popular among their contemporaries than those who went only twice a month or less. There were, however, no significant differences between the two groups in respect to honesty, persistence, moral knowledge, and suggestibility (*15*). Aside from technical questions which may be raised concerning the extent to which the two groups were equated in all respects other than attendance at motion pictures and concerning the validity of the methods employed to measure the children's behavior, it is also necessary to inquire whether the differences resulted from going or not going to the movies. A child's school work, for example, may be poor because he spends too much time in motion picture theaters instead of studying, or he may go to the movies frequently because he has little interest in studying and hence has more free time to do so. Delinquents went to the movies frequently and, according to their own testimony, were affected somewhat by what they saw (*16*) ; such a finding, however, certainly does not prove that motion pictures are the "cause" of the delinquent acts. The motion pictures, therefore, may affect behavior as a contributing factor.

The monumental research project on motion pictures and, to a lesser degree, on other media, which was conducted for the Information and Education Division of the American War Department during the last war by Hovland, Lumsdaine, Sheffield and their associates (*21*) has been frequently mentioned as propaganda was being analyzed in previous chapters. At this point a brief summary of other results from their project will be given as an aid in understanding film propaganda. Although the results tend more or less to agree with the interpretation of those derived from the Payne studies, they are sounder than any heretofore produced. The investigators displayed a maximum of statistical sophistication and evolved experimental designs from which conclusions could be validly drawn. They never studied, for example, the effect of a film by examining only an experimental group to which the picture had been exhibited. Instead they always sought to examine simultaneously a comparable control group which had not seen the film and, whenever possible, they measured both groups before and after the experimental one had been exposed to the film.

A training film on map reading, for example, could efficiently transmit definitions and general concepts, but such a film did not help the men apply what they had learned to specific situations. On the whole men could learn facts equally well from a motion picture or a film strip. In one instance, the film strip proved more effective because its particular pedagogical technique was superior to that of the motion picture. More was learned from a film if an instructor gave an explanation beforehand concerning its contents or if he reviewed its contents afterwards. Preliminary instruction, moreover, was more efficient than a review at the end: it clarified in advance many of the points in the film and it also stimulated men's interests in what they were to see, so that they learned more even about those points which the instructor had not mentioned. Here, then, is evidence that some factual material can be learned from perceiving a motion picture, but that actual performance may not be improved. It is clear, too, that the medium has advantages as a teaching tool only when its techniques are good and when the audience is properly motivated to learn.

Studies were made of men's reactions to a series of films called "Why We Fight" which sought to give the American version of why and how this country entered World War II as well as of the principles behind the conflict. A distinction was drawn by the investigators between the "facts" of the films and the opinions or attitudes related or not related to the events portrayed therein. The knowledge of the soldier audience was clearly affected by the motion pictures: the men had a strong tendency to learn what the producers of the films wished them to learn whether it was a thought like "the heavy bombing attacks on Britain were part of an attempt by the Nazis to invade and conquer Britain" or one like "September 18, 1931, marks the date of the Jap invasion of Manchuria." Nine weeks after the pictures had been seen, however, few men remembered what they had learned.

The effect of the films on the audience's attitude was less dramatic. A picture, "The Battle of Britain," which showed how the British resisted German air attacks in the fall of 1940, did *not* make more men feel that "the British are doing all they possibly can to win the war" or that "the British are doing their fair share of the fighting." On the other hand, one called "Prelude to War," which portrayed the aggressive policies and practices of the Axis countries, convinced some men of the strength of the German air and ground forces and of the correctness of the statement that the Nazis would try to "close all our churches and make everyone worship Hitler" if they were ever able to defeat the United States. The same film, however, did not induce more men to believe that "Germany, Italy, and Japan could not have been stopped from conquering the world without our going to war," nor did it significantly increase the number who agreed that "when the war is over we must see to it that the German people can never again exist as a nation." The films, in short, could affect knowledge without affecting attitude and the effect on attitude, when there was one, tended to be smaller than that on knowledge.

The effect on attitude, it was shown in addition, varied over a period of nine weeks. On some issues the same proportion of men maintained the same attitude; on others, the proportion decreased, which seemed to show that the effect was only temporary; and on still others the proportion increased. The increase suggests that the reactions to motion pictures can be delayed and that the learning of a general attitude may require time.

Finally, men's "morale" was measured by a questionnaire which asked them, for example, to rate the ésprit of their company or to indicate their willingness to select overseas duty rather than remain in the United States. The orientation pictures did not appreciably affect their answers. It would seem, therefore, that films could change knowledge without affecting attitudes or this verbal behavior called "morale" and that, even when they did change attitudes, "morale" was not necessarily affected. Pre-action responses, in different words, could be learned but action did not necessarily follow. For action depended on more than changes in knowledge and attitude.

Motion pictures, according to these findings in their entirety, can lay the psychological groundwork for certain types of action without inducing that action. It is dangerous, however, to apply this generalization to the normal, civilian population which sees commercial films. In the first place, all of the subjects in the War Department studies were males of combat age; conceivably but not at all probably, younger and older males as well as females may react differently. They were all Americans, and there may be something distinctive about the responses evoked by films in this society in comparison with their effects upon people in

Borneo or Belgium. Most of the pictures, moreover, were seen as part of the Army's regular routine. Perhaps the element of compulsion affected the men's reactions. Most important of all, the men in these investigations as well as the children in some of the Payne studies had only a relatively brief contact with the films. Ordinarily intentional and unintentional propaganda is repeated during years of seeing motion pictures, not simply for one or two performances. The cumulative effect of motion pictures—not after nine weeks or eighteen months but after years—can still be tremendous, although the influence of any one picture by itself is not startling. The War Department films, as the investigators themselves point out, frequently did not contain the stimuli which might be expected to evoke related personality responses, and they were seeking to change attitudes and actions of crucial importance to men at the time. Commercial films, on the other hand, eventually run almost the entire gamut of social stimuli: the learning opportunities are much more extensive. All types of attitudes are involved, both the crucial and the trivial, and these can be gradually but thoroughly reinforced before they are expressed in action.

Psychological Techniques of Motion Pictures

Most motion picture propagandists must initially solve the perceptual problem of inducing people to enter the building in which the picture is projected. The entertainment value of the films is so universally recognized in modern societies that little or no propaganda is required to convince people that motion pictures are a source of drive-reduction. Sporadic attempts are made in the United States to increase the business of commercial theaters through advertisements and publicity which pay tribute to the entertainment offered by movies as well as to their stabilizing and respectable nature. Such propaganda has been stimulated by the competing and less expensive entertainment offered by the radio. The theater owner, whose overhead costs remain more or less constant, makes every effort to lure more people into his palace on nights when attendance is small: week-day admission charges are lower, sometimes better known films are exhibited (with inferior pictures being relegated to weekends when people may be expected to come anyhow), and variations of a lottery are scheduled. Patrons are assured that the broadcasting of an important event like a prize fight can also be heard from the stage of the theater.

Much of commercial sub-propaganda, however, is devoted to publicizing not the motion picture industry in general but particular productions. All pictures are advertised in extravagantly laudatory and hence almost meaningless "previews" which the patron must perceive if he sits through an entire performance. Picture titles and frequently the names of their principal actors shine out from the marquee of the theater and are mentioned unblushingly on posters in front of the theater. The local newspaper carries an advertisement and sometimes also free publicity and reviews about them. Except for the marquee, these vehicles can stress almost any aspect of the film: its unusual title, the book or play from which the story has been adapted, almost certainly the featured players, favorable reviews quoted in or out of context, the cost of the production, the general theme, the ban imposed elsewhere, and even the names of the author of the script, the composer of the music, the producer, or the director. A song in the picture is heavily plugged, and by neither a coincidence nor a miracle does it often come to pass that its title is the same as that of the picture. In the United States the star is an especially important stimulus which provokes interest in a picture because movie patrons identify themselves so easily with him or her. A vast jungle of publicity, consequently, is sown to build up and then reinforce appropriately favorable and exciting responses. Prominent actors and actresses and those wishing to become prominent, therefore, have their own publicity agents who are aided by the studio's agents to inundate the press and magazines with pictures of their clients and with news of their everyday but most unusual and bizarre lives. The love life of the Hollywood notables receives its full measure of synthetic limelight, but equally important in an atomic age is considered a star's preferences for rhubarb or for being alone. Motion picture magazines exist which are devoted exclusively to idolizing every aspect of Hollywood and the motion picture industry. It has been estimated (*34*) that before the last war more newspaper reporters and columnists were assigned to Hollywood than to any other city in the United States except New York and Washington.

The publicity for a picture frequently begins before its script has ever been written, especially when the producer has decided to invest a significant portion of his budget. Each preliminary detail—the cost of the story, the search for and the finding of the stars, the anticipated cost, etc.— is described breathlessly and in great detail by the company's publicity agents, is more or less dutifully reported by the press, and is certainly trumpeted by the motion picture magazines. During production the publicity flood continues: incidents on the set, minor or major illnesses of the players, witty and not so witty observations by any of the people associated with the picture, etc., are the materials which are calculated to evoke expectancy among movie patrons and which cause them, at any rate, to learn of the film's existence *in utero*. A glittering "world premiere," which usually occurs in Hollywood or a large city but which sometimes "honors" some small site mentioned in the picture, is followed by a national advertising campaign to prepare people for the great moment when the picture will reach their community. Throughout the campaign the special brand of newspaper and radio columnist who specializes in chatty or intimate details concerning the industry has been functioning in a manner that fortunately is practically inimitable in other fields of human endeavor. If the build-up has been the least bit successful, many thousands of Americans flock to the first-run houses and are willing to pay more for their tickets than if they had waited a few weeks or months to see the same picture at their local theaters. This world-shaking publicity has made them impatient, or they wish to maintain status with their friends by having seen the very, yes, the very latest picture.

But the most powerful auxiliary response of all among

Americans is: "Let's go to the movies tonight." A question may follow: "What's playing?" And then the sad, sad reply: "I don't care, I just want to see a movie." Such a reply brings great joy to the local exhibitor and some grief to the producer of a particular film, but the latter does not sigh too deeply unless his pictures are excluded from a one-theater community.

When once the individual is confronted with a film—and he may be perceiving the picture because he just wants to go to the movies, because his interest has been aroused by a story in a motion picture magazine, because the speaker suddenly uncorks a film during his lecture, or because as a student he cannot very well leave the classroom—he almost certainly will perceive its contents. For one thing, the screen is the only point of brilliant illumination in the darkened room, and the sounds from the film are usually more intense than the coughs, the conversations, and the crackling of paper beside him. In a commercial theater, his main interest may be in the featured picture but, to see it or perhaps to take full advantage of everything to which his ticket entitles him, he must also perceive the other pictures on the same program, such as another feature in which he has little or no interest, a newsreel, a documentary, a so-called educational film like a travelogue, etc. Sometimes the feature picture functions merely as the bait in behalf of another picture. Hollywood during the last war, for example, produced a series of short pictures which were dedicated to helping the war effort and improving national morale. These pictures were seldom promoted, but instead were inserted into the regular programs. Brief advertisements by local merchants which are flashed on the screen represent the crudest and most obvious exploitation of this propaganda advantage.

Any motion picture is able to evoke innumerable personality responses which can lead to pre-action or action responses. The spectator knows that a picture has been produced in a studio and is therefore not a direct reflection of life; nevertheless sometime during the film or perhaps throughout he attributes a certain degree of reality to what he is seeing and hearing. Fixation upon the screen reduces the strength of competing responses which might destroy the illusion, and the images he perceives soon come to represent, for the time being, real people in real situations. The artistry of the medium, moreover, enables him to identify with the characters, to project onto them his own impulses, and to rationalize if need be their shortcomings because for the moment such weaknesses are also his own weaknesses. The telescoping and manipulation of time as well as the limiting of the stimuli which the script and the focusing of the camera accomplish evokes within him a continuous series of responses that are almost never aroused so quickly or so efficiently in his normal life. The effect upon him may be heightened by the accompanying music which is rich in appropriate associations for anyone living in our culture. No completely adequate or generally applicable description of his experiences can be given, as anyone knows who has sought to describe what has gone on within himself or who has read the attempts of men everywhere from ancient to modern times to describe the nature of the esthetic experience. Certainly, however, the camera's ability to highlight any detail—whether it be the movement of a finger in a mystery film or the functioning of scientific apparatus in an educational film—is one of the prime factors contributing to a picture's propaganda or educational effectiveness. The same effects can be secured in the animated cartoon which, though it lacks the realism of the motion picture, is able to manipulate the stimuli more arbitrarily so that even adults can be made to experience genuine emotions.

There are other factors present in the motion-picture situation which make films effective and which thus aid the propagandist. The spectator is a member of an audience unless he has the wealth or the political position to command a special performance. He is stimulated, consequently, by the presence of other people and by their expressions of approval or disapproval. He may project his own feelings onto them, or he may seek to conform to what he perceives or imagines to be their reactions. The motion picture provides him, in addition, with the only or the most impressive contact he ever has with aspects of his society. If he is a respectable member of the respectable middle class, his direct experiences with bankers, prostitutes, gangsters, Koreans, and the well-to-do probably approach zero, but from motion pictures he learns—or he thinks he learns—how these individuals behave. He may remind himself that the movies are all make-believe, and it is true that other media may have given or may continue to give him information and misinformation about these groups of people. The impression he receives from motion pictures over a period of time, however, is likely to be vivid and to persist. In addition, the auxiliary responses which have been built up and reinforced by motion-picture publicity can also function as related responses: movie patrons like a picture because they are interested in the star, and publicity has built up that interest.

Newsreels and documentaries possess a prestige of their own. The spectator may not be aware of the limited number of stimuli they present. He is likely to forget that the camera has had to be focused, the film has had to be cut, and the production has had to be edited. Instead he imagines that he is witnessing reality pure and untouched. Many newsreel cameramen are like journalists, except that they use a camera instead of a typewriter; they therefore search for the newsworthy or the newsworthy angle which may or may not contain all the picturable facts in the situation. The impression created by the newsreel shot, as a result, may not differ appreciably from that provided by the press or the radio. A smooth-sounding voice on the sound track "interprets" the event being portrayed and thus affects the audience's perception of it. It seemed to be standard practice during the last war, for example, for the newsreel voice in the United States to heap scorn and abuse upon pictures of Axis prisoners. Music rather than the human voice may do the slanting, a practice at which the producers of newsreels for the Nazia were adept (27). In their attempt to be entertaining and to avoid, whenever possible, the controversial, newsreel companies unintentionally carry on propaganda. Mr. Roosevelt's appearance in a newsreel seemed

always more impressive than that of any of his four opponents during a national election, although the companies
conscientiously tried to show no bias by allocating approximately the same amount of film space to both major candidates.

Continued patronage of the motion picture theater depends on the satisfactions which people secure from seeing
the films. For this reason the producer has every good reason to produce enjoyable pictures and to present actors and
actresses who are well liked; and, by featuring the name of
his company, to secure prestige credit for the future. And
the exhibitor has just as pressing a reason to exhibit only
pictures which will please the public and add to the prestige
of his theater. By and large, Americans seem easily satisfied by motion pictures. "It wasn't a very good picture,"
many of them say afterwards, "but . . ."—and the string
of rationalizing and genuine *but's* can be strung out indefinitely :

> "but it killed time."
> "but I always enjoy watching her in any show."
> "but I liked the music."
> "but it was interesting while it lasted."
> "but I was thrilled by the co-feature."
> "but I had a good cry (or laugh) anyway."
> "but the acting was excellent."
> "but the theater was air-conditioned."
> "but it was a relief to forget my problems for a while."
> "but I saw it with my girl (or fellow)."
> "but I won a set of dishes."

The motion picture, like the radio, must rely on a mass
appeal and hence tends to bring little or no satisfaction to
those groups—such as the critics, the highly educated, and
the snobs—who consider themselves very enlightened and
sophisticated. Nor does Hollywood produce films of direct
interest to Negroes and other minority groups: their contribution to the over-all box-office receipts is too small. The
displeasure of the enlightened and sophisticated sometimes
also displeases producers who wish to be liked—and patron-
ized—by everybody and who consider that they themselves

belong among the élite. Some of them, therefore, are tempted to realize more of the potentialities of the motion picture than the box office allows. A few in fact who have already reaped the money rewards granted by Hollywood and our society succumb to temptation and produce first-rate pictures. A segment of public opinion, in an exaggerated word, accelerates progress.

Plays

What has been said concerning motion pictures applies almost as well to their neglected parent, the stage. The presence of real actors, however, sometimes makes the spectator more conscious of the fact that he is witnessing a play and not a chunk of reality. For he himself and not a camera selects the particular stimuli on the stage to which he responds, and few theaters possess acoustics which can compete in efficiency with sounds projected by motion picture equipment. At the same time, as every skilful actor and actress knows, the spectators at a play can affect the quality of the acting on the stage. A responsive audience inspires the players, just as inspiring players cause an audience to respond with enthusiasm. This interaction, which sometimes resembles sparks jumping between two widely separated electrodes, places the audience in a more active role and affects many of them deeply and some of them even permanently.

In the inspired words of the Code of the Motion Picture Association of America, "Everything possible in a play is not possible in a film because of the larger audience of the film, and its consequential mixed character." It is true that the number of theater-goers in America is smaller and more restricted than that of movie-goers: with the single exception of New York City, there are relatively few theaters in the United States and their price of admission is almost always higher. The salaries paid by motion picture producers, moreover, have attracted a considerable part of the acting talent away from the "legitimate" stage, which, however, still retains for almost all of them its traditional prestige. As a result, the stage is much less important as a propaganda vehicle so far as quantity of propagandees is concerned.

From other propaganda viewpoints, as the Hollywood Code implies, the stage has many advantages. The cost of producing a play is usually much less—unless a lavish musical comedy or operetta is involved. For this simple reason, a producer may be willing to run the risk of presenting a play which "goes off the boards" in a short while or never even reaches Broadway because it was called a fiasco during its tryout in the provinces. The intentional propagandist who represents a minority group on a slim budget can afford to use this medium when his wildest ambitions do not include a Hollywood production. A play, moreover, can be adapted to a much smaller audience that represents only two or three of the social classes in society rather than five or six. The appeal can be narrower, the propaganda more blatant, and the general tone subtler and more sophisticated. Many critics and movie-patrons seem so shocked to observe how the plot of a play is manhandled when it is made into a scenario in Hollywood. Manhandling, they should see, is required if the play is to appeal to a wider scattering of social groups.

Plays have additional propaganda advantages. In areas which have not yet been invaded by the motion picture, they may be the only propaganda vehicle through which many people's ears and eyes can be reached simultaneously. The Soviet Union, for example, has employed small dramatic companies to entertain and propagandize people who live in more isolated sections. Then the sight and sound of live people seem to have an appeal that their celluloid or electrical images do not quite possess. For this reason, vaudeville in the United States never quite dies. The more palatial motion picture houses still profitably present "stage shows" which display talent usually inferior to the actors and actresses in motion pictures. During the last war, American soldiers abroad who had access to motion pictures, nevertheless, thoroughly enjoyed and appreciated the entertainment provided by the "live" USO. Plays in some form or another, therefore, will continue to be one of the forces reflecting and moulding public opinion in our society.

Meetings

As a result of the growth of the radio, the meeting as a propaganda medium has declined in importance. Many more individuals can be reached through a broadcast. It is easier though sometimes more expensive for speakers to go to a radio studio than to hire a hall and induce people to enter it. Meetings, however, retain an important function which radio has not appreciably usurped: under certain circumstances they can lead more directly to action when the radio produces only pre-action responses. Labor leaders call their rank-and-file together before a strike begins. Conspirators meet to discuss and conclude the details of the coup they plan. Conversions to religious faiths occur during and immediately after revival meetings. Contributions are made to the cause promoted by the propagandist as his hat is passed during the meeting or displayed afterwards. In addition, the less formal meeting on the street corner or in a public place like Hyde Park in London possesses the perceptual advantage of being able to reach people who otherwise would not hear the propaganda either because they consider it of little interest if it is broadcast or because the propagandists themselves do not have access to the mass media of communication. Finally, the speaker at a meeting can continually respond to his audience as they respond to him—at this point the communication slips away from propaganda into the field of persuasion.

Various devices are utilized to attract an audience. A formal meeting is promoted in any of the other media and the audience may be promised, in addition to the speaker or speakers, another attraction such as music, a preliminary parade, entertainment, etc., all of which are calculated to produce auxiliary responses. The speaker at a street-corner meeting faces an especially difficult problem when he begins his propaganda: he has no audience. After having selected a site where people are likely to congregate or be permitted by the police to do so—either because they pass by anyhow or because, as in Hyde Park, they can be expected to appear in order to listen or be entertained by the propaganda—and after calling attention to himself by mounting a platform, a box, or a ladder, he must employ some compelling stimuli if people are to stop and listen. Perhaps his voice or appearance is exotic. Perhaps he displays a flag or some kind of printed announcement. Perhaps he simply sings or has some of his associates break out in song. He can usually promote an audience by having some of his own adherents pose at the outset as attentive listeners. The sight of them then suggests to other people that a meeting is taking place and that evidently the speaker is interesting or entertaining the group already gathered.

The members of an audience at a meeting perceive not only the voice of the speaker but also his general appearance and gestures. As a result, they feel that they can secure a more adequate impression of his personality as well as of his voice. In addition and of greater importance, those who attend a meeting constantly stimulate one another and hence give rise to and are affected by a whole series of responses which people can provoke in other people: projection, identification, conformity, displacement, etc. At many meetings, moreover, the audience does not remain completely passive in relation to the speaker as the radio audience must during the time that the speech is in progress. There can be applause, heckling, and ostentatious inattention which radio listeners know they cannot convey to the speaker. Individuals at a meeting, therefore, can become convinced that as personalities they or their neighbors are actually and actively participating in what is going on, and their ensuing behavior they can consider to be a result of their own decision and not of the propaganda employed by the speaker. Here is one of the explanations for the violent reactions which crowds can display, although it is by no means the complete explanation. The crowd or the mob spirit, moreover, can sometimes be deliberately engineered by the propagandist's claque which represents itself as a genuine segment of the audience. If the speaker seeks discussion, he may have a supporter with feigned spontaneity raise the first question or the one to which he is eager to respond.

The radio listener may turn off or tune out the speaker without appearing impolite, but many members of a meeting hesitate to leave even when they have grown bored or exasperated. Sometimes people in the face-to-face situation have had to exert themselves to attend the meeting and hence they are reluctant to go, lest they miss some satisfaction which might be theirs if they remain seated. At other times they may have been charged an admission fee and do not want to cheat themselves by hearing only a portion of what they have paid for. Or they may be adhering to the unwritten social custom of being courteous to the speaker. The moment a few courageous or uninhibited members of the audience do withdraw, however, the sense of responsibility of those remaining may be weakened and they too may be able to depart. Those who are hostile to a speaker, therefore, can deliberately and devastatingly rise and leave, in order to begin an outward flow. Naturally people at an informal streetcorner meeting feel less compelled to remain, and the speaker there is under the constant fear of losing his audience. Since people do come and go, moreover, he must frequently repeat his central themes but, lest he offend those who hang on, with some minor variations.

The prestige of a meeting as a propaganda vehicle is variable. It can be low, which is usually the situation on the streetcorner or in places like Hyde Park or, in New York City, Columbus Circle. It can be increased tremendously when the audience realizes that the speech is being simultaneously broadcast: what is carried over the radio they consider important and what is important tends to make them more submissive. The hall itself can add or subtract prestige. Madison Square Garden in New York City is one of the traditional sites for political rallies during a national campaign not only because its size enables the speakers to address many thousands but also because the building has become associated in people's minds with power and significance. It may also be felt that an organization that can afford to hire an arena like the Hollywood Bowl must be influential and that, regardless of the fact, it must have mass support. A large hall, however, involves a grave risk for the propagandist: it may not be completely full when the meeting begins, and empty seats provide excellent stimuli to evoke apathy in the audience and to inhibit the development of an ésprit de corps.

Rumors

A much less formal and unpredictable vehicle of propaganda is the rumor which may be spread either unintentionally or intentionally. Unintentional rumors are frequently called gossip and are disseminated because they bring some kind of satisfaction both to him who passes on the tale and to him who receives it. Lumley (*29*) points out that "people gossip most frequently about *departures from the code,* departures on the side of over-aggression, departures on the side of looseness, relaxation." Gossips may be securing vicarious sexual satisfaction, they may be expressing their own latent or not too latent hostilities, or they may be seeking some kind of public recognition from the tales they spread, but at the same time they are helping to perpetuate aspects of their culture. Rumors during war time more or less spontaneously arise because people are afraid, aggressive, or deluded by their own wishes. "Most rumors, and most gossip too," two students of these subjects say (*1*), "are far from idle"; rather "they are profoundly purposive, serving important emotional ends."

During the last war, as has been indicated previously, the intentional spread of rumors constituted an important part of what was termed "black propaganda." Outside of war the deliberate use of rumors for propaganda purposes is usually called a "whispering campaign." Two writers (*28*) once asserted that organizations exist in the United States whose sole function is the spreading of rumors in behalf of paying clients. These groups are said to have circulated false stories concerning a disease allegedly flourishing among workers in a competitor's factory; to have employed actors to pose in public places as innocent conversationalists praising a certain brand of tire or raincoat in a loud voice; to have hired women who feigned anger when stores did not sell the sponsor's gloves; to have helped break strikes by, having bogus salesmen express informal but potent criticisms of unions to the workers' wives. It is impossible to estimate the extent of such practices, since for obvious reasons the tricks are concealed even in the reminiscences of public relations counsels. Mud-slinging during American political campaigns usually includes a quota of stories which, after being planted, then circulate on their demerits. Such rumor-mongering, in fact, has an ancient and dishonorable history (2). Nero's fiddling as Rome burned, for example, is said to have been a tale which probably had no basis in fact but which was spread and accepted by a "distressed populace"; his counter-propaganda which pinned the blame for the conflagration on the unpopular Christian sect proved more effective at the time if not for posterity.

Regardless of their origin, rumors undergo rather violent changes as they are passed along. Although these changes seem to follow some vaguely stated psychological principles (3), there are so many different distortions which can occur that it is rather difficult for the propagandist to predict the precise fate of the tale he wishes to spread. What he can do is to fabricate a statement which has some small basis in fact, which pertains to an ambiguous situation, and which can act as a stimulus to set off drives and habitual responses already present in prospective propagandees. It is much easier to enumerate these characteristics of a good rumor, the writer learned after attending conferences designed to spread rumors to enemy countries during the last war, than to invent the tale which at a given moment is likely to possess those characteristics. At any rate, after the rumor has been designed, the propagandist must kiss it fondly good-bye and leave the rest to propagandees who thus become unintentional propagandists in his behalf.

Rumors are psychologically effective partially because they float about as concealed rather than as revealed propaganda. The intentional or unintentional objective of the rumor-monger is not appreciated and hence at least one conflicting response in the propagandee is eliminated. Much also depends on the prestige of the rumor-monger. The spinster's gossip, for example, may be immediately dis- credited if she has the reputation for spreading lies or dis- tortions. But crucial in the acceptance or rejection of a rumor are the pre-existing attitudes and knowledge within the individuals who hear the report. On the other hand, as Allport and Postman (*4*) guess during their discussion of commercial whispering campaigns, the weakness of a rumor which is informally transmitted "lies in the fact that the listener does not regard the topic as important."

Considerable energy has been devoted to the problem of counteracting rumors. As in all counter-propaganda, the opponent of rumors is faced with a dilemma: silence means allowing the rumor to spread unchecked, but rebuttal gives currency to what is considered falsehood. During the last war, both the American government and private "rumor clinics" sought to combat demoralizing rumors in the United States, but each employed a different approach. In the words of Allport and Postman (*5*), government officials believed that "to smother a rumor with facts is better than to single it out for disproof." When nasty rumors could be anticipated or when they were discovered, an agency like the Domestic Branch of the Office of War Information stimu- lated the release of relevant facts without ever mentioning the rumors. In the interests of discounting rumors in gen- eral—as well as in promoting over-all security—slogans and posters were devised which propagandized against rumor- mongering or "careless" and "loose" talk, but not against specific rumors.

The privately organized "rumor clinics" approached the problem by first collecting the current crop of rumors and then debunking them with facts—when facts were or could be made available. Approximately forty newspapers and magazines in the United States and Canada employed this technique. "Most of the clinics," Allport and Postman (*6*) report, "invited their readers to become 'rumor reporters,' and interested readers became their principal source of supply." There were no radio clinics because it was felt that dial-twisting members of the audience might hear the rumor and not the counteracting facts and because one experiment demonstrated that listeners could recall the rumors more readily than they could the facts. After 1943, however, the clinics died off: the "rumor reporters" lost interest in collecting rumors, disliked to "snoop," and had never been very competent at detecting rumors anyhow; the columns were not syndicated; "in some cases editors found" the column "too complex and too time-consuming a feature to maintain"; and progress in the war itself was accompanied by fewer rumors (7).

As the war against Germany ended, Frenchmen were disappointed in the fruits of victory: peace did not diminish the hardships they were enduring. One scapegoat became the American Army which was being reorganized on French soil for the war against Japan. Rumors concerning that Army, therefore, began to appear. Some of them had a real basis in fact, for men about to go from one war to another are not in a peaceful frame of mind. Besides, few Americans were trained or able to avoid injuring French sensibilities. Other rumors were without foundation or were based upon inadequate knowledge. It was said, for example, that Americans had failed to bomb certain I.G. factories in Germany during the war because of pressure from "the trusts"; that surplus food and clothing of the American Army in France was being destroyed and not distributed to the needy French; that French roads were being ruined during the spring thaws by heavy American trucks; etc. American authorities interested in Franco-American relations were convinced that simple denials from American sources would not diminish the circulation of these rumors. They decided, therefore, to provide friendly French journalists with the facts—at least when the Army's public relations officers were willing to make those facts available. The tale concerning the damage to the French highways was counteracted not by minimizing or justifying the damage which actually was occurring but by publicizing the American promise to pay for the necessary repairs.

Parades

A parade is a kind of meeting without motion or a play without plot and with relatively little continuity. As a propaganda medium it solves the perceptual problem with great ease. Propagandees are interested in the crowd, the pageant, the music, and other features of the spectacle. The infrequency with which parades are staged, moreover, adds to their attractiveness. Both the bystander and the parader immediately perceive that many people are observing and perhaps being affected by the spectacle. The sound of martial music seems to have an almost irresistible psychological attraction in our society: it is associated with other stirring events in the past and its very rhythm increases suggestibility. Large organizations like the American Legion regularly include parades in their agenda in order to give their members and the public a sense of unity, which in fact the group may or may not possess. The parader himself, moreover, actively contributes to the success of the enterprise and thereby commits himself to the sponsoring group.

CHAPTER 21

The Value of Analysis

Pᴜʙʟɪᴄ opinion, propaganda, and the media of communication have now been analyzed. One more question, which is not an idle one, remains to be asked: what is the value of such an analysis? This question must be raised because an analysis of one or more of these problems is time-consuming and hence must be adequately justified.

Seldom does analysis occur for its own sake. The traditional comma-counting of Chaucer does not bolster the United Nations nor does it teach parents how to make their children happier. But presumably the pursuit of this kind of unimportant fact brings pleasure at least to the analyst and maybe even to a small coterie of scholars.

The leader and the propagandist cannot very well deny that analysis is useful. They may object to a particular kind of analysis, but they themselves are always analyzing people either systematically or intuitively. Otherwise they would be dethroned or defeated by their own ignorance.

It is the citizen and the propagandee who are often somewhat aghast when analysis is attempted. The opposition here assumes many forms. Analysis, it is said, is arduous or boring. Analysis interferes with the delights of life and makes people self-conscious. Analysis can also be sterile and lead to mere passivity—we must act from our blood and not from our brains, the romantics and the fascists have always insisted.

The last charge is a very serious one. It has been voiced very powerfully and plausibly by Mumford (*1*) who, without becoming either romantic or fascist, has maintained that during the interim between the two world wars "analysts of propaganda, exposing the rhetorical devices of persuasion, themselves put over one of the biggest frauds of our time: namely, the conviction that the important part about a statement is not its truth or falsity, but the question whether someone wishes you to believe it." The correctness of this observation may be admitted without discrediting analysis. The analysts Mumford has in mind were superficial. They forgot to remind their audiences again and again that analysis is only a first step and that the second step is evaluation and action stemming from the analysis.

The Complexities

It is well to recognize that the analysis of public opinion and propaganda is indeed complex. For this reason, it *is* arduous and it may be boring. Before tears are shed and all attempts at analysis abandoned, the complexities of the task should be recalled in horrifying detail. After the worst is known and known completely and concisely, then nothing more dreadful can happen and maybe something better can be found.

The complexities are of four orders. There is, first of all, the problem of defining terms. There is the problem of measurement. There is the problem of placing data within the framework of a consistent set of theories. And there is the ogre of interaction among numerous factors.

Admittedly there is little social agreement concerning the meaning of the terms "public opinion" and "propaganda." The situation is depressing. Unless observers view approximately the same phenomena, it is highly unlikely that their conclusions or generalizations will reveal any degree of unanimity. Public opinion is a loose term, and propaganda tends to be employed as an epithet. Poorly defined and "fighting" words produce confusion, not understanding. On the other hand, very simple semantic devices are available to discover or to indicate the meanings of words. Public opinion, though essentially a journalistic phrase, can be given a rather precise referent by considering both the issue at hand and the attitudes of the people whose behavior is being subjected to scrutiny. It is a little more difficult to arrive at a sensible definition of propaganda: it has been shown that a purely formal procedure runs smack into the problems of science and value when the activity connoted by this word is distinguished from that suggested by "education." But science and value are very important problems in their own right—difficult, yes—which no serious man wishes to avoid and which, in fact, no man can avoid.

Complexities also result from inadequate information. It is tempting to be glib about people's attitudes and to maintain that public opinion is reacting favorably or unfavorably to a particular issue. Actually, an adequate measure of a sample of public opinion on most issues is almost

always a delicate undertaking not merely because $\sqrt{\dfrac{p \times q}{n}}$

is involved in determining the confidence to be accorded the results but also because the nature, strength, and behavioral importance of attitudes cannot be ascertained with dispatch or without error. It is likewise simple to assert that a propaganda campaign will be, is, or has been successful or unsuccessful without stopping to determine whether the assertion is true or false and, if true, why and how the success or failure has come about. Actually people's reactions to propaganda, it has been proposed, involve perceptual, personality, pre-action, and action responses, no one of which can be immediately grasped except by the clairvoyant. Finally, the contents of a communications medium like the newspaper seem obvious and apparent: it is only necessary to read the printed words and to glance at the illustrations. The story behind the story, however, usually remains quite elusive, and the contents of many issues quickly become unmanageable unless they are quantified in some way or other. Suitable methods, however, exist which enable all these various types of information to be collected.

Each of the methods either immediately or ultimately involves contact with people. The contact with a sample may be direct: a poll, a market survey, a panel, an attitude scale, an experiment, and an open or a prolonged interview require communication between the investigator or his paper-and-pencil surrogate and the individuals whose attitudes or behavior is being measured. Participant observation, it has been shown, is also another direct method that can yield useful information. There are second-hand methods such as reading the report of a journalist or listening to an eye-witness. There are third-, fourth-, and *nth*-hand methods which usually are based on documents like sales records, election returns, or the tally on the number or prisoners who have surrendered. These documents may also be far removed from actual observation, as are discrete facts about a society's economic, political, or social systems; historical facts; or facts arranged to reveal trends. Questions concerning the chance sampling, the biasing sampling, and the instrument errors need to be raised in connection with each of these methods which have, therefore, certain advantages and generally numerous disadvantages. The disadvantages, however, should prove neither inhibiting nor discouraging. Some method has to be employed to be able to say anything about anyone. Even introspection, which is a method of collecting data, must be utilized to gain self-knowledge. It is certainly better to be acquainted with the pitfalls of a method than to be ignorant of the mistakes that are being committed or to assume that no method at all is being used just because the particular act of measurement has no elaborate title. Know thy errors and correct them—or, if no correction is possible, at least acknowledge fallibility.

Even when the meaning of the terms is carefully specified and even when precise measurements are feasible, insight into public opinion and propaganda cannot be guaranteed. Information is helpful only when it can be incorporated into a set of principles which indicate relationships and thus suggest explanations of the past and predictions for the future. The principles governing public opinion and propaganda are not sturdy because too little is known systematically about human behavior. In the preceding chapters, at any rate, an attempt has been made to extend some of the principles underlying individual behavior into the sphere of the inter-individual behavior which is public opinion and propaganda. Here, too, there is no reason to feel dismayed or disagreeable. Throughout history, as has been suggested, every man has had to learn some theory about people in order to survive at all satisfactorily. From some other viewpoint the various theories have been filled with fallacies and fancies, but they have been able, nevertheless, to withstand some pragmatic test. Constantly better theories are needed not only by scientists but also by ordinary men and women not preoccupied with the gathering of systematic knowledge.. Fads about theories always flourish but the less accurate theories perish, however slowly. Again the reach must be toward improved theories, again people must remind themselves that their theories are not infallible, again it must be recognized that facts about people are never in a "raw" state but have been collected for a purpose which itself is a theory or presupposes one.

Finally, complexities are encountered in an analysis of public opinion and propaganda because human behavior is truly indivisible. The people whose attitudes constitute public opinion and the propagandees who are the targets of propaganda have always been socialized in a particular society before they come within the purview of the analyst or the interested observer. Their cultural and personal past, therefore, already clings to them in the form of habits which are aroused or not aroused by socially significant stimuli. Then, as public opinion becomes actual and external and as propaganda proves effective or ineffective, the habits of the people themselves are changed. The change in habits results in other changes. During their lifetime, the people may react differently—or more or less intensely—in similar situations, and hence there are changes in public opinion and propaganda. As parents they may socialize their children differently or as citizens they may change the socializing institutions, and hence there are changes in culture and eventually in public opinion and propaganda. This process continues endlessly like a spiral.

Such a spiral has pursued the reader and the writer at every turn. In fact, it is possible to point out the basic struggle of the entire book by briefly recapitulating merely a few of the various forms the same problem has assumed in almost every chapter:

Social Behavior: the response of a personality depends on the stimulus, and the effects of the stimulus depends on the habits (attitudes, knowledge, etc.) which the personality already possesses.

The Nature of Public Opinion: public opinion is an outgrowth of a social organization or group, and that organization or group is affected by public opinion.

The Cultural Background of Public Opinion: a society's institutions reflect its methods of socialization, and those methods reflect the institutions; leaders change people, and people change leaders.

The Behavior of Public Opinion: people possess certain characteristics since they are members of groups, and they belong to groups because they possess those characteristics.

The Mechanics of Polling: polls are employed to measure public opinion, but the act of polling people can have an effect upon the attitudes being measured.

The Evaluation of Polls: the reliability of a poll is significant only when it is valid, and its validity depends upon its reliability; a poll can determine how people intend to vote, but the knowledge of people's voting intentions may affect the way they actually do vote.

Intensive Measures of Public Opinion: through a panel, public opinion can be constantly measured, but constantly measuring the attitudes of the panel members may change their behavior; a skilled observer can ascertain public opinion by participating in the life of a community, but his presence there alters the situation and hence may affect public opinion.

The Importance of Public Opinion: the politicians and the diplomats of a country influence and are influenced by public opinion, although the influence may be greater in one direction than in the other under varying circumstances.

The Nature of Propaganda: unintentional propagandists tend to perpetuate the culture which has produced them; all propagandists are affected by the public opinion which they seek to change.

The Perception of Propaganda: people selectively perceive the propaganda they are able and wish to perceive, and propaganda affects their perceptual skills and attitudes.

Personality and Propaganda: propaganda evokes certain habitual responses which are then strengthened, weakened, or altered as a result of being evoked by the propaganda.

The Learning of Propaganda: atrocity stories during a war are eagerly learned because people have a conscious or unconscious interest in this type of material, and that interest is whetted by propaganda; the interest, therefore, provokes the propaganda and the propaganda provokes the interest.

Propaganda and Action: satisfaction from propaganda can sometimes be obtained only by action, but action usually occurs only when satisfaction is reasonably certain.

The Printed Media: magazines with mass circulations cater to public opinion and eventually have some impact on that opinion which subsequently requires additional editorial changes.

Radio: Americans with superior education listen less frequently to the radio because programs are not so well adapted to their interests as they are to those with an inferior education, and the programs are not adapted to their interests because they listen less frequently.

The Media of Sight and Sound: Hollywood films give foreigners a bizarre conception of America, and foreigners with such a conception expect and demand films which confirm what they have come to believe.

Diagrams are supposed to clarify a complex problem. But, if the problem is really complex, then the diagram can hardly be simple. The diagram on the next page seeks merely to indicate the interacting relationship between public opinion and propaganda appearing in any social situation. At the center is "public opinion" which represents the habits prevalent among most of a group's inhabitants. Around the circumference are the various stages in the execution of propaganda; in the conventional order the "propagandist" comes first and then all the rest follow in clockwise fashion until "action" and the "propagandist" are reached. Almost all the arrows have tips at both ends to indicate the complexities. They signify the essential circularity of the process, the numerous interactions which can occur, and the interrelatedness of social behavior. People's personality responses, for example, may result from pre-existing habits prevalent in the group ("public opinion"), from the propaganda they have perceived ("perception"), or from whatever habits they have previously acquired during the propaganda campaign ("pre-action"). When they are evoked, the responses affect public opinion, the individual's perception, and the learning required by the propaganda. And so it goes: round and round, but ever changing. The one arrow between "propaganda" and "public opinion" and all

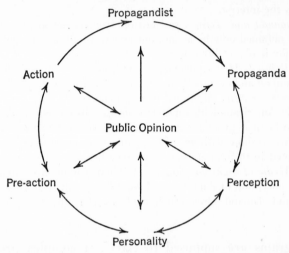

the arrows involving the "propagandist" are single-tipped, since the propagandist must first produce propaganda and the propaganda must then be perceived before public opinion and people can be affected.

At this point no one should be chided for being tempted to give up the ghost and to refuse to concern himself seriously with the analysis of public opinion and propaganda: anything that goes round and round cannot be encompassed by a sensible or simple theory. The ghost which is abandoned, however, is more than the analysis of these two phenomena; it is the study of all human behavior. For, regardless of terminological differences, the same complicated interaction and interrelation protrudes itself whenever any kind of social phenomenon is analyzed in some detail. Myrdal (2), for example, refers to a "principle of cumulation" to describe the dynamics of white-Negro relations in the United States, especially in the South. The Negro's standard of living, this sociologist points out on an abstract level, is low; as a result, he is unable to receive the training which is necessary to obtain regular and well-paid employment; his standard of living, therefore, remains low. This low standard of living, furthermore, has other consequences which include, according to Myrdal, "poverty, ignorance, superstition, slum dwellings, health deficiencies, dirty appearance, disorderly conduct, bad odor, and criminality." The low standard is due in part to discrimination by the whites; the Negro, consequently, acquires or retains the very characteristics which justify the discrimination because his living standard is low. More discrimination leads to an accentuation of the characteristics and to a further increase in discrimination. Less discrimination leads to a change in the characteristics and to a further decrease in the discrimination.

Karl Marx drew upon the Hegelian dialectic when he tried to analyze the interaction he observed in society. This dialectic suggests that each thesis generates an antithesis, out of the conflict between which emerges a synthesis. The ruling class as thesis, according to Marx's best-known analysis, produces an antithesis, another class; after a period of class conflict, a new society comes into being. In modern times, he visualized socialism as the synthesis of the struggle between the bourgeoisie and the proletariat. It is possible to criticize Marx's formulation as being glib or unspecific, but here it is necessary to make only one point: evidently Marx was so impressed with the problem of interaction that he called that problem a principle.

Perhaps the fact that thinkers as diverse as Myrdal and Marx have had to push their analyses down similarly crooked paths is not consoling to the individual with a penchant for straight highways in his intellectual processes. This is not entirely a personal matter. For crooked paths do not become straight when men earnestly wish them to be straight. It is sheer delusion to imagine that a segment of public opinion or propaganda—which in turn is a segment of human behavior—can be analyzed by neglecting the entire social context. Parts of the context may be neglected, in fact have to be neglected, but the omission must be made deliberately and constantly recalled.

The Analytic Attitude

Indeed, much, too much must be known before there can be a complete analysis of public opinion and propaganda. Such an ideal analysis may be summarized in one long sentence. The information to be specified is signified by blank spaces that are preceded by numbers in parentheses:

The (1) _____ PUBLIC OPINION of this (2) _____ group on the issue of (3) _____ is confronted with a PROPAGANDIST whose identity is (4) _____, whose background is (5) _____, whose resources are (6) _____, whose intentional or unintentional objectives are (7) _____, and whose PROPAGANDA in the communication media of (8) _____ employs the devices of (9) _____ while competing with (10) _____; as a result, the PROPAGANDEES do or do not perceive the propaganda because of (11) _____, do or do not react to it because of (12) _____, do or do not learn something because of (13) _____, and do or do not act because of (14) _____.

The fourteen problems can be indicated in greater detail by repeating the capitalized words of this gargantuan, awkward sentence and by suggesting the nature of the information that is required to fill in the spaces after each number:

PUBLIC OPINION

1. *In what form?*
   external vs. internal; actual vs. latent; momentary vs. enduring
2. *Of which group?*
   family, association, region, social class, nation, etc.
3. *On what issue?*
   political, economic, social, religious, etc.

PROPAGANDIST

4. *Who is he?*
   name, organization, occupation, etc.
5. *What is his background?*
   social class, personality, propaganda experience, etc.

6. *What are his resources?*
   financial, prestige, etc.
7. *What objectives does he seek?*
   deliberate intentions vs. possible and unforeseen consequences

PROPAGANDA

8. *In which media of communication?*
   social background, source of control, propaganda content, psychological techniques
9. *In what ways?*
   underlying themes: frequency of usage, prominence, etc.
10. *Against what competition?*
    other communication media, conflicting propagandas, contrary customs

PROPAGANDEES

11. *Is the propaganda perceived or not perceived?*
    because of: audience size, stimulus intensity, repetition, stimulus context, auxiliary responses, variation, simplification
12. *What is the initial reaction to the propaganda?*
    because of: audience composition, related responses, repetition, variation, auxiliary-related responses
13. *What is learned or not learned?*
    because of: response strength, propaganda recognition, prestige and submission, counter-propaganda, reinforcement, recency, limitation, learning ability
14. *What reaction occurs or does not occur?*
    because of: urgency, indicated action, sampling, drive reduction, primacy

The need for information on all these points is reasonably evident. The form of public opinion, the group, and the issue are specified at the outset to indicate, respectively, the types of attitude, the propagandees, and the aspects of society involved in the situation. Here is the over-all frame of reference whose relation to the culture of the group can be demonstrated. The term "public opinion," if it is to be more than a loose term, must refer to specific people and their psychological reactions to certain stimuli in their environment.

As a second step the propagandist is carefully identified and, when possible, and analysis is made of him and the resources at his disposal. It is he who provides the stimuli to which people react or which affect public opinion. Many of the exposés of propaganda are confined to unmasking the propagandist. More than unmasking is required to understand the role he is playing in society and the reasons that have led him to adopt that role.

The propaganda stimuli themselves are examined in the third place. Unlike persuasion, propaganda usually appears in one of the formal media of communication: these need to be understood by determining their role within society and the psychological devices they are able or unable to employ. An analysis of the propaganda's content, it has been shown in Chapter 13, cannot be made in its own right; instead it must be based upon either the intentions of the propagandist or the reactions of the propagandees. The competitor of a propagandist can be another communication medium, another propaganda campaign, or contrary customs within the society.

On the fourth and last level are the propagandees whose perceptual, personality, pre-action, and action responses are determined as precisely as possible. Frequently it seems necessary only to observe the action responses and to ascertain, for example, how citizens actually vote, whether people purchase the product, or which enemy troops surrender under specified conditions. The action response is the acid test of the propagandist's success or failure, but in many ways it is a crude and unsatisfactory test. It does not indicate how people have reacted and hence it obscures the reasons for their subsequent actions. Without a knowledge of the reasons the propagandist may find it difficult to employ the past as a guide to the future, and the propagandee or the propaganda analyst cannot, respectively, understand or predict future propaganda. Any action, moreover, is usually the result of innumerable factors; unless a detailed psychological analysis of them is made, there is always the danger that behavior will be attributed solely to the propaganda which, in reality, may be only a contributing factor.

Without question a thorough analysis is quite utopian. Few individuals—whether they be leaders, propagandists, propagandees, or citizens—ever have the patience or the facilities to procure information which can give a satisfactory answer to the fourteen questions that have been raised. Consider the seventh question concerning the objectives of the propagandist. A complete analysis requires a minute examination of the propagandist's personality and perhaps only a psychoanalysis can yield insight into his unconscious drives. Similarly the reactions of the propagandees—questions 11 through 14—seldom can be ascertained, inasmuch as each individual tends to be unique and that uniqueness becomes intelligible only when each is examined in his own right.

In practice, the analysis of public opinion and propaganda cannot be thorough or complete. Both for the leader-propagandist and the citizen-propagandee the compromise solution is to adopt an analytic attitude. The professional analyst who cannot procure all the information he needs and the non-professional who almost never can do so must approach their problems in a spirit of inquiry and objectivity. Such an attitude can never lead them to believe that theirs is the definitive analysis, but at least it can enable them to appreciate what is known and what is unknown. In Chapter 18, for example, certain exercises have been proposed to permit readers to appreciate the propaganda that inevitably appears in the newspapers they see. Nobody can be expected to read his daily paper with such suspicion and with so many reservations. The kind of informal analysis suggested in that chapter would make newspaper reading a real chore. Ordinarily, too, few people are tempted to compare the treatment accorded the same story by two or more different newspapers. All that is frequently needed, however, is an attitude regarding the press, not the continual application of a set of techniques. That attitude can cause readers to keep an open mind, to realize that inevitably their paper has its biases and so necessarily gives them a more or less oblique account of events. Without such an attitude they are vulnerable to misinformation and dogma. This does not mean that the cry, "It's propaganda," should be perpetually raised. Of course the press prints propaganda, but it also prints facts. From time to time—or as often as possible or as necessary—it is wise to seek to establish the distinction.

This analytic attitude enables the investigator to make compromises and to make them deliberately for a specific purpose. He knows that his analysis is limited, he appreciates the extent of its limitations, but he is content with the restricted results. If the value of a slogan is being discussed, it may be necessary for the advertiser only to see whether its use has promoted or discouraged sales. If the talents of a publicity agent are being questioned, it may be sufficient to observe how much of his material actually finds its way into print or onto radio programs. A far-flung analysis is not required to understand this metaphysical gem which has been lifted from a "dry" tract published in the United States:

. . . No man has a right to seduce another man's wife or daughter, or to build a slaughter house on the public square, or to sell the public poisoned food, or to sell cocaine, morphine, or any other deadly and habit forming drug promiscuously to the public, no matter how much individuals crave it. . . . How, then, can we justify ourselves in granting the avaricious, ruthless, heartless, conscience-less, and lawless liquor interests a license to sell liquor, and say to them that for so much revenue they may transform hundreds of thousands of men and women into gibbering, staggering, reeling, cursing, fighting, irresponsible drunkards, criminals, murderers, and vagabounds? . . .

Admittedly a more complete analysis of the propaganda involved in these three situations would produce helpful insights, but it is doubtful whether those insights would be worth the extra labor.

In other situations, information is simply unavailable and can never be made available. An understanding of Nazi propaganda even at the present time would be greater if more were known concerning Goebbels. That astute propagandist, however, committed suicide before a complete analysis of his personality had been made—and psychoanalyzing the dead on the basis of their words and deeds is a most risky procedure. Similarly, most propagandees—or even a sample of them—are often not available for questioning and analysis. Under such circumstances, consequently, all that can be done is to make sagacious inferences concerning what has taken place.

Certainly errors are likely to be committed when psychological processes are ascribed to people on the basis of admittedly inadequate information. The alternative, however, is silence. Silence is less perilous but obviously sterile. In real life, moreover, the quest for meaning is always strong, and events and people are or must be made meaningful even when adequate data are missing.

The drawing of inferences is especially dangerous when the individual is not aware of what he is doing, when he imagines that his own introspections and meditations possess the quality and power of omniscience. As a matter of fact, he may simply be projecting his own personality upon the event or the other people, and thus his analysis of public opinion and propaganda is really a self-analysis couched in general terms. An awareness of what he is doing can make him more cautious as he draws his inferences. There is a vast difference between a cocky statement which asserts that public opinion is reacting favorably to a particular event and one which modestly points out that undoubtedly public opinion is favorable because—and there follow the evidence and reasoning which have led to the inference.

Two important short-cuts, moreover, can be employed to help simplify the analysis of public opinion and propaganda, provided that the analyst's attitude is intentionally analytical. An over-all knowledge of culture and society is relevant to all fourteen questions which can be raised. The classification of public opinion into momentary or enduring, the role of the medium of communication in the lives of people, or the nature of the auxiliary responses which propagandees do or do not possess—these are illustrations of the kinds of information that a knowledge of culture and society can offer at least in preliminary form. Such knowledge, moreover, is part of the equipment of all who live in a group by virtue of the fact that they have been socialized therein and continually participate in its affairs. Foreigners from anywhere cannot usually be trusted to give an accurate account of the country they are visiting or inspecting; and their analyses of its public opinions and its propagandas are likely to be similarly biased. But it must be hastily added that the inhabitants themselves, in spite of their experiences during socialization and thereafter, are not infallible guides. They may be so emotionally involved that objective judgment cannot be anticipated from them. Their perceptions may be so blunted by frequent contact with their fellows that they fail to make the brilliant and original observations which sometimes characterize the analyses of foreigners. Knowledge of culture and society, therefore, is relatively easy to acquire, but its reliability and validity have to be perpetually assayed. The analyst should realize that he is not an objective seer who can lean back and penetrate the human mysteries surrounding him: he must make a pulling-himself-up-by-his-bootstraps effort to understand and then appraise himself as the measuring instrument.

The other short-cut is through time. The moment any amount of thought is given to a problem concerning human beings it almost appears as though absolutely everything from the first amoeba or from the original cave-dwellers must be taken into account. For the human organism is involved, and it behaves as it does because of the long struggle of its predecessors in the process of evolution. Culture is involved, and people learn habits from their culture because it too has gone through a long developmental process. Everything, however, cannot be considered simultaneously by finite man, no matter how intense his philosophical or scientific ambitions happen to be. At some point a halt must be called and, in like manner, at some point the analyst of public opinion and propaganda must shout: here shall I go and no farther. The "here" may be the present— the analyst rests content with discovering what people think by means of a poll without inquiring into the cultural, personal, and present reasons therefor. The "here" may be a segment of the past—the student seeks to discover why a man became a propagandist without inquiring systematically into the effect his propaganda had upon people. The "here" may be a portion of the future—the propagandist pre-tests a new campaign without showing any appreciation whatsoever for the relation that campaign has to social change.

The arbitrary halting of time provides the only exit from the interaction and interrelationships indicated by the diagram in the previous section. Let A equal public opinion. Let B equal propaganda, or one of the factors on the circumference of the circle. Then the diagram suggests that A affects B and B affects A. But when B is affected by A, it is no longer B but B'; B' then makes A into A'; A' changes B' into B''; etc. When a politician is affected by public opinion, for example, he becomes a slightly different person. As a propagandist he makes public opinion slightly different. Public opinion then changes him again. The analyst may consider only one phase of this process because he cannot do everything at once.

Evaluation

There is a fifteenth question which was not included in the schema above, which is more difficult than any of the others to answer, and which without doubt is the most important of all. That question involves the problem of value. Is the propaganda, it must be asked, "good" or "bad"? Should or should not public opinion be affected or express itself in a particular way?

This question admittedly does not belong to science and analysis which seek out truth wherever they must, regardless of the consequences. Certainly analysis can be cool and objective and produce non-evaluated results. Such results, however, have their consequences the moment they are communicated to people. Someone evaluates them and thus intentionally or unintentionally recommends a course of action. Since analysis inevitably leads to value judgments, it is necessary to ask whether the analyst and the evaluator should be the same person. If they are the same person, then the interest in value may bias the results—the scientist tries to prove a thesis or an ax is ground—and the analyst's ability to assemble the facts and to throw them into theoretical form does not guarantee his competency to evaluate the consequences of the analysis. If they are different persons, then the evaluator may misinterpret the results of the analysis with which he is not so thoroughly acquainted.

The interest of the leader and the propagandist in the analysis of public opinion and propaganda stems directly from their own value judgments. They wish to become better acquainted with people because they have previously decided to influence them. Here value stimulates or biases the quest for knowledge, and knowledge is utilized in behalf of value.

In the case of the citizen and the propagandee, however, the relation between value and analysis is more difficult to establish. They may have no consciously determined value as they make or become acquainted with an analysis, and they often do not know how to utilize additional knowledge when they have acquired it. Analysis is employed, rather should be employed to aid them in finding a value.

Any knowledge is a dangerous thing if it leads to value judgments without the simultaneous realization that the judgments are being made. The crude debunking of propaganda, as Mumford's statement at the start of this chapter suggests, may achieve passivity or skepticism as a by-product. The student who has merely learned that propagandists employ particular symbols is likely to seek out examples of those symbols in the propaganda that surrounds him without ever asking himself whether the symbols refer to real conditions or are stimulating him to engage in worthwhile action. After the analysis has been made, the question of value must be deliberately posed, or otherwise some value will be blindly—perhaps unwisely—selected. A technician can seize upon prose, poetry, and prayer and say: "Ah ha, propaganda, let's see which devices are being employed." Thinking cannot cease after a communication has been categorized. The citizen and the propagandee must proceed more or less as follows:

Ah ha, propaganda or maybe education. Let's see what objective is being sought and which devices are being employed to attain that objective. Is this education or propaganda? Is the propagandist or educator aware of what he is trying to do and of the possible consequences of his activity? What will be, what are, or what have been the effects of this communication upon people? Which people?

Now that these and many other questions have been answered, I must still make a decision: is this communication "true" or "false," "good" or "bad" in terms of my own standards and those of the society in which I live? *What am I going to do about it?*

People in democratic countries are often bewildered by the forces affecting them. They are drawn hither and yon by conflicting propagandas. They feel vaguely that their responses are unsatisfactory, but they have neither the training nor the opportunity to evaluate what is happening, what should be happening to them. Even a small amount of analysis—or the adoption of an analytic attitude—can help them discover what is happening and what will happen. What should happen they can decide afterwards with a profounder appreciation of the factors involved. It is encouraging to note in this connection that techniques are available to produce more reliable and valid analyses.

This, then, is the importance of analysis to the citizen and the propagandee: it can help them find facts or can enable them to adopt an analytic attitude toward social situations. Analysis, in different words, can lead to truth, but that truth will not set men free—or make them happier—until they evaluate it and act upon it. Analysis is only a first step and its relation to the second step, evaluation, is most intricate.

It is intricate for two compelling reasons. In the first place, facts in themselves do not automatically or unequivocally lead to value judgments. Leaders, for example, may reliably and validly measure public opinion. How should this knowledge then affect the policies they adopt? They may feel that other values are involved in addition to the democratic conviction that leaders should be responsive to public opinion. They may show more concern for latent rather than actual or for internal rather than external public opinion. Even if they believe that public opinion in actual and external form should be the decisive factor, the policies which best implement that opinion are not derived directly from it. People want lower prices, peace, or freedom from fear—but there can still be disagreement concerning the means to attain those ends. From another viewpoint, the citizen who becomes acquainted with the facts of public opinion has his own decision to make, and that decision does not spring full-grown out of the facts. Should he conform to what is the will of the majority? Should he try in his humble way to change the attitudes of that majority? Should he neglect the facts altogether by forgetting them?

Similarly the discovery that a communication is propaganda or employs a specific propaganda device contributes a more or less objective fact which, however, is not a value judgment. Propaganda itself is neither good nor bad. Its immediate and far-flung consequences must be taken into account before its goodness or badness becomes apparent. The use of repetition or simplification in any context, for example, is often unavoidable. The task of evaluation proceeds from the fact and seeks to appraise the results of any propaganda device.

The other reason why it is difficult to jump from analysis to evaluation is this: verbal truths about people are accepted more readily as intellectual propositions than they are as bases for action. Social scientists who spend valuable time describing how their society functions may profit very little in their private lives from the hard-earned insights. They may sneer at those who would improve society. They may continue to remain gullible. They may persist in torturing themselves and their families with the thought, for example, that they too must be conventional. Psychiatrists are able to describe graphically and convincingly the behavioral peculiarities of a disturbance from which they themselves still suffer. People can say that they are doing wrong and yet be unable to prevent themselves from so acting. Enough of the fundamental dynamics of war are known to men of good or bad will, but the threat of war is ever upon civilized and uncivilized countries.

This vast discrepancy which can exist between knowing something about people on the one hand and appraising and acting upon that knowledge on the other indicates again the complexity of human behavior. Truths may be grasped verbally, but verbal knowledge can prove a less decisive determinant of behavior than older and stronger habits and attitudes. The society and the individual himself often conspire to reward the ancient habits more heavily than the new insight. Analysis does not solve human problems: it describes the situation and it suggests the consequences of following specified paths.

It is, therefore, sad to remind ourselves that no easy route to earthly paradise exists. There is only the faith that decisions which include a consideration of relevant facts will be better than those which spring from ignorance and impulse. This does not mean that men must be cool, calculating machines. It cannot mean this because human drives can never be completely controlled by verbal calculations. What is needed is as much reason as possible before the emotion plunge into action occurs. Analysis is the method which provides either facts or a critical and inquiring attitude toward information that is not factual or that is semifactual. Without analysis the feeling is likely to emerge that men are fatalistically tossed about by an irrational, unintelligible destiny. With analysis there is the beginning of self-control and social control, but neither can be guaranteed.

Men have been eager to learn to control and adjust to their physical environment. The process has been slow and painful, but they seem convinced that by and large the struggle has been fruitful. They have also been eager— though less so—to learn about themselves and their social environment, presumably in order to achieve happier or better lives or to realize more of their potentialities. An earthly paradise may recede, its nature may remain a mystery, but somehow human values change. Analysis is a tool which aids men in their recurrent effort to improve their values and themselves. At all times the task of increasing wisdom carries with it the obligation to make wiser decisions, and decisions are wiser when they follow analysis.

██ **REFERENCES** ████████████████████

References are arranged alphabetically by chapter. The exact citation is indicated, whenever necessary, at the end of each reference. References recommended as supplementary reading are preceded by an asterisk.

Chapter 1. The Importance of People

1. Hull, Clark L. *Principles of behavior.* New York: Appleton-Century, 1943.

Chapter 2. Social Behavior

1. Doob, Leonard W. The behavior of attitudes. *Psychological Review,* 1947, v. 54, pp. 135–156.
2. * Hilgard, Ernest R. & Marquis, Donald G. *Conditioning and learning.* New York: Appleton-Century, 1940. Chap. 2.
3. * Miller, Neal E. & Dollard, John. *Social learning and imitation.* New Haven: Yale University Press, 1941. Chap. 2.
4. ————. *Idem.* Pp. 49–51.
5. Warner, W. Lloyd & Lunt, Paul S. *Yankee city series: Vol. I, The social life of a modern community; Vol. II, The status system of a modern community.* New Haven: Yale University Press, 1941, 1942.

Chapter 3. The Nature of Public Opinion

1. Ellwood, Charles A. *An introduction to social psychology.* New York: Appleton-Century, 1917. P. 155.
2. * Warner, W. Lloyd & Lunt, Paul S. *Yankee city series: Vol. II, The status system of a modern community.* New Haven: Yale University Press, 1942.

Chapter 4. The Cultural Background of Public Opinion

1. Dollard, John. *Criteria for the life history.* New Haven: Yale University Press, 1935. Pp. 14–15.
2. * Ford, C. S. Society, culture, and the human organism. *Journal of General Psychology,* 1939, v. 20, pp. 135–179.
3. Jenkins, William O. A review of leadership studies with particular reference to military problems. *Psychological Bulletin,* 1947, v. 44, pp. 54–79.
4. * Kardiner, Abram. *The individual and his society.* New York: Columbia University Press, 1939. Chaps. 1–4.
5. * Murdock, George Peter. *Our primitive contemporaries.* New York: Macmillan, 1934. Pp. 24–26.
6. Newman, Horatio H.; Freeman, Frank N.; & Holzinger, Karl J. *Twins: a study of heredity and environment.* Chicago: University of Chicago Press, 1937. Chap. 12.

Chapter 5. The Behavior of Public Opinion

1. Allport, Floyd H. The J-curve hypothesis of conforming behavior. *Journal of Social Psychology,* 1934, v. 5, pp. 141–183.
2. Allport, Gordon W. *Personality.* New York: Holt, 1937. Pp. 330–332.
3. ———— & Postman, Leo. *The psychology of rumor.* New York: Holt, 1947. Chap. 8.
4. ————. *Idem.* Pp. 70–72, 87–89, 112–113, 117–118.
5. Bartlett, F. C. *Remembering.* New York: Macmillan, 1932. Pp. 247–248.

6. Cantril, Hadley. Public opinion in flux. *Annals of American Academy of Political & Social Science*, 1942, v. 220, pp. 136–152.

7. ————. The use of trends. *In*: Cantril, Hadley & Associates, *Gauging public opinion*. Princeton: Princeton University Press, 1944. Pp. 226–230.

8. ————. *Idem*. P. 226.

9. ————. *Idem*. P. 230.

10. ————. *Idem*. P. 228.

11. Carmichael, L.; Hogan, H. P.; & Walter, A. A. An experimental study of the effect of language on the reproduction of visually perceived form. *Journal of Experimental Psychology*, 1932, v. 15, pp. 73–86.

12. Dollard, John. *Caste and class in a southern town*. New Haven: Yale University Press, 1937. Chap. 16.

13. * ————; Doob, Leonard W.; Miller, Neal E.; Mowrer, O. H.; & Sears, Robert R. *Frustration and aggression*. New Haven: Yale University Press, 1939. Chaps. 1–3.

14. Doob, Leonard W. Variability and culture. *Psychological Monographs*, 1936, v. 47, no. 212, pp. 375–380.

15. * Freud, Sigmund. *Civilization and its discontents*. New York: Cape & Smith, 1930.

16. Hartshorne, Hugh & May, Mark A. *Studies in deceit*. New York: Macmillan, 1928.

17. * Hayakawa, S. I. *Language in action*. New York: Harcourt, Brace, 1939.

18. James, William. *The principles of psychology*. New York: Holt, 1890. Vol. 1, p. 121.

19. Johnson, Wendell. *People in quandaries*. New York: Harpers, 1946.

20. Katz, Daniel & Schanck, Richard L. *Social psychology*. New York: Wiley, 1938. Chap. 3.

21. Korzybski, Alfred. *Science and sanity*. Lancaster, Pa.: International Non-Aristotelian Library Publishing Company, 1945.

22. Myrdal, Gunnar. *An American dilemma*. New York: Harpers, 1944. Chap. 4.

23. Sumner, William Graham. *Folkways*. Boston: Ginn, 1906. Pp. 16–18 & chap. 13.

Chapter 6. Sampling Public Opinion

1. Cantril, Hadley, et al. The use of small samples. *In*: Cantril, Hadley & Associates, *Gauging public opinion*. Princeton: Princeton University Press, 1944. Chap. 12.
2. ———. *Idem*. P. 171, italics theirs.
3. Crespi, Leo P. & Rugg, Donald. Poll data and the study of opinion determinants. *Public Opinion Quarterly*, 1940, v. 4, pp. 273–276.
4. * Gallup, George & Rae, Saul Forbes. *The pulse of democracy*. New York: Simon & Schuster, 1940. Pp. 46–47.
5. ———. *Idem*. Chap. 5.
6. Garrett, Henry E. *Statistics in psychology and education* (second edition). New York: Longmans, Green, 1939. Pp. 41–44, 98–108, 200–205, 226–228.
7. Hansen, Morris H. & Hurwitz, William N. Relative efficiencies of various sampling units in population inquiries. *Journal of American Statistical Association*, 1942, v. 37, pp. 89–94.
8. ———. On the theory of sampling from finite populations. *Annals of Mathematical Statistics*, 1943, v. 14, pp. 333–362.
9. ———. A new sample of the population: sampling principles introduced in the Bureau's monthly report on the labor force. *U. S. Department of Commerce*, Bureau of the Census, September 1944. P. 3.
10. ———. *Idem*. Pp. 4–5.
11. * Hauser, Philip M. & Hansen, Morris H. On sampling in market surveys. *Journal of Marketing*, 1944, v. 9, no. 1, pp. 26–31. P. 31.
12. * Hilgard, Ernest R. & Payne, Stanley. Those not at home: riddle for pollsters. *Public Opinion Quarterly*, 1944, v. 8, pp. 254–261.
13. Katz, Daniel. The polls and the 1944 election. *Public Opinion Quarterly*, 1944, v. 8, pp. 468–487.

14. Katz, Daniel. The interpretation of survey findings. *Journal of Social Issues,* 1946, v. 2, no. 2, pp. 33–44. P. 43.
15. McNemar, Quinn. Sampling in psychological research. *Psychological Bulletin,* 1940, v. 37, pp. 331–365. Pp. 343–346.
16. ————. Opinion-attitude methodology. *Psychological Bulletin,* 1946, v. 43, pp. 289–374. P. 335.
17. Mosteller, Frederick. The reliability of interviewers' ratings. *In:* Cantril & Associates, *op. cit.* Chap. 7.
18. Rugg, Donald. How representative are "representative samples"? *In:* Cantril & Associates, *op. cit.* Chap. 11.
19. * Stock, J. Stevens. Some general principles of sampling. *In:* Cantril & Associates, *op. cit.* Chap. 10.
20. Travers, R. M. W. Who are the best judges of the public? *Public Opinion Quarterly,* 1942, v. 6, pp. 628–633.
21. Wilks, S. S. Representative sampling and poll reliability. *Public Opinion Quarterly,* 1940, v. 4, pp. 261–267. P. 263.
22. * Williams, Douglas. Basic instructions for interviewers. *Public Opinion Quarterly,* 1942, v. 6, pp. 634–641.

Chapter 7. The Mechanics of Polling

1. Benson, Edward G.; Young, Cyrus C.; & Syze, Clyde A. Polling lessons from the 1944 election. *Public Opinion Quarterly,* 1945, v. 9, pp. 467–484. Pp. 474–480.
2. * Cantril, Hadley & Fried, Edrita. The meaning of questions. *In:* Cantril, Hadley & Associates, *Gauging public opinion.* Princeton: Princeton University Press, 1944. Pp. 4–6.
3. Cartwright, Dorwin. Public opinion polls and democratic leadership. *Journal of Social Issues,* 1946, v. 2, no. 2, pp. 23–32. P. 28.
4. Crespi, Leo P. The cheater problem in polling. *Public Opinion Quarterly,* 1945, v. 9, pp. 431–445.

5. * Doob, Leonard W. Some factors determining change in attitude. *Journal of Abnormal and Social Psychology*, 1940, v. 35, pp. 549–565.
6. Franzen, R. Symond & Lazarsfeld, Paul F. Mail questionnaire as a research problem. *Journal of Psychology*, 1945, v. 20, pp. 293–320.
7. Gallup, George. A scientific method for determining reader-interest. *Journalism Quarterly*, 1930, v. 7, pp. 1–13. P. 4.
8. * ———— & Rae, Saul Forbes. *The pulse of democracy.* New York: Simon & Schuster, 1940. Pp. 102–103.
9. Jenkins, John G. Dependability of psychological brand barometers: I. the problem of reliability. *Journal of Applied Psychology*, 1938, v. 22, pp. 1–8.
10. * Katz, Daniel. Do interviewers bias poll results? *Public Opinion Quarterly*, 1942, v. 6, pp. 248–268.
11. ————. The polls and the 1944 elections. *Public Opinion Quarterly*, 1944, v. 8, pp. 468–482. P. 473.
12. ————. The interpretation of survey findings. *Journal of Social Issues*, 1946, v. 2, no. 2, pp. 33–44. Pp. 36–37.
13. McNemar, Quinn. Opinion-attitude methodology. *Psychological Bulletin*, 1946, v. 43, pp. 289–374. P. 331.
14. * Mosteller, Frederick. The reliability of interviewers' ratings. *In:* Cantril & Associates, *op. cit.* Pp. 100, 102.
15. National Opinion Research Center. Reference in Cantril & Associates, *op. cit.,* p. 115.
16. Rugg, Donald. "Trained" vs. "untrained" interviewers. *In:* Cantril & Associates, *op. cit.* Chap. 6.
17. * ———— & Cantril, Hadley. The wording of questions. *In:* Cantril & Associates, *op. cit.* P. 28.
18. ————. *Idem.* Pp. 37–38.
19. ————. *Idem.* P. 26.
20. ————. *Idem.* P. 41.
21. Salstrom, William; Katz, Daniel; et al. Interviewer bias and rapport. *In:* Cantril & Associates, *op. cit.* Chap. 8.

22. Turnbull, William. Secret vs. nonsecret ballots. *In*: Cantril & Associates, *op. cit.* Chap. 5.

23. Williams, Frederick & Cantril, Hadley. The use of interviewer rapport as a method of detecting differences between "public" and "private" opinion. *Journal of Social Psychology*, 1945, v. 22, pp. 171–175.

Chapter 8. The Evaluation of Polls

1. Allard, Winston. A test of propaganda values in public opinion surveys. *Social Forces*, 1941, v. 20, pp. 206–213.

2. Barry, Herbert, Jr. A test for negativism and compliance. *Journal of Abnormal & Social Psychology*, 1931, v. 25, pp. 373–389.

3. Blankenship, Albert B. *Consumer and opinion research*. New York: Harpers, 1943. Pp. 163–173.

4. Burtt, Harold E. & Falkenberg, Don R. The influence of majority and expert opinion on religious attitudes. *Journal of Social Psychology*, 1941, v. 14, pp. 269–278.

5. * Campbell, Angus. The uses of interview surveys in federal administration. *Journal of Social Issues*, 1946, v. 2, no. 2, pp. 14–22. P. 15.

6. ———. *Idem.* P. 18.

7. * Cantril, Hadley. The use of trends. *In*: Cantril, Hadley & Associates, *Gauging public opinion*. Princeton: Princeton University Press, 1944. P. 221.

8. ———. The intensity of an attitude. *Journal of Abnormal & Social Psychology*, 1946, v. 41, pp. 129–135.

9. ——— & Fried, Edrita. The meaning of questions. *In*: Cantril & Associates, *op. cit.* P. 22.

10. Cartwright, Dorwin. Public opinion polls and democratic leadership. *Journal of Social Issues*, 1946, v. 2, no. 2, pp. 23–32. P. 27.

11. Connelly, Gordon M. Now let's look at the real problem: validity. *Public Opinion Quarterly*, 1945, v. 9, pp. 51–60. P. 52.

12. Crespi, Leo P. "Opinion-attitude methodology" and the polls—a rejoinder. *Psychological Bulletin*, 1946, v. 43, pp. 562–569. P. 566.

13. ———. *Idem.* P. 562.

14. Dollard, John. Under what conditions do opinions predict behavior? Unpublished paper delivered before Joint Meeting of the Washington Statistical Society and the Washington Chapter of the Institute of Mathematical Statistics, Washington, D. C., March 9–10, 1944.

15. Doob, Leonard W. An "experimental" study of the Psychological Corporation. *Psychological Bulletin,* 1938, v. 35, pp. 220–222.

16. ———. Some factors determining change in attitude. *Journal of Abnormal & Social Psychology,* 1945, v. 35, pp. 549–565.

17. * Field, Harry H. & Connelly, Gordon M. Testing polls in official election booths. *Public Opinion Quarterly,* 1942, v. 6, pp. 610–616.

18. Gallup, George & Rae, Saul Forbes. Is there a bandwagon vote? *Public Opinion Quarterly,* 1940, v. 4, pp. 244–249.

19. ———. *The pulse of democracy.* New York: Simon & Schuster, 1940. Chap. 20.

20. Gleeck, L. E. 96 congressmen make up their minds. *Public Opinion Quarterly,* 1940, v. 4, pp. 3–24. P. 8.

21. Goldman, Eric F. Poll on the polls. *Public Opinion Quarterly,* 1944, v. 8, pp. 461–467. Pp. 463–464.

22. Gurfein, M. I. & Janowitz, Morris. Trends in wehrmacht morale. *Public Opinion Quarterly,* 1946, v. 10, pp. 78–84.

23. Hartmann, George W. Judgments of state legislators concerning public opinion. *Journal of Social Psychology,* 1945, v. 21, pp. 105–114. P. 107.

24. Hyman, Herbert. Do they tell the truth? *Public Opinion Quarterly,* 1944, v. 8, pp. 557–559.

25. Jenkins, John G. & Corbin, Horace H., Jr. Dependability of psychological brand barometers: II. the problem of validity. *Journal of Applied Psychology,* 1938, v. 22, pp. 252–260.

26. Katz, Daniel. Three criteria: knowledge, conviction, and significance. *Public Opinion Quarterly,* 1940, v. 4, pp. 277–284. Pp. 280–281.

27. Katz, Daniel. The measurement of intensity. *In*: Cantril and Associates, *op. cit.* Chap. 3.

28. ————. The interpretation of survey findings. *Journal of Social Issues,* 1946, v. 2, no. 2, pp. 33–44. P. 40.

29. ————. *Idem.* Pp. 34–35.

30. Kriesberg, Martin. What congressmen and administrators think of the polls. *Public Opinion Quarterly,* 1945, v. 9, pp. 333–337. P. 334.

31. Kulp, Daniel H., II. Prestige, as measured by single-experience changes and their permanency. *Journal of Educational Research,* 1934, v. 27, pp. 663–672.

32. * LaPiere, Richard T. Attitudes vs. actions. *Social Forces,* 1934, v. 13, pp. 230–237.

33. ————. *Idem.* P. 235.

34. Lazarsfeld, Paul F. "Panel" studies. *Public Opinion Quarterly,* 1940, v. 4, pp. 122–128. Pp. 122–123.

35. ————; Berelson, Bernard; & Gaudet, Hazel. *The people's choice.* New York: Duell, Sloan and Pearce, 1944. Pp. 107–109, 167.

36. Lewis, George F., Jr. The congressmen look at the polls. *Public Opinion Quarterly,* 1940, v. 4, pp. 229–231.

37. ————. *Idem.* P. 230.

38. Link, Henry C. An experiment in depth interviewing on the issue of internationalism vs. isolationism. *Public Opinion Quarterly,* 1943, v. 7, pp. 267–279.

39. ———— & Freiberg, A. D. The problem of validity vs. reliability in public opinion polls. *Public Opinion Quarterly,* 1942, v. 6, pp. 87–98. Pp. 91–92.

40. Marple, Clare H. The comparative susceptibility of three age levels to the suggestion of group vs. expert opinion. *Journal of Social Psychology,* 1933, v. 4, pp. 176–186.

41. Moore, Henry T. The comparative influence of majority and expert opinion. *American Journal of Psychology,* 1921, v. 32, pp. 16–20.

42. Nielsen, Waldemar A. Attitude research and government. *Journal of Social Issues,* 1946, v. 2, no. 2, pp. 2–13.

43. Noyes, Charles E. & Hilgard, Ernest R. Survey of consumer requirements. *In*: Blankenship, Albert B. (ed.), *How to conduct consumer and opinion research.* New York: Harpers, 1946. Pp. 272–273.

44. Skott, Hans E. Attitude research in the Department of Agriculture. *Public Opinion Quarterly,* 1943, v. 7, pp. 280–292.

45. Wheeler, David & Jordan, Howard. Change of individual opinion to accord with group opinion. *Journal of Abnormal & Social Psychology,* 1929, v. 24, pp. 203–206.

Chapter 9. Intensive Measures of Public Opinion

1. Allport, Gordon W. & Postman, Leo. *The psychology of rumor.* New York: Holt, 1947. Chap. 2.

2. ———. *Idem.* Pp. 3–6.

3. ———. *Idem.* P. 180.

4. ———. *Idem.* Chaps. 4–10.

5. Barth, Allan. The bureau of intelligence. *Public Opinion Quarterly,* 1943, v. 7, pp. 66–76. Pp. 73–74.

6. Campbell, Albert A. Two problems in the use of the open question. *Journal of Social & Abnormal Psychology,* 1945, v. 40, pp. 340–343.

7. Dollard, John. *Caste and class in a southern town.* New Haven: Yale University Press, 1937. P. 17.

8. ———. *Idem.* Chap. 3.

9. * ——— & Horton, Donald. *Fear in battle.* New Haven: Institute of Human Relations, 1943. P. 75.

10. * Doob, Leonard W. War reactions of a rural Canadian community. *Journal of Abnormal & Social Psychology,* 1941, v. 36, pp. 200–223. Pp. 203–205.

11. Ferguson, Leonard W. A study of the Likert technique of attitude scale construction. *Journal of Social Psychology,* 1941, v. 13, pp. 51–57.

12. Garrett, Henry E. *Statistics in psychology and education* (second edition). New York: Longmans, Green, 1939. Pp. 318–319.

13. * Guttman, Louis. A basis for scaling qualitative data. *American Sociological Review,* 1944, v. 9, pp. 139–150.

14. Guttman, Louis & Suchman, Edward A. Intensity and a zero point for attitude analysis. *American Sociological Review*, 1947, v. 12, pp. 57–67.

15. * Harper, Manly H. Social beliefs and attitudes of American educators. *Teachers College, Columbia University, Contributions to Education*, 1927, no. 294. Pp. 37–38.

16. * Harrisson, Tom & Madge, Charles (eds). *War begins at home*. London: Chatto & Windus, 1940. Pp. 16–25.

17. Hyman, Herbert. Do they tell the truth? *Public Opinion Quarterly*, 1944, v. 8, pp. 557–559. P. 558.

18. Koop, Theodore F. *Weapon of silence*. Chicago: University of Chicago Press, 1946. P. 106.

19. Lazarsfeld, Paul F. "Panel" studies. *Public Opinion Quarterly*, 1940, v. 4, pp. 122–128. Pp. 127–128.

20. * ———. The controversy over detailed interviews— an offer for negotiation. *Public Opinion Quarterly*, 1944, v. 8, pp. 38–60.

21. ———; Berelson, Bernard; & Gaudet, Hazel. *The people's choice*. New York: Duell, Sloan and Pearce, 1944. Pp. 3–5.

22. ———. *Idem*. Pp. 85–86.

23. * Likert, Rensis. A technique for the measurement of attitude. *Archives of Psychology*, 1932, v. 22, no. 140.

24. Lockley, Lawrence C. Market description—quantitative and qualitative. *In*: Blankenship, Albert B. (ed.). *How to conduct consumer and opinion research*. New York: Harpers, 1946. Pp. 17–18.

25. * Murray, Henry A. & Morgan, Christiana D. A clinical study of sentiments. *Genetic Psychology Monographs*, 1945, v. 32, nos. 1 & 2.

26. Nielsen, Waldemar A. Attitude research and government. *Journal of Social Issues*, 1946, v. 2, no. 2, pp. 2–13. Pp. 6–7.

27. * Thurstone, L. L. & Chave, E. J. *The measurement of attitude*. Chicago: University of Chicago Press, 1929.

28. *US* ("Mass-Observation's Weekly Intelligence Service"), February 10, 1940, no. 2, p. 2, italics theirs.
29. * Warner, W. Lloyd & Lunt, Paul S. *Yankee city series: Vol. 1, The social life of a modern community.* New Haven: Yale University Press, 1941. Chap. 3.

Chapter 10. The Importance of Public Opinion

1. Bruner, Jerome S. *Mandate from the people.* New York: Duell, Sloan and Pearce, 1944. Pp. 223–227.
2. Cantril, Hadley. *The psychology of social movements.* New York: Wiley, 1941. Pp. 171, 184, 191–193.
3. ———. The use of trends. *In:* Cantril, Hadley & Associates, *Gauging public opinion.* Princeton: Princeton University Press, 1944. P. 228.
4. Childs, Harwood L. *An introduction to public opinion.* New York: Wiley, 1940. Pp. 22–34.
5. Connelly, Gordon M. & Field, Harry H. The nonvoter—who he is, what he thinks. *Public Opinion Quarterly,* 1944, v. 8, pp. 175–187.
6. * Davis, Allison; Gardner, Burleigh B.; & Gardner, Mary R. *Deep south.* Chicago: University of Chicago Press, 1941. Chap. 8.
7. * Dollard, John; Doob, Leonard W.; Miller, Neal E.; Mowrer, O. H.; & Sears, Robert R. *Frustration and aggression.* New Haven: Yale University Press, 1939. Chap. 7.
8. Doob, Leonard W. Communication of information about the United States. *Journal of Consulting Psychology,* 1946, v. 10, pp. 45–50.
9. ———. *The plans of men.* New Haven: Yale University Press, 1940. Chap. 12.
10. Fraser, Lindley. *Germany between two wars.* London: Oxford University Press, 1945. Pp. 97–101.
11. Gallup, George & Rae, Saul Forbes. *The pulse of democracy.* New York: Simon & Schuster, 1940. Chaps. 9–17.
12. Geldard, Frank A. & Harris, Chester W. Selection and classification of aircrew by the Japanese. *Ameri-*

can Psychologist, 1946, v. 1, pp. 205–217. Pp. 211–212.

13. Gleeck, L. E. 96 congressmen make up their minds. *Public Opinion Quarterly,* 1940, v. 4, pp. 3–24. Pp. 8, 12.

14. ———. *Idem.* P. 14.

15. Goldman, Eric F. Poll on the polls. *Public Opinion Quarterly,* 1944, v. 8, pp. 461–467. P. 465.

16. Hartmann, George W. Judgments of state legislators concerning public opinion. *Journal of Social Psychology,* 1945, v. 21, pp. 105–114. Pp. 107, 110–112.

17. Holcombe, A. N. *Government in a planned democracy.* New York: Norton, 1935. Pp. 47–49.

18. Kardiner, Abram. *The psychological frontiers of society.* New York: Columbia University Press, 1945. Chaps. 2 & 14.

19. Kriesberg, Martin. What congressmen and administrators think of the polls. *Public Opinion Quarterly,* 1945, v. 9, pp. 333–337.

20. Kuhn, Ferdinand, Jr. Letting the whole world know. *Survey Graphic,* 1946, v. 35, pp. 492–497, 512–513.

21. * Lazarsfeld, Paul F.; Berelson, Bernard; & Gaudet, Hazel. *The people's choice.* New York: Duell, Sloan and Pearce, 1944. Figure calculated from data given on p. 54.

22. * Lippmann, Walter. *Public opinion.* New York: Macmillan, 1922.

23. ———. *The phantom public.* New York: Harcourt, Brace, 1925. Chaps. 4, 5, 15.

24. Schanck, Robert L. A study of a community and its groups and institutions conceived of as behavior of individuals. *Psychological Monographs,* 1932, v. 43, no. 195. Pp. 36–40.

25. Smith, Charles W., Jr. *Public opinion in a democracy.* New York: Prentice-Hall, 1942. P. 346.

26. ———. *Idem.* Pp. 120–122.

27. Spykman, Nicholas John. *America's strategy in world politics.* New York: Harcourt, Brace, 1942.

28. Wyant, Rowena & Herzog, Herta. Voting via the senate mailbag. *Public Opinion Quarterly,* 1941, v. 5, pp. 359–382, 590–624. Pp. 372–374.

Chapter 11. The Nature of Propaganda

1. Chen, William Keh-Ching. The influence of oral propaganda material upon students' attitudes. *Archives of Psychology,* 1933, v. 23, no. 150. Pp. 23, 27–28.
2. Doob, Leonard W. *Propaganda.* New York: Holt, 1935. Pp. 79–88.
3. ———. *The plans of men.* New Haven: Yale University Press, 1940. Chaps. 3–6.
4. Experimental Section, Research Branch, Information and Education Division, U. S. War Department. *Experimental studies of army educational films.* 1948. Chap. 2.
5. Freeman, Ellis. *Social psychology.* New York: Holt, 1936. Pp. 263–265.
6. * Henderson, Edgar H. Toward a definition of propaganda. *Journal of Social Psychology,* 1943, v. 18, pp. 71–87.
7. Lasswell, Harold D. & Blumenstock, Dorothy. *World revolutionary propaganda.* New York: Knopf, 1939. Pp. 10–11, footnote.
8. Linton, Ralph. *The study of man.* New York: Appleton-Century, 1936.
9. * Lumley, Frederick E. *The propaganda menace.* New York: Appleton-Century, 1933. P. 44.
10. Martin, Everett D. Our invisible masters. *Forum,* 1929, v. 81, pp. 142–145. P. 145.
11. Remmers, H. H. Propaganda in the schools—do the effects last? *Public Opinion Quarterly,* 1938, v. 2, pp. 197–210.
12. Smith, Bruce Lannes; Lasswell, Harold D.; & Casey, Ralph D. *Propaganda, communication, and public opinion.* Princeton: Princeton University Press, 1946. P. 121, italics theirs.
13. Warburg, James P. *Unwritten treaty.* New York: Harcourt, Brace, 1946. P. 17.

Chapter 12. The Propagandist

1. Doob, Leonard W. The utilization of social scientists in the Overseas Branch of the Office of War Information. *American Political Science Review,* 1947, v. 41, pp. 649–667.
2. Federal Communications Commission. *Statistics of the communications industry in the United States.* Washington, D. C.: U. S. Government Printing Office, 1944. Pp. 248–249.
3. * Lasswell, Harold D. The person: subject and object of propaganda. *Annals of American Academy of Political & Social Science,* 1935, v. 179, pp. 187–193. P. 191.
4. ———. *Idem.* Pp. 191–192.
5. ———. *Idem.* P. 190.
6. Lee, Alfred McClung. Trends in public relations training. *Public Opinion Quarterly,* 1947, v. 11, pp. 83–91.
7. * Rosten, Leo C. *The Washington correspondents.* New York: Harcourt, Brace, 1937. Chap. 6.
8. ———. *Idem.* Pp. 328–329.
9. ———. *Idem.* Pp. 244–248.
10. ———. *Idem.* Pp. 220, 225.
11. * Smith, Bruce Lannes. The political communication specialist of our times. *In:* Smith, Bruce Lannes; Lasswell, Harold D.; & Casey, Ralph D., *Propaganda, communication, and public opinion.* Princeton: Princeton University Press, 1946. Pp. 35–54.
12. ———. *Idem.* Pp. 57–62.
13. ———. *Idem.* Pp. 54–56.

Chapter 13. The Content of Propaganda

1. Berelson, Bernard. The effects of print upon public opinion. *In:* Waples, Douglas (ed.), *Print, radio, and film in a democracy.* Chicago: University of Chicago Press, 1942. Pp. 41–65.
2. * Dollard, John & Mowrer, O. Hobart. A method of measuring tension in written documents. *Journal of Abnormal & Social Psychology,* 1947, v. 42, pp. 3–32.

3. Dollard, John & Mowrer, O. Hobart. *Idem.* Pp. 14–15.

4. Fairbanks, Helen. Studies in language behavior: II. The quantitative differentiation of samples of spoken language. *Psychological Monographs,* 1944, v. 56, no. 255, pp. 19–38.

5. Geller, A.; Kaplan, D.; & Lasswell, Harold D. The differential use of flexible and rigid procedures of content analysis. *Experimental Division for the Study of War Time Communications* (Library of Congress), March 1, 1943, no. 12.

6. Gerth, H. H. & Mills, Wright. *From Max Weber: essays in sociology.* New York: Oxford University Press, 1946. P. 66, footnote.

7. Hamilton, Thomas. Social optimism and pessimism in American Protestantism. *Public Opinion Quarterly,* 1942, v. 6, pp. 280–283.

8. Herma, Hans; Kris, Ernst; & Shor, Joseph. Freud's theory of the dream in American textbooks. *Journal of Abnormal & Social Psychology,* 1943, v. 38, pp. 319–334.

9. Janis, Irving L.; Fadner, H.; & Janowitz, Morris. The reliability of a content analysis. *Public Opinion Quarterly,* 1943, v. 7, pp. 293–296.

10. Jones, Dorothy B. Quantitative analysis of motion picture content. *Public Opinion Quarterly,* 1942, v. 6, pp. 411–428.

11. Kaplan, Abraham & Goldsen, Joseph M. Reliability of certain categories for classifying newspaper headlines. *Experimental Division for the Study of War Time Communications* (Library of Congress), May 15, 1943, no. 40.

12. Katz, Daniel. The content of news programs and of newspapers. *In:* Lazarsfeld, Paul F., *Radio and the printed page.* New York: Duell, Sloan and Pearce, 1940. Pp. 207–213.

13. * Kingsbury, Susan M.; Hart, Hornell; & Associates. *Newspapers and the news.* New York: Putnam's, 1937.

14. Kris, Ernst. The "danger" of propaganda. *American Imago,* 1941, v. 2, pp. 1–42.

15. * ———— & Speier, Hans. *German radio propaganda.* London: Oxford University Press, 1944.

16. ————. *Idem.* P. 291.

17. ————. *Idem.* Chap. 10.

18. Lasswell, Harold D. *Propaganda technique in the world war.* New York: Knopf, 1927.

19. ————. The world attention survey. *Public Opinion Quarterly,* 1941, v. 5, pp. 456–462.

20. ————. Communications research and politics. *In:* Waples, *op. cit.* Pp. 101–117.

21. * ————. Describing the contents of communication. *In:* Smith, Bruce Lannes; Lasswell, Harold D.; & Casey, Ralph D., *Propaganda, communication, and public opinion.* Princeton: Princeton University Press, 1946. Pp. 75–76.

22. ———— & Blumenstock, Dorothy. *World revolutionary propaganda.* New York: Knopf, 1939.

23. ———— & Associates. The politically significant content of the press: coding procedures. *Journalism Quarterly,* 1942, v. 19, pp. 12–23.

24. * Lee, Alfred McClung & Lee, Elizabeth B. (eds.). *The fine art of propaganda.* New York: Harcourt, Brace, 1939. Pp. 23–24, italics theirs.

25. ————. *Idem.* P. 131.

26. ————. *Idem.* P. 24, italics omitted.

27. Lumley, Frederick E. *The propaganda menace.* New York: Appleton-Century, 1933.

28. Mann, Mary Bachman. Studies in language behavior: III. The quantitative differentiation of samples of written language. *Psychological Monographs,* 1944, v. 56, no. 255, pp. 41–74.

29. Walker, Gayle Courtney. A yardstick for the measurement of country weekly service. *Journalism Quarterly,* 1930, v. 7, pp. 293–302.

30. Waples, Douglas; Berelson, Bernard; & Bradshaw, Franklyn R. *What reading does to people.* Chicago: University of Chicago Press, 1940. Chap. 4.

31. * Willey, Malcolm M. *The country newspaper.* Chapel Hill: University of North Carolina Press, 1926.
32. Woodward, Julian Laurence. *Foreign news in American morning newspapers.* New York: Columbia University Press, 1930.
33. Wyant, Rowena & Herzog, Herta. Voting via the senate mailbag. *Public Opinion Quarterly,* 1941, v. 5, pp. 359–382, 590–624.

Chapter 14. The Perception of Propaganda

1. Barton, Samuel G. The radio panel. *In:* Blankenship, Albert B. (ed.), *How to conduct consumer and opinion research.* New York: Harpers, 1946. Chap. 14.
2. * Burtt, Harold Ernest. *Psychology of advertising.* Boston: Houghton Mifflin, 1938. Pp. 158–167.
3. ———. *Idem.* Pp. 168–175.
4. ———. *Idem.* Pp. 199–208.
5. Chakotin, Serge. *The rape of the masses.* London: Routledge, 1940. Chap. 4.
6. Chappell, Matthew. Factors influencing recall of radio programs. *Public Opinion Quarterly,* 1942, v. 6, pp. 107–114. Pp. 107–108.
7. * ——— & Hooper, C. E. *Radio audience measurement.* New York: Stephen Daye, 1944. Pp. 1–2, italics theirs.
8. ———. *Idem.* Pp. 140–147.
9. ———. *Idem.* Chap. 9.
10. Fiske, Marjorie & Lazarsfeld, Paul F. The office of radio research. *In:* Blankenship (ed.), *op. cit.* Pp. 143–144.
11. Hooper, C. E. The coincidental method of measuring radio audience size. *In:* Blankenship (ed.), *op. cit.* Chap. 12.
12. Lehman, A. W. & Allen, George H. The new cooperative analysis of broadcasting. *In:* Blankenship (ed.), *op. cit.* Chap. 11.

13. Roslow, Sydney & Kelly, Nelle. The personal interview-roster method of radio measurement and its application. *In*: Blankenship (ed.), *op. cit.* Pp. 175–176.
14. Swann, Carroll J. What we know and don't know about the value of position. *Printers' Ink,* February 28, 1947, v. 218, pp. 32–33, 82, 84. P. 32.

Chapter 15. Personality and Propaganda

1. Benson, Lawrence E. Mail surveys can be valuable. *Public Opinion Quarterly,* 1946, v. 10, pp. 234–241.
2. * Biddle, William W. Propaganda and education. *Teachers College, Columbia University, Contributions to Education,* 1932, no. 531. Pp. 29–31.
3. Burtt, Harold Ernest. *Psychology of advertising.* Boston: Houghton Mifflin, 1938. Chaps. 5–6.
4. Experimental Section, Research Branch, Information and Education Division, U. S. War Department. *Experimental studies of army educational films.* 1948. Chap 2.
5. Goode, Kenneth. *Advertising.* New York: Greenberg, 1941. P. 108.
6. Hilgard, Ernest R. & Marquis, Donald G. *Conditioning and learning.* New York: Appleton-Century, 1940. Chap. 3.
7. Lee, Alfred McClung & Lee, Elizabeth Briant (ed.). *The fine art of propaganda.* New York: Harcourt, Brace, 1939. Pp. 23–24.
8. * Lockley, Lawrence C. Market description—quantitative and qualitative. *In*: Blankenship, Albert B. (ed.), *How to conduct consumer and opinion research.* New York: Harpers, 1946. Pp. 16–17.
9. ——. *Idem.* Pp. 12–14.
10. Lucas, D. B. & Benson, C. E. *Psychology for advertisers.* New York: Harpers, 1930. Pp. 71–72.
11. Miller, Clyde R. *The process of persuasion.* New York: Crown Publishers, 1946. Chap. 12.
12. Nixon, H. K. *Principles of advertising.* New York: McGraw-Hill, 1937. Chap. 4.

13. Poffenberger, Albert T. *Psychology in advertising.* Chicago & New York: A. W. Shaw, 1925. Chap. 3.
14. ——— & Franken, R. B. Type face appropriateness. *Journal of Applied Psychology,* 1923, v. 7, pp. 312–329.
15. Wakeman, Frederic. *The hucksters.* New York: Rinehart, 1946.

Chapter 16. The Learning of Propaganda

1. Allport, Floyd H. *Social psychology.* Boston: Houghton Mifflin, 1924. P. 305, italics his.
2. * Burtt, Harold Ernest. *Psychology of advertising.* Boston: Houghton Mifflin, 1938. P. 64.
3. * Experimental Section, Research Branch, Information and Education Division, U. S. War Department. *Experimental studies of army educational films.* 1948. Chap. 4.
4. ———. *Idem.* Chap. 8.
5. ———. *Idem.* Chap. 6.
6. Freifeld, Sidney A. Nazi press agentry and the American press. *Public Opinion Quarterly,* 1942, v. 6, pp. 221–235. Pp. 231–234.
7. Gordon, Matthew. *News is a weapon.* New York: Knopf, 1942. Chap. 5.
8. Hollonquist, Tore & Suchman, Edward A. Listening to the listener. *In:* Lazarsfeld, Paul F. & Stanton, Frank N., *Radio research 1942–1943.* New York: Duell, Sloan and Pearce, 1944. Pp. 269–270.
9. Koop, Theodore F. *Weapon of silence.* Chicago: University of Chicago Press, 1946. Chap. 12.
10. Lazarsfeld, Paul F.; Berelson, Bernard; & Gaudet, Hazel. *The people's choice.* New York: Duell, Sloan and Pearce, 1944. Chap. 6.
11. Lockley, Lawrence C. Market description—quantitative and qualitative. *In:* Blankenship, Albert B. (ed.), *How to conduct consumer and opinion research.* New York: Harpers, 1946. P. 13.

12. * May, Mark A. *A social psychology of war and peace.* New Haven: Yale University Press, 1943. Chap. 2, pp. 134–135.
13. Miller, Neal E. Experimental studies of conflict. *In:* Hunt, J. McV., *Personality and the behavior disorders.* New York: Ronald Press Co., 1944. Chap. 14.
14. Padover, Saul K. *Experiment in Germany.* New York: Duell, Sloan and Pearce, 1946. P. 50.
15. *Printer's Ink,* April 14, 1932, v. 159, p. 20.
16. * Read, James Morgan. *Atrocity propaganda 1914–1918.* New Haven: Yale University Press, 1941. Chaps. 2 & 4.
17. ———. *Idem.* Chap. 5.
18. ———. *Idem.* P. 3.
19. ———. *Idem.* Pp. 37–38, 49–50, 187.
20. Rosten, Leo C. *The Washington correspondents.* New York: Harcourt, Brace, 1937. Chap. 3.
21. ———. *Idem.* P. 73.
22. * Taylor, Edmond. *The strategy of terror.* Boston: Houghton Mifflin, 1940. Pp. 70, 103, 206.
23. Warburg, James P. *Unwritten treaty.* New York: Harcourt, Brace, 1946. P. 18.

Chapter 17. Propaganda and Action
1. Burtt, Harold Ernest. *Psychology of advertising.* Boston: Houghton Mifflin, 1938. Pp. 344–345.
2. Flynn, John T. *God's gold.* New York: Harcourt, Brace, 1932. P. 484.
3. * "Glim, Aesop." *How advertising is written—and why.* New York: McGraw-Hill, 1945. P. 4.
4. * Gordon, Matthew. *News is a weapon.* New York: Knopf, 1942. P. 7–8.
5. * Gruening, Ernest. *The public pays.* New York: Vanguard, 1931. Chaps. 3–5.
6. * Kris, Ernst & Speier, Hans. *German radio propaganda.* London: Oxford University Press, 1944. Pp. 344–353.
7. ———. *Idem.* Pp. 423–443.

8. Kris, Ernst & Speier, Hans. *Idem.* P. 326.
9. Levin, Jack. *Power ethics.* New York: Knopf, 1931. Chaps. 9–10.
10. Thompson, Carl D. *Confessions of the power trust.* New York: Dutton, 1932. Chaps. 37–40.

Chapter 18. The Printed Media

1. Allport, Gordon W. & Faden, Janet M. The psychology of newspapers. *Public Opinion Quarterly,* 1940, v. 4, pp. 687–703.
2. Avenarius, Ferdinand. *Das Bild als Verleumder.* Munich: Georg D. W. Callwey, no date. Pp. 22–23.
3. * Borden, Neil H.; Taylor, Malcolm D.; Hovde, Howard T. *National advertising in newspapers.* Cambridge: Harvard University Press, 1946. Chap. 3.
4. ————. *Idem.* Pp. 12–13.
5. ————. *Idem.* Pp. 35–36.
6. Burtt, Harold Ernest. *Psychology of advertising.* Boston: Houghton Mifflin, 1938. Pp. 208–209.
7. * Casey, Ralph D. Communication channels. *In*: Smith, Bruce Lannes; Lasswell, Harold D.; & Casey, Ralph D., *Propaganda, communication, and public opinion.* Princeton: Princeton University Press, 1946. Pp. 16–23.
8. Christman, Henry. "Nobly save or meanly lose." *Survey Graphic,* 1946, v. 35, pp. 436–440. P. 440.
9. * Ernst, Morris L. *The first freedom.* New York: Macmillan, 1946. Chap. 4 & pp. 279–292.
10. ————. *Idem.* P. 84.
11. ————. *Idem.* P. 116.
12. ————. *Idem.* P. 117.
13. Freifeld, Sidney A. Nazi press agentry and the American press. *Public Opinion Quarterly,* 1942, v. 6, pp. 221–235. Pp. 226–231.
14. Gallup, George. A scientific method for determining reader-interest. *Journalism Quarterly,* 1930, v. 7, pp. 1–13. P. 9.

15. Gordon, Matthew. *News is a weapon.* New York: Knopf, 1942. Pp. 67–74.
16. Irwin, Will. *Propaganda and the news.* New York: McGraw-Hill, 1936. Chaps. 2–4.
17. * Johnson, Gerald W. *What is news?* New York: Crofts, 1926. Pp. 48, 63–64.
18. * Lazarsfeld, Paul F. *Radio and the printed page.* New York: Duell, Sloan and Pearce, 1940. Pp. 218–240.
19. * Lee, Alfred McClung. *The daily newspaper in America.* New York: Macmillan, 1937.
20. Ludeke, H. C. The survey applied to editorial problems. *In:* Blankenship, Albert B. (ed.), *How to conduct consumer and opinion research.* New York: Harpers, 1947. Pp. 189–190, 205.
21. Lundberg, George A. The newspaper and public opinion. *Social Forces,* 1926, v. 4, pp. 709–715. P. 713.
22. McKenzie, Vernon. Treatment of war themes in magazine fiction. *Public Opinion Quarterly,* 1941, v. 5, pp. 227–232.
23. Miller, Merle. Freedom to read: magazines. *Survey Graphic,* 1946, v. 35, pp. 462–467. Pp. 463, 466.
24. ———. *Idem.* P. 466.
25. Morris, Charles. *Signs, language, and behavior.* New York: Prentice-Hall, 1946. P. 23.
26. Mott, Frank Luther. Newspapers in presidential campaigns. *Public Opinion Quarterly,* 1944, v. 8, pp. 348–367. P. 362.
27. * Rosten, Leo C. *The Washington correspondents.* New York: Harcourt, Brace, 1937. Pp. 97–98, chap. 10.
28. Stewart, Kenneth. Freedom to read: newspapers. *Survey Graphic,* 1946, v. 35, pp. 452–455, 513–514.
29. White, Llewellyn & Leigh, Robert D. *Peoples speaking to peoples.* Chicago: University of Chicago Press, 1946. Pp. 69–70.
30. Winship, Elizabeth C. & Allport, Gordon W. Do rosy headlines sell newspapers? *Public Opinion Quarterly,* 1943, v. 7, pp. 205–210.

Chapter 19. Radio

1. Ackerman, William C. The dimensions of American broadcasting. *Public Opinion Quarterly,* 1945, v. 9, pp. 1–18. P. 9.
2. ———. *Idem.* Pp. 7 & 10.
3. ———. *Idem.* P. 6.
4. Cantril, Hadley & Allport, Gordon W. *The psychology of radio.* New York: Harpers, 1935. Chap. 6.
5. ———; Gaudet, Hazel; & Herzog, Herta. *The invasion from Mars.* Princeton: Princeton University Press, 1940. Pp. 139–144.
6. Chappell, Matthew N. Factors influencing recall of radio programs. *Public Opinion Quarterly,* 1942, v. 6, pp. 107–114.
7. * ——— & Hooper, C. E. *Radio audience measurement.* New York: Stephen Daye, 1944. Pp. 12, 88–95, Chap. 6.
8. ———. *Idem.* Pp. 13–14.
9. ———. *Idem.* Pp. 96–105.
10. * Eisenberg, Azriel L. *Children and radio programs.* New York: Columbia University Press, 1936. P. 52.
11. ———. *Idem.* P. 53.
12. ———. *Idem.* P. 51.
13. ———. *Idem.* Pp. 63–66.
14. * Ernst, Morris L. *The first freedom.* New York: Macmillan, 1946. P. 295.
15. ———. *Idem.* P. 155.
16. ———. *Idem.* P. 158.
17. ———. *Idem.* P. 159.
18. * Federal Communications Commission. *Public service responsibility of broadcast licensees.* Washington, D. C.: U. S. Government Printing Office, 1946. P. 11.
19. ———. *Idem.* P. 36.
20. ———. *Idem.* Pp. 37–39.
21. ———. *Idem.* P. 12.
22. ———. *Idem.* Pp. 3–9, 18–36.
23. ———. *Idem.* P. 15.
24. ———. *Idem.* Pp. 46–47.

25. Federal Communications Commission. *Idem.* P. 39.
26. ———. *Idem.* P. 14.
27. ———. *Idem.* Pp. 42–43.
28. ———. *Twelfth annual report.* Washington, D. C.: U. S. Government Printing Office, 1947. Pp. 5, 9–10.
29. * Field, Harry & Lazarsfeld, Paul F. *The people look at radio.* Chapel Hill: University of North Carolina Press, 1946. Pp. 133–141.
30. ———. *Idem.* Pp. 54–55.
31. ———. *Idem.* Pp. 126–127.
32. ———. *Idem.* Pp. 97, 102.
33. ———. *Idem.* Pp. 101–102.
34. ———. *Idem.* Pp. 5–7.
35. ———. *Idem.* Pp. 50–51.
36. ———. *Idem.* Pp. 66–68.
37. ———. *Idem.* Chap. 2.
38. Kerwin, Jerome G. *The control of radio.* Chicago: University of Chicago Press, 1934. Pp. 8–16.
39. * Lazarsfeld, Paul F. *Radio and the printed page.* New York: Duell, Sloan and Pearce, 1940. Pp. 15–20.
40. ———. *Idem.* Pp. 21–47.
41. ———. *Idem.* Pp. 135–136.
42. ———. *Idem.* Pp. 259–263.
43. ———. "Panel" studies. *Public Opinion Quarterly,* 1940, v. 4, pp. 122–128. P. 125.
44. MacDougald, Duncan, Jr. The popular music industry. *In:* Lazarsfeld, Paul F. & Stanton, Frank N., *Radio research 1941.* New York: Duell, Sloan and Pearce, 1941. Pp. 65–109.
45. Meine, Frederick J. Radio and the press among young people. *In:* Lazarsfeld & Stanton, *op. cit.* P. 193.
46. ———. *Idem.* Pp. 201–208, 218–222.
47. Stewart, Kenneth. Freedom to read: newspapers. *Survey Graphic,* 1946, v. 35, pp. 452–455, 513–514. P. 452.
48. * White, Llewellyn. *The American radio.* Chicago: University of Chicago Press, 1947. Pp. 199, 200.
49. ———. *Idem.* Pp. 200–203.

50. White, Llewellyn. *Idem.* P. 144.
51. ———. *Idem.* Pp. 35, 145–148.
52. ———. *Idem.* Pp. 44–48.
53. ———. *Idem.* P. 206.
54. ———. *Idem.* P. 60.
55. ———. *Idem.* Pp. 54–59.
56. ———. *Idem.* P. 69.
57. ———. *Idem.* P. 66.
58. ———. *Idem.* Chap. 5.
59. ———. *Idem.* P. 75.
60. ———. *Idem.* Pp. 80–82.

Chapter 20. The Media of Sight and Sound

1. * Allport, Gordon W. & Postman, Leo. *The psychology of rumor.* New York: Holt, 1947. P. vii.
2. ———. *Idem.* Pp. 159–169.
3. ———. *Idem.* Chap. 8.
4. ———. *Idem.* Pp. 183–184.
5. ———. *Idem.* P. 15.
6. ———. *Idem.* P. 23.
7. ———. *Idem.* Pp. 24, 28–29.
8. Bruner, Jerome S. & Fowler, George. The strategy of terror: audience response to Blitzkrieg im Westen. *Journal of Abnormal & Social Psychology,* 1941, v. 36, pp. 561–574.
9. Casey, Ralph D. Communication channels. *In:* Smith, Bruce Lannes; Lasswell, Harold D.; & Casey, Ralph D., *Propaganda, communication, and public opinion.* Princeton: Princeton University Press, 1946. P. 16.
10. * Charters, W. W. *Motion pictures and youth.* New York: Macmillan, 1933.
11. ———. *Idem.* Pp. 7–11.
12. ———. *Idem.* Pp. 13–18.
13. ———. *Idem.* Pp. 17–25.
14. ———. *Idem.* Pp. 25–35.
15. ———. *Idem.* Pp. 11–12.
16. ———. *Idem.* Pp. 35–43.

17. Dale, Edgar. *The content of motion pictures.* New York: Macmillan, 1933. (Summarized by Charters, *op. cit.,* pp. 47–52.)

18. ———. *Children's attendance at motion pictures.* New York: Macmillan, 1933. (Summarized by Charters, *op. cit.,* pp. 44–47.)

19. * Ernst, Morris L. *The first freedom.* New York: Macmillan, 1946. Chap. 6.

20. ———. *Idem.* Pp. 221–222.

21. * Experimental Section, Research Branch, Information and Education Division, U. S. War Department. *Experimental studies of army educational films.* 1948.

22. * Inglis, Ruth A. *Freedom of the movies.* Chicago: University of Chicago Press, 1947. Pp. 43–44.

23. ———. *Idem.* P. 6.

24. ———. *Idem.* Pp. 116–117, 152–171, 180–181.

25. ———. *Idem.* P. 45.

26. Jones, Dorothy B. Quantitative analysis of motion picture content. *Public Opinion Quarterly,* 1942, v. 6, pp. 411–428.

27. Kracauer, Siegfried. *The conquest of Europe on the screen: the Nazi newsreel 1939–1940. Experimental Division for the Study of War Time Communications* (Library of Congress), May 1, 1943, no. 50.

28. Littell, Robert & McCarthy, John J. Whispers for sale. *Harper's Magazine,* 1936, v. 172, pp. 364–372.

29. Lumley, Frederick Elmore. *Means of social control.* New York: Appleton-Century, 1925. P. 223, italics his.

30. Lynd, Robert S. & Helen Merrell. *Middletown in transition.* New York: Harcourt, Brace, 1937. Pp. 403–418.

31. * Rosten, Leo. *Hollywood.* New York: Harcourt, Brace, 1941. P. 355.

32. ———. *Idem.* P. 357.

33. ———. *Idem.* Pp. 358–360.

34. ———. *Idem.* P. 7.

35. Thorp, Margaret Farrand. *America at the movies.* New Haven: Yale University Press, 1939. P. 3.

36. Wanger, Walter.   120,000 American ambassadors. *Foreign Affairs,* 1939, v. 18, pp. 45–59.
37. White, Llewellyn & Leigh, Robert D.   *Peoples speaking to peoples.*   Chicago: University of Chicago Press, 1946.   P. 80.
38. ———. *Idem.*   P. 81.

Chapter 21. *The Value of Analysis*

1. Mumford, Lewis. *Values for survival.*   New York: Harcourt, Brace, 1946.   P. 39 footnote.
2. Myrdal, Gunnar. *An American Dilemma.*   New York: Harpers, 1944.   Pp. 1065–1070.

The entry for an author frequently includes pages in which his publication as numbered in the References is cited without specific mention of his name